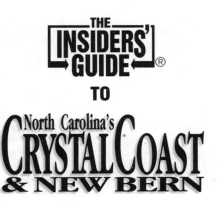

THE INSIDERS' GUIDE ®

TO

North Carolina's
CRYSTAL COAST
& NEW BERN

THE INSIDERS' GUIDE ®

TO

North Carolina's CRYSTAL COAST & NEW BERN

by
Tabbie Nance
and
Janis Williams

By The Sea
Publications
Inc.

Published and distributed by:
By The Sea Publications, Inc.
Hanover Center
P.O. Box 5386
Wilmington, NC 28403
1-800-955-1860

●

Fourth Edition
1st Printing
Copyright 1995 by By The Sea Publications, Inc.
Jay Tervo, Publisher
Printed in the United States of America

●

This book is produced under a license granted by:
The Insiders' Guides®, Inc.
P.O. Box 2057
Manteo, NC 27954
(919) 473-6100

●

●

ISBN 0-912367-73-3

Preface

Welcome to *The Insiders' Guide to North Carolina's Crystal Coast and New Bern*. This guide is designed to give you an Inside perspective on this beautiful coastal area. Use it like a road map, and keep it handy. If you are a newcomer, you'll learn about each area in our Area Overviews chapter. You'll find out about favorite spots and special events. If you've been around awhile, you're sure to enjoy our sidebars and learn about a place or two you didn't know existed. Keep this guide handy for all your visiting relatives and friends.

This book is divided into two major parts. The first section deals with the beautiful Crystal Coast, which includes all of Carteret County and Swansboro. The nickname Crystal Coast was given to the Carteret County beach area several years ago by the Carteret County Chamber of Commerce. It was hoped the name would attract visitors to the county's crystal waters and brilliant beaches, and it has. The second section of this book addresses the historic city of New Bern. Best known as the site of Tryon Palace, the city offers so much to visitors and guests. New Bern is the second-oldest town in North Carolina and is rich with history.

We've packed this book with chapters that deal with just about every topic you can imagine, including History, Restaurants, Accommodations, Vacation and Year-round Rentals, Shopping, Nightlife, Annual Events and Festivals, Camping and more. We even suggest places to launch and store your boat, have a picnic, get a surf report, rent a boat, go for a hike and play a round of golf. There are also chapters on schools, churches, relocation services, industry, sports and parks. The service directory offers a wealth of information including libraries, town halls, tax rates, emergency services and bus and taxi services. You'll also find information about buying or building a home and renting.

We've provided some general maps to help you see the overall picture. These are site detailed and should be used in conjunction with your regular road map. We also offer the following general hints. U.S. 70 takes on a different name in each town it passes through (Main Street in Havelock, Arendell Street in Morehead City and Cedar and Live Oak streets in Beaufort). N.C. 58 takes on a new name in each of the beach towns it passes through (Fort Macon Road east or west in Atlantic Beach, Salter Path Road between Atlantic Beach and Indian Beach and Emerald Drive in Emerald Isle). The Crystal Coast, New Bern and Havelock are within the 919 telephone area code. A recent change has brought a new area code, 910, to the area. The dividing line is at the Carteret County-Onslow County line, which is marked by the White Oak River. Phones on the Carteret County side remained in the 919 area code, and phones on the other side changed to 910. Because of this change, dial 910 to reach Swansboro and Wilmington. All telephone numbers in this book are in the 919 area code unless otherwise noted. Milepost numbers are given to help locate places on the beach.

Besides the Crystal Coast and New Bern, you'll also discover information about our neighboring city of Havelock, which is rich in history and continually growing. Home to Marine Corps Air Station Cherry Point and associated Naval Aviation Depot, Havelock is the largest city in Craven County.

We offer you daytrip itineraries to a few getaway spots including Ocracoke, the Outer Banks, Wilmington, Oriental and Belhaven.

From a map, the entire area seems to be little more than a highway. But the Crystal Coast and New Bern have much to offer visitors and residents. If your are visiting the area, don't expect to see it all in one trip. If you have relocated to the area, we urge you to spend a weekend now and then exploring the many treasures that surround you.

This is the fourth edition of *The In-siders' Guide® to the Crystal Coast and New Bern*. We've tried to include as many as the wonderful sights, sounds and tastes of the area as possible. We've done our best to ensure that all the information is accurate; however, we know there is always room for improvement. Let us know what you think so that future editions can accommodate your ideas and suggestions. Write to us in care of The Insiders' Guide, Inc., P.O. Box 2057, Manteo, North Carolina 27954.

Our hope is that the coast's lure and its varied pleasures will suit you as well as they do us and other Insiders. We trust this book will be a helpful guide to the area and that you will enjoy exploring, revisiting or living on the Crystal Coast and in New Bern.

— Tabbie and Janis

About the Authors

Tabbie Nance moved to Carteret County 12 years ago to work as a reporter/ photographer for the local newspaper. A North Carolina native, she was reared on a small farm in Guilford County and graduated from High Point College, now University, with degrees in media communications and human relations. Tabbie's travels throughout the United States, New Zealand and Europe have given her a special insight into the kind of information travelers and newcomers want and need.

Tabbie is the director of school-community relations for the Carteret County School System. She is involved in various community volunteer activities, including serving on the Core Sound Waterfowl Museum board and as a child advocate through the court's guardian *ad litem* program. She also works as a freelance writer, and this is her fourth year as coauthor of *The Insiders' Guide to North Carolina's Crystal Coast and New Bern.*

Tabbie lives in an old restored house in Beaufort. She enjoys working on the house, running, biking, swimming, cooking, camping, traveling, needlework and playing with her sister's kids. Tabbie also competes in road races and triathlons. She has completed an Ironman triathlon (2.4-mile swim, 112-mile cycle and 26.2-mile run) and loved it.

Janis Williams moved to Carteret County 15 years ago to publish an entertainment magazine, *The Maritimes,* with a friend. To their surprise, it worked, and they eventually learned how to do it. She worked as managing editor for eight years before starting out on her next venture, a retail clothing business. For six years she learned how that was done, but, realizing that it wasn't the 1980s anymore, she closed the store last fall just in time to update *The Insiders' Guide* — something she's wanted to do since the book's beginnings on the Crystal Coast.

This, for her, is what "life on the edge" is all about — being allowed to try something interesting and learn how to do it in the process. It's quite a change from her earlier years in Washington, D.C., where she felt defined by degrees and a career track. That wasn't nearly as challenging as defining her life herself.

Winters Janis works with her husband managing the galley aboard their charter sailboat, *Good Fortune,* in the Florida Keys and Bahamas. She's also aboard whenever possible in the summers in Beaufort.

Acknowledgements

My part of this book couldn't have been completed without the help of many, many people. Thanks to all those who shared with me and took time to lend a hand. My special thanks go to Havelock's Brenda Wilson and Mary Kurek who provided a wealth of information about their town. Thanks also to my parents, Buddy and Tabbie Nance, who instilled in me an appreciation and love for North Carolina; my sister, Miriam Lewis, for always supporting and loving me; my mentor, Rodney Kemp, a Moreheader with contagious love for Carteret County; and my friend, Ralph Merrill, a Beaufort native who provides invaluable humor breaks and long runs.

— Tabbie

I would like to list the names of all the kind people who returned my calls and helped take the chase out of updating this year's book. Your names are numerous, and I will find you in 1995 to personally thank you face to face. I am especially grateful for the time and assistance of Susan Moffat at the Swiss Bear Downtown Revitalization Corporation Office in New Bern who reviewed the entire New Bern section offering refinements and updates for me to pursue. She streamlined my time on the road. Much more than thanks, actually great gratitude, to Jay Tervo for his leap of faith in believing that I had the grit to communicate by computer. And for helping prove him right, I thank my neighbor Sharon Guthrie who set me up and was always available to bail me out.

— Janis

I would like to express my deepest appreciation to Tabbie and Janis for the excellent job they did in making this edition of *The Insiders' Guide to the Crystal Coast and New Bern* possible!

Tabbie, thanks for yet again another fine effort. And Janis, welcome aboard — it is good to have you with us! I would like to thank The North Carolina Travel and Tourism Division and Bald Head Island for color photography and photographers Scott Taylor, Bill Benners, Cathy Crowell and Irv Hooper for their wonderful contributions to making this book so much fun to flip through. And for sure, endless thanks go to the ever more competent and expanding staff at Insiders' Guides Inc., including but not limited to Theresa Shea Chavez, Giles Bissonnette, Beth Storie, Michael McOwen, Mike Lay, David Haynes, Gina Twiford, Julie Ross and the rest of the gang whose faces I do not yet know but whose efforts I am much thankful for.

— JCT

Photo: Scott Taylor

Boats of all types still sail the Crystal Coast.

One to one.
Person to person.
Face to face.
Welcome to
Personal Banking.

Welcome
to Wachovia.

Main Office	Main Office
New Bern	Morehead City
401 Tryon Palace Drive	800 Arendell Street
New Bern, NC 28563	Morehead City, NC
(919) 638-6121	(919) 726-7181

Table of Contents

Preface v
About The Authors vii
Acknowledgements viii

Crystal Coast
Getting Around
   The Crystal Coast 1
Area Overviews 5
Restaurants 29
Accommodations 59
Vacation Rentals 75
Camping 87
Shopping 93
Attractions 115
Kidstuff 135
Annual Festivals
   and Events 141
Nightlife 151
Fishing, Water Sports
   and Beach Access 159
Marinas 175
Sports, Fitness and Parks 179
Golf 189
Ferries 192
Arts 197
Places of Worship 203
Service Directory 205
Real Estate
   and Neighborhoods 215
Schools and Child Care 243
Retirement and
   Senior Services 249
Volunteer Opportunities 257
Hospitals and Medical Care 259
Higher Education
   and Research 265
Commerce and Industry 269
Military 271

New Bern
New Bern 273
Restaurants 281
Accommodations 291
Camping 297
Shopping 301
Attractions 307
Kidstuff 315
Annual Events and Festivals 317
Nightlife 323
Fishing and Water Sports 326
Marinas and the
   Intracoastal Waterway 327
Sports, Parks and Fitness 332
Golf 335
Arts 337
Places of Worship 342
Service Directory 345
Real Estate
   and Neighborhoods 349
Schools and Child Care 363
Retirement and
   Senior Services 365
Volunteer Opportunities 369
Hospitals and Medical Care 373
Higher Education
   and Research 378
Commerce and Industry 379
Airports 381
Havelock 383
Oriental 399
Daytrips 403
Index of Advertisers 413
Index 415

Directory of Maps

Regional Overview .... Inside front cover
Beaufort 13
Down East 23
New Bern 275

Photo: Scott Taylor

A lonely skiff awaits the coming dawn.

Carteret County
Chamber of Commerce

3615 Arendell Street • P. O. Box 1198
Morehead City, N.C. 28557

Welcome to the Crystal Coast of North Carolina!

We are glad you are here and are sure you will enjoy our wonderful county. We have miles of beautiful beaches, wonderful restaurants, unique shopping, fun fishing and boating, and interesting historical sites. Please take time to enjoy all and return often. If we can be of help, stop by the Commerce Development Center at 3615 Arendell Street, Morehead City from 8:30 am to 5:00 pm, Monday through Friday, or call us at (919) 726-6350 or 1-800-622-6278. If you are interested in receiving visitor information, contact our local tourism department at (919) 240-1832 or 1-800-786-6962.

Once again, we are glad you are here!

Sincerely,

Phyllis

Phyllis Ford
President
Carteret County Chamber of Commerce

(919)726-6350 • (800)622-6278 • (919)726-4215 FAX

Getting Around
The Crystal Coast

By land, sea or air, more and more people arrive year-round to visit or relocate to the Crystal Coast and historic New Bern. Getting to the area is half the fun by sea or air, but 95 percent of the millions estimated to visit our shores annually arrive by land.

From the north by land, either I-95 or U.S. Highway 17 will take you to U.S. Highway 70. From the west, I-40 will take you to Highway 70, and from the south, I-95 runs into U.S. Highway 70. Traveling from the south, you also have the option of following U.S. Highway 17 to U.S. Highway 24 to U.S. Highway 58 to the Crystal Coast. From the east, travelers who will persevere to see the last of North Carolina's Outer Banks after Ocracoke must reserve space for the 2¼-hour ferry ride to Cedar Island. At the ferry landing, N.C. 12 continues a short distance to intersect with U.S. Highway 70 W. at Atlantic, it's point of origin. From here, it's an astonishing ride Down East through lowland fields of junkus and spartina marsh grasses and fishing villages to Beaufort, the Crystal Coast or on to Havelock and New Bern.

By air, you can reach New Bern by commercial carrier, or fly into New Bern or Beaufort by private plane. By water, the Intracoastal Waterway provides access to the Crystal Coast via Morehead City, Beaufort, Swansboro and Emerald Isle. To reach New Bern by water, slip into Pamlico Sound and head up the Neuse River.

When you get to either New Bern or the Crystal Coast, you'll find that a car is almost essential. There isn't a public bus service in either place, and a look at the map will show you that most communi-

The Cape Lookout Lighthouse has been guiding boats to safety since 1859.

ties are far enough apart to make a car a must. Each of the major towns has one or more cab companies to supplement transportation, but a car of your own is the best way to get around.

If you've brought your bicycle, there are some marked bike routes, but remember you're in a tourist area, and vehicle

Photo: Scott Taylor

These horses live on Carrot Island off Beaufort.

that it has many names as it traverses Carteret County. In Morehead City, it's Arendell Street, the main street through town. It's the Morehead-Beaufort Causeway. In Beaufort, it's Cedar Street until it takes a left turn and becomes Live Oak Street. And by any name, it's always well trafficked.

From Morehead City to Swansboro the main thoroughfare is Highway 24. Recent construction has partially four-laned the highway, and new bridges across both Broad Creek and Gales Creek offer lovely views of Bogue Sound.

Milepost markers run parallel to the beach on the 30-mile island and will help you find your way around Bogue Banks on the Crystal Coast. Mile 1 begins on the east end of the island at Fort Macon.

Upon arrival to the Crystal Coast, stop in at one of the Carteret County Tourism Development Bureau's visitors centers located in Morehead City on U.S. 70 and at Cape Carteret on N.C. 58, or at the North Carolina Ferry Division's visitors Center at the Cedar Island terminal. The friendly staff at all locations will help you with maps and brochures and will answer immediate questions. And, regardless of your Crystal Coast destination, have a safe and pleasant trip, relax and take time to explore the area's rich resources.

traffic is often heavy. Beaufort has a marked bike route; a routing guide is available at the Welcome Center on Turner Street. Biking in residential sections on Bogue Banks, especially in the Emerald Isle area, is safe and pleasant.

Now, about the roads within the area. Highway 70 is generally very easy to drive from New Bern through Havelock and on to Morehead City, Beaufort and Down East. From Beaufort east, however, Highway 70 is a two-lane highway that winds between canals and marshes, but the road is adequately wide and always in excellent repair. This area is great for bird watching. Another important detail to remember about Highway 70 is

Photo: NC Travel & Tourism Div. Clay Nolen

The Traditional Wooden Boat Show is held each May at Beaufort.

Somehow, our rural roads don't seem so lonely anymore.

It used to be when you drove on the rural roads in your area you felt a little isolated. Sometimes lonely.

Well, not anymore. Sprint Cellular proudly announces expanded service to many towns that were once just a lot of static on a cellular phone.

Our expanded coverage not only makes rural roads a little less lonely, it allows you to use your Sprint Cellular phone in more places in North Carolina than any other cellular company.

So, now you can take us with you almost anywhere you want to go. And vice versa.

Call us today. Find out why more people are using Sprint Cellular.

Sprint Cellular

Call 1-800-409-4343

Crystal Coast
Area Overviews

The Crystal Coast is such a diverse and dynamic place that just one introduction to the entire area wouldn't do it justice. So, we have divided the county into geographic sections. Each chapter of this book features information in the following order: Bogue Banks, Beaufort, Morehead City, Swansboro, Down East and Western Carteret County. If you are looking for a restaurant on the beach, go to the Restaurant chapter and look for the "Bogue Banks" section. If you're looking for accommodations in Beaufort, go to that chapter and flip to the "Beaufort" section.

We're starting the Crystal Coast section of the book with a brief introduction to each geographic area. The chapters that follow focus on specific subjects such as shopping, attractions, marinas, fishing and water sports, neighborhoods and much more.

You're sure to find this information helpful, and you'll learn a little bit more about the area as you go through this book. There is a lot to enjoy on the Crystal Coast, so take your time. We'll still be here!

Bogue Banks

Bogue Banks is the narrow island that runs from Fort Macon in Atlantic Beach on the east to Emerald Isle on the west. The 30-mile-long island is connected to the mainland by high-rise bridges at each end. Through the years, the island has continued to attract visitors and residents. There are many second homes, condominiums and hotels on the island.

N.C. 58 stretches from one end of the island to the other and is marked with mileposts (MP). The MP series begins with mile 1 at the east end of the island and continues along the road to mile 21 on the west end. Throughout this book, we have given the MP as part of the address for places on Bogue Banks.

All Bogue Banks development, both business and residential, is along Highway 58. A ride from one end of the island to the other on Highway 58 and down a few of the side streets can give you a quick overview of the island communities and what they offer. From several points along the road you can see the sound and the ocean at the same time.

There are basically five

As N.C. 58 passes through the different communities, it often takes on a new name. In Atlantic Beach, its called Fort Macon Road. East Fort Macon Road is the strip between the old fort and the main intersection in town. West Fort Macon Road is the strip between that intersection and the western edge of town. Salter Path Road is what the longest stretch of the highway is called — it goes from Atlantic Beach, through Pine Knoll Shores, Indian Beach and Salter Path. In Emerald Isle, the highway is called Emerald Drive. It really isn't as confusing as it sounds — it's just one two-lane road with lots of names.

areas on the island, although they blend together. Atlantic Beach is at the far east end of the island and borders the town of Pine Knoll Shores. Indian Beach surrounds the small unincorporated community of Salter Path, and Emerald Isle is at the far west end of the island. Each town has its own personality and points of interest. Glancing at the maps in this chapter might help you get an overall picture of how these towns combine into Bogue Banks.

Atlantic Beach

Atlantic Beach had its beginning in 1887 when a pavilion was built on the beach. The one-story building had a refreshment stand and areas for changing clothes. The popularity of surf bathing was growing, and guests at the Atlantic Hotel in Morehead City (which stood at the site of today's Jefferson Motor Lodge) were taken to the sound side of Atlantic Beach by sailboat. The guests then walked across the island to the ocean.

Later, a large two-story pavilion was built on the island, and a boardwalk was built from the dock to the pavilion. Supplies were carted over the sand dunes by ox cart. In 1916, the first pavilion and 100 acres were bought by Von Bedsworth and the 100-room Atlantic View Beach Hotel was built. The hotel later burned. By 1928, a group of county citizens developed a plan, built a toll bridge from Morehead City to today's Atlantic Beach, and constructed a beach resort complete with a dining area, bath houses and a pavilion. Just a short year later, the entire complex

was destroyed by fire. A New York bank took possession of the property, and some of the buildings were restored. A new hotel was built. In 1936 the bridge was sold to the state, and the toll charges were dropped. In 1945 Morehead City resident Alfred Cooper bought the property, and in 1953 a drawbridge replaced the old bridge. In the late 1980s, the drawbridge was replaced by the high-rise bridge.

Today, Atlantic Beach has a year-round population of about 2,000, that swells to about 35,000 during the summer. The current town board and residents are working to improve the waterfront area known as The Circle, found at the southernmost end of the Atlantic Beach Causeway.

Pine Knoll Shores

Incorporated in 1973, Pine Knoll Shores is located in the center of Bogue Banks. This planned community was developed by heirs of Theodore Roosevelt and is called one of the state's most ecologically sensitive communities. The town's 1,400 residents share their community with the N.C. Aquarium, Theodore Roosevelt Natural Area and the Bogue Banks Public Library.

The N.C. Aquarium is one of the state's three aquariums. It offers educational exhibits, displays and a meeting area for civic and special-interest groups (see Attractions). Theodore Roosevelt Natural Area is a 265-acre maritime forest owned and protected by the state (see Parks). The area lies around the N.C.

Aquarium and is one of the few remaining maritime forests on North Carolina's barrier islands.

Pine Knoll Shores officials stress the importance of protecting existing maritime forests in town and enforce regulations that decrease the amount of maritime forest acreage that can be cleared for development. The town itself owns significant forest tracts.

A historic marker stands at the corner of Highway 58 and Roosevelt Boulevard noting the area of the first landing of Europeans on the North Carolina coast. Giovanni da Verrazzano, a Florentine navigator in the service of France, explored the state's coast from Cape Fear north to the present Kitty Hawk in 1524. His voyage along the coast marked the first recorded European contact with what is now North Carolina.

Indian Beach

Indian Beach is a resort and residential town located near the center of Bogue Banks. Incorporated in 1973, the town offers residents and visitors a fishing pier and wide, beautiful beaches for sunbathing, surf fishing and water sports. Quite a few condominiums, camping areas and restaurants are located in this area and are profiled in various chapters within the Crystal Coast section.

The town surrounds the unincorporated community of Salter Path. So, there is actually an "east" Indian Beach and a "west" Indian Beach.

Salter Path

Much of the quaintness of Salter Path was lost when modern development began moving in. Now, the community's modest homes seem crowded together. But the character of the community can still be seen in the close family ties, the fishing boats beside the homes and the fish nets being mended in the yards.

The first families to settle in Salter Path came over from Diamond City (see Attractions), which at the time was the largest community on Shackleford Banks, the 9-mile-long island that is now part of Cape Lookout National Seashore. By 1897, about 500 people lived in Diamond City and had erected stores, a school, a post office and church buildings.

Diamond City was a whaling com-munity, and the center of the community was a large hill that was used as a look-out. Once a whale was spotted, the men would jump into boats and row after the whale and, if successful, harpoon and kill the creature.

Two hard storms in the late 1890s con-vinced many Diamond City residents it was time to leave the island. Houses were cut into sections, tied to skiffs and floated or sailed across the water. Once at the new homesites, the houses were recon-structed. Many settled on Harkers Island, in the Shackleford Street area of Morehead City or in Salter Path.

Legend has it that the name Salter Path originated with Joshua Salter, a Broad Creek area resident who often came by boat from the mainland to the beach area to fish and hunt. A path was made from the sound area where he anchored his boat to the oceanfront. Folks called the walkway Salter's Path, and the name stuck.

Many locals credit the early residents of Salter Path with bringing shrimp into the culinary limelight. Once considered only a menace by fishermen, they were plentiful. After local residents began to eat them, the seafood soon became a marketable item throughout the county and all coastal areas.

Emerald Isle

Stories say this end of the island was originally home to nomadic Indians and whalers. It is also said that about 15 families, perhaps from Diamond City, came here in 1893 and settled at Middletown, a small section of the island that is now part of Emerald Isle.

Other than those small groups, Emerald Isle was largely unsettled until the 1950s. Several years after Atlantic Beach was developed as a seashore resort, a Philadelphia man named Henry K. Fort bought the land that now makes up most of Emerald Isle and about 500 more acres on the mainland in what is today the town of Cape Carteret. Fort planned to tie the two areas together with a bridge and de-

velop a large resort. When support for constructing a bridge could not be raised from the state or county, he abandoned the project. A ferryboat was later operated in the area where he had hoped to put a bridge. The ferry carried motorists and pedestrians between the beach and mainland and landed on the beach near Bogue Inlet Pier, which was the first recreational spot at the island's west end.

Today, a modern high-rise bridge provides guests access from the mainland to Emerald Isle and the western end of Bogue Banks. The Cameron Langston Bridge spans the Atlantic Intracoastal Waterway and offers, from the top, a great view of area land formations, the waterway and Bogue Banks.

Emerald Isle has a year-round population of 2,434 and a seasonal population of 16,000. The town's $1.4-million municipal complex and community center offers large meeting rooms, a full basketball court and a gym area (see Sports and Fitness Centers). The town's residential and business sections line Emerald Drive (Highway 58). Several new housing areas have been developed west of the high-rise bridge in the area surrounding the Coast Guard Station.

Photo: Scott Taylor

Don't miss the wild horses on Carrot Island in Beaufort.

PROFESSIONAL PROFILE

Real Estate
EMERALD ISLE REALTY

The local experts in Emerald Isle real estate!

Ray Eatmon's local knowledge and experience is a proven asset to both buyers and sellers.

A graduate of the Realtor's Institute, Ray has excelled in sales and service since 1988. Treating customers and clients like friends and family is a trademark of Ray's service and the unwritten rule at Emerald Isle Realty. When you need the best in professional service, rely on a local expert!

Ray Eatmon, GRI

Emerald Isle Realty
7501 Emerald Drive
Emerald Isle, NC 28594
(800) 849-3315

Beaufort

Beaufort is a small seaport brimming with charm and history. It is quietly different from most coastal towns. Once you've walked along the wooden boardwalk and tree-lined streets, heard the tolling church bells and smelled the salt air, you will come to understand the special feeling Beaufort gives.

Beaufort is the third oldest town in North Carolina and was named for Henry Somerset, the Duke of Beaufort. The town was surveyed in 1713, nearly 20 years before George Washington's birth.

Beaufort was incorporated in 1722 and has been the seat of Carteret County since that time. The English influence is apparent in the architecture and, more noticeably, in the street names: Ann and Queen, for Queen Anne; Craven, for the Earl of Craven; Orange, for William the Prince of Orange; Moore, for Col. Maurice Moore; and Pollock, for the governor at the time of the survey.

Beaufort offers a glimpse at a relatively unspoiled part of North Carolina's coastal history. The town has made great strides in the restoration of many of its

Photo: Scott Taylor

Wildlife is abundant in the marshes of Eastern North Carolina.

oldest structures. Much of that can be credited to the Beaufort Historical Association, which was organized in 1960 to celebrate the town's 250th anniversary. The first home "plaqued" was the Duncan House, c. 1790, at 105 Front Street. To be plaqued, a home must be at least 80 years old and have retained its historic and architectural integrity. Through the years, the Beaufort Historical Association has moved old structures threatened with demolition to an area on Turner Street. For more information about the Beaufort Historic Site see the Attractions chapter.

The town's designated historic district is between Gallant's Channel and the east side of Pollock Street and between Taylor's Creek and the south side of Broad Street. (Taylor's Creek is the body of water the boardwalk and downtown area face, and Gallant's Channel flows under the drawbridge.) The one-block area of the county courthouse is also included.

Beaufort's historic houses and sites each have their own story to tell. Many structures and areas are listed on the Na-tional Register of Historic Places. The house with the most lively history is the Hammock House of 1698. Considered Beaufort's oldest standing house, it once stood so close to the water that visitors could tie a skiff (small boat) to the front porch. Through the years, dredging changed the creek's course, and now the house stands one block back from the creek. Robert Turner, who had the town plotted in 1713, lived in the house, as did Nathaniel Taylor, who donated the Old Burying Ground to the town. The house later served as an inn or "ordinary" and Blackbeard, the fiercest of all pirates, was a regular guest. Legend has it that Blackbeard hung one of his wives from a live oak tree in the front yard, and neighbors can still hear her screams on moonlit nights. The house was used as accommodations by the Union Army during the Civil War. Hammock House is privately owned.

The Old Burying Ground on Ann Street is an interesting place to wander and look at the types of grave markers as well as the messages they bear. Deeded to the town in 1731, the Old Burying

Beaufort

DOWNTOWN

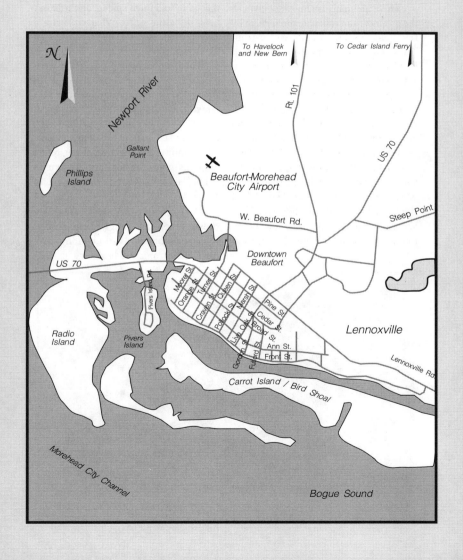

Ground was declared full in 1825, and the General Assembly said no more burials would be allowed. The town was ordered to lay out a new graveyard, but the town's people did not support the act and continued to bury their loved ones in the Old Burying Ground until the early 1900s. The north corner of the graveyard is the oldest section.

There are many interesting graves in the grounds, and tours are often given by the Beaufort Historical Association. Those buried here include Capt. Josiah Pender, whose men took Fort Macon in 1861; James W. Hunt, who had the distinction of marrying, making his will and dying the same day; Esther Cooke, mother of Capt. James W. Cooke, who once commanded the Ironclad *Albemarle*; the Dill child, who was buried in a glass-top casket; the common grave of the *Crissie Wright* crew, who froze to death when the ship wrecked on Shackleford Banks in 1886; and the child who died aboard a ship and was brought to Beaufort in a keg of rum for burial — keg and all.

With the town's waterfront revitalization project in the late 1970s, Beaufort took a new direction. The renovation involved tearing down many old waterfront structures not considered salvageable and building the existing wooden boardwalk, docks and facilities. With this, businesses were encouraged to stay or move to the downtown waterfront. Soon word about the "new" old town spread, and it hasn't been the same since. What was once a coastal hideaway is now a favorite spot for visitors traveling by car or boat.

As you enter Beaufort from the west, you will cross the Grayden M. Paul Bridge. The bridge's namesake was Grayden Paul, a lively 96-year-old historian who was best known for his songs, poems and tales about Beaufort and Carteret County. He lived on Front Street with his wife, Mary Clark, known as "M.C.," until his death in the summer of 1994.

Drawbridges in coastal areas are slowly becoming things of the past as more and more towns are choosing to replace these romantic bridges with con-

Photo: Carteret County Museum of History

Bogue Banks Life-Saving Station opened in 1905 under the supervision of Keeper Alexander Moore.

crete high-rises. And that's the case for this old landmark. Because of the increased traffic, plans are in the works to replace the drawbridge in the next few years. The only sticking point is where to locate the new high-rise bridge.

Beaufort is home to a number of attractions, including the North Carolina Maritime Museum and Watercraft Center and the Rachel Carson Component of the North Carolina National Estuarine Research Reserve.

Beaufort's Nearby Communities

LENNOXVILLE

Lennoxville is the community closest to Beaufort. The area begins at the east end of Front Street and continues to the east end of Lennoxville Road. This is primarily a residential area with the exception of Beaufort Fisheries and Atlantic Veneer (see Commerce and Industry). At one time, there were several tomato canneries in the community. Lennoxville is surrounded by water: Taylor's Creek on the south and North River on the north.

NORTH RIVER

North River is a small community that lies to the north of Beaufort on Merrimon Road. The community can be reached by traveling east on U.S. 70 out of Beaufort and continuing straight at East Carteret High School. (A right turn at the school would take you to the Down East area.) Baseball pitcher Brien Taylor put the community of North River on the map in 1991 when, as a high school senior, he

A young surfer tries his luck on Bogue Banks.

signed a $1.55 million contract with the New York Yankees.

SOUTH RIVER

The South River community actually lies to the north of the North River community. Named for the body of water it nestles beside, South River is primarily a fishing-based community. Many of this community's early residents came from Lukens. Today, much of the land is owned by recreational hunters and businesses, and there are several private airstrips in the area. Many artifacts and Indian pottery pieces have been found in the South River area throughout the years.

MERRIMON

The community of Merrimon lies to the west of South River. This rural area borders the Neuse River and Adams Creek, which is a stretch of the scenic Intracoastal Waterway. The seaport of Oriental is just across the Neuse River and, on most days, is visible.

In recent years, a few neighborhood developments have sprung up around South River, Merrimon and the Intracoastal Waterway. Sportsman's Village, Jonaquin's Landing and Indian Summer Estates offer waterfront and mainland lots.

HARLOWE

Harlowe is the community that lies off N.C. 101 between Beaufort and Havelock. Part of the community is in Carteret County and part is in Craven County. Harlowe is primarily a farming area, as it has always been.

Morehead City

Morehead City is the county's largest city. A look into the history of the city starts with an early land prospector from Virginia by the name of John Shackleford. In 1714, Shackleford saw a future for the area and purchased 170 acres at the mouth of the Newport River, stretching from Bogue Sound on the south to Calico Creek on the north.

The land became known as Shepard's Point after it was purchased in 1723 by David Shepard. The community grew but was not incorporated until 1861.

In 1852 the state decided to extend a railroad line to connect Raleigh with the coast; several towns vied for the location since it would bring growth to their communities. For a while, it was considered inevitable that it would end in Beaufort. To make a bid for the rail business, a new town named Carolina City was formed by the Carolina City Company. The company purchased 1,000 acres at the western end of the Shepard's Point land, and Carolina City lots went on sale in 1855.

John Motley Morehead, who was elected governor of the state in 1840 and again in 1842, came to the coast in 1856 when he was put in charge of extending the railroad to the coast. He began to buy land in what is now, appropriately, Morehead City. In 1857, he began selling lots at public auction. Gov. Morehead also established the planetarium in Chapel Hill, a state school for the blind and the school of business at the University of North Carolina at Chapel Hill.

In May 1858, Gov. Morehead described the area: "The City of Morehead is situated on a beautiful neck of land or dry plain, almost entirely surrounded by salt water; its climate salubrious; its sea breezes and sea bathing delightful; its drinking water good and its fine chalybeate spring, strongly impregnated with sulfur, will make it a pleasant watering place . . . ."

The sale of the land was successful, Gov. Morehead was successful in his bid for the end of the railroad, and Morehead City was incorporated. When the state Legislature authorized the incorporation of the town, surveyors laid out the streets and named the primary ones after men who had been influential in the settlement of the area — Fisher, Arendell, Bridges, Evans, Shackleford and Shepard.

At that time, the only roads entering the county were sandy, narrow lanes, so most of the influential visitors arrived by rail, steamer or sailboat.

One of the first commercial buildings in Morehead City was the Macon Hotel at the corner of Arendell and Ninth streets. Constructed in 1860, this three-storied building was a landmark for 80-some years.

The town was started just in time to be taken over by the Union forces when they attacked Fort Macon on April 26, 1862, thus ending for a time any significant development. Even after the end of the War Between the States, Morehead City was not able to get its commercial life active again until about 1880 when the shipping industry began to bring business to town. In the early 1880s, a new Atlantic Hotel was built in Morehead City, replacing the old Atlantic Hotel that

had been destroyed by a hurricane. Located where the Jefferson Motor Lodge now stands, the Atlantic Hotel had 233 rooms and claimed to have the largest ballroom in the South. It drew the cream of the state's society to the coast until it was destroyed by fire in 1933.

In 1911, the city began a program of road improvement to alternately "pave the way" and keep up with the town's slow but steady growth.

Crab Point is one area that grew as a result of road improvement. Crab Point is what Moreheaders call that part of the city that is east of Country Club Road and north of the 20th Street Bridge over Calico Creek. The area got its name because when tides came in, crabs got trapped on the shoreline. Then locals would go and have an easy time catching them. In the early days, Crab Point served as a port and had windmills for grinding grain and generating power for lumber companies. A private cemetery in the area has graves dating back to the early 1700s.

Swansboro

From its origins as the site of an Algonquian Indian village at the mouth of the White Oak River to its current status as the "Friendly City by the Sea," Swansboro continues to be a lovely place to visit and, both because of its relatively mild climate and the warmth and friendliness of its residents, a comfortable place to live.

The history of the town of Swansboro began about 1730, when Jonathan and Grace Green moved from Falmouth, Massachusetts, to the mouth of the White

Oak River. With them, and owning half of the property, was Jonathan Green's brother, Isaac. They lived there about five years until Jonathan Green died at the early age of 35. His widow married Theophilus Weeks, who had moved with his family from Falmouth to settle on Hadnot Creek a few miles up the White Oak River.

After their marriage, Weeks moved into the Green family home on the Onslow County side of the White Oak River. He soon purchased the interest of Isaac Green to become sole owner of the large plantation. Weeks first farmed, then opened a tavern and was appointed inspector of exports at the thriving port. In 1771, he started a town on that portion of his plantation called Weeks Wharf, selling 48 numbered lots recorded as being "in the plan of a town laid out by Theophilus Weeks," thus earning him the title of founder of the town.

Originally called Week's Point, then New-Town-upon-Bogue was established by law in 1783. The General Assembly named the town Swannsborough, in honor of Samuel Swann, former speaker of the N.C. House of Representatives and longtime Onslow County representative.

Another name that became well-known in Swansboro (the later version of the town's name) was that of Otway Burns. During the War of 1812, this native son became a privateer with his schooner, the *Snapdragon*. His participation during this "Second War of Independence" was acclaimed as an act of brav-ery and patriotism. After the war, he returned to the trade of ship building and was later appointed keeper of the lighthouse at Portsmouth where he died in 1850. He is buried in Beaufort's Old Burying Ground.

Swansboro's port continued to prosper, particularly because of the nearby pine forests that produced the lumber, tar, pitch and other naval items shipped through the port. It continued to prosper until the end of the War Between the States. Then, gradually, the town came to support itself with farming and fishing.

The town is water-oriented, situated on the Intracoastal Waterway and along the mouth of the White Oak River, with the Atlantic Ocean easily accessible through Bogue Inlet. A good many fishing boats call Swansboro home port, and many residents keep sportfishing boats at marinas in Swansboro or Cedar Point.

The town's historic commission supervises the restoration of many of the town's oldest structures. Several of these fine structures now house businesses, while others remain private residences.

Down East

The term "Down East" refers to the area that stretches from the North River, just east of Beaufort, to Cedar Island. This is a beautiful area that includes marshes, canals and undisturbed areas, particularly as you get closer to Cedar Island.

In the past, the livelihood of the Down East people depended on the water. Today, some still rely on the water, but many work in Beaufort or Morehead City or travel to Air Station Cherry Point in Havelock. Still, that tie and love for the water is obvious by the number of boats, fish houses and seafood businesses.

There are no incorporated towns in the Down East area, so it is governed by the county. Activities center around the churches, volunteer fire and rescue squads, post offices, schools and local stores. Most of the communities lie along U.S. 70, which is the main road in the Down East area.

While some outsiders refer to the Down East area as almost anything east of the capital city of Raleigh, Insiders know that the real Down East does not begin until you cross the North River Bridge. The history of this area is rich and could fill volumes. We'll just give you a very brief overview below.

Bettie is the first Down East community you reach after leaving Beaufort on Highway 70. It lies between the North River Bridge and the Ward's Creek Bridge. The next community is **Otway**, named for famous privateer Otway Burns, who is buried in Beaufort's Old Burying Ground.

Straits is the name of the community that surrounds the road going to Harkers Island. It is also the name of the body of water that lies between the Straits community and the island. The spelling of Straits is shown on early maps as "Straights." Later, cartographers probably noticed the name was not applicable to a water course, so they changed the spelling to Straits, meaning narrows. Years ago, Straits was a farm community, and a substantial amount of cotton was grown here. Straits United Methodist Church, c. 1778, was the first Methodist Church built east of Beaufort.

Originally called Craney Island, **Harkers Island** was once the home of a thriving band of Tuscarora Indians. By the turn of the 20th century, all that remained of the native Indian settlement was a huge mound of sea shells at the east end of the island, now called Shell Point. Folks say the Indians were attempting to build a shell walkway through the water to Core Banks.

In 1730, George Pollock sold the island to Ebenezer Harker of Boston, Massachusetts, who began living on the island. Later he divided the island among his three sons, and the divisions he used, "eastard," "westard" and "center," have remained unofficial dividers ever since. The Harker heirs did not part with their land for years, so the island population remained sparse. By 1895 there were still fewer than 30 families living on the island. The population grew when folks from the Shackleford Banks community of Diamond City left because of the devastation of the hurricanes. Some loaded homes on boats and brought them to the safer ground. With this new surge in population, schools, churches and businesses sprung up. Still, the island was isolated. Ferry operations to the mainland began in 1926, with the ferry leaving from the west end of the island and docking in the Gloucester community. A bridge to the island was built in 1941. The island is home to the National Park Service Office and Core Sound Waterfowl Museum.

The **Smyrna** community was named in 1785 from a deed that conveyed 100 acres from Joseph Davis to Seth Williston. The land was on Smunar Creek, and the spelling was later changed to Smyrna.

Deep Hole Point was the first name for **Marshallberg**. Folks say that clay dug from there to be used to fill ramparts and cover easements at Fort Macon left a large hole, thus the name. It was later named for Matt Marshall, who ran the mailboat from Beaufort. **Marshallberg** lies on a peninsula formed by Sleepy Creek and Core Sound.

Graham Academy was established in Marshallberg by W.Q.A. Graham in 1880 at the head of Sleepy Creek. Curriculum prepared students for college, and those who did not live in town stayed in the school's dormitories. Monthly board was about $5.50 per student, and the school's attendance in 1892 was 126. The Academy was destroyed by fire in 1910.

Gloucester was named in the early 1900s by Capt. Joseph Pigott for the East Coast town in Massachusetts that he loved. A ferry once ran between Gloucester and Harkers Island.

Williston was named for John Williston who was one of the area's first settlers. The community has long been nicknamed "Beantown," though why is still a point of confusion. Some say it was because of the large amount of beans that were grown in the community, and others say it was because residents had a reputation for loving beans. Williston United Methodist Church was built in 1883.

Davis was settled by William T. Davis in the 1700s and was a farming village. People worked the water and the land to make a living. Farm crops, such as cotton and sweet potatoes, were taken by sailboat to Virginia to be sold or traded for needed items (flour, sugar, cloth). Davis residents were known as "Onion Eaters." Some folks say the name came from the number of green onions grown in the community, and others say it was because Davis Shore people simply liked onions. An Army camp was opened in Davis during World War II, and some of the old buildings remain along the water's edge.

Stacy is really made up of two even smaller communities: Masontown and Piney Point. The post office was opened in 1885. Stacy Freewill Baptist Church is more than 100 years old.

Originally called Wit, **Sea Level** is still the fishing community it has always been. In 1706, Capt. John Nelson was granted about 650 acres by the King of England, and that land is today's Sea Level. Sailors' Snug Harbor, the oldest charitable trust in America, opened a facility for retired merchant marines there in 1976. The original facility of its type opened in 1833 on Staten Island. Sea Level Extended Care Facility is a nursing home on Nelson's Bay. A satellite clinic of Carteret General Hospital now operates alongside the nursing home.

Atlantic was settled in the 1740s and was originally called Hunting Quarters. The first post office opened in 1880, and the name was changed to Atlantic. The community's nickname is Per, and old timers refer to their home as Per Atlantic. In the 1930s progress arrived in the form of paved roads. A ferry once operated between Atlantic and Ocracoke. Atlantic is home to two of the East Coast's largest seafood dealers, Luther Smith & Son Seafood Company and Clayton Fulcher Seafood Company.

Insiders' Tips

The Crystal Coast offers great "secret" fishing spots, like the back side of Shackleford Banks and the jetty at Fort Macon.

Down East

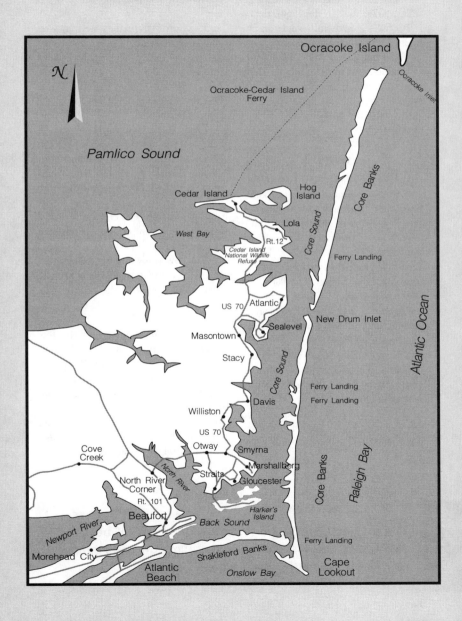

Cedar Island was known by that name until two post offices were established in the early 1900s. Then the east end of the island became known as Lola and the west end as Roe, each with its own post office and school. In the 1960s, the two post offices closed, and a new one was opened. The whole island became known as Cedar Island again. Locals still use the old names, and some homes on the island date back to the 1880s. Many locals widely accept the fact that Cedar Island is the site of the so-called "Lost Colony" (see Oral History).

Newport/ Western Carteret County

Carteret County's only incorporated town west of Morehead City on Highway 70 is **Newport**. The town continues to grow along with Marine Corps Air Station Cherry Point in Havelock. The last census showed a population of 2,569, meaning the town grew by 1,000 people in the past 10 years. Chartered in 1866, Newport was first supported by logging, farming and fishing. Today, many residents work at Cherry Point.

Newport offers many quiet residential areas, a school, stores, a town hall and a public library. Called "the town with old-fashioned courtesy," Newport is home to the Newport Pig Cooking Contest each April. The town has a strong volunteer fire department and rescue squad.

Northeast of Newport is the community of **Mill Creek**. This is mainly a farming community, including a large blueberry farm, which can be reached from Newport or Highway 101 out of Beaufort.

Highway 24 traces the waterfront west along Bogue Sound, from Morehead City to Onslow County. The highway passes through several old settlements and some new communities, then across the White Oak River into Onslow County and the town of Swansboro.

From Cape Carteret, Highway 58 goes west through the Croatan National Forest through several old settlements including Peletier, the Hadnot Creek community and Kuhn's Corner and then into Jones County. If you turn east on Highway 58 from Cape Carteret, you'll cross a high-rise bridge and enter the beach town of Emerald Isle.

The newest town in the western part of the county is **Cedar Point**, the westernmost point of the county. The town was established in 1713 but not incorporated until 1988.

Cape Carteret is one of the few "planned" communities in Carteret County. It was chartered in 1959, and the late W.B. McLean began the development of the town. The first homes were built on the Bogue Sound waterfront near the foot of what is now the B. Cameron Langston Bridge, the high-rise bridge built in 1971 to replace the ferry. The

town grew slowly and today is complete with stores, a town hall, fire and rescue departments and a school.

Several communities dot the western part of the county. **Bogue** stretches along Highway 24 several miles west from Cape Carteret and is home to the U.S. Marine Corps Auxiliary Landing Field. **Ocean** is an old community and was once a small thriving village with one of the county's first post offices. **Broad Creek** is another old timer, once made up almost exclusively of commercial fishermen and their families. Some of these fishermen came to the area as much as 100 years ago; others came from Diamond City on Shackleford Banks after the horrible hurricanes forced them to vacate. Today, there is a school and lots of new residential developments.

Kuhn's Corner marks the intersection of Highway 24 that leads to **Stella**, which was once a thriving community with stores, a couple of mills, a good many farmhouses and even a couple of huge plantation houses.

Photo: Scott Taylor

Almost everybody loves fresh seafood.

Crystal Coast
Restaurants

Seafood is the featured entree in most Crystal Coast restaurants. In all coastal Carolina areas, deep fried used to be the typical way restaurants prepared seafood. But today, restaurant-goers have a choice of steamed, broiled, baked, grilled, blackened or fried seafood in addition to many creative entrees exclusive to each restaurant.

Still, fried hushpuppies continue to be a local favorite and are often used to rate restaurants. Hushpuppies are made with corn meal, flour, eggs and sugar. Some folks add some chopped onion, others add sweet milk. Once blended, the mixture is dropped by the spoonful into hot fat and fried to a golden brown. Oldtimers say the name derived from cooks tossing bits of fried batter to yapping 'coon dogs in an effort to quiet them.

Most natives were reared on conch and clam chowders. Now newcomers are discovering these treats. Conch chowder is made with the whelk of a conch shell, and clam chowder is made with the white meat of the clam. To easily remove the meat, locals recommend freezing the shell; once thawed, the meat can be easily pulled out. Traditional chowder is made with chopped meat, water, butter, salt, pepper and diced potatoes. For a different flavor, you might also add squash, onions and spices.

Collards have long been a mainstay in the diet of most locals, especially those living Down East. A "mess" of collards cooking in the kitchen creates an unforgettable aroma that you either love or hate.

Collards are leafy green vegetables that grow almost year round in this area. Most locals say the best way to cook collards is with a streak-of-lean salt pork or some fat back added to the pot and then topped off with a few new red potatoes and some cornmeal dumplings. Cornmeal dumplings are unique to the coastal area and are basically cornmeal, water and salt shaped into small patties and dropped into the collard pot for about 15 minutes.

There is nothing like a traditional Down East clam bake. You won't find eating like this on any restaurant menu. But, you can luck out and catch a school or fire department putting on a clam bake to raise money. If that happens, our advice is to drop all your plans and head on over for some real good food.

It is said that the idea for the clam bake came from the Native Americans who taught early residents to cook clams, fish and corn in the steam of hot stones. Today, there are businesses that have large steamers for hire. Modern-day clam bakes offer clams, chicken, sweet potatoes, white potatoes, onions, carrots, corn, and sometimes a few shrimp. They are all steamed together in a net bag or cheesecloth and served with melted butter. This is not the time for table manners, so use your fingers!

Peelers, pickers, jimmies, white bellies, hens, steamers, paper shells or soft shells — no matter what you call them, they're still crabs. Learning the difference between the names and the stages of a crab's life is the hard part. Knowing when crabs are ready to shed and are marketable as soft shells is important to the livelihood of many Crystal Coast fishermen. Understanding the process a crab goes through to become a soft shell is an art. After the crabs are caught, either in crab pots or by trawlers, they are sorted and separated.

A peeler is a crab that will, if all goes well, become a soft crab within 72 hours. They are carefully handled and put in vats where they can go through this molting process. Jimmies are the large crabs that measure six inches from upper shell tip to tip, and steamers or pickers are just regular crabs. The sure way to tell if a crab is a peeler is by the pinkish-red ring on the outer tip of the flipper or back fin. Those that complete the molting process are sold live or dressed. Many are packed with damp sea grass, refrigerated and shipped live to restaurants in New York. Most are sold dressed because live soft shells are delicate to handle and have a limited life of about three days. Locals consider soft shells a delicacy, and favorite ways to prepare them include battering and lightly frying or sauteing in butter and wine.

Shrimp burgers are very popular and are little more then fried shrimp on a hamburger bun with slaw and just the right special sauce. Each restaurant has its own sauce, which is the secret to a great shrimp burger. Some places have come up with variations (oyster burgers, clam burgers), but it's all basically put together the same way. And, oh, what a wonderful lunch it makes.

There are increasing numbers of fast food and chain restaurants finding their way to the Crystal Coast. Most of these places seem to locate on U.S. 70, which is the main artery through the area. You'll find Burger King, Hardee's, McDonald's, Bojangles, Pizza Inn, Shoney's, Taco Bell, KFC, Wendy's and many more. These places balance out the number of seafood spots and provide diners with a greater variety of restaurants from which to choose. This guide does not review those restaurants because you are probably already familiar with their fare.

Planning and Pricing

When planning your lunch or dinner outing, we recommend you call ahead to verify the information offered in these restaurant profiles and to check the hours or seating availability. Although most of the restaurants in the area are locally owned and have been in business for years, a few will change hands during the off season. While we seek to be as accurate as possible, these changes often mean a modification of menu items. Some area restaurants traditionally close in the winter, and some that remain open limit menu items to ensure freshness.

Mixed drinks are available in restaurants and lounges in all the towns throughout the Crystal Coast except Newport. You won't find mixed drinks in the Down East area or any other unincorporated area except in the Bogue Banks' community of Salter Path. Most restaurants do serve wine and domestic and imported beer, and some allow brown bagging.

Some restaurants in the area offer special discounts to early diners, and many have discounts for senior citizens and for children's dinner menu items.

Because of the large number of restaurants on the Crystal Coast and the limited space in this chapter, we have reviewed restaurants that continue to be favorites. There are certainly other restaurants here; check the local phone book

and newspaper advertisements for other suggestions. We have designed these brief reviews in hopes of making your selection easier, but we know you will want to try several of the establishments in town to get a full taste of local favorites. Restaurants are arranged alphabetically according to their location. We have given the milepost (MP) number for those on N.C. 58 on Bogue Banks to help you find them more easily.

We have also arranged a price code to give you a general idea of the cost of a dinner for two, including appetizers, entrees, desserts and coffee. Because entrees come in a wide range of prices, the code we used reflects an average meal — not the most expensive item or the least expensive item. Also keep in mind that these prices are based on a full dinner, so a lighter dinner would be less expensive, and a dinner with cocktails, wine and extras would be more expensive. For those restaurants that do not serve dinner, the price code reflects the cost of lunch fare. These codes do not reflect gratuity or the state's 6 percent sales tax. Most of the dinner establishments listed honor major credit cards and take reservations.

The price code used in the reviews is as follows:

Less than $20	**$**
$21 to $35	**$$**
$36 to $50	**$$$**
More than $51	**$$$$**

Bogues Banks

Atlantic Beach

BISTRO BY THE SEA
401 Money Island Dr., MP 1¹ᐟ⁴   *247-2777*
$$

Bistro By The Sea is a local favorite for dinner. This small restaurant is beside Sportsman's Pier and offers a casual atmosphere and fine food. A favorite appetizer is the roasted peppers and Italian sausage. Salad favorites include the Caesar with char-grilled tuna and the leafy spinach with shrimp. Seafood entrees vary nightly according to freshness and avail-

Photo: Scott Taylor

Waiting on a shrimpburger.

The REX

★ ★ ★ ★ ★ ★ ★ ★ ★ ★ ★ ★ ★ ★

Eastern North Carolina's Most Exclusive Caterer

Tastefully Serving Groups From 10 to 1,000

★ ★ ★ ★ ★ ★ ★ ★ ★ ★ ★ ★ ★ ★

ITALIAN BUFFET
Tuesday, Friday & Saturday

★

FEATURING
Northern & Southern Italian Specialties
Live Lobster & Italian Clam Bar

★

PIANO MUSIC
Every Saturday Night

★

MAGICIAN
Every Tuesday Night

★

THE MARINO FAMILY
Serving The Crystal Coast Since 1948

Highway 70 West • Morehead City, NC 28557

Announcing The Rex at St. Regis
North Topsail Beach
(910) 328-4999

(919) 726-5561

ability. We recommend the char-grilled filet mignon or rib eye, liver in orange liqueur or stir-fried chicken with rice and wontons. Pasta creations include seafood cheese-filled pasta shells, eggplant Parmesan and capellini with pesto, vegetables and scallops. Sandwiches are also available, along with a tempting selection of desserts. Bistro By The Sea has a bar area and serves mixed drinks, beer and wine.

BOURBON STREET CAFE

MP 3   *808-2888*
$$

Bourbon Street Cafe is tucked in a corner in Atlantic Station Shopping Center, but it is not to be missed. The cafe serves Cajun and creole creations for lunch and dinner. Favorite appetizers are barbecue shrimp and conch fritters. Gumbo ya-ya is a traditional New Or-

leans' chicken and sausage gumbo. Try the grilled chicken salad made with chicken marinated in honey and bourbon. Entrees include pasta jambalaya with chicken, shrimp and sausage, shrimp scampi and chicken dishes with creole rice. One favorite is seafood lasagne with shrimp, scallops and spinach. Daily and nightly chalkboard specials are also offered. For dessert try the bread pudding with whiskey sauce or the chocolate pecan pie. Bourbon Street Cafe offers guests a fine selection of wines and beers along with mixed drinks. Reservations are encouraged.

CHANNEL MARKER
RESTAURANT & LOUNGE

Atlantic Beach Causeway   *247-2344*
$$-$$$

Channel Marker specializes in grilled

fish and aged beef. Overlooking Bogue Sound, the restaurant offers waterfront dining and has all ABC permits. House specialties include grilled fish, land and sea combinations, seafood platters, steak and shrimp kebabs and broiled lobster tails. A grilled or broiled fish is offered each night, and the chef also prepares cold plate entrees, grilled chicken breasts and stuffed flounder. Desserts include French silk, lime and lemon pie and bananas foster. The dock in front of the restaurant is available for those arriving by boat, and the adjoining lounge (see the Nightlife chapter) has all ABC permits and a good selection of wines and beers. The restaurant can accommodate groups of up to 100.

No Name At The Beach

MP 3   240-2224
$$$

No Name At The Beach offers the same great menu as the sister restaurant in Beaufort, plus a few extras. Guests will find great pizza, all kinds of subs, Greek entrees, hamburgers, cheeseburgers, spaghetti, lasagna and other pasta dishes. The Greek salad is loaded with feta cheese and served with a loaf of garlic bread. The chef's salad is piled high with meats and cheeses. Guests can enjoy a limited selection of seafood and steaks. No Name also serves sandwiches and chicken and offers desserts, including baklava. No Name At The Beach offers dine-in or drive-through service.

DJ Shooters
Restaurant and Lounge

MP 4³/⁴   240-1188
$$

DJ Shooters serves a country breakfast with farm fresh eggs, a variety of

meats, omelettes, cream chipped beef, homemade corned beef hash and fruit waffles. The lunch and dinner menu is filled with selections of fresh local seafood, juicy steaks and tender baby back ribs. Steamed shrimp, crab legs and fillet of flounder or trout are offered along with plentiful combination platters and surf and turf specials. Other menu items include pork chops, chicken and ribs. DJ Shooters has a good repeat business among locals and visitors alike. They offer specials to senior citizens and children. The restaurant serves wine, beer and mixed drinks.

HARPER'S OCEANFRONT
AT THE JOLLY KNAVE
Oceanfront, Atlantic Beach Circle   726-8222
$-$$

The Jolly Knave offers casual indoor and outdoor oceanfront dining. Voted as providing the "best oceanview on the island," the outside second-floor deck is a great place to dine and enjoy the view of the Atlantic Ocean and beach. Appetizers include potato skins, wings, shrimp, beef ribs and oyster cocktails. They offer all kinds of sandwiches (club, barbecue, chicken breast), burgers and salads. Dinner entrees include seafood (try the combination platter broiled or fried), steak, pasta, barbecued beef ribs and daily specials. The chef also serves pizza, fajitas, soups and cold plates, and a child's menu is offered. This establishment has all ABC permits. For information about the lounge, see our Nightlife chapter.

W.B. KELLI'S
Atlantic Beach Causeway   247-1094
$$$

Kelli's has become known for its Angus beef and great seafood. Appetizers include crab-stuffed mushrooms and chicken fingers. Entrees feature rib eye, prime rib, stuffed flounder and shrimp, lobster, chicken and all kinds of seafood, broiled, grilled, fried or panned in butter. There is a variety of land and sea combination platters available. Entrees include a garden or spinach salad, baked potato, fries or wild rice and rolls. There is a fresh fish special each day. Guests can park cars in front or dock boats at the lounge deck. Patrons often enjoy a drink in the lounge or on the deck before or after dinner (see Nightlife).

MAN CHUN HOUSE RESTAURANT
MP 1¹/²   726-8162
$$

Man Chun House has been serving wonderful Chinese food for many years and has an excellent reputation. The restaurant features a complete Chinese menu and has a few American menu items. The egg drop and won ton soups are tasty, and the hot and sour soup is wonderful. Marinated barbecued ribs and egg rolls are favorite appetizers. So is the famous flaming pu-pu platter that has a selection of several appetizers. Favorite entrees include marinated beef with snow peas and vegetables, shrimp and peas, chicken and broccoli, scallops with vegetables, sesame chicken, duck, lobster and sweet and sour shrimp and chicken. The restaurant has all ABC permits and serves beer and wine. Man Chun offers a take-out service too.

NEW YORK DELI
Crow's Nest Shopping Center   726-0111
Atlantic Beach Causeway
$

This is the place for authentic deli food, and it is wonderful. We recommend a Manhattan Cheesesteak — heck, order two cheesesteaks and we'll join you. They

serve overstuffed sandwiches, subs, great kraut, chili dogs, homemade soups and salads. They also have one of the area's best supplies of imported beers and wines. Deli meats and cheeses are also available for you to take home and create your own feast. New York Deli offers take-out or eat-in service, catering, party trays, gift baskets and a retail wine shop.

SKIPPER'S COVE RESTAURANT AND LOUNGE
MP 2   726-3023
$$-$$$

Skipper's Cove is a popular restaurant that offers an extensive buffet and entertainment. The restaurant's famous all-you-can-eat buffet is served every day from 4 to 10 PM. It features all types of seafood — shrimp, fish, clams, crabs, scallops, oysters and more — along with beef,

chicken, roast, ham, pasta, barbecue, soups, salads, vegetables and breads. A complete dinner menu is also available and features seafood, steaks, chicken and more. Entrees are served with a choice of potato and a visit to the salad bar. Guests will find homemade salad dressing and tempting desserts. Skipper's Cove offers banquet facilities. Entertainment varies and includes the house six-piece band playing beach, country and Top 40 for dining and dancing.

Pine Knoll Shores

CLAMDIGGER RESTAURANT
Ramada Inn, MP 8¼   247-4155
$-$$

Open for breakfast, lunch and dinner, the Clamdigger in the Ramada Inn prides itself on serving made-from-scratch items. You'll find fluffy omelettes for breakfast and prime rib sandwiches for lunch. Dinner entrees include steaks and all kinds of seafood. The Clamdigger features authentic Mexican cuisine every Friday at lunch. There is a special every evening — oysters on Monday, rib eye on Tuesday, seafood combination on Wednesday, shrimp on Thursday, flounder on Friday, lobster and shrimp on Saturday and steak and shrimp on Sunday.

PARADISE RESTAURANT
Sheraton Resort, MP 4³/⁴   240-1155
$$-$$$

In the Sheraton Resort, Paradise serves breakfast, lunch and dinner in a quiet, casual atmosphere overlooking the hotel pool and the ocean. Lunch guests can enjoy creative sandwiches, speciality burgers, grilled chicken and stir-fried entrees. Dinner appetizers include such treats as escargot tempura (snails lightly fried and served in garlic butter) and crabmeat cocktail. The dinner menu features seafood, steaks and pasta. A few of our favorites are the flounder stuffed with crabmeat, grilled swordfish, veal marsala, filet mignon, scallops and shrimp over fettuccine noodles. The restaurant has all ABC privileges.

TRADEWINDS
Royal Pavillion, MP 5¹/²   726-5188
$$-$$$

Tradewinds is in the newly renovated Royal Pavillion Resort. The restaurant offers diners good variety and features a wonderful Sunday brunch with a large selection of entrees, breads, fruits and desserts. Dinner entrees include seafood, aged prime beef, pasta and chicken along with soups and salads. Try the Jack Daniels rib eye or one of the other house specialities. Tradewinds often features live

entertainment and offers banquet and meeting facilities. Guests can also enjoy the Passport Lounge next door.

Indian Beach/Salter Path

BIG OAK DRIVE IN
Heart of Salter Path, MP 10¹/²   247-2588
$

Turn on the blinker and stop the car. Big Oak has the best shrimp burger on the Crystal Coast — that's the vote of an Insiders' poll. While others serve a good shrimp burger, Big Oak serves a great one. They've been at it for 18 years. Other goodies you'll find include barbecue sandwiches, burgers, hot dogs, chicken sandwiches, pizza and even BLTs. Big Oak has plates of barbecue, fried chicken, chicken salad and shrimp as well as mighty good french fries, onion rings and slaw. But it's that shrimp burger that will keep you coming back!

CRAB SHACK
On Bogue Sound, MP 10¹/²   247-3444
$$

Tucked back off the main road, The Crab Shack offers diners excellent seafood and a wonderful view of Bogue Sound — the restaurant actually hangs over the water. This is one of the our favorite places for steamed crabs in addition to shrimp and crab legs. Yum! The restaurant has an extensive seafood menu and will fry, grill, pan in butter or broil your choice. For the landlubber, there is rib eye, chicken and hamburger steak. The Crab Shack serves wine, beer and has set ups for those wishing to brown bag their favorite beverage. The outside deck is a great place to relax.

FRANK AND CLARA'S
RESTAURANT & LOUNGE

MP 11   247-2788
$$-$$$

Frank and Clara's is a local favorite and is also very popular with visitors. The restaurant offers a variety of dinner choices that include seafood and steaks. Insider favorites are the crab cakes, cut-to-order char-grilled steaks and flounder stuffed with your choice of crabmeat, shrimp, scallops or oysters. Each meal is prepared to order. Dinner entrees come with cheese and crackers, a salad and homemade dressings, a cup of clam chowder, hushpuppies or rolls, and a potato, fries or rice. There are special entrees for senior citizens and children. Beside the Salter Path Post Office, the restaurant has all ABC permits. Come early — Frank and Clara's has lots of repeat business so

there might be a short wait. There is also an upstairs lounge.

FROST SEAFOOD
HOUSE AND OYSTER BAR

MP 10³/⁴   247-3202
$$

In the heart of Salter Path, Frost's serves all kinds of seafood and has an oyster bar. The restaurant serves dinner every day and all three meals in the summer, including all-you-can-eat breakfast specials. Frost serves seafood, steaks, chicken, barbecue, lobsters and fresh vegetables. Local favorites include shrimp scampi, popcorn shrimp and snow crab legs. Frost's offers seafood prepared Salter Path-style from family recipes and has the best hushpuppies around. The restaurant has facilities to accommodate private parties and offers a take-out service.

During the summer, a line of hungry people forms, so we suggest you go early. Frost Seafood Market is just the place to get fresh local seafood to prepare at home.

SQUATTER'S SEAFOOD RESTAURANT
MP 11   247-3464
$$-$$$

This is the place to go if you are really hungry for seafood. The all-you-can-eat dinner buffet includes a salad, seafood and dessert bar. There you will find popcorn shrimp, fish, snow crab legs, crab cakes, clam strips, deviled crabs, shrimp creole, seafood casserole, lasagna, meatballs, game fish, vegetables and chef's specials. If those don't suit your fancy, try any of the seafood, steak or chicken entrees from the full menu. Squatter's offers a breakfast buffet, early bird specials and special menus for senior citizens and children.

Emerald Isle

BUSHWACKERS RESTAURANT
100 Bogue Inlet Dr.   354-6300
$$

Bushwackers is known for its fun wait staff, spectacular oceanfront view and great decorations. It is a favorite dinner spot for fresh seafood prepared in a variety of ways, although broiled and steamed are the specialties, along with steaks, chicken and other entrees. Their appetizer menu is extensive, even including gator and shark bites. We love the blooming onion and the stuffed clams. Entrees feature fresh seafood, char-grilled Angus steaks, prime rib and more. Try the rock 'n' roll cheesecake for dessert. The Safari Lounge is a great place to meet friends and make new ones. Bushwackers has all ABC permits and serves beer and wine. Come enjoy an island dining adventure.

RUCKER JOHNS
A RESTAURANT & MORE
140 Fairview Dr., MP 19¹/²   354-2413
$$

Rucker Johns offers great food and fun for the entire family. The restaurant is just off the main road and is one of our favorites. The restaurant prepares each dish to order and offers fresh seafood, pasta, barbecued shrimp, beef ribs, steaks, chicken and pork chops. Favorite appetizers include the fried calamari and shrimp cooked in beer, hot crab dip and sultry chicken wings. For lunch, try the grilled Cajun chicken salad, the spinach salad with hot bacon, the coastal pasta salad, any of the juicy burgers or a creative sandwich. Dinners feature seafood — shrimp, crab cakes, fish, seafood pasta — steaks and ribs. Rucker Johns has all ABC permits and has a restaurant in Wilmington. The "More" in their name refers to the lounge (see our Nightlife chapter).

Beaufort

BEAUFORT GROCERY CO.
117 Queen St.   728-3899
$$-$$$

Beaufort Grocery Co. is a favorite of locals and visitors. In a relaxed atmosphere, Chef Charles Park offers fine cuisine in a restored town grocery store. The lunch menu consists of creative salads (try the smoked fish salad), soups and sandwiches. Favorites are the gougeres (herb pastries stuffed with crab, shrimp, chicken or egg salads), smoked turkey, country ham and cheese on sourdough or chicken salad with apples on a croissant. Dinner starts with such creative appetizers as Oriental pork ribs marinated in dried fruit, fabulous Carolina crab cakes, or the fisherman's soup filled with shrimp, scal-

RUCKER JOHNS

A RESTAURANT AND MORE . . .

rucker johns

Quality Foods Prepared Fresh to Order

Seafood • Pasta • Steak • Chicken • Ribs

Lunch & Dinner All Day, Every Day, Year Round

MasterCard - Visa - American Express - All ABC Permits - Casual

- Serving you in two locations -

140 Fairview Drive	5511 Carolina Beach Road
Emerald Isle, NC 28594	Wilmington, NC 28412
(919) 354-2413	(910) 452-1212

lops, clams, fish and vegetables. For your entree, we suggest fresh grouper encrusted with crabmeat and asparagus with a sauce, grilled turkey steak served with corn salsa or filet mignon. The dinner menu features fresh seafood, choice steaks, chicken, duck and lamb. Early diner's specials are also offered. Top your meal off with raspberry cheesecake or any other dessert. Entrees are served with a salad, fresh vegetables and bread. Beaufort Grocery Co. offers a wonderful Sunday brunch, a take-out menu and a full delicatessen with meats, cheeses, homemade salads and breads. There is also a small bar area; the restaurant has all ABC permits.

115 QUEEN STREET

115 Queen   728-3899

$$$$

115 Queen is the perfect restaurant for a special dinner or if you just want to travel a little bit without leaving Beaufort. Let Chef Charles Park take you away with his culinary creations. 115 Queen offers the ultimate in international cuisine. Each week the menu changes to feature a different cuisine from around the world. It might be German, African, Thai, Hungarian, Chinese, French — whatever direction Chef Park wants to go. His inspiration for menus comes from books, travels and friends. Each menu is arranged with several selections in each of the four or five courses. Reservations are recommended and can be made next door

at Beaufort Grocery Co. 115 Queen is open for catering and special parties.

CLAWSON'S 1905 RESTAURANT

429 Front St.   *728-2133*
$$

Clawson's 1905 is a wonderful mix of old and new. The restaurant is housed in what was Clawson's General Store back in the early 1900s and is decorated with what could have been some of the wares available. But the menu items are new creations. Two local lunch favorites are the dirigible, a hearty baked potato stuffed with seafood, vegetables or meats, and the French dip, roast beef on a toasted roll with au jus for dipping. Other lunch items include overstuffed sandwiches, burgers, salads, soups and seafood plates. Dinner appetizers include vegetables lightly battered and quick fried, cheese fries, ribs and shrimp. Entrees offered are grilled, fried or sauteed seafood, zesty ribs, steaks, chicken and pasta. Clawson's serves mixed drinks, wines and domestic and imported beers. This place gets crowded during the summer months, so go a little early. To save time, lunch orders can be faxed to 728-2692.

FINZ GRILL & EATERY

330 Front St.   *728-7459*
$

Finz is the perfect place to relax, enjoy good food and visit with friends. Guests can sit inside at a table or at the bar or on the back porch that hangs over Taylor's Creek. Finz serves breakfast, lunch and dinner on varying days, so call ahead. Breakfast items include eggs, omelettes, pancakes, country ham and more. Lunch and dinner focus on sandwiches, subs, burgers, soups (try the wonderful gumbo or black bean) and baskets that might include grilled, blackened or fried seafood and steaks and pasta dishes. Finz

prides itself on offering seafood caught by local fishermen, many are their friends and customers. Items vary depending on the catch and could include fresh Spanish mackerel, king mackerel or flounder. Finz has great desserts, all ABC permits and a popular bar.

FRONT STREET GRILL

419 Front St.   *728-3118*
$$-$$$

This new American bistro focuses on seafood, grilled meats, pasta and other creative entrees served for lunch and dinner. The lunch menu includes soups, creative salads with grilled tuna, hot fried chicken or shrimp, overstuffed sandwiches with grilled chicken, turkey and smoked cheese or fish, crab cakes and pasta. Dinner appetizers include hot crab dip, pepper-fried calamari and black bean and goat cheese quesadillas. Suggested entrees include herb-encrusted tequila grilled shrimp, seared tuna and grilled beef with tomato chutney. Nightly chalkboard specials are also featured. Try the chocolate raspberry truffle cheesecake and Key lime cheesecake for dessert. Front Street Grill has all ABC permits plus an extensive beer and wine selection. Espresso and cappuccino are also available. Reservations are suggested.

HARPOON WILLIE'S RESTAURANT & PUB

300 Front St.   *728-5247*
$$

Why not relax and dine overlooking Taylor's Creek and an island chain that is home to roaming ponies? That's what Harpoon Willie's offers, so come on in. The restaurant operates on two menus — a dinner menu and a bar menu. Dinner appetizers include crab cakes, steamed clams, seafood gumbo and stuffed shrimp.

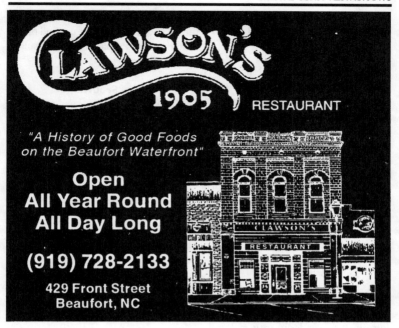
Entrees focus on fresh local seafood and certified Angus beef. Diners can enjoy the daily catch broiled, baked, blackened, fried, steamed or sauteed. Favorites include shrimp Alfredo, savory scallops, baby back ribs, rib eyes and seafood platters. The bar menu features soups, salads, burgers and seafood. The restaurant has all ABC permits and offers wine and domestic and imported beers. Harpoon Willie's pub is next door. A ferry to Shackleford Banks and Carrot Island leaves the restaurant dock several times each day during the summer.

NET HOUSE
STEAM RESTAURANT & OYSTER BAR
133 Turner St.   *728-2002*
$$-$$$

    The Net House specializes in steamed seafood, has a raw bar and is a favorite among locals and visitors. Guests can enjoy an atmosphere of weathered pine and nautical antiques in this family owned and operated business. Try the creamy clam chowder, conch chowder, crab soup or seafood bisque for lunch or as a dinner appetizer. Sandwiches, salads and seafood are also offered for lunch. Dinners are wonderful, whether you like seafood steamed, broiled, panned in butter or lightly fried. Favorites include steamed crabs, clams, oysters and shrimp or the broiled platter that includes flounder stuffed with crabmeat, scallops, oysters and shrimp. For dessert, the Net House is known for its famous Key lime pie. The Net House has all ABC permits

No Name Pizza & Subs

408 Live Oak St.   728-4978, 728-4982
$

This is the best place for pizza, according to our own personal survey. It is also a great place for subs (everything from meatball to vegetarian), burgers and spaghetti with meatballs. The Greek salad is loaded with feta cheese and is served with a loaf of garlic bread. No Name also serves pasta dishes, Greek dishes, sandwiches and chicken. The baklava is wonderful. The menu is the same for lunch and dinner, and you'll leave satisfied and feeling like you got your money's worth. No Name offers dine-in or drive-through service.

Purple Pelican

Town Creek Marina   728-2224
$$-$$$

Owner Martha Bourne offers Beaufort diners a wonderful treat at Purple Pelican. Above Town Creek Marina, this restaurant is a local favorite, offering lunch, dinner and a bar menu. Diners can enjoy the spectacular view of Gallant's Channel and the Intracoastal Waterway while dining inside or on the deck. Lunch features grilled fish, a variety of seafood, chicken sandwiches, soups, salads and burgers. The dinner menu emphasizes fresh local seafood, chicken, beef and pasta entrees with nightly specials. Try one of the many homemade desserts to top off your meal. You can be sure of a creatively prepared meal and good service here. The bar menu features lighter fare and finger foods. The Purple Pelican has all ABC permits, wines and domestic and imported beers. Reservations are suggested, and off-season hours vary, so call ahead. An elevator is available for guests needing assistance reaching the second floor. Martha also operates

Bogue's Pocket on the Morehead City waterfront. She can arrange on- and off-site catering; the Purple Pelican is available for private parties.

The Spouter Inn

218 Front St.   728-5190
$$$

The Spouter offers waterfront dining at its best. Guests enjoy a small dining area that extends over the water and provides a wonderful view of the Beaufort Inlet and Taylor's Creek. Summer diners can eat on the outside dock and enjoy the sunshine. There are always chalkboard specials. One lunch favorite is the half and half, which includes a cup of clam chowder and half of the sandwich of your choice. The Out Island, which is shrimp, mushrooms, onions, cheese, tomatoes and sprouts served on rye, or Buster's Hideout, a soft shell crab in a pita pocket, are popular as are the salads and club sandwiches. The Inn's clam chowder is filled with clams, potatoes and vegetables. Dinner entrees include baked grouper, grilled dolphin, prime rib, chicken, lobster and veal. For a real taste of local seafood, try the seafood supreme — baked grouper, shrimp, backfin crabmeat with mornay sauce. Dessert favorites include crepes, parfaits and a sinful peanut butter pie. Don't miss Spouter's Sunday champagne brunch. The Spouter Inn has all ABC permits.

Morehead City

Anchor Inn
Restaurant & Lounge

2806 Arendell St.   726-2156
$$-$$$

The Anchor Inn Restaurant is well known by locals and visitors for fine food and quality service. For 25 years, the res-

taurant has offered creative entrees and is open for breakfast and dinner. Guests are offered a variety of omelettes, waffles, fruits, pancakes, quiches, biscuits and muffins at the hearty breakfast. Dinners are served by candlelight and include Black Angus beef and prime rib, fresh local seafood, fresh pasta and chicken dishes. Seafood is prepared in a variety of ways — blackened, grilled, broiled or fried. A special diet menu is also offered, and there are daily breakfast and dinner specials. Desserts are unsurpassed and include their famous Toll House Pie and Chess Pie. Private banquet and meeting rooms are available, and the restaurant has all ABC permits. The adjoining lounge often features live entertainment.

BOGUE'S POCKET CAFE
708 Evans St.   247-5351
$$-$$$

Bogue's Pocket Cafe is another one of our favorites. Don't let the outside fool you. Some of the best gourmet cooking on the coast goes on inside. Bogue's Pocket is famous for creative preparation and sauces and fine service. This is the perfect place to bring that special person or guests or to gather with a few friends and enjoy a fine meal. Diners will find homemade soups, salads and entrees with special flair. Owner Martha Bourne features a limited, always changing dinner menu to ensure fresh quality. Emphasis is on homemade sauces and the freshest seafood and meats. Entrees include seafood, pasta, chicken and beef. Finish the meal off with a tempting homemade dessert. Bogue's Pocket has all ABC permits and serves beer and wine along with a nice selection of coffees. Try this establishment's sister restaurant, Purple Pelican at Town Creek Marina, Beaufort. Martha can arrange on- and off-site catering.

CALYPSO CAFE

506 Arendell St.   240-3380
$$$

Calypso Cafe offers tropical cuisine in a casual atmosphere for dinner. Each dish is carefully prepared, and the results are fabulous. Selections vary depending on availability and freshness. Guests can start with an appetizer: black bean torta, baked stuffed jalapenos or curried potato bisque. Entrees focus on local seafood presented with island fruits and spices. Favorites include the shrimp curry with tropical salsa, grilled fish with ginger salsa and New York strip with caramelized onions. You'll also find pork loin, pasta, seafood fajitas and blackened or grilled seafood. Desserts, such as paradise pie (a brownie and ice cream covered with strawberry puree) are sure to tempt. Guests can dine at table, at the bar or on the patio. The cafe serves mixed drinks, wine and beer, but is best known for the creative cocktails.

CAPT. BILL'S
WATERFRONT RESTAURANT

701 Evans St.   726-2166
$$-$$$

This family-style restaurant has been serving lunch and dinner on the Morehead City waterfront for 51 years. John and Diane Poag own Capt. Bill's today, and the tradition of good food continues. The menu features fresh local seafood and homemade items, including sauces, dressings, soups and hushpuppies. Daily lunch specials include an entree (baked chicken, pepper or ham steak,

chicken and pastry, shrimp or beef stew), two vegetables and hushpuppies for $3.95. Monday is all-you-can-eat fish day, and Friday is all-you-can-eat fish and popcorn shrimp day. Wednesdays and Saturdays are conch stew days. Capt. Bill's also offers cold plates, salads, seafood casseroles, seafood combination plates, Cajun-style catfish, steaks, chicken and sandwiches. Items approved by USA Weight Loss Center and the Diet Center are available along with an extensive children's menu. Desserts are made from family recipes and include the original Down East Lemon Pie. Diners can come by boat or by car, but don't leave without samples of the 13 flavors of fudge made at the restaurant or without stopping by the gift shop. Capt. Bill's Catering Service can take care of any event.

CHARTER RESTAURANT

405 Evans St.   726-9036
$$-$$$

On the Morehead City waterfront, the Charter specializes in fresh local seafood and is open for lunch and dinner. Diners have a good view of the Morehead City waterfront, the state port and the surrounding water because the dining area actually hangs over the water. Lunches offer all kinds of seafood, along with ribs, hamburger steak, soups and salads. Our favorite is Crabby Dan, hot crabmeat heaped on an English muffin and topped with a tomato slice and cheese. There are always lunch specials along with a full menu. Dinner appetizers include such creations as oyster supreme, clam chowder, seafood bisque and wonderful marinated grilled shark bites. Entrees include homemade crab cakes, shrimp and flounder stuffed daily, prime rib and live lobsters. Seafood is steamed, fried or broiled. Chicken, charbroiled steaks and barbe-

cue ribs are also offered. The restaurant's salad bar includes vegetables, breads, pasta and cheese. Our recommendations for dessert: Granny's Apple Caramel Pie or homemade Toll House Pie. The Charter offers menus for senior citizens and children and has all ABC permits.

EL'S DRIVE-IN
3600 Arendell St.   726-3002
$

El's has been a Carteret County tradition since 1959. This is an old-fashioned drive-in — that means you are waited on by car hops and sit in your car and eat. El's has great burgers, hot dogs, fries and shakes. Try a shrimp or oyster burger, a BLT, a fish or steak sandwich, a shrimp or oyster tray or fried chicken. This is a favorite lunch and dinner spot for locals, so go early to get a parking place. And don't forget to lob a french fry or two out the window to the waiting sea gulls.

NIKOLA'S
Fourth and Bridges Sts.   726-6060
$$-$$$

Nikola's serves Northern Italian cuisine with a warm, Old World charm. This is the perfect place to take someone special or to gather with a group of close friends. The 1920s two-story Victorian house provides eight separate dining rooms, and guests can enjoy five course meals as well as à la carte selections. Meals include a choice of appetizers, homemade soups or pasta, tossed green salads, two vegetables, an entree, dessert and beverage. Creative entrees could be fresh seafood, red snapper, veal marsala, filet mignon, steak pizzaiola or fettuccine Alfredo. Favorites include the spinach soup, any of the made-from-scratch pas-

Menhaden Industry

Jule Wheatly remembers when Beaufort merchants used their sense of smell as an economic indicator. They could judge the winter business season by the smell in the air. When merchants and residents awoke to the smell of fish cookin' at the town's menhaden plants, they knew things were going well and money was coming into the town.

When the 45-year-old president and general manager of Beaufort Fisheries was growing up, Beaufort was home to three menhaden plants, and there were just as many in Morehead City. Now, his is the only plant left in the county.

"The town of Beaufort's first name was Fishtowne," Mr. Wheatly said. "I remember when there were so many menhaden boats stacked along the Beaufort waterfront that they had to get a court order to get the owners to move them so other boat traffic could get through the creek."

Menhaden is an oily, high protein fish that is processed into fish meal, oil and solubles (see Commerce and Industry). Menhaden, often called

The Menhaden Chantymen.

fatbacks or shad, are a restless fish that move in huge schools up and down the coast.

Wheatly's grandfather, the late Claude Wheatly Sr., joined the late Will Potter in partnership to buy the plant in about 1934. Jule Wheatly began working at the plant in 1973 and became president-general manager in 1983.

"Fishing is so much different now than it was back then," Mr. Wheatly said. "Now, we depend on speed, and it is strictly business." Planes are used to spot menhaden schools and direct the boats to them. The factory is capable of processing 4 million fish every 24 hours. Annual production at Beaufort Fisheries varies from 80 to 160 million fish.

"There are more menhaden out there now than ever," Mr. Wheatly said. "If we quit fishing, you would see large fish kills on the beaches." He noted large menhaden kills within the last few years in Maine, Massachusetts and elsewhere. The growing menhaden population is attributed to the closure of fish meal plants along the coast — many being forced out of business by environmental groups and other lobbying organizations.

Continually, there are proposals and regulations being applied to the menhaden fishing business, including the restricting of fishing within 3 miles of shoreline. Beaufort Fisheries catches the majority of its fish within one-eighth of a mile of shore.

"It takes a lot of coast to do fishing," Mr. Wheatly said. "We survived through bad prices, through low catches and through bad weather, but we'll have trouble surviving all these regulations."

Beaufort Fisheries employs between 70 and 90 workers and has three boats. With the ability to carry 2.5 million fish, *Coastal Mariner* is the plant's newest vessel. The *Gregory Poole* can carry 1.5 million fish, and the smaller *Taylor's Creek* can handle about 600,000.

Men leave these larger boats in small purse boats to surround the fish. A purse net is used to surround the fish and is so called because it is drawn shut like a handbag. In early years, workers pulled the fish-ladened nets up from the water by hand. In order to synchronize the pulling and lifting, the men sang songs, or chanteys as they were called. Today, the nets are pulled up with hydraulic lifts.

John Henry Pritchett was one of those men who did the work by hand. Like many African Americans from Beaufort, Mr. Pritchett, who was 74 years old when he died last April, worked in the menhaden business.

"Singin' was the way we got those fish up," Mr. Pritchett once said. "It made us pull together — kept us in rhythm. You'd sing before you'd bend down to pull. There weren't any engines to raise those fish. You had to do it by hand. After they got this hydraulic stuff, you didn't have to sing chanteys."

With the introduction of hydraulic equipment, he knew the old work songs the crew sang would be forgotten. To keep these work songs alive, he and fellow former fishermen formed The Menhaden Chanteymen in 1988.

"We're trying to keep these chanteys alive," Mr. Pritchett said in an interview months before his death. "Those songs are old. Folks were singin' them before we were old enough to go on the boats."

Mr. Pritchett retired from the menhaden business in 1986 after working for 46 years, most of that time as an engineer. "I first stopped around 1980, but every year they wanted me to go back. They needed an engineer, so I went."

The Menhaden often perform locally at the N.C. Maritime Museum in Beaufort and have performed at Carnegie Hall in New York. The group has appeared on CBS's *Sunday Morning with Charles Kuralt*. They have also given performances for the North Carolina State Legislature and many other groups.

Mr. Pritchett's favorite chantey was "Going Back to Weldon." One man would sing the opening and the crew would respond. The response is noted in all capital letters.

Going Back to Weldon
I'm going back to WELDON, WELDON, WELDON.
I'm going back to WEL-DON,
To get a JOB IN THE WELDON YARD.
Chorus:
Oh, I'm going back to WELDON, WELDON, WELDON.
Oh, I'm going back to WEL-DON,
To get a JOB IN THE WELDON YARD.
Oh, Captain, if you FIRE ME, FIRE ME, FIRE ME.
Captain, if you FIRE ME,
You've got to FIRE MY BUDDY TOO.
Chorus:
Oh, the captain's got a LUGER, LUGER, LUGER.
Oh, the captain's got a LU-GER,
And the MATE'S GOT AN OWL'S HEAD.
Chorus:
I don't want no WOMAN, WOMAN, WOMAN.
I don't want no WO-MAN,
Who's got HAIR LIKE A HORSE'S MANE.
Oh, I don't want no WOMAN, WOMAN, WOMAN.
I don't want no WO-MAN,
Who's got HAIR LIKE A HORSE'S MANE.
Chorus:
Oh, the house is on FIRE, FIRE, FIRE.
Oh, the house is on FI-RE,
And it's ALMOST BURNING DOWN.
Oh, the house is on FIRE, FIRE, FIRE.

Oh, the house is on FI-RE,
And it's ALMOST BURNING DOWN.

Another favorite was "Drinking of the Wine."

Drinking of the Wine
Well, drinking of the WINE, WINE, WINE.
Oh, drinking of the WINE, THAT HOLY WINE.
Well, you ought to been to HEAVEN TEN THOUSAND YEARS,
DRINKING OF THE WINE.
Oh, two white HORSES SIDE BY SIDE.
None can ride them but the SANCTIFIED.
That's why you ought to been to HEAVEN TEN THOUSAND YEARS,
DRINKING OF THE WINE.
I got a mother in the PROMISED LAND,
I'm never going to STOP UNTIL I SHAKE HER HAND.
That's why I should have been to HEAVEN TEN THOUSAND YEARS,
DRINKING OF THE WINE.
Two white HORSES SIDE BY SIDE.
One of them HORSES I'M BOUND TO RIDE.
Well, you ought to been to HEAVEN TEN THOUSAND YEARS,
DRINKING OF THE WINE.
I know you love WINE, WINE, WINE.
I know you love, that WINE, THAT HOLY WINE.
That's why you ought to been to HEAVEN TEN THOUSAND YEARS,
DRINKING OF THE WINE.
If my mother ASKS FOR ME,
Brother, won't you tell her I'm on my WAY TO GALILEE.
Oh, Lord, I'm on my way to the WINE, WINE, WINE.
Well, drinking of the WINE, THAT HOLY WINE.
Ought to been to HEAVEN TEN THOUSAND YEARS,
DRINKING OF THE WINE.

tas, broiled rack of lamb, flounder sauteed in almondine sauce and shrimp scampi. Nikola's has all ABC permits.

OTTIS' WATERFRONT RESTAURANT
711 Shepard St.   *247-3474*
$$-$$$
Here you'll enjoy a variety of cooking — blackened, Cajun, pan-fried, sauteed, grilled and broiled. Appetizer selections include calamari served with sweet and sour sauce, crab-stuffed mushrooms and blackened shrimp served spicy. Diners can enjoy steamed oysters, clams, shrimp and snow crab legs in season. Menu entrees vary and feature fresh grilled seafood, steaks, pasta, chicken and local specialties. Try the baked orange roughy in a champagne-dijon mustard, roasted salmon topped with basil butter, the blackened shark fillet topped with salsa or the cajun spiced tuna. Other favorites

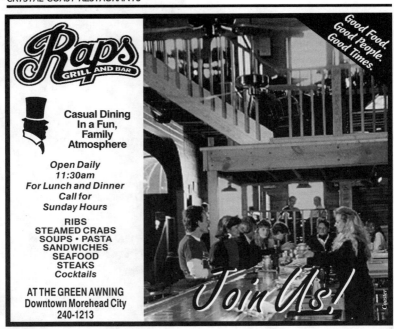
are choice rib eye, New York strip steaks, pasta primavera and chicken marsala. Ottis features an extensive selection of California wines, and the restaurant has all ABC permits and a good selection of beers. Ottis' Restaurant can also cater any affair.

RAPSCALLIONS

715 Arendell St.   *240-1213*
$$

Raps is a favorite for lunch, dinner or drinks served up in a casual 1890s family atmosphere. House specialties include steamed clams and crabs, a true Philly cheesesteak, the original Raps Burger and seafood Alfredo. Guests will also find ribs, crab legs, soups and steaks. Raps has a wonderful taco salad and dressed-up hamburgers, seafood gumbo and overstuffed sandwiches. Lunches feature

a light and lively special that could be shrimp salad one day and a delicious fruit plate the next. The bar at Raps is a popular gathering place on weeknights and weekends. Bar patrons can enjoy hot popcorn and watch the wide-screen television.

REX RESTAURANT

U.S. 70 W.   *726-5561*
$$-$$$

Rex is a true Italian restaurant that has been pleasing locals and visitors alike since 1947. A family business now in its fourth generation, Rex is a popular lunch and dinner spot. The restaurant focuses on Italian foods, fresh local seafood and choice steaks. Favorite appetizers are the clams casino and the hot seafood antipasta. Entrees are creative and include veal and eggplant parmigiana, manicotti, lasagna, linguine with red clam sauce and more. We recommend the evening Italian buffet. Rex is also famous for pizzas and fresh breads. Dessert favorites include Italian rum cake, homemade cheesecakes and homemade pastries. Rex has all ABC permits, an extensive line of wines and beers and a small bar area for relaxing, where live entertainment is often provided. Contact the Rex with your catering needs, and let them design a cake for any occasion.

RIVERWALK DELI & CAFE
714 Shepard St.
Morehead City Waterfront   808-2166
$

Riverwalk offers lunch and dinner in casual surroundings. Try the antipasto, chef's salad, or shrimp, chicken or tuna salad garnished with veggies, cheeses and fruits. There is always a soup, lunch and dessert special. Sandwich selections include turkey with provolone cheese, roast beef with Swiss, shrimp in pita bread and the popular Salty Dog, a quarter-pound beef frank anyway you like. The deli offers imported meats and cheese along with side dishes such as creamy potato salad, cole slaw and pasta salad. Riverwalk serves beer and wine.

SANITARY FISH
MARKET & RESTAURANT
501 Evans St.
Morehead City Waterfront   247-3111
$$

Sanitary has been a landmark on the Morehead City waterfront for 55 years. In 1938 Ted Garner and Tony Seamon, both now deceased, opened a waterfront seafood market in a building rented for $5.50 per week with the agreement that no beer or wine would be sold and that the premises would be kept clean and neat. The name Sanitary Fish Market was

chosen by the partners to project their compliance. When 12 stools were set up at the counter, the first seafood restaurant on the city's waterfront was in business. Today, son Ted Garner Jr. operates the family-oriented business. Customers will find old favorite menu items plus many new additions. Best known for fresh seafood, the restaurant also offers steaks, poultry, pork and pasta entrees. Seafood is served broiled, steamed, grilled or fried. Lunch features always include a good selection of vegetables. Appetizers vary and include shrimp and clam cocktails, shrimp salad, clams on the half shell, homemade chowders and soups. Dinner favorites include seafood combination platters, charbroiled Angus beef, grilled chicken and steamed Maine lobster along with cold plates of shrimp, shrimp salad and crabmeat, fried shrimp and fish and rib eye. Sanitary Fish Market offers fresh local seafood for those who prefer to dine at home.

SUMMER PALACE
CHINESE RESTAURANT
3402 Arendell St.   726-6000
$

Summer Palace offers Mandarin, Szechuan and Cantonese cuisine. The lunch and dinner buffets and a full menu offer a variety. The lunch menu offers a wide selection served with chicken wings or egg rolls. Lunch includes such favorites as beef with broccoli or vegetables, shrimp chow mein, sweet and sour pork or chicken, and chicken Cantonese. Dinner appetizers include the popular pu-pu tray with a variety of items, fantail shrimp, steamed or fried dumplings and a good selection of soups. Entrees feature chicken, duck, beef, seafood and pork. Two favorites include the Peking duck served with scallions and Chinese pancakes and the orange beef. Hot and spicy items are noted. Summer Palace offers a children's menu and an American menu including chicken. Take-out service is available.

THE WATERFRONT
SEAFOOD DELI & CAFE
Jib of Shepard St. and Evans St.   *247-3933*
$

This small cafe is in the jib, or triangle, between Shepard Street and Evans Street and across from Ottis' Waterfront Restaurant. The breakfast menu offers traditional favorites and specializes in breakfast steak, bacon, ham and cheese sandwiches and eggs served on buns or toast. The lunch and dinner menu features seafood platters, crab cake sandwiches, shrimp burgers, hamburgers, hot dogs, soups, salads and more. Dinner specials also include pasta dishes and grilled or blackened fish dishes. You'll also find steamed clams and oysters, along with a good selection of beer and wine. Takeout lunches are also offered and are convenient for boaters or anyone on the go. Patrons can either eat in the cafe, outside in a grassy park in front of the cafe or take their meals with them.

WEST SIDE CAFE
4370-A Arendell St.   *240-0588*
$$-$$$

West Side Cafe is a favorite among locals and regulars. This upscale cafe offers creative lunches and gourmet dinners. The lunch menu offers soups (try the almost famous tomato soup), specialty sandwiches, burgers, dogs, subs and salads. Favorites include the pastrami, knockwurst and Swiss grilled on rye with Russian dressing; the stadium dog with slaw, kraut and chili; the grilled shrimp salad; and the smoked turkey sandwich.

While lunch is wonderful, dinner is where the West Side Cafe shines. Favorite appetizers are glazed shrimp, seafood potstickers with Oriental dipping sauce and soups. Salads offered include grilled shrimp or grilled lemon herb chicken over mixed greens. Entrees include shrimp and sun-dried tomatoes in a cream sauce over linguine, grilled beef in a cognac cream sauce and sauteed breast of chicken in a raspberry glaze. Fresh fish can be broiled, grilled or sauteed. Each week a "temptations" menu is prepared to accompany the regular dinner menu. This special menu might feature shrimp and veal, roasted Cornish game hen, or scallops and bananas with pasta. Special appetizers, wines and desserts for the week are also highlighted. West Side Cafe has all ABC permits and serves beer, wine, select coffees and wonderful juices. There is a full deli offering homemade salads, meats, cheeses and fresh baked goods, and live entertainment is often provided.

MRS. WILLIS' RESTAURANT
3004 Bridges St.   *726-3741*
$-$$

Mrs. Willis and her family have been offering home-cooked meals since 1949. The restaurant actually began in the home of "Ma Willis" as a barbecue and chicken take-out specializing in mini-lemon pies. Customers ate right in the kitchen, which is now Capt. Russell's lounge. In 1956, the restaurant moved into the garage, which is the front of today's restaurant, and additions were made through the years. The restaurant is a favorite of locals and visitors who want a meal made from family recipes without going to the trouble themselves. Specialties include fresh pork barbecue, local seafood, charcoal steaks and fresh vegetables. We recommend the Down East conch chowder for starters and then the prime rib — it is truly the best around for the value. Other entree suggestions include the seafood combination plate, chicken livers, pork chops, stuffed crab, rib eye or roast beef. There is a special every day and night. Mrs. Willis' can accommodate groups of any size and has all ABC permits.

Swansboro

CAPT. CHARLIE'S RESTAURANT
N.C. Hwy. 24 at Front St.   326-4303
$$

Capt. Charlie's restaurant specializes in fresh seafood, prime rib and steaks. Fried seafood is still popular, although there are plenty of other choices. Try the stuffed flounder or broiled shrimp and scallops. The steaks have developed a following too. Well-cooked food served in ample amounts brings people back to Capt. Charlie's again and again. With all ABC permits, you can have a drink while you wait for your dinner or with it if the mood strikes you.

RIVERSIDE DELI & CAFE
108 W. Corbett Ave.   326-1830
$-$$

Riverside Deli & Cafe features a well-stocked deli offering marvelous fresh salads of all kinds, deli-sliced cold cuts, a wide variety of cheeses and a great selection of wines and beers. Cafe diners are treated to a view of the White Oak River and can eat at the bar or tables downstairs or upstairs. The cafe serves breakfast, lunch and dinner, specializing in sandwiches and salads. A favorite is the reuben with spicy kraut. Riverside offers a private dining room upstairs and a catering service. The staff can handle banquets, meetings and receptions.

YANA'S YE OLDE DRUGSTORE RESTAURANT
Front St.   326-5501
$

Just about everybody who is anybody in Swansboro eats at Yana's at some time during the week. Whether it is the food or the company that attracts you, once you've been in, you'll come again and again. Breakfast specialties are many, and all are cooked to order. Lunch can include a variety of sandwiches or soups, but the Bradburger, an all-beef hamburger with egg, cheese and bacon, lettuce and tomato, is worth a sample. And the desserts, well, see for yourself!

WHITE OAK RIVER CAFE
N.C. 24   326-6121
$$-$$$

This charming cafe overlooks the White Oak River and features authentic Italian seafood. Luncheon items include creative and hearty pizzas, deli sandwiches on freshly baked breads and salads, and there are always specials. Dinner appetizers might include antipasto or roasted peppers and fresh baked breads filled with tomato, ham or spinach. Entrees include pasta, lasagne, seafood, veal, chicken and wonderful homemade sauces. We suggest the lemon and basil flounder or the swordfish pesto. Early bird dinner specials are offered. And you just can't resist the pastries baked fresh daily — eclairs, napoleons or cheesecakes. White Oak River Cafe offers fresh deli and bakery items each day and has all ABC permits. Come enjoy a touch of Southern Italy.

Down East

DRIFTWOOD RESTAURANT

Cedar Island   225-4861
$$

Locals refer to everything at this complex by simply saying, "the Driftwood." On the banks of Core Sound, the Driftwood includes a motel, restaurant, campground, gift shop, convenience store and hunting guide service. The restaurant is known far and wide for the Friday and Saturday night prime rib special and seafood buffet. Other entrees offered include all types of seafood, including fresh crabmeat, shrimp salads, five-seafood combination plates and soft shell crabs. You'll also enjoy ham, pork chops, chicken, barbecue and a children's menu. The restaurant is beside the Cedar Island-Ocracoke Ferry Terminal. This is a very popular restaurant year round, and we suggest you call for the off-season schedule. For information about the motel, see the Crystal Coast Accommodations chapter, and for information about the campground, see the Camping chapter.

ISLAND RESTAURANT

Harkers Island   728-2214,728-2247
$-$$

Liston and Carolyn Lawrence have been serving island residents and guests for 14 years from the same location. Open for breakfast, lunch and dinner, Island Restaurant offers everything from pizza and sandwiches to seafood platters and prime rib. Shrimp and eggs, along with all the traditional dishes, are served for breakfast. The lunch menu includes hamburgers, subs, pizza and spaghetti. Sandwiches range from oyster and shrimp burgers to flounder and crab sandwiches, and there is a take-out service. The restaurant's prime rib special and week-end seafood buffet just can't be beat and are well worth the drive no matter where you are. There is a full menu that includes shrimp and fish dinners, roast pork and cold seafood platters. You can have your meal prepared as you like it — fried, broiled, steamed or charbroiled. The "little mates menu" offers plenty selections for children.

SEA LEVEL INN & RESTAURANT

Sea Level   225-3651
$$

Twelve miles from the Cedar Island ferry terminal, Sea Level Inn and Restaurant offers casual waterfront dining on Nelson's Bay off Core Sound. The restaurant serves lunch and dinner most weekdays, dinner on Friday and Saturday and breakfast and a lunch buffet on Sunday. The breakfast menu offers traditional Southern items. There is usually a hot lunch special, along with salads, seafood plates and sandwiches. Fresh local seafood and beef are favorites on the dinner menu, and everything is cooked to order. For information about the inn, see the Accommodations chapter.

Western Carteret County

BUTCHER BLOCK CAFE

Chatham St., Newport   223-5336
$

This cafe has a reputation for serving up ample portions of well-prepared, home-style food. Breakfast is a time for pancakes, steak and eggs, omelettes and homemade biscuits. For lunch or dinner, guests will enjoy steak, seafood, roast turkey, chicken and pastry and more. Of course, there are sandwiches, soups and salads, and there are daily lunch and dinner specials. Butcher Block Cafe is in downtown Newport.

GRANNY'S DINER

U.S. 70, Newport   223-6106
$

Granny's Diner offers country cooking in a family atmosphere. Open at 5:30 AM every day, Granny's serves a hearty breakfast that can't be beat. You'll find pork tenderloin, hamburger gravy on toast, eggs and all your favorites. For lunch and dinner, the menu features such entrees as barbecue ribs, steak, chicken and fish. Each Friday and Saturday night features prime rib and seafood, which draw quite a crowd. The homemade banana pudding keeps folks coming back. Granny's serves three meals a day Monday through Saturday. On Sunday, it's open for breakfast and lunch only.

FAIRWAY RESTAURANT

N.C. 58, Cape Carteret   393-6444
$-$$

The Fairway Restaurant is a popular lunch spot for golfers, construction workers, business people, tourists and locals. Guests will find salads, quiche, specialty sandwiches, homemade soups and creative burgers. Dinner turns to steak and local seafood, and one of the specialties of the house is the prime rib. Done to perfection, exactly the way you request, it's moist and delicious. Fairway is closed on Sunday.

THE FLYING BRIDGE

N.C. 24, Cedar Point   393-2416
$-$$

The Flying Bridge has an advantage several other area restaurants don't have: You can eat overlooking the Intracoastal Waterway and a neighboring sandy island. The Flying Bridge has three parts: a restaurant serving lunch and dinner, and

featuring fresh grilled seafood, pasta, chicken, veal and steaks; a steam and raw bar offering oysters, clams, crabs and shrimp; and a ship's store deli, bakery and seafood market offering subs, bagels, and seafood. The restaurant and bar have all ABC permits. The restaurant offers daily specials and wonderful desserts.

MAZZELLA'S ITALIAN RESTAURANT

N.C. 58, Cape Carteret   393-8787
$$

About 2 miles north of Cape Carteret is Mazzella's. This is an authentic Italian restaurant that offers excellent dinners. This family-owned and -operated business provides only the finest Italian cuisine and has diners coming back again and again. Guests will find a number of creative entrees along with fresh pastas, homemade sauces, seafood and more, even sandwiches and pizzas.

T & W OYSTER
BAR AND RESTAURANT

N.C. 58, near Cape Carteret   393-8838
$-$$

T & W has been satisfying customers since 1972 with steamed oysters, shrimp cocktail and homemade clam chowder followed by plenty of seafood entrees. Try a single seafood, a combination of two or more seafood items, steak, chicken or a hamburger. Guests will also find sandwiches and burgers made with fried shrimp, oysters, scallops or fish. T&W serves beer or wine and has an ABC license for brown bagging. Don't let the line fool you. The restaurant can accommodate parties of close to 400, and the bar can handle plenty who stop by to feast on steamed oysters.

Photo: Irv Hooper

This shrimp boat is off early to fill its hold with fresh seafood.

Inside
Accommodations

The Crystal Coast is a diverse resort area, and most accommodations are near natural or historic attractions. You have many attractive choices full of our history and hospitality. Pick from oceanfront or soundside rooms, efficiency suites and cozy bed and breakfast inns.

On the beach, as in all beach areas, rates vary according to proximity to the water. If you are considering a location away from the water in order to save money, you might want to find out what access to the ocean or sound is provided and if it is within walking distance.

The Crystal Coast is, more and more, a year-round resort. There really is no "off season" anymore when visitors aren't here in some abundance, so it is always wise to make reservations in advance. Many establishments offer attractive weekend getaway packages and winter rates. The area is also a popular site for meetings and conventions. The larger hotels offer meeting rooms and convention facilities, as does the Crystal Coast Civic Center in Morehead City.

Each establishment has a different deposit and refund policy. While some require a deposit equal to one night's accommodations in advance, others will simply hold your reservation on your credit card. Often, a 24-hour notice is sufficient for a full refund, but some require as much as a three-day notice. Because of the area's popularity, extending your stay can be difficult but not impossible. Some places require up to 72-hours' notice for extensions past your originally scheduled departure date.

Many of the area's lodgings offer non-smoking rooms by request. The older inns restrict smoking to certain areas and often do not offer facilities to accommodate small children. North Carolina law prohibits pets in hotels and motels, although some lodgings make provisions for them.

This guide doesn't attempt to list all the accommodations available on the Crystal Coast. Rather, we've provided a sampling of some of our favorites. For more information about lodging, contact the Carteret County Tourism Development Bureau, P.O. Box 1406, Morehead City, NC 28557, (800) SUNNY NC or 726-8148. The bureau operates visitors centers located at 3409 Arendell Street (Highway 70) in Morehead City and on Highway 58, just south of the intersection of Highways 58 and 24.

For the purpose of comparing prices, we have placed each accommodation in

The deep roots of sea oats help to anchor the sand dunes. The plant is protected by law, so don't even think of harvesting a few, even if they're dead.

Insiders' Tips

a price category based on the rate for a double-occupancy room per night during the summer season. Winter rates can be substantially lower. Rates shown do not include state and local taxes. We've tried to be accurate, but amenities and rates are subject to change. It's best to verify information when making reservations. You'll find that most of these establishments accept major credit cards, but ask when you're making your reservation if it's important to you.

$25 to $52	$
$53 to $75	$$
$76 to $99	$$$
More than $100	$$$$

Atlantic Beach

The accommodations we'd recommend on the beach are just too numerous to list. Here, we offer a small sample of the many great places available to you from full-service resorts to family and angler favorites. We also suggest you contact condominium developments on the beach (see Vacation Rentals) because most offer attractive vacation rates.

SHOW BOAT MOTEL

Atlantic Beach Causeway   726-6163
$-$$

With easy access to Bogue Sound, this motel offers lodging and water sports at affordable rates. Guests can fish from the motel wharf, complete with a fish cleaning table, or take a dip in the pool. All rooms have refrigerators, and guests can enjoy picnic areas and grills. The motel offers family, corporate and AARP rates and is open all year. Also on site is Wreckreational Divers, 240-2244, a full-service dive shop for those who like to go "down under."

SUNDOWNER MOTEL

Atlantic Beach Causeway   726-2192
$-$$$

This older hotel offers quiet, clean waterfront accommodations to anglers and families. Kitchenettes are available, and patrons are given free boat launching and a wet slip during their stay. Complete with a pool, the motel has picnic tables, barbecue grills, brewed coffee and storage spaces. There is even a cozy wood stove for those chilly evenings.

OCEANANA RESORT MOTEL

E. Fort Macon Rd. MP 1$^{1/2}$ 726-4111
$$-$$$

This comfortable, no-frills motel on the ocean provides guests with lots of extras. It offers a pool, children's play area, fishing pier, picnic tables and grills, country club golf privileges, free patio breakfast in season, beach chairs and a patrolled beach. Guests can choose from standard rooms, oceanfront rooms or suites, all including refrigerators. The Oceanana closes for the season the first weekend in November and reopens two weeks before Easter.

HOLLOWELL'S MOTEL

E. Fort Macon Rd. MP 1$^{3/4}$ 726-5227
$-$$$

Hollowell's is a family-oriented motel operated by Russell and Betty Hollowell. It is three blocks, an easy walk, from the ocean, restaurants and shopping. Guests are offered quiet rooms, kitchenettes, cottages, bridal suites and a swimming pool with slide. All rooms have telephones, cable TV and HBO.

BUDGET INN

221 W. Fort Macon Rd. MP 2$^{1/2}$ 726-3780
$-$$$

This clean, comfortable motel was recently remodeled and offers family and commercial rates by the day, week or month. There is a pool, and all rooms have HBO and phones. Efficiencies are also available. The motel is an easy three-block walk from the ocean and is close to restaurants, shopping areas and the main beach amusement circle.

DAYS INN SUITES

Salter Path Rd. MP 2¹ᐟ²   247-6400
$$-$$$$ (800) 972-3297

Days Inn Suites are truly nice rooms, arranged with a hallway entrance and bath and sleeping area on the main floor. Two steps down will take you to a sunken sitting area and onto a private porch with a wonderful view of Bogue Sound. Rooms offer either king-size or two double beds and microwaves; all have refrigerators and coffeemakers. There is an outdoor pool,

boat ramp, dock, and slips are available by reservation. Summer rates vary for weekdays and weekends. The inn is within walking distance of the beach and is near shopping areas and restaurants.

SHERATON ATLANTIC BEACH RESORT

Salter Path Rd. MP 4¹ᐟ²   240-1155
$$$-$$$$ (800) 624-8875

The Sheraton is a full-service beach resort. All rooms offer guests a refrigerator, microwave and coffeemaker. Each has a private balcony. Suites are available with a bedroom and living room plus a Jacuzzi. The staff can arrange anything from same-day dry cleaning to a chartered sailboat. Meals are available in the resort's Paradise Restaurant (see Restaurants), and Harry's Island Bar has live weekend comedy shows. Overlooking the ocean is

Molly's Beachside Bar, offering, in season, casual food fare and beverages. Alongside Molly's is a fishing pier for anglers, and Woody's nightspot (see Nightlife) is favored by guests and locals alike for dance music and beverages. Catering and full banquet services are available for small or large meetings.

Pine Knoll Shores

WINDJAMMER INN

Salter Path Rd. MP 4¹/²   247-7123
$$$-$$$$ (800) 233-6466

Attractive inside and out, the Windjammer Inn offers all oversize and oceanfront rooms with private balconies, refrigerators, cable, HBO and two phones. The glass-enclosed elevator is an unexpected surprise and offers a great view. Guests may use the oceanfront pool and a private beach area with lifeguard and beach service. Enjoy complimentary coffee each morning. There is a two-night minimum during summer weekends and a three-night minimum on holiday weekends. We recommend you get a room on the top floor and relax.

SEA HAWK MOTOR LODGE

Salter Path Rd. MP 4³/⁴   726-4146
$$$ (800) 682-6898

This comfortable and newly remodeled lodge offers all oceanfront rooms with balconies or patios, phones, color cable TV and refrigerators. Connecting double rooms are also available. A coffee shop is open in season. A pool is situated in the middle of a large, grassy lawn facing the ocean. Guests especially enjoy lazing on the lawn in the late evening.

HOLIDAY INN OCEANFRONT

Salter Path Rd. MP 4³/⁴   726-2544
$$$-$$$$ (800) HOLIDAY

Holiday Inn services and accommodations here are further enhanced by the oceanfront location. The inn offers 114 guest rooms. Guests enjoy the pool, 800 feet of private beach and a picnic area along with special golf and tennis privileges. The Palms Restaurant and Oasis Lounge are located in the inn. Open year-round, the inn can accommodate small or large groups for vacations or meetings.

The Quiet Place
At Island Mile Post 5

Morehead City, NC - On the Ocean in Pine Knoll Shores
(919) 726-5168 - In U.S. TOLL FREE 800-682-7057

ATLANTIS LODGE

Salter Path Rd. MP 5   726-5168
$$-$$$$ (800) 682-7057

Set among the beautiful live oaks on the oceanside, the Atlantis Lodge was among the first hotels built on Bogue Banks. Its patrons are faithful and never disappointed. Most units are arranged as suites, offering efficiency kitchens, dining, living and sleeping areas. All have patios or decks facing the surf, cable TV and other expected amenities. Recreation areas, equipment and complimentary beach services are extended to guests. Lifeguards are on duty during the summer months. The outdoor pool is a quiet place for sunning and swimming. A third-floor lounge is offered with adjoining library. Unlike most hotels, the Atlantis makes provisions for pets. Packages are available in the fall and spring.

ROYAL PAVILLION RESORT

Salter Path Rd. MP 5¹ᐟ²   726-5188
$$-$$$$ (800) 533-3700

This is the newest oceanfront resort and conference center on Bogue Banks. Many remember it as the former John Yancey Motor Hotel; however, after ex- tensive renovations, the new resort offers 150 light and airy guest rooms. Many rooms are equipped with special amenities, including complete efficiency kitchens. An outdoor pool, 1,500 feet of private beach, cable service and local activities arrangements provide guests with an abundance of leisure-time choices. Guests may arrange for use of any of the four conference rooms and service of the resort's Tradewinds Restaurant.

IRON STEAMER RESORT

Salter Path Rd. MP 6³ᐟ⁴   247-4221
$$-$$$ (800) 332-4221

The Iron Steamer, so named because of the remains of a Civil War blockade runner visible from the resort's pier at low tide, is on a quiet stretch of the island. Favored by families and anglers, it has 49 oceanfront rooms and a 1,000-foot lighted pier complete with tackle shop, fishing gear rentals and a 24-hour snack bar. Rooms are available with refrigerators and private balconies. Guests have access to the beach, pool and pier. Its operating season runs from Easter to Thanksgiving.

RAMADA INN OCEANFRONT

Salter Path Rd. MP 8¹/⁴   247-4155
$$$-$$$$ (800) 338-1533

On the ocean in a quiet mid-island residential area, this seven-floor inn offers all oceanfront rooms with double or king-size beds. Each room has a small private balcony, and guests have access to the beach, pool, golf and tennis privileges, the Cutty Sark Lounge and the Clamdigger Restaurant, a favorite of locals who know all about the weeknight specials. Meeting and banquet facilities are available. Open year round, the Ramada Inn offers attractive weekend packages during the late fall and winter.

Salter Path

WILLIAM-GARLAND MOTEL

Salter Path MP 10¹/²   247-3733
$-$$

This small family-owned motel has eight rooms and three mobile units. Nine are efficiencies, and two provide simple sleeping accommodations. Don't expect anything fancy, but do expect a family atmosphere and clean surroundings.

Guests have access to the ocean via a nature trail walkway (about 200 yards) and to Salter Path Dunes Natural Area, a 20-acre natural area perfect for walking, sunning and picnicking. William-Garland Motel is beside Big Oak Drive-In, home of the famous shrimpburger.

OAK GROVE MOTEL

Salter Path MP 10¹/²   247-3533
$-$$

This motel has impressed us because it's so tidy and always looks cool in the shade of live oaks, even on the hottest days. It has one- and two-story stone-sided units offering guests standard rooms and efficiency apartments. The motel is a family facility and has lots of repeat business. They do not take one-night reservations on weekends.

Emerald Isle/Cape Carteret

ISLANDER MOTOR INN

Islander Dr.   354-3464
$$-$$$ (800) 354-3464

The Islander is on the ocean in Emerald Isle and, although the rooms do not

The Atlantic Coast Hotel, opened in the spring of 1932, was one of the first resort hotels on Bogue Banks.

Photo: Carteret County Museum of History

A Brogue All Their Own

Down East is the area in Carteret County that begins at the North River Bridge just east of Beaufort and continues to Cedar Island. Natives of the Down East area have a brogue all their own that combines Old English sayings and pronunciations with terms coined and used by elders. As modern ways encroach on these communities and more people leave the area to take jobs elsewhere, the unique Down East brogue seems destined to lose its purity.

Even North Carolina natives don't always understand Down Easters terms. A few of the terms you might need to know before you wander off are offered below. Listen carefully.

Addle/Addled: dazed or confused. He was *addled* by all the new fishin' laws.

Blow: wind or windy conditions. There's going to be a *blow* tonight.

Cam (calm): There are several degrees of cam. "Cam" indicates no wind but possibly some motion in the water. "Slick cam" means a stillness in the air and the water.

Catawampus: out of line or crooked. She turned the whole thing *catawampus*.

Common: not in good taste; to act below oneself. What he did was common.

Cut: a small body of water that cuts away from the main body and leads to land.

Ding batter or **Dit Dot**: someone from out of the area, or from "off."

Off: somewhere out of the Down East area. He married a girl from off.

He ain't ugly: means he is handsome.

I think: used in agreement.

Ill: irritable or angry. Mom's *ill* with sister for not behaving.

Jot: to write.

Landin': the shore. I'm going down to the *landin'*.

Merkle bush: a type of myrtle bush; said to keep bugs away.

Mommick: to bother, harass or aggravate. I have been *mommicked* this day.

Nary: none. I haven't heard *nary* a word.

Purty: pronunciation of pretty, but often used to mean unattractive. He sure is *purty* with that black eye and dirty hair.

Run a'ground: to finish, end anything; unable to move. I've eaten so much I've *run a'ground*.

Scrape: a bad or undesirable situation. I'm in a *scrape* now.

Skiff: a small, usually cabinless, boat There will be a few *skiffs* in the creek today.

Slam: an intensifier usually meaning completely. He loaded the pot *slam* full of hard crabs.

directly face the water, most offer a wonderful east-west view of the sea and beach. The two-story brick motel offers guests easy beach access, a pool, a luxurious lawn area, a restaurant and a lounge. Some rooms have kitchenettes, and others have microwaves and small refrigerators. The inn has large meeting rooms.

PARKERTON INN

Hwy 58 N.   393-9000
$$

Newly opened for summer 1994, the Parkerton Inn is just north of the intersection of highways 58 and 24. It is especially convenient for guests overnighting for the summer outdoor drama, *Worthy Is The Lamb*. Guests may choose any of several room arrangements including kitchenette efficiencies and rooms for the handicapped. Golf packages are offered, and a complimentary continental breakfast is included.

HARBORLIGHT GUEST HOUSE

332 Live Oak Dr.   393-6868
$$$-$$$$ (800) 624-VIEW

Situated on a spectacular peninsula on Bogue Sound off Highway 24, the Harborlight Guest House offers bed and breakfast accommodations among its seven suite or room arrangements. The rambling three-story inn, once a restaurant used by the ferry service, is particularly graced by its views, 530 feet of shoreline and a quiet setting close to Emerald Isle beaches and attractions. Gourmet breakfasts are served in the dining room and waterfront terrace or privately for guests in the luxury upstairs suites. Open year round, the inn offers its 20-person capacity conference room for seminars, weddings and other group gatherings.

Beaufort

The majority of accommodations in Beaufort are historic bed and breakfast inns that offer charming surroundings, memorable views and hospitality. All are located in the historic district and within walking distance of the waterfront, boardwalk, shopping areas, restaurants, the N.C. Maritime Museum and historic sites.

Room arrangements and breakfast specialties vary in each inn. Most do not have facilities for young children or pets, and many limit smoking to certain areas of the house. There are two large hotel-like inns, Beaufort Inn and Inlet Inn. Both are relatively new and were constructed in the old Beaufort style, as required by the Beaufort Historic Preservation Commission.

BEAUFORT INN

101 Ann St.   728-2600
$$$ (800) 726-0321

On Gallant's Channel, Beaufort Inn offers guests 41 rooms, all with private porches complete with rocking chairs for viewing waterway activity. Rooms are furnished in early American decor incorporating local arts and crafts.

Owned and operated by Bruce and Katie Ethridge, the inn opened in 1987 and has become well known for its complimentary breakfasts. A typical breakfast, served in a cozy dining room with a fireplace, includes Katie's breakfast pie, croissants, cereal, Danish pastries, fresh juice and coffee. The inn has one large meeting room and two smaller meeting rooms, which accommodate 18 to 20 people. An exercise room and dock slips are available, and Katie can loan you a bike or help you with area information.

The Inlet Inn
Bed & Breakfast

Built near the site of the original Inlet Inn of the 19th century, today's inn by the same name still plays host to boaters. The Inn is directly across from the Town Docks on Taylor Creek, and near all historic points of interest.

From French doors leading to private porches, to cozy rooms with fireplaces, the Inn offers simple elegance in a beautiful setting. Open all year. 36 rooms. Continental breakfast, complimentary wine, newspaper included.

Inlet Inn and Conference Center
601 Front at Queen Streets
Beaufort, North Carolina (919) 728-3600

PECAN TREE INN
Bed & Breakfast

"A magnificent Victorian home located in the heart of the Beaufort Historic District, one half block from the waterfront."

(919) 728-6733

AAA   **116 Queen Street • Beaufort, NC 28516**

CAPTAIN'S QUARTERS
BED & BISCUIT

315 Ann St.   728-7711
$$$-$$$$

This two-story white home with its luxurious wraparound porch offers guests the quiet elegance of a Victorian summer at the shore. You'll find Ruby, Capt. Dick Collins and daughter Polly to be delightful hosts.

The three upstairs bedrooms feature private powder rooms and baths. House traditions include a homemade continental breakfast and a toast to the sunset each evening, which is celebrated with wines and fresh fruit juices. The Collins family assists guests with area information, reservations and services, including use of a PC, modem and fax machine. Payment by personal check is preferred.

THE CEDAR'S INN AT BEAUFORT

305 Front St.   728-7036
$$$-$$$$ (800) 732-7036

Standing at the corner of Front and Orange streets, the two stately homes that make up the inn are surrounded by flower and herb gardens that color each room and flavor the specialties served by the inn's restaurant. Both houses, c. 1768 and 1851, have been completely restored and furnished with period pieces. The Grady family extends its comfortable hospitality in every detail. Guests are offered 16 rooms and suites with private baths and second-floor porches with rocking chairs. Some rooms are designed with separate sitting rooms, and others have fireplaces. The inn is open all year, and a full breakfast is included in the price.

Fine Dining and Lodging by the Sea

The Cedars Inn
At Beaufort

305 Front Street, Beaufort, North Carolina 28516, (919) 728-7036

DELAMAR INN BED & BREAKFAST
217 Turner St.
$$$ 728-4300

Delamar Inn, c. 1866, is restored to its original charm and accommodates guests in three antique-furnished guest rooms with private baths. The Scottish charm and hospitality of hosts Mabel and Tom Steepy begins with a breakfast of homemade breads and muffins, jams, cereals and fruits and extends to helpful arrangement of their guests' plans to enjoy the beaches, explore the town by bicycle, charter a boat or whatever suits the moment. Cookies and refreshments await at the day's end. The Steepys welcome guests year round.

INLET INN
601 Front St.   728-3600
$$$-$$$$

The 37-room Inlet Inn opened in 1985 on the same block of Front Street occupied by the original Inlet Inn of the 19th century. Today's inn offers harborfront rooms with a sitting area, bar, refrigerator and ice maker. Many rooms open onto private porches. Others offer cozy fireplaces or window seats for viewing the Cape Lookout Lighthouse, Beaufort Inlet and Beaufort waterfront from the best vantage available. Guests are served a continental breakfast of homemade pastries, fruits, coffee or tea in the lounge where they are invited between 5 and 7 PM for wine and cheese. Boat slips, a courtyard garden, the rooftop Widow's Walk Lounge and an on-site meeting room are also available for guest use year round.

LANGDON HOUSE

135 Craven St.   728-5499
$$-$$$$ *No credit cards*

Innkeeper and restorer of the Langdon House (c. 1733), Jimm Prest provides around-the-clock extras that make a difference — fishing poles in the morning, full beach baskets for an afternoon picnic, sightseeing suggestions, wine in the evening or aspirin in the middle of the night. He'll suggest the best jogging route, arrange for sail or motor boats and make reservations for dinner. Guests are accommodated in four rooms, each with a private bath, and are offered a full and scrumptious breakfast, usually involving Jimm's orange pecan waffles. Jimm takes everything from reservations to responsibility for his guests' good time, but he doesn't take credit cards.

PECAN TREE INN

116 Queen St.   728-6733
$$$-$$$$

This 1860s two-story Victorian home, complete with gingerbread trim and turrets, is a charming seven-guestroom bed and breakfast remodeled by hosts Sue and Joe Johnson. Each spacious room has special character, all have private baths, and the romantic one — the bridal suite — has a Jacuzzi. A stay at the inn includes an expanded continental breakfast served in the formal dining room or on the inviting wraparound front porch. You will enjoy Susan's freshly baked homemade muffins, cakes and breads, fruit, cereal and specially ground coffee. The Johnsons are glad to assist with daytrip plans or arrange for box lunches, beach chairs or bicycles. They encourage simple relaxation on the cool porches overlook-

ing the inn's ever-expanding herb and flower gardens.

Morehead City

BEST WESTERN
BUCCANEER MOTOR LODGE

2806 Arendell St.   726-3115
$$-$$$ *(800) 682-4982*

The Buccaneer Motor Lodge has 91 attractive rooms with refrigerators, some with a king-size bed and Jacuzzi. Guests are offered complimentary full, hot breakfasts, newspapers, free local calls, cable TV, HBO and ESPN. Meeting and banquet facilities are available. Special rates apply for corporate, commercial and military guests, and golf, fishing and other packages are available. The lodge is located beside Morehead Plaza for shopping and is a short driving distance from Atlantic Beach. The Anchor Inn Restaurant and Lounge is beside the motel (see Restaurants).

COMFORT INN

3012 Arendell St.   247-3434
$-$$$ *(800) 422-5404*

The Comfort Inn, like others in the national hotel chain, offers reliably comfortable rooms, a pool and complimentary continental breakfast each morning. Convenient to the Crystal Coast Civic Center and all beach and historic attractions, the Comfort Inn has 100 rooms and additional meeting facilities to accommodate any gathering. Local phone calls are free; fax service is available; each room has cable TV. Golf and fishing packages are also available. The inn is conveniently near Shoney's, Hardee's and the Morehead Plaza. Corporate, AARP and AAA discounts are also offered.

ECONO LODGE CRYSTAL COAST

3410 Bridges St.   247-2940
$-$$ (800) 533-7556

The Econo Lodge is an easy two blocks from the Crystal Coast Civic Center and offers 56 rooms at very attractive rates. Amenities include color cable TV, free HBO and local calls, a pool and complimentary continental breakfasts. Guests are offered real values on special packages for golf, tennis, deep-sea fishing, sailing, scuba diving, historic tours, shopping trips, dinner cruises and other area activities.

HAMPTON INN

4015 Arendell St.   240-2300
$$-$$$ (800) 538-6338

Hampton Inn, overlooking Bogue Sound, offers beautiful views of the waterway and the island of Bogue Banks.

The 120-room inn has a fresh nautical decor. Guests enjoy an outside pool and deck area, free continental breakfasts served in a sunroom, free accommodations for children and an exercise room. There is a meeting room and plenty of parking. Restaurants and shopping areas are nearby.

Down East

There are a few motels in the Down East area, and they're featured here. For information about campgrounds, see the Camping chapter. Alger Willis Fishing Camps, Davis, 729-2791, and Morris Marina Kamps & Kabins, Atlantic, 225-4261, provide cabins on Core Banks. For more information about these two businesses, see the Ferry chapter.

DRIFTWOOD MOTEL

Cedar Island   225-4861
$-$$

Guests at the Driftwood will find 37 rooms in this older motel. Located at the Cedar Island-Ocracoke Ferry Terminal, rooms offer two double beds and a television. There are no phones in the rooms, so this is a good place to escape from it all. The motel complex also has a restaurant (see Restaurants), campground (see Camping), gift shop, grocery store and a guide service for hunting and fishing. The motel closes from mid-January to mid-March.

CALICO JACK'S INN & MARINA

Island Rd., Harkers Island   728-3575

This 24-room motel offers comfortable accommodations during summer and fishing seasons with two double beds and a restaurant. The marina accommodates boats up to 50 feet and offers gas and diesel fuel, supplies, refreshments and a complete tackle shop. Charter boats are also available.

FISHERMAN'S INN

Harkers Island   728-5780
$

This six-room motel faces the water and is owned and operated by Don and Linda Flood. The Floods also have a cottage with a full kitchen and bath available. The inn offers a marina, campground, boat slips, tackle and bait shop and charters.

HARKERS ISLAND FISHING CENTER

Harkers Island   728-3907
$-$$

Harkers Island Fishing Center has a 20-room motel that sits back off the road. Rooms offer standard, no-frills accommodations. Ten efficiencies are available and contain two double beds, a refrigerator and a stove. Guests have easy access to the marina, boat ramp and charter boats. The island location is a good jumping off point for Cape Lookout, Shackleford and North Core Banks.

SEA LEVEL
EXTENDED CARE FACILITY

Sea Level   225-4611
Cost determined by amount of care required

Sea Level Extended Care Facility provides long-term care as well as day-to-day care for those in need of attention. The facility has a guest program that allows vacationers to bring a family member requiring special care along. The program is used by many people who want a vacation but find it difficult to leave their relative behind. Contact the facility for more information about this program.

SEA LEVEL INN AND RESTAURANT

Sea Level   225-3651
$

On Nelson's Bay, Sea Level Inn offers rooms in a variety of accommodations. Guests can opt for a comfortable, traditional-style motel room, an efficiency apartment with all the necessary amenities, or a one-bedroom apartment with space to entertain and relax. For a special occasion, why not treat yourself to the nicest accommodation we know of — a very private waterfront suite complete with a large stone fireplace, screened porches, a kitchen area, a Roman tub and a wet bar. The inn has a lighted fishing pier for boat docking and fishing. All accommodations are available by day or week. See the Restaurants chapter for additional information.

Photo: Scott Taylor

A boy, a sunny day and a couple of life jackets fortell a great day on the water.

Crystal Coast
Vacation Rentals

The Crystal Coast is the perfect place to vacation. If this is your first visit, you are about to discover why so many people come back year after year. The climate is moderate year round, the scenery is spectacular, the people are friendly and welcoming.

Now, let's make your stay on the coast as easy as possible. There are about 10,000 "beds" for rent on the Crystal Coast. That's the figure the Tourism Development Bureau, 726-8148 or (800) SUNNY NC, uses, and those options range from small fishing units near the pier — perfect if you spend all your time surf casting or pier fishing — to plush condos. All you need to do is make a few simple decisions, starting with when to visit the coast.

The Rate Season

Rental rates change according to the season, and that's sometimes confusing. To add to the confusion, not all rental agencies on the Crystal Coast use the same season schedule. It's always best to check with each company for specific season/rate changes.

Generally, most rental agencies on the east end of Bogue Banks use two seasons: in-season (Memorial Day through Labor Day) and off-season (any other time). On the west end of Bogue Banks, many rental agencies use these descriptions: prime season (mid-June through mid-August), mid-season (May through mid-June and mid-August through September), off-season (September through November and March through April) and winter (December through February).

Vacation rentals can vary from $275 a week to more than $1,500. Costs can be as much as 25 percent to 30 percent less in off-season than in-season. For that reason, and because the weather is relatively warm year round, many people decide to vacation here in the "shoulder seasons" of spring, fall and winter. Decide what you need, and call rental agencies listed in the following pages or others listed in the phone directory to see what is offered.

Most visitors to the Crystal Coast come in the months of June, July and August. Tourism plays a big part in the county's economy. The average visitor stays 4.2 nights, and all together, visitors have an estimated $237,187,240 annual impact on the Crystal Coast.

Types of Accommodations and Locations

Rental agencies can help you find the perfect place, whether that's the fisherman's cottage close by the pier, the family cottage within walking distance of the beach or the oceanfront condo with all the amenities of home. Rental costs vary with the type of accommodation and the location. Always check rental brochures or with an agent about the location. This is very important if you are planning to walk to the beach. Carrying chairs, coolers and an umbrella while watching out for your children can make a short trip seem a lot longer if you are

several rows back from the water. Of course, generally speaking, the farther away from the water, the less expensive the rental rate.

Here's the general idea of what location descriptions mean. Oceanfront means facing the ocean with no physical barrier, road, property lines, etc., between you and the beach. Oceanside means you can walk to the beach without crossing a major road, but there might be other rows of houses between your cottage and the ocean. Soundfront means the cottage fronts the sound and you have easy access. Soundside means you are on the sound side of the road and in walking distance of the sound. Often, soundside cottages and developments offer guests access to the ocean and beach by means of a walking path.

Pets

If you plan to bring a pet, tell the agent. Some places allow them and charge an additional fee, and others don't allow them at all. Vacationers who choose to violate this rule are subject to losing their deposit and eviction. Boarding kennels are available on the Crystal Coast. Check the Animal Services section of the Service Directory in this book.

Furnishings and Equipment Rentals

If you are renting an apartment or condo, it will likely be fully furnished. Most rental brochures list the furnishings (small appliances, TVs, VCRs, stereos, toasters, microwaves) and note other items provided, such as beach chairs and umbrellas, hammocks and grills. You might only need to bring your sheets and towels, or you can rent those from the rental company. If not, there are a few

independent agencies that rent linens along with other extras, such as baby furniture, extra folding beds, etc. Check our Service Directory. In many of the units, a telephone is available for local calls and for credit card or collect long distance calls. Some do not have phones, so if that's important, check ahead.

Occupancy

Most vacation rentals are offered on a weekly basis, particularly in the summer. If you would like just a few days at the beach, check with an agency and see what can be arranged. Everything is more flexible in the off-season. Each rental unit is governed by rules and regulations spelled out in rental brochures and contracts.

Other Tips

Renting vacation accommodations is a business on the coast, so approach it that way. Be sure to read the rental agreement carefully, and ask questions if there is anything you don't understand. By getting all your questions answered, you can often reduce the number of items you

Spring and fall at the Crystal Coast offer visitors a more relaxed atmosphere with fewer motorists and no crowds on the beaches or at restaurants.

Insiders' Tips

bring and make it an enjoyable vacation for everyone. If you are a smoker, check to see if smoking is permitted. If you are planning a house party, let the agent know in advance. If large parties are prohibited and you ignore this rule, you could be evicted and lose your money.

Most visitors who arrange rentals on the Crystal Coast are family-oriented people who prefer a quiet, relaxed beach vacation.

Rental Companies

The Crystal Coast offers numerous cottages and condos to choose from, but you need to shop early. Many places are booked early in the year. Below is a listing of just a few of the many Crystal Coast companies that handle rentals. If you spot a particular place you would like to rent, just jot down the location and contact one of these rental companies. Or, simply tell the company representative what you want in the way of size and location and let them guide you. Most can send a picture-illustrated brochure featuring the available cottages and condos to help you make your choice. We have alphabetically arranged these companies and given their telephone numbers for your convenience.

Bogue Banks

Alan Shelor Rentals, 240-7368, (800) 786-7368, offers condo and cottage rentals in Atlantic Beach and Pine Knoll Shores.

Century 21 — Coastland Realty, 354-2060, (800) 822-2121, handles rentals of

cottages and condos in a variety of styles and prices in Emerald Isle.

Coldwell Banker Spectrum Properties has two offices. The Atlantic Beach office can be reached at 247-5366, (800) 334-6390, and the Emerald Isle office can be reached at 354-3040. Both offices offer condo and cottage rentals along Bogue Banks from Atlantic Beach to Emerald Isle.

Colony By the Sea, 247-7707, has oceanfront and ocean view one- and two-bedroom condo units.

Emerald Isle Realty, Inc., 354-3315, (800) 849-3315, offers about 600 vacation properties in Emerald Isle, Atlantic Beach and Pine Knoll Shores.

ERA Carteret Properties Rental, 354-3005, (800) 448-2951, has a large selection of cottages and condos in Emerald Isle.

Gull Isle Realty, 726-7679, (800) 682-6863, handles vacation rentals of cottages and condos from Atlantic Beach west to Salter Path.

Ketterer Realty, 354-2704, offers

oceanfront home, beach cottage and condo rentals in Emerald Isle.

LOOK Realty, 354-4444, (800) 849-0033, handles cottages and condo units in Emerald Isle.

Ocean Resorts Inc. - Condo Rentals, 247-3600, (800) 682-3702, handles the vacation rentals for the condo subdivisions of Dunescape Villas, Island Beach & Racquet Club and Beachwalk Villas at Pine Knoll Shores.

Realty World — Clark Realty, 354-3313, (800) 722-3006, handles many Emerald Isle vacation rentals of condos and cottages.

Sands Oceanfront Resorts, 247-2636, (800) 334-2667, handles vacation rentals for Sands Villa Resort, A Place At the Beach and Sea Spray, all in Atlantic Beach.

Sound 'n Sea Real Estate, 247-7368, (800) 682-RENT, has vacation houses and condos rentals in Atlantic Beach and Pine Knoll Shores.

Sun-Surf Realty, 354-2658, (800) 553-SURF, handles the rental of more than 200 homes, cottages and condos from Emerald Isle to Pine Knoll Shores.

Tetterton Management Group, Atlantic Beach, 247-3096, (800) 334-2727; Indian Beach 247-1000, (800) 334-6866, offers a variety of vacation cottages and condo rentals along the beach.

Whaler Inn Beach Club, 247-4169, (800) 525-1768, features attractive oceanfront one- and two-bedroom condominiums for rent by the day or week.

Williams & Co., 247-7347, (800) 626-3113, handles many vacation rentals of

condos and cottages in Atlantic Beach and Pine Knoll Shores.

Windward Dunes, 247-7545, (800) 659-7545, is an eight-story condo development in Indian Beach that offers 50 oceanfront one- and two-bedroom units.

Information about timeshare or interval ownership follows at the end of this chapter.

Beaufort

Beaufort offers no condos to vacationers, but there are a few rental apartments and houses available. Rates vary for one night, a week or longer.

While a few people advertise their own rentals with a sign out front, most list them with local agents. If you are looking for a rental in Beaufort, we recom-

mend you contact a Beaufort real estate company, look in the *Carteret County News-Times* or ask another Insider.

Down East

A drive Down East, particularly on Harkers Island and Cedar Island, will turn up several nice rental cottages/ houses. Many of these are not handled by a real estate agency; they simply have the owner's name and a phone number posted out front. Most rental places are booked year after year by the same people, so we suggest you find the one you are interested in and make arrangements early.

Timeshare, Interval Ownership

There are several developments on the Crystal Coast set up for interval owner-

ship, or timesharing. Billed as a way to have a lifetime of affordable vacations, the plan is set up so you actually purchase a block of time, one or more weeks in length, for a specific unit. Each year, the time you purchased is yours at that unit. Of course, your plans may change one year. With almost all of the companies you can exchange your week on the Crystal Coast for another location, some around the nation or world.

Before you arrange to buy into an interval ownership condo, there is a maintenance fee to consider. Once you pay off the note, you receive the deed to your week in your specific unit. Some organizations do put restrictions on resale, even after you own the time in that unit, so check on that before you put your name on the dotted line.

The unit will be completely furnished,

down to the linens, dishes and pans, so you just stop by the supermarket to pick up food, bring in your suitcases, unload the sporting equipment, and you'll be set for the duration. Each of these interval-ownership facilities is loaded with amenities, and each one is different.

If you are seriously considering purchasing into a timeshare or interval ownership property, give the resort a call and arrange a tour. A few of the facilities on the Crystal Coast that offer interval or fractional ownership are listed here.

Peppertree, 247-2092, has units in various sizes and locations. There are one-, two- and three-bedroom units, many with an ocean and sound view. Owners also can use the facility property year round. This allows owners who might live nearby to come to the beach and park and use shower facilities as well as all the other amenities. The facility offers something to non-property owners as well — a daily club membership that you might want to use if you move to the area but live somewhere other than on the beach. For a fee, you can park at the resort and use its private beach house for your visits to the shore. Peppertree has four pools, three outdoor and one indoor, and a security guard.

Sands Oceanfront Villas, 247-2636, offers units for timeshare purchase. Each unit has two bedrooms and is fully furnished.

Spectrum Resort Properties, Inc., 354-3070, offers fractional ownership of resort properties. This concept involves 10 individuals owning a 10th of a deeded interest in resort property. For this, each individual gets five weeks occupancy of the condos; weeks and holidays rotate each year. Two weeks are left for maintenance.

Whaler Inn Beach Club, 247-4169, features attractive oceanfront one- and two-bedroom condominiums. Completely furnished, the units offer fully equipped kitchens complete with dishwashers and all the kitchenware and utensils vacationers need. Units also offer balconies for relaxing and washers/dryers for cleaning up. Owners have immediate and full access to the ocean and sandy beaches in front of the club as well as to the club's heated pool and Jacuzzi. Ownership also allows those living or visiting nearby to continue to use the facility for parking, beach access, showers, swimming and other amenities. Whaler Inn is part of Interval International, allowing owners access to more than 11,000 resorts worldwide. Whaler Inn's helpful staff can offer more information about the beach club.

Photo: Scott Taylor

This great white heron is off for some early morning fishing.

Crystal Coast
Camping

Camping is certainly not for everyone, but for some it is the best way to relax and enjoy the beauty of the surrounding area. The Crystal Coast has a variety of camping opportunities, from rent-a-space RV camping with all the conveniences of home to tent camping with no conveniences at all. Primitive camping is offered at Cape Lookout National Seashore, Bear Island and in the Croatan National Forest (see the Attractions section).

Camping along the coast is popular all year because of the mild winter climate. Summer campers may need to create shade with tarps or overhangs to protect themselves from the sun's blistering rays. Campers will find beach camping a little different from mainland camping. Longer tent stakes may be needed in the sandy soil to hold things down in strong ocean breezes. Netting is almost a must, except in the dead of winter, to protect against the late-afternoon and early-morning mosquitoes and "no-see-ums," which are barely visible flying insects. A roaring fire and a good insect repellent often help, too. If you aren't fond of plastering yourself with pesticides, try mixing Avon's Skin So Soft with water and spraying it on. This mixture will fend off most insects and keep you smelling good at the same time. It works to protect dogs, too.

There are no designated camping sites on Cape Lookout National Seashore, and camping is allowed everywhere except on the small amount of privately owned land, which is marked. Bear Island has quiet, secluded campsites. Cape Lookout and Bear Island are only accessible by boat or ferry. Croatan National Forest, which includes land in Carteret and Craven counties, offers campers two options: Stay in one of the two planned campgrounds or pitch a tent anywhere on National Forest land that isn't marked for private use.

Overnight fees vary from campground to campground and usually depend on the location (whether oceanfront or off the beaten path) and the facilities offered. Fees for commercial campgrounds range from $10 to $30 a night, and reservations are suggested. There is no charge to camp at Cape Lookout National Seashore or at some sites in Croatan National Forest.

Most piers along Bogue Banks also offer RV and tent spaces (see the Fishing, Water Sports and Beach Access chapter).

There is nothing like camping beneath Cape Lookout Lighthouse, watching the light sweep the beach and listening to the rolling waves.

Insiders' Tips

ARROWHEAD CAMPSITE

MP, 11 1/2, Hwy. 5

Indian Beach   247-3838

On Bogue Sound in the middle of Bogue Banks, Arrowhead Campsite offers guests 12 acres with full-hookup, tent sites and clean restroom/shower facilities. Most types of water activities, such as sailing, shelling, fishing and clamming, can be enjoyed in the sound. A boat ramp, pier and protected-swimming area also are offered, and ocean access is just 600 feet away. Popular restaurants, shops and a grocery store are within walking distance. The campground has a lot of regulars who come year after year, so reservations are a good idea. Arrowhead is closed in the dead of winter.

SALTER PATH FAMILY CAMPGROUND

MP 11 3/4, Hwy. 58, Salter Path   247-3525

This campground offers areas on the ocean or the sound in the middle of Bogue Banks. The campground has been owned by the Lindsay family for 27 years. The sites have electrical outlets, water taps and picnic tables, and most have sewer and cable hookups. Guests are offered shower facilities, volleyball, basketball, fishing, wind surfing, laundry, a camp store, boat ramp, pond and dump station. This campground is within easy walking distance of a grocery store, restaurants and shops. It is open mid-March through early November. Reservations are suggested, and it might save you a few bucks to check out the weekly and monthly rates. Clam rakes are available at the office for guests at the exorbitant cost of 15¢ per hour, and users are asked to contribute one clam to the campground saltwater aquarium. (They also provide instructions for fixing your catch!)

WATERSPORTS RENTALS & RV CAMPGROUND

MP 12, Indian Beach   247-7303

This camp spot is on Bogue Sound right across the road from the Indian Beach Pier. This water sports equipment rental business offers spaces for RV full-hookup camping and tents. The business offers rentals of sail and motor boats, jet skis, as well as lessons on how to use that equipment and how to water ski (see the Fishing, Water Sports and Beach Access chapter).

BEACHFRONT RV PARK

MP 19 1/4, Hwy. 58, Emerald Isle   354-6400

With about 158 full-hookup and tent camping sites, Beachfront RV Park is oceanfront beside Bogue Inlet Fishing Pier. Park owners pride themselves in offering pleasant surroundings and clean bath houses. A camp store with RV supplies, a dump station, a pier, surf fishing and a game room are available. Seafood restaurants are within walking distance. The campground is closed from early December to early March.

HOLIDAY TRAV-L-PARK RESORT
MP 21, Hwy. 58, Emerald Isle   354-2250

This oceanfront camping resort offers 365 grass sites with full-hookups, along with a host of amenities including paved streets, shower facilities, shaded tent sites, a complete grocery store with RV supplies and LP Gas, a yogurt shop, a recreation hall, a dump station and an outdoor swimming pool. Beach and recreation rentals are available for umbrellas, chairs, mopeds and bicycles. Guests have access to basketball and tennis courts, a shuffleboard area and a go-kart track. A summer activity director lines up live entertainment, so there is always something going on for those who want to stay active. There is also plenty of peace and quiet for others. In business since 1976, Holiday Trav-L-Park enjoys a large re-peat business. The park is the site of the huge Emerald Isle Beach Music Festival in mid-May. Storage facilities are available for campers, boats and motor homes. The park is within walking distance of grocery stores, restaurants, movie theaters and shops and is open all year except two or three weeks in late December and early January.

BRIDGEVIEW FAMILY CAMPGROUND
MP 21, Hwy. 58, Emerald Isle   354-4242

Bridgeview is near the foot of the high-rise bridge connecting Bogue Banks with the mainland. The campground sits back off the highway and fronts Bogue Sound. About 113 RV and tent sites are offered along with a boat ramp, swimming pool and fishing pier. Several lots are wooded, and picnic tables and a playground area are featured.

WHISPERING PINES CAMPGROUND
Hwy. 24
12 miles west of Morehead City   726-4902

Situated on Bogue Sound, Whispering Pines has 140 full-hookup sites, a swimming pool, paddleboats, 18-hole miniature golf, a freshwater pond and fishing. The camp store and the park are open all year. The park offers a mail and phone message service. Whispering Pines offers special off-season monthly rates.

TOMMY'S FAMILY CAMPGROUND
Hwy. 24, Cedar Point   393-8715

On the Intracoastal Waterway between Cape Carteret and Swansboro, Tommy's offers 42 full-hookup sites and about 10 tent sites amid shady weeping willow trees. A favorite among fishermen and their families, the campground provides a boat ramp and basin as well as a storage area for campers and boats. Tommy's is open all year.

BEAR ISLAND
Hammock's Beach Rd. west of Swansboro
Ranger Station   326-4881

Access to Bear Island is provided from Hammock's Beach State Park (see the Attractions and the Ferry chapters) or by private boat. The 3.5-mile island offers primitive, private camping at designated spots for a small fee. All campers must register with the park office on the mainland before going over to Bear Island. There is a bathhouse located in the center of the island, but that is a good distance from the camping areas. Camp sites for boaters are also offered, but some are tricky to get to because of the shallow water. Campers are advised to travel light because it is a half-mile to mile walk from the ferry landing to some sites. To mini-mize human disturbance of nesting loggerhead sea turtles, Bear Island is closed to camping during the full moon phase of the months of June, July and August.

GOOSE CREEK RESORT
Hwy. 24, 7 miles east of Swansboro   393-2628

Goose Creek Resort offers facilities for family camping on Bogue Sound. Campers will find a boat ramp, pool, water slide, game room, heated/air conditioned bathhouse, camp store, tent sites, a 250-foot fishing pier, basketball, skiing, clamming and crabbing and a dump station. The resort is open year round, and all 300 sites offer full-hookup services.

COASTAL RIVERSIDE CAMPGROUND
216 Clark Ln., Otway   728-5155

Otway is a small Down East community just east of Beaufort. This campground has all the extras you would expect, plus a security gate to ensure privacy. Guests will find 57 sites with hookups and additional tent sites. This shady campground is on North River and has a pier, pool, boat ramp, bath house, store, game room and dump station. They also offer RV and boat storage and seasonal rates. The campground is open all year.

CEDAR CREEK
CAMPGROUND & MARINA
Hwy. 70, Sea Level   225-9571

Cedar Creek caters to family camping with shady sites and easy access to Core Sound and Drum Inlet. Guests will find a swimming pool, flush toilets, hot-water showers, a dump station, boating, fishing, horseshoes and basketball, along with 20 sites with full hookups and 35 without. Parts of the campground and marina are open all year, although the facilities are only fully operational between April 1 and November 30. About

12 miles from the Cedar Island-Ocracoke ferry terminal, Cedar Creek also offers an RV storage area.

DRIFTWOOD CAMPGROUND
Hwy. 12, Cedar Island　　　　225-4861

This waterfront campground is beside the Cedar Island-Ocracoke ferry terminal and has 65 sites. Swimming, fishing, volleyball, horseshoes and video games are offered along with a bath house, store and dump station. The campground is open March 1 through December 15. This campground is part of the Driftwood complex, which includes a restaurant (see the Restaurant section), a motel (see Accommodations) and a convenience store/grill. Driftwood is well-known for hunting and fishing guide service and its great food.

CAPE LOOKOUT NATIONAL SEASHORE
Ranger Station, Harkers Island　　728-2250

Cape Lookout National Seashore (see the Attractions section) offers waterfront primitive camping at its best. This is the place to go if you want privacy. You might see a ranger or a few anglers around the cabins (see Down East Accommodations) or folks around the lighthouse keeper's quarters; otherwise, you are on your own. Imagine sitting around the fire at dusk, listening to the waves roll on the beach and watching the sweeping light of the Cape Lookout lighthouse as it cautions boaters of shallow water — water as far as you can see, with the Atlantic Ocean to one side and Core Sound to the other. There are no developed campsites, no bath houses (there is a toilet at the lighthouse), no fees and no access without a boat. So how do you get to this wonder-land? You can take your boat or take a ferry. Ferry service is provided by several concessionaires permitted by the National Park Service (see our Ferry chapter) and numerous charter boats. Like all National Parks, some restrictions apply, so talk to a ranger before scheduling your trip.

CEDAR POINT TIDELAND TRAIL
1 mile north of Cape Carteret
Ranger Station　　　　　　638-5628

This is one of the two planned camping sites in Croatan National Forest. Sitting beside the White Oak River, the area offers 50 camping spaces, drinking water, toilets and an unpaved boat ramp. Cedar Point can be reached by following the signs from Highway 58 about a mile north of Cape Carteret. The Cedar Point Tideland Trail, an interpretive nature trail, is located here and offers a short loop, a 1-hour walk, and a 2-hour walk (see the Attractions chapter).

CROATAN NATIONAL FOREST
Hwy. 70, Ranger Station　　　638-5628

Croatan National Forest is made up of 157,000 acres spread between Morehead City and New Bern. Recreational areas are available for a day's outing or for overnight camping. The forest has two planned camp sites, Cedar Point and Neuse River, where you will find drinking water, bathhouse facilities and trailer space. Primitive camping is permitted all year, and campfires are allowed. Much of the park is closed November through March, except Cedar Point and primitive camping sites, which are open year round. For more information on Croatan National Forest, see our Attractions chapter.

Photo: Scott Taylor

The Crystal Coast is often a study in contrasts.

Crystal Coast
Shopping

Shopping is a favorite activity for many visitors to the Crystal Coast, so you'll find plenty of unusual stores and unique boutiques to explore.

Initially, a newcomer or visitor in the area may find it difficult to locate what he or she needs because there are no single, all-inclusive large shopping centers or malls. However, the shops do exist. There are mini-malls, strips of shops and several good-size shopping centers. The combination is enough to allow you plenty of places to find what you need.

Because the Crystal Coast is considered a resort area, you'll find plenty of shops that cater to the beachgoer or surfer. If you're looking for a beach souvenir, a gift for someone back home, the perfect-fitting swimsuit, a special T-shirt or a romantic beach wrap, you can find them. If you need clothing or equipment for your favorite summer sport, you will find many brands of goods including everything from surf boards to tennis togs. Because this is a resort area, some of the shops close in the winter, particularly those shops on Bogue Banks.

Grocery shoppers on the Crystal Coast have several large chain stores and seafood shops to chose from as well as seafood markets and roadside fruit and vegetable stands.

We have designed this section to offer you a brief look at a few of the shops in each Crystal Coast community. Antique shops, decoy shops and flea markets are listed separately at the end of this section. There is no way we could mention every shop that warrants your attention, so ex-plore on your own, and ask around. Other Insiders will be delighted to share information with you.

Bogue Banks

Most Bogue Banks' shopping is focused on the active lifestyle of beachgoers — both residents and visitors. Shops offer swimwear, water sport accessories, casual wear, seashells and souvenirs. Here is a sampling of some of the shops you'll find on Bogue Banks, beginning in Atlantic Beach and wandering west to Emerald Isle. We have given the milepost (MP) number for the shops on N.C. 58 (the main road on the island).

Atlantic Beach

Bert's Surf Shop, MP $2^{1/2}$, stocks swimwear, activewear and beach T-shirts as well as a large variety of sports equipment and sunglasses. Bert's also has a shop in Emerald Isle. **Marsh's Surf Shop**, Atlantic Beach Causeway, offers everything from dresses and shorts sets to T-shirts and jackets for men, women and children. There are plenty of surf items too — sunglasses, surfboards, swim suits, beach bikes and all the accessories.

Sandi's Beachwear, MP $2^{1/2}$, just remodeled and offers a wide variety of swimwear and activewear at this store and the one in Beaufort. **Atlantic Beach Surf Shop**, MP $2^{3/4}$, offers quality beachwear as well as casual and officewear. They offer footwear, jewelry and sunglasses along with surfboards, beach bikes and

all the accessories. **Davis Beachwear Shop**, on The Circle, has been in business for years and carries a complete line of sportswear and swimwear for ladies, men and children.

Presents, Atlantic Beach Causeway, is the place to shop for unique gifts, gourmet foods, toys, decorator and garden items, stationery and gift baskets. **Catco**, Atlantic Beach Causeway, offers distinctive hand-created nautical jewelry. **Wings**, MP $2^{1/4}$, has two beach-oriented retail stores within the same block carrying lots of T-shirts, bathing suits, casual apparel and shorts, along with shells and jewelry.

Hi-Lites, MP $2^{1/4}$, specializes in discounted clothing in juniors, misses and plus sizes with emphasis on sporty separates. You'll also find swimsuits, belts, earrings, bags and hats. **Tony's Beach Shop**, MP $4^{3/4}$, is across from the Sheraton. The store offers everything from 24 flavors of ice cream and yogurt to swimwear and boogie boards. Tony's also offers gifts and souvenirs and has hermit crabs and the largest selection of seashells in the area.

ATLANTIC STATION SHOPPING CENTER

Atlantic Station, MP 3, offers a variety of shops. The center is anchored by **Atlantic Station Cinemas** and **Pak-A-Sak Food Store**. **Outer Banks Outfitters** is just the store for your hard-core fishing friends. This is a marine electronics store that, along with radios, stereos and spotlights, carries fishing tackle, clothing, jewelry and much more.

Beach Book Mart offers a great selection of paper and hardback books at reduced prices. Beside the movie theater, Beach Book Mart also offers a good selection of local books along with bestsellers, cookbooks and much more.

Other shops include **Kites Unlimited**, which offers hundreds of wind-borne treasures in designs and sizes and for all ability levels; **Atlantic Photo** provides film processing services; and **Video City** offers a wide selection of movies. **Coastal Crafts Plus** features the work of more than 30 crafters in a large building. Patrons will find pottery, jewelry, paintings and wood crafts.

The **Bake Shoppe Bakery** can tempt you with donuts, bagels, fresh breads, pies and some health food items. **Great Mistakes** offers savings on brand name clothing for women and men. **Special Moments** can arrange anything for any occasion. The shop offers gift baskets, balloons, cards, stationery, gourmet candy and coffee, mugs, stuffed animals, T-shirts, souvenirs and more. Let them create a fabulous gift arrangement for that special moment. **Sunsplash** offers beach and rock 'n' roll souvenirs, posters and blacklights as well as boogie board rentals.

Across Highway 58 from Atlantic Station Shopping Center is **Coral Bay Shopping Center**, MP 3. This small center includes **Eckerd Drug Store** and **Food Lion** supermarket.

Pine Knoll Shores

There are no outright shopping areas in Pine Knoll Shores. This residential town does offer a convenience store and several hotels and piers with gift shops or tackle shops.

Salter Path, Indian Beach

There are a few places to shop in Salter Path and Indian Beach. **Village Gift Shop & Beach Wear**, MP 11, offers beachwear, T-shirts, shell items, gifts, jewelry, hats, suncatchers and lots more. **Fishin' Fever**, MP $11^{1/2}$, is a seafood market and tackle shop. There is sure to be someone to tell you where to go wet a line, what bait to use that day and how to prepare your catch. They also sell fresh seafood in case you're unlucky.

Old Island Store, MP $11^{1/2}$, offers gifts, souvenirs, shells and baskets. **Island Rigs**, MP 12, is a watersport rental business (see the Fishing, Water Sports and Beach Access chapter) that also offers water sport accessories and beachwear; **Food Dock**, MP $11^{1/4}$, is the local grocery store.

Emerald Isle

Shops line Emerald Drive (Highway 58) and are in Emerald Plantation (see below). Here, we have included a sampling of the shops you'll find in town.

Fran's Beachwear, MP $19^{1/2}$, is celebrating its 22nd year in business. The shop carries an excellent selection of swimwear from the daring to the shy, along with sporty and dressy separates and a wide range of shoes, accessories and souvenirs. **Fran's Gifts** (same location and number) offers such collectibles as Tom Clark Gnomes, Dept. 56 Snow Village and Precious Moments. You'll also find gifts, jewelry and accessories.

Bert's Surf Shop, MP $19^{1/2}$, was the town's first surf shop. The shop stocks beach clothing for all ages, skateboards, windsurfing equipment and surfboards. Bert's always has activewear, sunglasses, hats and beach T-shirts. **Wing's**, MP 19, is filled with T-shirts, bathing suits, casual apparel and shorts, along with shells and jewelry.

Emerald Plantation, MP $20^{1/4}$, offers

residents and visitors stores in a court-yard-type setting. The center is anchored by **Food Lion, Revco Drug Store, Sound Ace Hardware** and **Emerald Plantation Cinema 4**. Also in Emerald Plantation, **Tom Togs Factory Outlet** sells a large selection of well-known clothing brands at drastically reduced prices. Inside you will find items for women, men and children along with accessories. Make sure to check Tom Togs out before you pay full price elsewhere.

The Gazebo carries fountains, patio furniture, hammocks, planters, weather vanes, stepping stones, plants, outdoor lighting, trees, shrubs and bird feeders. **Elly's Personal Touch** is packed with children's clothes, games, books and all kinds of gifts including stained glass, pot-tery, decoys and wreaths. **Emerald Isle Books & Toys** has books and magazines for all ages. **Country Store** offers baskets, windsocks, flags, cards, wreaths, brass, clocks and frames. It also has a Christmas shop.

Beaufort

The unique shops in Beaufort are sure to suit anyone's taste. Although there are others, most shops are along the downtown waterfront area. Because our generally mild climate attracts visitors year round, only a few of Beaufort's shops close in the winter. Beaufort's attractions — the waterfront, museum, historic sites and pubs — provide a mecca for those who find themselves in Beaufort with a born shopper. We couldn't possibly list all the

shops, so we hope you will do some exploring on your own.

Downtown/Waterfront

Fabricate Apparel specializes in clothes of natural fibers. The shop offers trendy, expressive clothes as well as conservative outfits for women, men and children. You'll find jewelry, belts, bags, a few shoes and T-shirts and sweatshirts that feature Beaufort scenes, environmental messages and drawings by M.C. Escher. **Sandi's Beachwear** offers swimwear and activewear along with all the accessories. There is also a Sandi's in Atlantic Beach.

Mary Elizabeth's caters to women seeking the career look in traditional clothing, shoes and all types of accessories. Mary Elizabeth's also offers sportswear and has some great sales, so keep your eyes open. **The Ladies' Shop** has been in business on Front Street for 23 years. The shop offers traditional apparel, sportswear and accessories and has a wonderful sale room that is loaded with real finds.

Stamper's Gift Shop sells fine china, all kinds of gifts and novelty items as well as an extensive line of collectibles by Gorman, Lee Middleton, Susan Wakeen, M.I. Hummels and Tom Clark Gnomes. Next door, **Stamper's Jewelers** offers a full line of jewelry items as well as engraving and excellent repair services. **Bird Shoal Peddler** offers fun gift items year after year. It's not unusual to find a feathered boa, a handmade hair clip, note cards with local scenes or a porcelain face mask at this shop.

For great ice cream or a few more souvenirs, stop by **The General Store** where you'll find all kinds of memorabilia to take home — hats, T-shirts, shells, saltwater taffy and jewelry. **Top Deck** is one of the best places in town for name brand clothing, shoes, T-shirts, casual wear, Ray Bans and things labeled "Beaufort." **The Harbor Shop** offers all kinds of things — baskets, rugs, stained glass, art, jewelry and, oh, so much more. Owner Rob Davis carries some cards, drawings and jewelry created by local artists. **La Vaughn's Pottery** has plenty of gourmet coffees and wines, some from North Carolina vineyards. As the name reflects, the store has pottery items along with furniture, knickknacks and jewelry.

Local artist Alan Cheek displays his work at **Down East Gallery**. Inside you will find artwork that will serve as a lovely reminder of time spent in the Beaufort seaport. Down East Gallery can also custom frame your art. On the Beaufort Historic Site, the **Mattie King Davis Art Gallery** features paintings, sketches, note cards, carvings, photographs, weavings and gifts created by local artists.

Ginny Gordon's Gifts and Gadgets is a wonderful place to go if you enjoy cooking, eating or just hanging around the kitchen. You'll find Calphalon cookware, cookbooks, every cooking utensil imaginable and lots of special things — sauces, wines, aprons, coffees and more. Ginny has a store in Morehead City too. **Jackson Press** carries cards and stationery, gifts, pottery and children's coloring books. The store also has a fine selection of imported items from Mexico, rugs and pillows from India, and gifts for that hard-to-buy-for person. **Chachkas** has creative gifts of hand-painted furniture, murals and accents along with jewelry and florals.

Scuttlebutt specializes in things that have to do with the sea and boating. Shoppers will find nautical books and charts, clocks, music, games, toys, models,

Harkers Island Native Focuses on Decoys, Traditions

Without ever taking an art lesson, David Lawrence has developed a talent for carving and painting. The Harkers Island resident's work is known throughout the state and region, and so is his commitment to preserving the carving traditions of the area.

His continuous commitment to the Core Sound Decoy Carvers Guild earned him the distinction of being named the 1994 Core Sound Decoy Festival Featured Carver.

Each year the festival highlights one carver. The person selected must represent the highest and best as a craftsman, with excellent skills as a carver. The group also looks for someone who demonstrates commitment, support and motivation to the guild.

"I've never had an art lesson in my life," David Lawrence said. "What you see is just what I call a God-given talent. I can't take full credit for it. All my work is just me trying to create something from what I see." Holding up a block of tupelo, he said "There is a lot of wood to take out to get to the duck."

Mr. Lawrence is doing his part to keep the tradition of carving decoys alive. His son, 25-year-old Corey, also carves and works with his father. Both live on Harkers Island.

"I'm real proud of Corey because he's my youngern' and he is carrying on the tradition," Mr. Lawrence said. "There's not many carvers that have sons carrying on the tradition." Mr. Lawrence said as a child Corey spent a lot of time in the shop watching him. Then Corey made one bufflehead and Mr. Lawrence made six and they hunted over them. Corey entered that decoy in the Chincoteague, Virginia, decoy festival and won a blue ribbon. Corey then carved seven decoys for the float tank competition in the Currituck decoy festival and won five blue ribbons. The fever had set in so much that wife Carol gave Corey the nickname "Chip" meaning "Chip off the old block."

Born on Harkers Island, Mr. Lawrence started hunting when he was 13 years old. He credits his mother's side of the family for developing his love of hunting and carving.

"The first carving I did was to replace decoy heads that had been knocked off," Mr. Lawrence said. "We couldn't buy new ones and, even if we could, we didn't have the money. In the early '70s I got serious about carving. I went goose hunting up in Delaware and stopped at a decoy factory on the way back. I'd never seen so many decoys in my life, and I bought a book about decoys. That excited me about carving."

After working as a graphic artist at the Naval Aviation Depot on Cherry Point Marine Base in Havelock and as a police officer at the N.C. State Port in Morehead City, Mr. Lawrence began working full time as a wildlife artist last January. He concentrates on art — whether it be carving, painting or designing.

Mr. Lawrence divides his time between his drawing board in the family den and his carving shop behind the house. At the drawing board he paints hunting and coastal scenes and portraits with acrylic paints. He carves ducks, shorebirds and even a fish or two. In the shop are black ducks, greenwing teal, buffleheads, ruddy ducks, redheads, pintails, canvasbacks, ringnecks and mallards.

"Most carvers today use power tools for the whole process, but I'm proud that I can still do it the old way," Mr. Lawrence said. "It's important to remember how to do it the old way so it wouldn't be a lost art form.

"There is a tradition of decoy carving in this coastal area, and it is very strong," he continued. "That tradition is being lost. Except for the old-timers, the young people will not know a thing about this if we don't save it. And that is just what the museum we are planning will do."

The planned Core Sound Waterfowl Museum will be built on National Park Service property at Shell Point on the east end of Harkers Island. There it will encompass a complete history of eastern North Carolina. The museum will include exhibits of artifacts, interpretive displays, a research library, galley space and a workshop area. A picnic area and a natural habitat area with live waterfowl are also planned.

The Core Sound Waterfowl Museum now operates from a temporary home beside the school on Harkers Island. This building provides office space and a small museum with decoy and hunting artifacts, carving demonstrations and a research library. The museum gift shop offers the area's finest carvings, waterfowl art, books and other gift items for waterfowl lovers.

For more information about the museum, contact the Core Sound Waterfowl Museum, P.O. Box 556, Harkers Island 28531, 728-1500.

"I used to hunt ducks and geese, then I raised them for several years," Mr. Lawrence said. "Once you've been that close to them it is hard to kill them. But I never killed anything unless we could eat it. This year I bought a hunting license for the first time in a long while so Corey and I could go out. But I think I'll be using the video camera more than the gun."

galleyware and lots more. **Chadwick House** is a retail interior design store offering lamps, prints, paintings, furniture, upholstery, wallpaper and window treatments. You'll find lovely accessories including glass vases, picture frames, baskets, garden ornaments and kitchen accents.

For **Nature's Sake** offers a unique line of gifts and products, all aimed at passing on the messages of conservation, preservation and peace. You'll find art as well as clothing. You'll discover savings on brand name clothing for women and men at **Great Mistakes**.

Somerset Square houses a number of shops. This two-story building is on Front Street at the south end of Turner Street.

Handscapes Gallery specializes in works by North Carolina artists and craftspeople and is the perfect place to find unique gifts and treasures. Owner Alison Brooks fills the shop with pottery, jewelry, paintings, glass and wood items. The **Rocking Chair Book Store** is celebrating its 16th year of offering visitors and residents alike books for adults and children. Be sure to check the selection of regional books, books on sailing and helpful book lights. You'll find owners Neva Bridges and Josephine Davis full of information, and they can order any book for you. The **Fudge Factory** makes creamy, sinful fudge on marble-top tables right in front of you from natural ingredients. **Containing Ideas** carries an extensive line of Patagonia apparel (jackets, pants, hats and accessories) and lots of T-shirts, bags and hats with environmental messages.

Bell's has been serving the people of Beaufort and visitors since 1918 and continues that same friendly, professional service today. Bell's Drug Store has fountain drinks, personal care items, over the counter drugs, a pharmacy, gifts and cards.

Just outside the downtown area is Gaskill's **True Value Farm & Garden Center** on Highway 70. Step inside and go back in time. Bo Sullivan and his helpful crew stock this country seed store with everything you need to get that garden going again, that lawn tamed, that house or boat fixed, or those animals fed.

Jones Village Shopping Center, on Highway 70 E., between the waterfront area and Beaufort Square and has three stores: **Pak-a-Sak Food Store**, a chain grocery store with a deli and lunch counter; **Revco Discount Drug**, a drug and gift store; and **Family Dollar Store**, a discount variety store.

Beaufort Square Shopping Center, on Highway 70 E. about 2 miles from the waterfront area, is anchored by **Byrd's**, a chain grocery store; **Eckerd Drug**, a drug and gift store; and **Coastal Coin Laundry. Holland's Shoes**, has been a mainstay and carries an excellent selection of shoes for the entire family with great prices to match. You'll find major brand name shoes, including Reebok, Nike, Rockport and Sperry, along with handbags, socks, laces, and shoe shining and cleaning items. **Lottie's Frocks & So Forth**, offers a good selection of ladies clothing and accessories.

Down East Trading Post shopping center opened over the winter and is on Highway 70 just east of Beaufort Square Shopping Center. **Food Lion**, a grocery store and deli, is the anchor store, and **Video Plus**, is the other tenant.

Morehead City

Morehead City offers the largest selection of shops on the Crystal Coast. Shopping opportunities are spread from one end of the city to the other and range from clothing boutiques and craft shops to book shops and marine hardware suppliers. Here we have tried to describe a few of the shops in the city and have arranged them by area.

Downtown/Waterfront

In the last few years the downtown/waterfront sections of Morehead City have seen quite a bit of revitalization. Projects provided for sidewalks, trees and benches along the waterfront, and more work is scheduled. Here is a small sampling of the businesses you will find.

Dee Gee's Gifts and Books is a tradition on the waterfront and continues to offer a huge selection of books, maga-

zines, cards and unique gifts. Dee Gee's features a special section of local and regional books and a children's section filled with educational books and games.

Waterfront Junction is the place to stop for craft supplies, needlework, prints, crewel embroidery and nautical gifts. The shop is well known for its custom framing as well as its stock of ready-made frames. **Taste Makers** offers a wonderful selection of gourmet food items, coffees, baked goods, wines and more. Let the staff create a gift basket for you or attend one of the cooking classes. **Windward Gallery** offers oils, watercolors and pastels by acclaimed local artist Alexander Kaszas and many others. Inside you will also find jewelry, pottery, scrimshaw and glass pieces. For clothing for women, **Lee's "Of Course"** has it — and they spe-

cialize in one-of-a-kind fashions for all sizes.

Branch's is a traditional office supply shop with lots of extras. You'll find gifts, home accessories, cards, and drafting, art and school supplies. **Carolina Office Supply** has a complete line of office supplies and paper products along with calendars, art supplies, pens and office furniture.

Mary's Flowers and Pastries, 801 Arendell Street, offers gorgeous fresh and silk flower arrangements, one-of-a-kind gift items and local creations. Mary and Rick Rogers also host a professional floral design school on-site. European pastries and gourmet coffees are featured. The shop offers a European-type breakfast and soups, salads and sandwiches for lunch. Tempting desserts and coffees are served throughout the day.

Through the Looking Glass creates distinctive floral arrangements for every occasion and offers crystal, exclusive gifts for that very special person and a Christmas shop. **Morehead City Floral Expressions** offers potted plants and flower arrangements. **Morehead Floral Market** features creative, unique arrangements and flowers for any occasion along with gourmet food and gift items.

City News Stand offers an endless number of magazines, greeting cards and books and just about any major newspaper. **Fannie's Attic** showcases antiques, collectibles, pottery, afghans, holiday items, art-to-wear, dolls, pottery, dried flowers, wind chimes, dolls and more.

Carolina City Smoked Seafood has delicious varieties of smoked seafood and spreads. Our favorites are the smoked salmon and smoked trout. Stop by for a sample, and check out their party trays. **Ottis' Fish Market** and **Carolina Atlantic** has been in business on the Morehead City waterfront for 45 years. If you don't catch it yourself, this is the place to go for all kinds of fresh, local seafood. Stop by and take some seafood home to enjoy later. Ottis' will even pack the cooler for you.

Sew It Seams has sewing patterns and notions, fabrics, books, and craft and quilting items. Classes are often taught here. **Parsons' General Store** is a wonderful collection of gifts, local crafts, books, home accessories, seasonal decorations and a sweet shop. Stop by **Crystal Coast Crafters** if you are looking for craft and art supplies of any kind, including stained-glass supplies. **Ginny Gordon's Gifts And Gadgets** offers a wonderful collection of cookware, cookbooks from near and far, every cooking utensil imaginable and lots of special things — sauces, coffees and more. Ginny also has a Beaufort store.

Around Morehead City

Here we have listed shops that are in the city but not clustered in a particular area or shopping center. The street address should make them easy to find.

The Painted Pelican, 4645 Arendell Street, features the work of local artists and craftspeople in the form of prints, pottery, shorebirds, jewelry, scrimshaw and much more. You'll also find an art gallery and frame shop. **Twin Book Stores**, 3805 Arendell Street, is the place to find thousands of new and used hardbacks, paperbacks, comic books, cookbooks and North Carolina books.

Diamond Shoal Jewelers, 4637 Arendell Street, offers a wonderful selection of jewelry and watches for men and women. Diamond Shoal specialists can also make repairs. Go to **EJW Outdoors**, 2204 Arendell Street, if you want to buy new fishing gear or repair old gear, get outdoor clothing or have your bike checked out. **Wind Creations**, 4109 Arendell Street, offers all kinds of special flags and banners and has a number of their unique creations on hand or will make special ones on order.

The **Gourmet Galley**, 4050 Arendell Street, offers gourmet cheeses, pastas, domestic and imported wines, some gourmet candies, spices and plenty of coffees. The shop is also where Carolina Swamp Sauces were created and are offered for sale.

Howard's Furniture Showrooms, 4024 Arendell Street, offers a full line of home furnishings, bedding, accessories and window treatments. Howard's staff also offers a complete home design service. Sharing the same building is **Superior Carpet & Appliance**. Superior offers top-of-the-line carpets and vinyl floorings, GE appliances and all types of outdoor furniture. Let Superior's staff install and service your carpet and appliances.

Auto Brite, 4303 Arendell Street, is the best place in town to pamper your car with a professional cleaning job and to get a car-related gift. While your car is being cleaned, you can look through car coffee mugs, tapes and CDs, shirts, cards or any number of small items for the maintenance and upkeep of your car.

Truckers Toy Store, Highway 70 W., carries all kinds of goodies to make your truck or car unique, from the utilitarian to the decorative. **Pine Ridge Arts & Crafts**, 5901 Arendell Street, offers art and needlework supplies, crafts, gifts and classes.

Inside **Colonial Carolina Pottery**, off Highway 70 W., you'll find china, crystal, glassware, brass, gifts, bird feeders, rugs, baskets, cookware, furniture, linens, candles, housewares and silk flowers. A separate department offers a huge selection of bath and bed linens and lamps. **Sunshine Garden Center** is next door and offers potted plants, silk flowers and arrangements, baskets, home decorations and every lawn and garden item imaginable.

MOREHEAD PLAZA

Morehead Plaza is between Arendell and Bridges streets and is anchored by **Belk**, a full-line department store; **Roses Stores**, a discount retail store; **Byrd's Food Store**, a grocery store with a good deli section; and **Eckerd Drugs**, a drug store and pharmacy. The **Light Within** is a wonderful store to explore. Inside you will find items that will help you focus on your overall health and healing. There are natural herbs, essential oils, mineral salts, books and tapes. The Light Within also offers a complete yoga school that teaches the full science of yoga. Day and evening classes are offered for all levels.

Maurice's carries trendy clothing for women and men. **Crystal Sports** offers sporting goods equipment, clothing, training shoes and related items as well as plaques and trophies ready to be personalized. **Radio Shack** is a comprehensive shop dealing with car and home stereo systems and most anything electronic.

At the back of Morehead Plaza, facing Bridges Street, is **Williams Hardware**, one of the best-supplied hardware stores in the area. It has a helpful staff that won't keep you waiting. **Anderson Audio** is the perfect place to look for that home or car stereo system or other electronic sound machine. **Crystal Coast Brass** cleans brass, silver and copper and sells items ranging from vases and cups to decorative pieces.

MOREHEAD PLAZA WEST

This strip of shops is behind Morehead Plaza and can be reached from Bridges Street. The largest store in the plaza is **Western Auto** where you can find everything you need for do-it-yourself auto repairs or have one of their mechanics do it for you. They have tires, batteries, accessories and cleanup kits, as well as bicycles. **Jewelers' Workbench** is our favorite place to go for custom-made jewelry – everything from wedding rings to placing a special piece in just the right setting. Owner Laurie Stinson can professionally handle any jewelry creation, repair or cleaning and offers her own designs for sale. Tired of your old jewelry? Bring it to Laurie and have it reborn.

PELLETIER HARBOR SHOPS

Pelletier Harbor Shops, 4428 Arendell Street, includes a number of specialty shops. For women's clothes, visit **The Golden Gull**, which features the latest fashions and accessories for ladies. **Lynette's** carries distinctive fashions for women. The shop offers lovely jewelry, handbags and all the accessories.

Knowledge of Christ Books & Gifts is a wonderful store filled with books, gifts, stained glass, collectibles, dolls, prints and paintings. The store also offers Bibles for adults and children. **Creative Lighting** is filled with fixtures for kitchens and baths along with cabinets and countertops of all types. You'll love the many unique chandeliers.

Over The Rainbow is a great place to shop for distinctive clothing, accessories and toys for that favorite little person. **Cameo Boutique** offers all types of lingerie for women plus a few items for men. There are also accessories, adult games, lotions, stockings and gifts.

ETC handles everything from denim to sequins. **Crystal Palate** features gourmet food items such as coffees and teas, cheeses and crackers, domestic and imported beers and wines and scads of those one-of-a-kind kitchen gadgets that are perfect as gifts — or for your own kitchen. **McQueen's Furniture and Interiors** has lovely home and office decorations, furniture, lamps, prints and accessories. **Consider the Lilies Florist** delivers and wires flowers and creates wedding flowers. If you are shopping for clothes and accessories for that favorite gentleman or lady, stop by **Graff's Fashions**. **Shoe Splash** can provide just the right shoes to go with any ensemble, and **Sun Photo** offers a reliable 1-hour color photo service.

THE MARKETPLACE

The Marketplace is at 4900 Arendell Street at the junction of Highway 70 and Country Club Road. **Rack Room Shoes** carries a wide selection of women's, men's and children's name brand shoes — everything from casual wear and dress wear to athletic wear, plus lots of handbags. The **Dress Barn** sells women's clothes at discounts. **Paper Plus** offers a variety of paper products for the office or the home. This is the place to go when planning your next party. If you want to stay in and watch a movie, pick from a wide selection at **Blockbuster Video**.

CYPRESS BAY PLAZA

Cypress Bay Plaza is between highways 70 and 24, and **Wal-Mart** is the plaza's largest store. Wal-Mart carries everything you can think of, and more — clothing, household items, toys, electronics, fabric/sewing/craft items, books and cosmetics. **Sears Roebuck And Co.** features appliances, hardware, clothing, shoes and an auto shop.

J.R. Dunn Jewelers features distinctive jewelry for men, women and children, along with many nautical creations. **Carolina Linen** has a large inventory of bed and bath accessories. Other stores in the center include **Food Lion** supermarket, **Revco Drug Store**, and **Gloria's Hallmark**. Shoppers will also find a **Baskin-Robbins Ice Cream & Yogurt Shop**, a couple of small take-out food shops, a video rental store or two and more.

Swansboro

Shops in Swansboro are basically in two areas — along the waterfront and along the highway. We suggest you take some time, walk along the White Oak River, shop a bit, enjoy lunch at one of

the restaurants and relax in Bicentennial Park.

The waterfront shops are clustered along Front Street. Inside **Russell's Olde Tyme Shoppe** you'll find country crafts, jewelry, handcrafted clothing, pottery, furniture, baskets, silk and dried flowers and kitchen and cooking items. Each purchase in Maxine Russell's store is placed in a handpainted shopping bag, a gift in itself. **Noah's Ark** offers special gifts for an adult or child. The shop carries women's and children's clothing, plenty of accessories, some toys, books and cassette tapes.

Keepsake Originals is on the second floor of the 1839 William Farrand Store. The shop features cards, unique rubber stamps, handmade alpine lace, beautifully crafted gift boxes, and soothing music on tape and CD. The **Southern Sampler** is just the shop if you are interested in quilting and crafts. The shop offers quilting supplies, a wonderful selection of fabrics, doll patterns, gifts and more, and quilting classes are taught.

Through the Looking Glass offers unique and memorable floral arrangements for any occasion along with candles, greeting cards, wines, and porcelain and crystal sculptures. The **Christmas House** is packed with all the seasonal items you can imagine and more. **Sunshine and Silks** features baskets, silk flowers, wreaths, ribbons, knickknacks, gifts and wood art.

Just across Highway 24 from Front Street is the **River Emporium General Store and Fudge Company**. This shop specializes in gourmet foods, coffees, candies, North Carolina products, wines, dip ice cream and souvenirs. Shoppers will also find Carolina Swamp Sauces, which were created right here on the coast. Open every day, the shop can prepare and mail gift baskets.

Down East

There are only a few Down East shops, but each is unique and well worth the trip. Because hours vary, we suggest you call ahead. Also, stop at the area grocery stores — many offer shoppers a selection of local crafts and gift items.

Lucky Duck's in Bettie is a wonderful shop filled with antique decoys, waterfowl carvings by local artists, wildlife art, gifts and accessories. Shopkeep Gail Corwin also carries a complete line of carving supplies.

The **Core Sound Waterfowl Museum Gift Shop** on Harkers Island is filled with unique Down East gifts, most of which have a waterfowl theme. There are decoys, wildlife art, books, cards, house flags and windsocks, clothing, bird houses and feeders and much more. The shop also features wonderful decoy and local history exhibits.

Somethin' Special in Smyrna features handmade baskets, decoys, stained-glass items, furniture, pillows, afghans and lamp shades, as well as craft supplies, cross-stitch patterns, thread and a good selection of fabric.

We couldn't fail to mention **Phil's Barbecue Sauce** in the Down East shopping section. Phil's Barbecue Sauce is a home creation of Philip Willis of Davis and is a spicy vinegar-based sauce that is great on grilled fish, pork and chicken. The sauce is sold in many local grocery stores.

Newport

Newport offers a number of shops in the downtown area, as well as a few along Highway 70, just outside the town.

In the downtown area you'll find **C.M. Hill Hardware**. This traditional hardware store carries everything from guns and fan belts to mowers and Westinghouse appliances. **Newport Garden Center** offers everything for the lawn and garden and also sells and services equipment. The center's greenhouse provides fresh, locally grown plants.

Turner Technical Service, U.S. 70A at Roberts Road, offers a full line of office machines and supplies. Representatives can repair all types of office machines. Patrons are provided a fax and copy service, including color copies.

Cape Carteret

The town's shopping center features **Piggly Wiggly**, a chain food store; **Kerr Drug Store**, a drug store and pharmacy; **Max-Way**, a discount clothing and supply store; and **McCauley Cleaners & Laundry**, a dry cleaners offering alterations and shoe repair. **West Carteret Medical Center**, is operated by Carteret General Hospital and is in the town's shopping center.

Western Carteret County

There are a number of good stores scattered throughout the western part of the county. Most communities have a convenience/gas store, a beauty salon and tanning booth, or maybe a craft and flower shop. We have listed a few of the stores you will find here.

Russell's Hardware, Highway 24, Bogue, offers a very wide variety of gardening and lawn supplies at reasonable

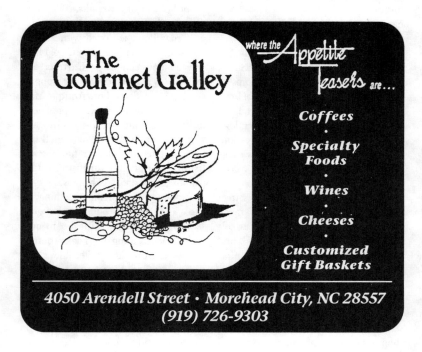

prices. It also carries standard hardware items plus feed for cattle, chickens, horses, pigs, dogs and cats. **Walston True Value Home Center**, Cedar Point, is an extremely well-equipped store with a wide variety of hardware and building products along with plants and gardening supplies. **Redfearn's Nursery** in Cedar Point has a variety of landscaping and potted plants, planters, garden seeds, fertilizers and herbicides or pesticides.

Wild Birds Unlimited, Cedar Point, is a fascinating shop offering special blends of bird seeds, unique feeders for a variety of animals, and books and videos on bird types and how to attract birds to your feeder. Wild Birds also has educational items for children, clothing and gifts.

Winberry Farm Produce, Highway 24, Cedar Point, and **Smith's Produce**, Highway 24, Ocean, are two well-known roadside stands that offer seasonal local vegetables, Bogue Sound watermelons and cantaloupes.

Antiques

Antique shops are plentiful along the Crystal Coast and offer furniture, accessories and more. If you are looking for antique decoys, check the next section in this chapter.

Beaufort offers several antique shops. **Carteret Antique Mall** is on the west side of the Beaufort drawbridge. Inside you'll find a variety of antiques such as old furniture, accessories, kitchen items, frames, glassware and toys. Consignment items are taken at this shop. The **Flea Market**, 131 Turner Street in Beaufort, has old furniture, toys, jewelry, kitchen items and hardware. A good number of old nautical items are usually around.

Also in Beaufort is **Waterfront Antiques & Collectibles**, 121 Turner Street, a cozy shop that has several rooms of items, including a large selection of brass and lots of plates and kitchen gadgets. There is also old furniture, trunks, jewelry, toys, advertising collectibles and children's clothing. **Ginny Agnew's Antiques & Collectibles**, 400 Front Street, is filled with lovely glassware, plates, rugs, jewelry and other pieces. **Craven Street Antiques & Collectibles**, 121 Craven Street, buys items and sells antiques, collectibles and furniture. Often you'll find some wonderful items from old Beaufort homes.

Morehead City is also home to a number of antique shops. **Cheek's Antiques**, 727 Arendell Street, is a good place to start your search. Long established, this shop has a variety of antiques certain to keep you busy browsing. The specialty is matching old sterling. **Seaport Antique Market**, 509 Arendell Street, offers more than a dozen vendors' booths set up in an attractive manner to give you an opportunity to see more than one collector's wares at a time. You'll find furniture, books, glassware, knickknacks, jewelry and even some clothing and accessories.

Swansboro's Front Street and the associated side streets offer several antique stores. A sampling of those shops is given here. **Lighthouse Antiques**, Front Street, fills a two-story historic house with antiques of almost every sort, from miniatures and furniture to clocks and dishes. One room features pottery, another Chinese antiques, and another children's furniture and toys. Shoppers will also find a few decoys, some rugs and jewelry. The **Barber Shop Antiques and Collectibles**, Front Street, features quilts, collectibles, dishes and furniture.

Cedar Point is dotted with antique shops. The town's 5-mile stretch of Highway 24 between Cape Carteret and Swansboro is a great place for stopping and browsing. **Swansboro Antique Mall**, offers a collection of booths representing many dealers showing their wares in a 12,500-square-foot building. You'll find kitchen collections, decoys, hunting and fishing equipment, furniture, quilts, paintings, toys, books, old radios and cameras, political memorabilia, clothing, tobacco and medical products and original stained glass. **Calico Village Antiques and Carpentry Shop** offers oak furniture, bric-a-brac, toys and collectibles. Next door is **The Grapevine**, a rustic old house with antiques, baskets and furniture. **Lazy Lyon's Auction Service** is behind Calico Village and is the site of frequent estate sales. Lazy Lyon's also has a shop on Front Street in Swansboro.

Decoys

Old working decoys and new hand-carved ones are plentiful in the area, and collecting these art forms is becoming very popular. Many shops along the Crystal Coast offer a few decoys, but the majority available, old or new, are sold by the collectors or from the crafter's home.

If you are looking for a decoy or two, keep your eyes open for yard signs and stop by the **Core Sound Waterfowl Museum** on Harkers Island for a flyer listing area decoy shops. The museum also sells decoys and has hundreds on display.

Most of the area's decoy shops are east of Beaufort and in the Down East area. Not all the "shops" are really shops. You might be browsing in someone's living room or garage and discover a real treasure. They advertise using signs along the road. But don't let that fool you. These guys aren't just messing around with some wood — they are creating works of art. One stop will prove that to you. Whether you are looking for carved ducks, geese or shorebirds, you are sure to find them along the Crystal Coast.

For hundreds of years, Carteret County has been well known for its excellent hunting grounds. The abundant waterfowl in this area were hunted by locals and sportsmen from near and far. Hunting clubs formed along the banks and duck blinds went up. With that popularity came the need to have decoys, so locals took to the task of chopping the forms of ducks and geese from blocks of wood. These working decoys were used to lure waterfowl to within firing range. As hunting became more and more popular, many hunters turned to cheaper, lighter plastic decoys. With that change, much of the carving stopped, and the art form was almost lost.

Core Sound Decoy Carvers Guild was formed about seven years ago to bring back the art of carving and to support those locals who had never quit chopping at blocks of wood. Of course, the ducks, geese and other waterfowl these men and women now craft are not all used in the water. Instead, many are collected, bought, sold and displayed. The Guild's membership is made up of handcarvers of working, decorative and realistic waterfowl, collectors, painters, taxidermists, photographers and breeders.

Each December the Guild hosts a large and impressive festival at Harkers Island Elementary School. Scheduled for the first weekend each December, the **Core Sound Decoy Festival** attracts local as well as nationally known carvers, goose callers and other artists. Decoys are judged, sold, displayed, made and auctioned. There are booths set up to display artifacts, promote conservation and preservation efforts and focus on wildlife clubs. But most of all, there are decoys, lots and lots of decoys. This is one educational festival not to be missed — even if you're not a collector. The 8th Annual Core Sound Decoy Festival is scheduled for December 2 and 3, 1995, on Harkers Island. For more information about Core Sound Decoy Carvers Guild, Core Sound Waterfowl Museum or area carvers and shops, contact the museum at P.O. Box 556, Harkers Island, North Carolina 28531, or call 728-1500.

Flea Market

There are two large flea malls in the area — one between Newport and Morehead City and the other outside Cape Carteret. Both are very active in the summer and have varying winter hours.

Newport-Morehead Flea Mall, Highway 70, is actually several large open-air buildings joined together. Dozens and dozens of vendors gather here to sell all kinds of items — crafts, appliances, clothing, food, books, antiques, artwork, vegetables, plants and hardware. **Cedar Point Open Air Flea Market**, junction of highways 24 and 58, offers a tremendous variety with booths rented to dealers who sell everything from baseball cards to original paintings. You'll also find handmade wooden items, plants, uniforms, clothing, cosmetics, produce and jewelry.

Photo: NC Travel & Tourism Division, Clay Nolen

Loggerhead turtles nest along the shores of the Crystal Coast.

Crystal Coast
Attractions

Ocean related activities and coastal parks are much of what make the Crystal Coast so distinct and different, so attractive to tourists and so protected by residents. Cape Lookout National Seashore, Fort Macon State Park, Hammocks Beach State Park, Theodore Roosevelt Natural Area, Rachel Carson Research Reserve, Hadnot Creek Farm and Cedar Island National Wildlife Refuge offer a wide variety of pristine beaches, maritime forests and waterways to enjoy and explore.

The unique cultural and natural histories of the area, our aquarium and museums enhance the visit of every tourist and the daily lives of every resident.

Among the attractions we've included in this chapter are a few of the interesting islands that surround the Crystal Coast. We've described county and local parks, along with sporting activities and annual events in the Sports and Fitness and Annual Events chapters. For attractions the whole family will enjoy, especially the kids, see our Kidstuff chapter.

General Attractions

NORTH CAROLINA
AQUARIUM AT PINE KNOLL SHORES
Salter Path Rd., Hwy. 58, MP 7   247-4003

The North Carolina Aquarium at Pine Knoll Shores is one of the most popular attractions on the Crystal Coast. One visit will tell you why.

Tucked away in the maritime forest of the Theodore Roosevelt Natural Area,

the aquarium bustles with activity from spring to fall. Visitors enjoy films, talks, programs and workshops on coastal topics. They also take part in field trips and other fun and educational activities. The Pine Knoll Shores aquarium is one of the state's three aquariums. Others are located on Roanoke Island and at Fort Fisher.

Each aquarium conducts a wide variety of activities and displays numerous exhibits and showtanks that are home to colorful fish and other marine life native to North Carolina waters. The aquariums educate the public about our state's fragile aquatic and marine resources. In fact, the aquariums were first called Marine Resources Centers. They were renamed in 1986 as part of their 10-year anniversary.

While all the programs and exhibits are designed to educate, there is a lot of fun involved too. The popular hands-on touch tanks allow everyone to get a feel for and close-up look at common marine animals. At the Pine Knoll Shores aquarium, visitors will find a collection of freshwater and saltwater plants and animals. The Precious Waters exhibit features a 2,000-gallon salt marsh tank with live alligators. Its accompanying video presentation explains the effect of coastal water quality on such conservation issues as loss of habitat.

A popular exhibit is the loggerhead nursery, where turtle hatchlings that have been injured, abandoned, or for some reason were unable to reach the sea are moni-

Photo: NC Travel & Tourism Division, William Ross

At the Harvey W. Smith Watercraft Center in Beaufort you can learn about building wooden boats.

tored until they can be safely released into the ocean. Each year, usually in May, the aquarium stages a Turtle Release trip (one of the aquarium's most popular events), at which time these sea turtles are returned to the open sea.

Other popular programs include Onboard collecting cruises, canoe trips, snorkeling instruction, saltwater fishing, interpretive beach walks and excursions to remote barrier islands. The nearby Alice Hoffman Nature Trail in the natural area provides a short, loop-trail hike. Interpretive trail brochures are available at the aquarium information desk and in the gift shop, which carries a wide and unique variety of educational and environmental items.

Admission fees are: adults, $3; senior citizens and active military $2; children (6 to 17 years old), $1; registered school groups, Aquarium Society members and children younger than age 6, free of charge. The admission fees have created a special fund to be used for renovations, improvements and expansion of the three existing aquarium facilities.

Membership in the Aquarium Society entitles participants to free admission, newsletters, calendars, special functions and discounts on programs and gift shop purchases. The three aquariums are open to the public year round. Some field trips, classes and workshops require a nominal fee to cover supplies. Aquarium hours are 9 AM to 5 PM Monday through Saturday and 1 to 5 PM on Sunday.

Insiders' Tips

A trip to Cape Lookout requires taking all your necessities with you, especially drinking water and sunscreen.

BEAUFORT HISTORIC SITE
100 Block of Turner St.
Beaufort   728-5225

The Beaufort Historic Site is a large area in the center of town that is home to a number of restored homes and buildings. Cared for by the Beaufort Historical Association, the site is available for tours of these old structures as well as classes, workshops and events throughout the year.

Most of the buildings were moved years ago to the site from other locations in town. These moves were necessitated in many cases by property owners who were ready to tear down an old structure to build a new one. Among the restored buildings on the site are those described below.

Josiah Bell House, c. 1825, is the large yellow house used as the welcome center for the Beaufort Historic Site. Its Victorian furnishings reflect typical customs of the era. **Samuel Leffers Cottage**, c. 1778, was once the schoolmaster's house. It is furnished in a primitive style and features a Beaufort-type roof line.

Carteret County Courthouse of 1796 was the county's third courthouse and is the oldest public building remaining in Beaufort. It has been restored with authentic furnishings. **Old County Jail**, c. 1829, is in excellent condition. Its three cells and jailkeeper's quarters were in use until 1954. There is a museum room in one of the cells. The **Apothecary Shop and Doctor's Office**, c. 1859, features a wonderful collection of medical instruments and memorabilia from the first county doctors and dentists.

R. Rustell House, c. 1732, is home to the Mattie King Davis Art Gallery. In its time, it was a typical Beaufort cottage and was owned by prominent early citizen Richard Rustell Jr.

Guided tours begin at the Josiah Bell House Monday through Saturday, 9:30 AM until 4:30 PM.

After a tour of the historic site, hop on the old English double-decker bus and listen to a guide as you pass through the town's historic district. Tours depart the historic site April through October on Monday, Wednesday and Saturday. In addition, the Beaufort Historical Association conducts its annual **Beaufort Old Homes Tour** during the last weekend in June (see Annual Events). Activities include tours of private and Association-owned homes, musical performances, an antique show and sale, military re-enactments and more.

For information about the Beaufort Historic Site or any of its activities, stop by the "yellow house" on the first block of Turner Street. We guarantee you'll wish you had a few more days in town.

N.C. MARITIME MUSEUM

315 Front St., Beaufort   728-7317

The N.C. Maritime Museum interprets North Carolina's historical alliances with the sea. The museum's theme, "Down to the Sea," celebrates the state's coastal heritage, maritime and natural history and natural resources.

The 18,000-square-foot building is all-wood construction, resembling facilities used in the 19th century by the U.S. Lifesaving Service, the forerunner of the U.S. Coast Guard. The museum's interior is designed to impart the feeling of being in the hold of a large ship. On the ground floor are exhibit areas, offices, an auditorium, a classroom, a library and a book shop.

The museum houses an impressive collection of ship models, ranging from sailing skiffs to full-rigged ships, including one model, the *Snapdragon*, was once captained by the privateer Otway Burns of Swansboro. Burns sailed the North Carolina coastal waters during the War of 1812. Other museum exhibits include native coastal birds, fish and mammal specimens, marine fossils, marine artifacts, decoys, small watercraft and salt water aquariums. The museum also houses a huge collection of sea shells, the Brantley and Maxine Watson collection, from international and local waters. The museum's library offers the best references and periodicals collection you'll find in maritime topics, and you're welcome to its use while there.

Museum programming reflects maritime history. Films, talks and lectures are conducted for the public in the large auditorium, and if you are looking for a special book on natural or maritime history or a navigational or topographical map, chances are the museum bookstore will have it.

The **Cape Lookout Studies Program** is a special educational program that began operating through the museum in 1989. It has been a smashing success. The program is actually an intense short course of study and can be designed to meet the needs of a particular group. Groups of eight to 15 people stay at the old Coast Guard Station on Cape Lookout to learn about and experience coastal ecology. Courses of study have included dolphin behavior, tern and turtle nesting, barrier island ecology and other marine-related subjects.

Each year, the museum conducts two major events that attract visitors from across the country: the **Strange Seafood Exhibition**, where brave gastronauts sample "under-utilized seafoods" such as

periwinkles in garlic butter, sea urchin bits and sun-dried mullet roe, and the **Traditional Wooden Boat Show**, which features beautiful handcrafted boats, music, boat races, talks, entertainment and displays (see our Annual Events chapter).

The museum is open year round and targets its programs and activities to interest visitors of all ages. Its **Summer Science School** for youngsters (see Kidstuff) addresses such subjects as sea shells, marine archaeology, pirates, fishing and salt marsh habitats. Field trips and programs for both adults and children range from how to harvest, clean and cook clams to hands-on trawl and dredge trips aboard a research vessel. A trained naturalist might take adventurers on a hike through the marshes, on a trek to look for waterfowl or on a boat ride to explore one of the area's many surrounding undeveloped is-

lands. Whatever the topic, a unique coastal experience is sure to follow.

There is no admission fee; museum hours are from 9 AM to 5 PM Monday through Friday, 10 AM to 5 PM Saturday and 2 to 5 PM Sunday.

HARVEY W. SMITH
WATERCRAFT CENTER
Front St., Beaufort   728-7317

The beautiful new watercraft center is an extension of the N.C. Maritime Museum and is located just across the street on Front Street. The watercraft center is the hub of the museum's **Small Craft Program**, which researches and preserves boat styles traditional to area uses. It is a busy, bustling arena of activity, where the sounds of hammers, saws and drills and the smells of wood chips and salt air bring back images of traditional boatbuilding and early seafarers. The center's viewing platform above the boat shop floor allows visitors to observe boats in the making. In addition to boatbuilding and restoration projects, the center offers classes in boatbuilding carpentry, oarmaking, lofting, tool making and halfmodeling. It also houses the **John S. MacCormack Model Shop**, where model builders construct scale models of a variety of vessels, including colonial merchantmen, local small craft and other interesting historical ships. There is no admission charge. Hours are 9 AM to 5 PM Monday through Friday; 10 AM to 5 PM, Saturday; 1 PM to 5 PM, Sunday.

CARTERET COUNTY MUSEUM OF HISTORY AND ART
100 Wallace Dr., Morehead City 247-7533

In 1985, the Carteret County Historical Society was given the old Camp Glenn School building, c. 1907, which had served the community first as a school and later as a church, a flea market and a print shop. The society moved the building from its previous location to Wallace Drive, facing the parking lots of Carteret Community College and the Crystal Coast Civic Center, just off Arendell Street in Morehead City. The members renovated the building and created a museum to show visitors and residents how life used to be in Carteret County. There are rotating exhibits with emphasis on the area's Native American heritage, schools, businesses and homes. The museum also houses the society's research library for use by those interested in genealogy and history. Monthly exhibits feature area artists, and there is a gift shop. The museum is open Tuesday through Saturday, 1 until 4 PM. There is no admission charge.

CORE SOUND WATERFOWL MUSEUM
SR 1335 Just east of the school
Harkers Island 728-1500

Established in 1988 as an outgrowth of efforts by the Decoy Carvers Guild, the museum is funded by its own membership, which now numbers more than 1,200. Truly a grassroots effort, the museum houses decoys from the collections of such renowned local carvers as Homer Fulcher and Eldon Willis. It has pieces by Jack Dudley, author of *Core Sound Waterfowl Heritage*, and a Dixon reproduction decoy. Also exhibited are the blue ribbon pieces from all past Core Sound Decoy Festival competitions in the decoy painting, gunning shore birds and best in show categories. The museum gift shop carries books, stationery, T-shirts, canvas geese and decorative decoys.

Plans are in progress to build a permanent museum building "at the end of the road" in Harkers Island next to the Cape Lookout National Seashore park service headquarters. The land has been acquired, and fund-raising efforts for the planned $2 million facility were kicked off at the 1994 Core Sound Decoy Festival in December. Membership categories range from $25 for individuals to various statuses of contribution support.

Insiders' Tips

Taking your dog to the Cape Lookout National Seashore islands is a good way to acquire an expensive citation. Dogs are allowed only if needed for sight assistance or if used with a permit for hunting during hunting season.

The
American Chamber
Music Festival

Call
808-ARTS
for more information

Offering internationally recognized artists and ensembles throughout the year.

North Carolina Maritime Museum
Beaufort, NC

CRYSTAL COAST AMPHITHEATER/ WORTHY IS THE LAMB

Hwy. 58
Pelletier   393-8373, (800) 662-5960

This 2,000-seat amphitheater overlooks the White Oak River in the little community of Pelletier, just north of Cape Carteret. The amphitheater is home to *Worthy is the Lamb*, an outdoor passion play depicting the life of Christ. The spectacular presentation is a sensitive, moving composition of art, spoken word and music with insightful, spiritual reflections that reveal a compelling portrait of the life and times of Christ.

This outdoor drama is the only fully orchestrated musical passion play in production. It features period costuming, ships, horses, chariots and pageantry. Sets have been carefully constructed to create a lifelike replica of the city of Jerusalem. State-of-the-art technology in computer-coordinated sound, lighting and special effects provide consistently outstanding performance quality. The soundtrack was recorded in London at the same historic English cathedral where soundtracks for

such movies as *Greystoke* and *Yentl* were produced.

Worthy is the Lamb performances are staged at 8:30 PM Thursday through Saturday from mid-June through August 31. From September 1 through 24, performances begin at 7:30 PM on Friday and Saturday only. Adult tickets are $11; senior citizens, $9; children ages 6 through 12, $6. Discounts are offered to groups of 15 or more and active military.

HADNOT CREEK FARM

3223-4 Hwy. 58, Swansboro   393-8185

Tucked back in the woods along the White Oak River, this natural heritage area can be tricky to find, but it's worth the search. The farm is located 5 miles north of Cape Carteret on Highway 58 behind the T&W Oyster Bar. It is marked by a Hadnot Creek Kennels sign and a brown state directional sign indicating NCCF, the **North Carolina Coastal Federation**. After the turn, a winding dirt road leads behind the restaurant, past farm land and into the woods. At the end of the road is the North Carolina Coastal Federation office where you can pick up

a trail guide and head into the natural area.

There are two trails: One is about 2.5 miles long; a shorter loop is a 30-minute walk.

The farm and natural heritage area is on a peninsula fronted by the White Oak River and flanked by Caleb's Branch on one side and Hadnot Creek on the other. The presence of rare and endangered plants and animals contributes to the site's significance. American alligators have been sighted in Caleb's Branch and, are thought to breed in the area. Other forest animals include bobcats, raccoons, opossums, deer and squirrels. Red-tailed hawks, merlins and osprey live here, too. Blueberry bushes, red flax, palmetto palms, a variety of ferns and elegant Jack-in-the-pulpits grow in abundance. At the lower elevations, miniature mud towers of crayfish dot the trail.

Guided tours are scheduled each Wednesday at 1:30 PM, and hikers should call ahead to register. The North Carolina Coastal Federation has also added fascinating new tours to the schedule between May and October. Each Friday a

boat trip into the sound notes the geographic effects of Bogue Inlet's changes on nearby islands and samples the bottom for indigenous marine life. Tuesdays bring an inlet and open beach investigation to observe the changes effected on Bogue Inlet and nearby beaches by modern and historic development. On Thursdays, the Croatan Forest Safari takes explorers into the land of carnivorous plants. Venus's-flytraps, sundews, butterworts and four varieties of pitcher plants proliferate in the Croatan. All trips are scheduled through the coastal federation office, and all but the trail tour require a small fee that is very well spent.

Tours

MYSTERY TOURS
Front St., Beaufort   728-6783, 728-6783

Docked in Taylor's Creek in front of the Beaufort House Restaurant, the 65-foot double-decked, *Mystery* tour boat cruises 18 miles of area waterways. Complete with a covered cabin and snack bar, the boat provides visitors with a water view of Beaufort's historic homes, wild

"banker" island ponies, salt marshes, bird rookeries, Morehead City State Port, Fort Macon, Shackleford Banks and other islands along the Intracoastal Waterway. Tours last 1½ hours and are conducted daily at 2, 4:30 and 7 PM, April through October. Costs are $8 for adults, $5 for children ages 6 through 12, and free for youngsters younger than 6. The *Mystery* also charters half-day fishing trips from 8 AM to noon and can make arrangements for dinner cruises. The boat is available for special occasion charters such as birthdays, weddings and anniversaries. Special interest trips can be arranged for birders, shell collectors and other groups.

CRYSTAL QUEEN

600 Front St.
Beaufort waterfront   728-2527
Docked in Taylor's Creek on the Beaufort waterfront, the colorful red, white and blue 82-foot paddle wheeler *Crystal Queen* is available for a variety of scenic tours. Licensed for 150 passengers, the *Crystal Queen* includes a snack bar with soft drinks, beer and wine on its fully enclosed, heated and air-conditioned lower deck. It also has a canopy and sundeck, complete with foul weather curtains, on its upper deck.

The tour boat offers several daily 1½-hour narrated sightseeing cruises in season. Two-hour evening dinner cruises are scheduled by reservation and usually have live musical entertainment aboard. Departure times for tours and dinner cruises are generally fixed during the summer months and change according to demand; call for departure times.

Tours take sightseers along the Morehead and Beaufort waterfronts, Shackleford Banks and surrounding waterways. The *Crystal Queen* also accepts private charters; you can choose your own route. Help is available with food planning and the boat has all ABC permits.

Group rates, active military and senior discounts are available; children 6 to 12 receive a reduced admission fee; children 5 and younger ride free. Call for rates, departure times and reservations or fax to 728-1644.

State and National Parks

The Crystal Coast is fortunate to have national, state and local parks scattered from one end of its borders to the other. Here, we offer a look at national and state parks. Local parks are described in the Sports and Fitness chapter. Our coastal area parks are dazzling with historic interest and natural beauty, so get out there and enjoy them.

FORT MACON STATE PARK
East Fort Macon Rd., Hwy 58, MP 0
Atlantic Beach   726-3775

Fort Macon State Park, at the east end of Bogue Banks, is North Carolina's most visited state park with more than a million visitors each year. Initially, the fort served to protect the channel and Beaufort harbor against attacks from the sea. Today, the danger of naval attack seems remote, but during the 18th and 19th centuries this region was very vulnerable. The need for defense was clearly illustrated in 1747 when Spanish raiders captured

Beaufort and again in 1782 when the British took the port town.

Construction of **Fort Dobbs**, named for Governor Arthur Dobbs, began here in 1756, but it was never completed. In 1808-1809, **Fort Hampton**, a small masonry fort, was built to guard the inlet. The fort was abandoned shortly after the War of 1812 and by 1825 had been swept into the inlet.

Designed by Brig. Gen. Simon Bernard and built by the U.S. Army Corps of Engineers, **Fort Macon** was completed in 1834 at a cost of $463,790. The fort was named for Nathaniel Macon who was speaker of the House of Representatives and United States Senator from North Carolina. The five-sided structure was built of brick and stone with outer walls 4.5 feet thick. The fort was deactivated after 1877 and then regarrisoned by state troops in 1898 for the Spanish-American War. It was abandoned again in 1903, was not used in World War I and was offered for sale in 1923. A Congressional Act in 1924 gave the fort and the surrounding land to the state of North Carolina to be used as a public park. The park, which is more than 400 acres, opened in 1936 and was North Carolina's first functioning state park.

At the outbreak of World War II, the Army leased the park from the state and, once again, manned the fort to protect a number of important nearby facilities. In 1944, the fort was returned to the state, and the park reopened the following year.

North Carolina Maritime Museum

◆ *20 years of Excellence* ◆
serving North Carolina

1975~1995

·CELEBRATING· TWENTY YEARS

- ◆ **Annual Wooden Boat Show** *[first weekend in May]*
- ◆ *Summer Science School for Children*
- ◆ *Annual Strange Seafood Exhibition*
- ◆ *Fall Cultural Heritage Event*
- ◆ *Wooden Boat Preservation and Construction*
  [Workshops and courses]
- ◆ *Natural History Lectures, Tours, and Field Trips [monthly]*
- ◆ *In-House Research Library*
- ◆ *Museum Bookstore [Large selection of navigational charts]*
- ◆ *Interpretive Exhibits*

Hours:	
M–F	9–5
Sat.	10–5
Sun.	1–5

315 Front Street ◆ Beaufort, NC 28516 ◆ [919] 728-7317
A Division of the NC Department of Agriculture, James A. Graham, Commissioner

Today, Fort Macon State Park offers the best of two worlds — beautiful, easily accessible beaches for recreation and a historic fort for exploration. Visitors are offered sandy beaches, a seaside bathhouse and restrooms, a refreshment stand, designated fishing and swimming areas and picnic facilities with outdoor grills. A short nature trail winds through dense shrub and over low sand dunes. There is abundant wildlife in the park, including herons, egrets, warblers, sparrows and other animals.

The fort itself is a wonderful place to explore with a self-guided tour map or with a tour guide. A museum and book shop offer exhibits to acquaint you with the fort and its history. The fort is open year round, and the museum is open daily June through Labor Day and on weekends throughout the year. Re-enactments of fort activities are scheduled periodically. Talks on Civil War history and a variety of field trips and nature walks are conducted year round. The fort is open daily from 9 AM to 5:30 PM. The fort office is open from 8:30 AM to 12:30 PM.

Beside the park is Fort Macon Coast Guard Base, home port of four large cutters and several smaller vessels. The base is charged with patrolling the area from Drum Inlet on Core Banks south to the North Carolina-South Carolina border (see our Military chapter).

THEODORE ROOSEVELT NATURAL AREA
Roosevelt Dr., MP 7
Pine Knoll Shores   726-3775

This little gem of a nature trail is located alongside the N.C. Aquarium on Roosevelt Drive in Pine Knoll Shores. Maintained and operated by Fort Macon State Park, the 265 acres have extensive maritime forests and freshwater ponds. The land was donated to the state by the family of Theodore Roosevelt, the country's 26th president. The forest attracts naturalists, birdwatchers and photographers. The nearby aquarium offers a nature trail guide that is available in the aquarium gift shop.

This soundside trail is a good place to see land birds. The marshes along this section of Bogue Banks are not extensive, so there are few marsh or water birds. The best birding along the trail is from mid-April through May or in late fall and winter. Mosquitoes tend to take over the trail from late spring through early fall, so come prepared.

RACHEL CARSON COMPONENT OF THE NORTH CAROLINA NATIONAL ESTUARINE RESEARCH RESERVE
430-B W. Beaufort Rd.
Beaufort   728-2170

Just across Taylor's Creek from the Beaufort waterfront is a series of islands that make up the Rachel Carson Component of the North Carolina National Estuarine Research Reserve. Most locals refer to the entire chain of islands as Bird Shoal or Carrot Island, the names the islands were known by prior to the state's land acquisition.

These islands are roughly 3.5 miles long and have an interesting recent history. Through the years, the land was privately owned by individuals or groups. In 1977, when the owner of 178.5 acres announced plans to divide the land and sell it in tracts, locals formed The Beaufort Land Conservancy Council and began collecting money and support for preserving the barrier island chain. They sought the aid of the Nature Conservancy, a national nonprofit organization dedicated to the protection of natural areas, and together the groups raised $250,000 from individuals and businesses for the

purchase of the islands. Now, the state of North Carolina manages the island reserve.

In the late 1960s, Congress recognized the need to protect coastal resources from pollution and the pressures of development. In particular danger were the nation's estuaries, those valuable, fragile areas where rivers meet the sea. So, the National Research Reserve was established. Now administered by the North Carolina Division of Coastal Management, the reserves are sites for walking, exploring and research and education on natural and human processes affecting the coast.

Estuary waters make up the bays, sounds, inlets and sloughs along the coast and are among the most biologically productive systems on earth. More than two-thirds of the fish and shellfish commercially harvested in coastal waters spend part or all of their lives in estuaries. So, the economy of many coastal areas depends heavily on the health of these environments. North Carolina is fortunate to have four protected sites: Zeke's Island,

Currituck Banks, Masonboro Island and Rachel Carson.

This site was named in honor of the late scientist and author, Rachel Carson, who did research on the islands in the 1940s and, through her research and writing, made people aware of the importance of coastal ecosystems. The Rachel Carson site is made up of salt marshes, tidal flats, ellgrass beds, sand flats and artificially created dredge spoil islands. It is a favorite spot for beachcombing, swimming, sunbathing and clamming, but camping is not allowed. Visitors are encouraged to leave everything — the animals, plants and research equipment — undisturbed. You'll need a boat to get there, and there are a few that can be hired to take you (see Ferries). You can volunteer to pick up litter while you visit, and site director Joyce Atkinson will make arrangements to transport you to and from the island.

The Rachel Carson site is home to a number of feral ponies descended from domesticated ponies that were taken to the islands to graze. They now roam the sandy expanse, living in small bands called harems, each consisting of one stallion, several mares and the year's foals. Bachelor males roam the island alone or in pairs. These are either older stallions who have lost their harem to a younger, stronger male or young stallions who have not yet challenged the dominant males. The ponies paw watering holes in the sand and often fight over the limited supply of water. As a result of the damage to the marsh caused by grazing and the seasonal food shortages that affect the ponies, reserve managers are considering different ways to protect the herd. The site is also home to about 160 species of birds.

For additional information about the Rachel Carson site, contact Joyce Atkinson, 728-2170. There is also an information sign about the reserve on Front Street in Beaufort across from the Inlet Inn.

HAMMOCKS BEACH STATE PARK
1572 Hammocks Beach Rd.
Swansboro 326-4881

Venture to Hammocks Beach State Park on Bear Island and be rewarded with one of the most beautiful and unspoiled beaches in the area. The park consists of a small area off Highway 24 just south of the residential area of Swansboro (watch for state directional signs) and a barrier island off the southernmost point of Bogue Banks. Loggerhead turtles come ashore at night during nesting season to nest above the tide line. Explorers can discover marine life in tidal creeks and mudflats. The island is accessible only by ferry (see our Ferry chapter), and camping is allowed (see our Camping chapter).

A bathhouse and snack bar provide the only shade and comfort facilities on the island, so go prepared. There's something about the access, the bathhouse ar-

chitecture and the walk from the ferry landing to the beach (about a half-mile) that feel like Sunday beach trips must have felt in the 1920s. The trip is a lot of fun.

CAPE LOOKOUT NATIONAL SEASHORE
131 Charles St., Harkers Island 728-2250

Cape Lookout National Seashore is one of America's few remaining undeveloped coastal barrier island systems. It includes about 28,500 acres of barrier island environment bounded on the north by Ocracoke Inlet and on the south by Beaufort Inlet. Three islands make up the 56-mile seashore: North Core Banks, also known as Portsmouth Island; South Core Banks, or Cape Lookout; and Shackleford Banks. Each island is distinctive in history and characteristics.

Cape Lookout National Seashore was authorized by the United States Congress to be included in the National Park System in 1966. The National Park Service maintains authority over the seashore.

The seashore's pristine ocean beaches offer surf fishermen, sunbathers and shell collectors a wonderful escape. Other recreational pursuits in the park include picnicking, primitive camping, migratory waterfowl watching and hunting. The area is noted for its natural resources. Animals and reptiles are the only permanent residents. The endangered loggerhead sea turtle nests on the beaches each summer and seldom nests any farther north. The park is an inviting habitat for plentiful resident and migrant birds. Raccoons, rabbits, nutria, a variety of insects, snakes and lizards are also among the park's permanent residents. Ghost crabs, mole crabs and coquina clams populate the beaches.

Cape Lookout National Seashore is surrounded by water and can only be reached by private or commercial boat.

For some sites, limited ground transportation can be arranged with the ferry operator prior to departure, as can accommodations (see our Ferry chapter). Camping is permitted anywhere in the park (see our Camping chapter) except in posted areas.

One objective of the National Park System in preserving the banks was to return them to their natural state, and the acquisition of privately owned cabins, which are visible from the Cape Lookout bight caused some ruffles. Some owners proved their points and were granted lifetime or 25-year leases on property that will revert to the National Park Service. No further development on the islands is allowed.

The **Cape Lookout Lighthouse** is still an active aid to navigation. The first lighthouse was built on Core Banks in 1811-1812 and was painted with red and white stripes. The current lighthouse was completed in 1859 as the prototype for other North Carolina lighthouses and wears its distinctive black and white diamond pattern. Visitors are welcomed in the restored lighthouse keeper's quarters; other associated structures (coal shed, etc.) are also preserved.

PORTSMOUTH VILLAGE

At the northernmost end of Core Banks at the Ocracoke Inlet is Portsmouth Village. The village was established in 1753 to serve as the main port of entry to several coastal communities. Named for Portsmouth, England, the port village was busy with lightering incoming vessels, an unloading and reloading process that allowed vessels passage through the shallow Ocracoke Inlet. During its heyday in the 1860s, the population numbered about 600. The village became less important when Hatteras Inlet opened.

From 1894 to 1934, the population of Portsmouth was mainly concerned with its lifesaving station. After a severe hurricane in 1935, the village population declined, and by the early 1970s, no year-round residents remained.

Today, the village looks much like it did in the early 1900s. The homes, cemeteries, church and pathways remain and are used by former residents and their descendants who spend time there. Struc-

tures that are not privately owned are maintained by the Park Service. Portsmouth Village was placed on the National Register of Historic Places in 1979 and is guided by policies of the National Historic Preservation Act.

SHACKLEFORD BANKS

Looking east from Fort Macon, Shackleford Banks is the island across the Beaufort Inlet. It stretches 9 miles east to Cape Lookout, bordered by the Atlantic Ocean on the south and Back Sound on the north. The island's sound side has long been a favorite weekend destination for residents escaping the car-accessible crowded beaches. The rock jetty is a favorite spot for anglers.

Shackleford Banks officially became part of Cape Lookout National Seashore on the first day of 1986. Until then, the island was dotted with cabins, or camps, that former banks residents and their descendants continued to use as getaway shelters. The acquisition of Shackleford Banks meant removing the structures and livestock that had been left to roam the island. Before 1986, the island was home to hearty herds of wild cattle, sheep, goats, pigs and horses. Today, only the horses have been allowed to remain.

The island was named for Francis Shackleford who was granted the land in 1705. Permanent residents once populated communities on Shackleford. The largest community was Diamond City at the east end. By 1897, about 500 people populated Diamond City in a community complete with church buildings, stores, a post office and a school. According to information provided in *Island Born and Bred*, a history/cookbook compiled by Harkers Island Methodist Women, the most growth occurred in the 1850s because of a boom in the local whaling industry.

New England whaling vessels visited the area as early as 1726. By 1880, six crews of 18 men from Diamond City were whaling off the banks' shores. The whalers were a hearty people and included families of Davises, Moores, Guthries, Royals and Roses — all names still common in Carteret County. When a lookout spotted a whale, crews would launch their small rowing boats to harpoon the creature. If successful, a crewman would signal villagers on shore by holding an oar in the air. Pots of boiling water would be waiting to process the blubber into valuable oil. Merchants in Beaufort and Morehead City sold the oil as lamp oil and used it as lubricating oil or to make soap. Whale bone was valuable in making corset stays, ribs for umbrellas and other items. They sold the rest of the whale as fertilizer.

East of Diamond City, across what is now Barden's Inlet, was the community of Cape Lookout. West of Diamond City was Bell's Island, a settlement known for bountiful persimmon trees. The western part of Shackleford Banks was known as Wade's Shore. Two hurricanes that followed each other closely in 1896 and 1899 convinced most island inhabitants to move to the mainland. Many moved their homes by boat to Harkers Island or Morehead City. Others resettled in Salter Path on Bogue Banks.

CEDAR ISLAND
NATIONAL WILDLIFE REFUGE
Lola Rd., Cedar Island   225-2511

This 12,500-acre wildlife refuge on the southern end of Cedar Island is maintained by the U.S. Fish and Wildlife Service, which provides a variety of services

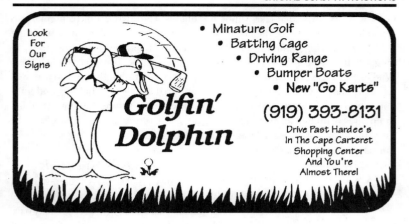
including areas for hiking, bird watching, launching boats, picnicking and hunting.

Waterfowl that are abundant during the year include mallards, black ducks, redheads, pintails and green-winged teals. Other wildlife at home in the refuge include raccoons, deer, bears, woodpeckers and river otters. In the spring and fall, this is a delightful picnicking and birdwatching destination.

The Cedar Island Wildlife Refuge was formed about 30 years ago to build waterfowl impoundments, primarily to help the black duck. All the planned impoundments have not been created and would require additional government funding. There are some restrictions for hunting on the impoundment.

The access is well marked on Cedar Island. Turn on Lola Road and follow it to the refuge office. One boat ramp is across from the office, and another is on the west side of Thorofare Bridge, the swing bridge on Highway 12 just west of Cedar Island. Although the swing bridge is being replaced by a high-rise, the ramp is expected to remain open.

CROATAN NATIONAL FOREST
141 E. Fisher Ave., New Bern   638-5628

Croatan National Forest is made up of 157,000 acres spread in a triangle between Morehead City, Cape Carteret and New Bern. Forest headquarters are located on Fisher Avenue, approximately 9 miles east of New Bern off Highway 70. Well-placed road signs make the office easy to find.

The name Croatan comes from the Algonquian Indians' name for "Council Town," which was once located in the area. Because of the forest's coastal location, you'll find many unique features here. Some of the ecosystems present are pocosins, longleaf and loblolly pine, bottomland and upland hardwoods.

Sprinkled throughout the Croatan are 40 miles of streams and 4,300 acres of wild lakes, some fairly large such as Great Lake, Catfish Lake and Long Lake. Miles of unpaved roads lace through the woodland providing easy, if sometimes roundabout, access to its wilderness.

The forest offers excellent hiking, swimming, boating, camping, picnicking, hunting and fresh and saltwater fishing. Boat access is provided at several locations. Rangers advise that lake fishing is generally poor because of the acidity of the water. All fishing, hunting and trapping activities are regulated by the N.C. Wildlife Resources Commission. The forest has several planned camping sites (see our Camping chapter), and primitive camping is permitted all year. Some areas of the forest close seasonally, and fees can vary, so call headquarters for current rates and availability.

As with all national forests, the Croatan's natural resources are actively managed to provide goods and services for the public. Pine timber is harvested and replanted each year, and wildlife habitat for a wide range of animals is maintained on thousands of acres. Endangered and sensitive animal and plant species are protected. The red-cockaded woodpecker is among the endangered animals that find safety here. More common animals that abound include the southern bald eagle, alligators, squirrels, otters, white-tail deer, black bears, snakes and wild turkeys.

The area is known for its beautiful wildflowers, including five genera of insectivorous plants, a combination rarely seen elsewhere. The insectivorous plants include pitcher-plants, round-leaved sundew, butterworts, Venus's flytraps and bladderworts, all of which die if removed from their natural habitat; it is against the law to disturb them. Pamphlets about the wildflowers and insect-eating plants are available at the park headquarters.

Because the Croatan is so expansive and undeveloped, it is best to pick up a forest map from the headquarters if you plan to explore extensively. For short daytrips or hiking excursions, site brochures are sufficient.

The summer 1994 fire in the Croatan affected mostly pocosin, which was for-tuitous. The insect-eating plants that proliferate in pocosin habitat are actually fire dependent, another reason not to try to take one home. It is expected that these plants will return in 1995 thickened, well nurtured after a good burning and hungry for bugs. Nature is stranger than fiction. No recreation areas were affected by the fire.

Crystal Coast Islands

The Crystal Coast is a composition of many islands bridged to the mainland and islands accessible only by boat. Many have been discussed earlier in this chapter, but there are others that are too interesting to omit.

Hog Island is on the northeast side of Cedar Island and is a couple hundred acres. The island is bordered by Back Bay, Pamlico Sound and Cedar Island Bay. The name of this island probably came from the wild hogs that roamed its expanse. Regardless, there was once a thriving little town named Lupton here. This island was inhabited until the mid-1900s and served as a trading point for people from Cedar Island.

Phillips Island can be seen from the top of the Morehead City-Beaufort highrise bridge. Looking north, this two-acre island is in the Newport River and is easy to identify because of the brick chimney poking through the trees — a remnant of an old menhaden (fish) processing plant once operated on the island. The island is privately owned and in 1993 was leased to the National Audubon Society, making it one of the newest in the society's North Carolina Coastal Sanctuary System. Considered one of eastern North Carolina's most important nesting sites for many species of wading birds including herons, egrets and ibises, Phillips Is-

The Lost Colony

The Lost Colony was not lost at all — just misplaced. That's what many locals believe.

The Lost Colony refers to the English colony established on the coast in 1587. Led by John White, three ships carrying 120 men, women and children left Plymouth to establish a colony in the New World. According to most historic accounts, when White returned in 1590 the colony had been evacuated and the colonists had vanished, never to be found.

Locally, there is a strong belief that John White's colony was not established on Roanoke Island at all, but on Cedar Island, which his colonists had never occupied.

When he found none of the settlers there, White declared the people lost. But the settlers weren't lost. They were just further south on Cedar Island. It was White and the returning crew who were lost.

That theory and facts to document it are offered by Melvin Robinson in a book, *The Riddle of the Lost Colony*, published in 1946. A copy of the book is housed in the North Carolina Collection at the Careteret County Public Library on Turner Street in Beaufort and is available for in-house reading.

Robinson supports his argument that Cedar Island was the site of the original settlement by using census reports and maps of land formations, inlets and surrounding islands.

One of the many interesting points Robinson makes is that the logs form John White's original voyage indicate the settlers were left at an island seven leagues, about 20 miles) from the harbor they entered. Roanoke is about 40 miles from the nearest possible point of entry at that time. On the other hand, Cedar Island is just about 20 miles from Ocracoke Inlet.

According to Robinson's research, there was a strong belief in the 1940s that the descendants of these colonists continued to live in Carteret County. The first official census in the United States, completed in 1790, reported a white population of 3,019 in Carteret County. Sixty people bore surnames of the original colonists.

Regardless of what you believe now about the so-called Lost Colony, a short review of Robinson's book will leave you considering new possibilities. Who knows? You might join some of the locals and be convinced the Lost Colony wasn't lost at all — just misplaced.

land has recently known less nesting activity. Birds are fickle that way.

Piver's Island is located on the west side of the Beaufort drawbridge and is about 20 acres in size. The island is home to the Duke University Marine Laboratory and Biomedical Center and the National Oceanic and Atmospheric Administration/National Marine Fisheries Service Beaufort Laboratory. The majority of the island was bulkheaded for the construction of these facilities that dominate the island.

Radio Island is located on the south

Worthy Is The Lamb *is an outdoor passion play depicting the life of Christ. Performances are at the Crystal Coast Amphitheater.*

side of the Morehead City-Beaufort Causeway. The island is about 200 acres and, for years, the east side has been a favorite beach spot for locals. Beachgoers can park and walk a few steps to the beach. Small boats and sailboards can be launched from the beach, and divers converge on the south end and walk into the water next to the rock jetty for some interesting diving near the beach. The south end of the island is owned by the U.S. government, and the broad cement ramp and pilings accommodate landing craft that transport deployed troops from nearby military bases. The N.C. State Ports Authority (SPA) owns the rest. A daytime-only beach access area with parking and toilet facilities is managed by the Carteret County Parks and Recreation Department on the east side.

In Swansboro, there is another island of historical significance. **Russell's Island**, formerly known as Huggins Island, was the site of Huggins Island Fort. That Confederate earthworks fort was apparently built in the final months of 1861 to guard Bogue Inlet and West Channel, the principle access channel from the inlet into Swansboro. The fort consisted of earthworks, an underground bunker or magazine and barracks. It had six cannon and was garrisoned in January 1862 by a 200-man company commanded by Capt. Daniel Munn. Two months later, the troops were ordered to remove their guns and ammunition and go to New Bern to aid in the defense of that town. At New Bern, the guns and ammunition were captured. Huggins Island Fort was never regarrisoned. All that remains of the former fort are the brush-covered earthworks.

Crystal Coast
Kidstuff

I went to find the pot of gold
That's waiting where the rainbow ends.
I searched and searched and searched
and searched
And searched and searched, and then —
There it was, deep in the grass,
Under an old and twisty bough.
It's mine, it's mine, it's mine at last ....
What do I search for now?

— Shel Silverstein

If the pleasure is the search, not the treasure, there's a lot of kid in you. For that kid, and any other kids you have onboard, great explorations are ahead on the Crystal Coast and in New Bern. Of course the beaches at the ocean's edge are hard for any kid to take lightly, and the adventures and challenges there are as endless as imagination. But, when you reach the what-do-I-search-for-now point, the choices present you with another bountiful quest.

Set out for fun in the jungle, on a pirates' island or on a water boggan slide. School up with other minnows at the North Carolina Aquarium, and explore things that live in the ocean. Make wonderful creations from stuff you find on the beach, or to go on a snorkeling ad-

venture in the sound. Ride a Ferris wheel and see forever. Take the helm of a bumper boat, or try your skills in a round of golf, mini style. We've got horseback rides on the beach, a fireman's museum and some of the best summer camps on earth. And, if you're really interested in how the seashore environment works, you'll have a ball in the North Carolina Maritime Museum's Summer Science School. The courses are short, and the classes are out in the wild for only a few hours each day, so it won't take your whole vacation.

When you've exhausted the suggestions we've listed and you're told, "Go fly a kite!," you actually can! Flying anything is best on a North Carolina beach, you know. The Wright Brothers knew.

Many of the sites for adventures that follow are also described in other chapters and, for further details, we have referred you to them. We just thought you might appreciate having a concentration here in case you have the misfortune of finding a pot of gold.

SUMMER CAMPS

The Crystal Coast area is home to some of the most prestigious summer camps in the eastern United States for

Knowledgeable mothers pack powdered meat tenderizer in their beach bags to soothe almost any kind of sting a kid may encounter on the beach.

Insiders' Tips

Fishing is fun for everyone.

campers 6 to 17 years old. On Bogue Sound in Morehead City is **Camp Morehead By The Sea**, 726-3960. Programs naturally lean toward water sports and traditionally focus on sailing.

On the Neuse River in Arapahoe is **Camp Seafarer** for girls, 249-1212, and **Camp Sea Gull** for boys, 249-1111. Both are operated by the YMCA Association of Raleigh, 832-4744, and offer programs for varied interests but with a love for the water. Sailing and watersports, including ocean excursions from the Morehead City waterfront outpost, horsemanship, archery, golf, tennis and riflery are offered.

For more information about these and other camps in the Crystal Coast area, see the Sports, Fitness and Parks chapter.

THE CIRCLE
Atlantic Beach, MP 2¹/⁴   *(no phone)*

Depending on your age, you may well think of The Circle when you consider Atlantic Beach. This was the site of the beach's first arcade, the Idle Hour. The Pavilion always had the best bands and was the birthplace of all things that were

cool. The younger kids were jostled all day and night on the rides in the center, and there was no place more fun than The Circle. It's still an active place for nightclubs that provide live music, dancing and entertainment far into the night, and it's the home of **Fun 'n' Wheels** amusements, 240-0050, which features the largest Ferris wheel on the island in the summer months and a go-cart track.

The Circle is undergoing a significant face-lift this year, thanks to the town of Atlantic Beach. Already, the boardwalk has been improved, and beach volleyball courts have been added. This year will see the razing of the old Pavilion building to provide beach access parking, burying of utility wires, paving, guttering and landscaping. The improvements will invite far more recreational use of The Circle in the summer of 1995.

JUNGLELAND
Salter Path Rd., Hwy. 58, MP 4¹/²
Atlantic Beach   *247-2148*

This large amusement park has something for the whole family. Here you will find bumper boats, miniature golf, an arcade, a snack bar and rides for the kids. Admission to the park grounds is free, and tickets (or day passes) are available for individual rides. The park is open daily at 11 AM from April through October. We find Jungleland one of the best places to keep kids amused for hours.

PIRATE ISLAND PARK

Salter Path Rd., Hwy.58, MP 10¹/²
Salter Path   247-3024

The family will enjoy an active day at this Salter Path park with two giant twister waterslides, kiddie slides, a pool and bumper boats. A lounge area, showers and lockers are available for use before a round of miniature golf or a turn through the video arcade. Hot dogs and snacks are available; you may choose to eat at the picnic area. Call for rates and hours.

PLAYLAND

204 Islander Dr., MP 20¹/²
Emerald Isle   354-6616

Playland in Emerald Isle has eight super-fast water slides and all sorts of rides for toddlers and youngsters, including bumper cars and boats as well as slick and grand prix tracks. Home of "the original" **Water Boggan**, 354-2609, and **Lighthouse Golf**, 354-2811, an 18-hole miniature golf course, Playland also has a snack bar and picnic area to keep the kids completely happy and give moms and dads a break. Playland is open daily during the summer months.

BOARDWALK BY THE SEA ARCADE

Islander Dr., Emerald Isle   354-4440

This is the hub of meet-and-greet activity for the younger set in Emerald Isle. Other than arcade games, the boardwalk features a beach volleyball court, a snack bar and a long boardwalk over the dunes to the beach. It's the place to see and be seen.

THE GOLFIN' DOLPHIN

Manatee St., Cape Carteret   393-8131

This expansive family entertainment complex, located off Highway 24 in Cape Carteret behind Hardee's, is where sports of all ages and stages can hone their competitive edges. The complex includes a 50-tee driving range, a baseball and softball batting range and an 18-hole miniature golf course. While the bigger kids are sharpening their skills, the little ones enjoy the arcade games and new bumper boats. The Golphin' Dolphin also has a snack bar and a pro shop that sells quality golf and baseball accessories. A party room is available for private birthday parties and celebrations. The complex is open daily, "9 AM until," from March through December.

WHITE SAND TRAIL RIDES

Hwy 12., Cedar Island   729-0911

Mount up, cowpokes. There are beach trails to explore on horseback about as far Down East as you can go before getting wet. Lots of packages are available, but Wayland Cato also offers a half-hour ride just for kids. The 45-minute drive from

Beaufort through Down East is a great exploration trip, too, with stops at Harkers Island to visit the Core Sound Waterfowl Museum and at the Cedar Island Wildlife Refuge (see our Attractions chapter). In fact, this trip could pretty much devour a whole day.

KITE FLYING
Kites Unlimited, Atlantic Station
Atlantic Beach   *247-7011*

Kites Unlimited sponsors Sunday morning kite-flying exhibitions at Fort Macon State Park that everyone is invited to join. Bring a kite because you'll want to try the things you see after the demonstrations. And competitions are natural. For the truly competitive kite fliers, the Carolina Kite Fest at Fort Macon in October (see our Annual Events chapter) is also sponsored by Kites Unlimited.

SPORTSWORLD
Hwy. 70 W., Morehead City   *247-4444*

The sport at Sportsworld is skating, and for the local crowd, it's the meet-and-compete spot for the younger-than-the-driving-age set. Sportsworld is well kept and supervised with all the right music and activity changes on the skating floor. A snack bar with arcade games is a comfortable vantage for viewing the skating without actually having to relearn the sport. Sportsworld is open year round. Call for hours and activities.

CARTERET LANES
Hwy. 70 W., Morehead City   *247-4481*

Everyone in the family can enjoy knocking down a few pins at Carteret Lanes. It's bowling in a family atmosphere with a games arcade and snack bar available. Of course leagues and competitions bring out the matching shirts, but the unpolished amateurs also have lots of fun. Carteret Lanes is open year round.

SUMMER SCIENCE SCHOOL FOR CHILDREN
N.C. Maritime Museum
315 Front St., Beaufort   *728-7317*

This popular summer program of the North Carolina Maritime Museum (see our Attractions chapter) is for students from 1st through 8th grades. The various hands-on study activities include explorations of delicate marine ecosystems with guidance of researchers and instructors at area marine laboratories. Maritime heritage projects are assisted by the museum staff. Classes are offered in one-week sessions for about three hours a day. Activities are often scheduled to take advantage of tides. Class sizes are small, activities are often wet and assistance is always handy. For schedules and applications, write or call the museum.

PROGRAMS JUST FOR KIDS
N.C. Aquarium, Hwy. 58
Pine Knoll Shores   *247-4004*

Everything at the North Carolina Aquarium (see our Attractions chapter)

Photo: NC Travel & Tourism Division, William Russ

When you get right down to it, it doesn't take much for the young in spirit to enjoy the beach.

will keep a kid fascinated, but each summer the aquarium plans programs and activities with a Kids' point of view in focus. Activities are scheduled each week through the summer months for kids from 4 to 11 years old. The 1¹ᐟ²-hour programs introduce preschoolers to marine life with live animals, craft projects, stories and films. The early grade students enjoy art projects, games and sea life videos; the older children learn about coastal environments and marine life via field trips as well as craft and live animal activities. Beginning snorkelers of any age are offered instruction on a regular basis at the aquarium during the summer months. Preregistration is required for all these activities, and we suggest making your reservations early.

ARTS AND DRAMA CAMPS
Morehead City Park and Recreation
1600 Fisher St., Morehead City   726-5083
Art camps and drama camps are scheduled throughout the year for school-age children during school breaks by the Morehead City Parks and Recreation Department. Usually full-day schedules for a specified number of days, the projects are goal oriented. For example, an art camp may create Halloween costumes, while a drama camp may create and present a Christmas musical. Participation fees are specified for each camp, and scholarships are often awarded by the Carteret Arts Council.

N. C. KIDSFEST
Morehead City Recreation Dept.   726-5058
Proposed in February, 1995, Kidsfest is planned to be an annual event occurring the first Saturday in June on the Morehead City Waterfront. The full-day early summer event is to be staged for and by children involving entertainment on two stages, educational tents, puppet shows, storytelling, a kazoo parade and booths where kids can sell products to benefit civic and charitable organizations focused on kids.

Kidsfest is planned to take place in the waterfront area between Harborview Towers and the Sanitary Restaurant.

Crystal Coast
Annual Festivals and Events

A full calendar of annually scheduled events reflects the year-round nature of this once seasonal resort as well as the highly valued salty traditions that spice the distinctive flavor of the Crystal Coast. While the simple pleasures of being here provide a full plate, plans that include any of the following events will graciously enlarge the feast.

February

Art From the Heart is an extraordinary two-week exhibition of original, innovative and traditional works created by selected area artists in mid-February. Proceeds benefit the local arts council and provide scholarships to Children's Art Camp. Carteret Arts Council in Morehead City, 726-9156, sponsors the exhibition.

The **American Music Festival** chamber music series continues its 1994-'95 schedule in late February. All concerts are performed in the auditorium of the North Carolina Maritime Museum in Beaufort. The series continues through May (see our Arts chapter). Call 808-ARTS or the museum, 728-7317, for details.

March

The **Homes and Gardens Show,** in early March assembles services, wares and expertise of local businesses focused on aspects of building, gardening and decorating. Gather ideas, good advice and the right products for do-it-yourself projects, or shop for professional services during the weekend show at the Crystal Coast Civic Center. For exact dates, call 247-3883.

The **St. Patrick's Day Festival** is a mid-March weekend of fun and games, corned beef and cabbage, music and wearing of the green in Emerald Isle. Benefits from the festival help support local craftspeople and civic organizations. For more information call 354-6350.

In mid-March the **N.C. Commercial Fishing Show** features boats and fishing equipment displays. For exact dates call

Photo: NC Travel & Tourism Division, William Russ

The Strange Seafood Exhibition — you simply cannot imagine the wierd stuff that comes out of the ocean that you can eat!

the Crystal Coast Civic Center in Morehead City, 247-3883.

Swansboro Oyster Roast offers all-you-can-eat oysters for one price. Proceeds from the roast support local charities and civic groups such as Meals on Wheels and Boy Scouts. Rotary Club, 354-6444, sponsors the mid-March event.

April

Newport Pig Cooking Contest takes place on the first weekend in April. Delicious "Down East" barbecue goes on sale after the contest. It's a huge barbecue competition in North Carolina and draws folks from all over for the best barbecue on earth, accompanied by homemade baked goods, live entertainment and children's activities. The event benefits numerous civic organizations and occurs in Newport Park on Howard Boulevard in early April. For more information call 223-7447.

Publick Days on Beaufort Historic Site in mid-April features the outdoor sale of flea market merchandise and crafts, entertainment, mock trials and exhibits. Proceeds benefit preservation of historic structures through the Beaufort Historical Association. If you have questions, please contact the Beaufort Historic Site at 728-5225.

On Easter weekend, The Beaufort Historic Site is the setting for a traditional **Easter egg hunt.** For more information call 728-5225. **Easter sunrise services** are celebrated at several locations across the county, many on the waterfront or beach. The local paper lists services the week before Easter.

Beaufort By-the-Sea Music Festival is a full weekend celebration for all ages and musical tastes in late April. Concerts scheduled on various stages located within a three-block area of downtown Beaufort include classical, country, traditional, jazz, rock and reggae. The Beaufort Business and Professional Association sponsors and schedules the weekend. Bring a chair or blanket to spread; call 728-6894 for details.

Lookout Spring Road Race in Morehead City offers 5K and 1-mile races in late April. Benefits from the event help local charities and civic organizations. For more information contact Lookout Rotary Club, 726-5831.

May

Annual Turtle Release returns rehabilitated sea turtles to their natural environment in late April or early May. Loggerhead and other types of turtles are taken offshore and released into the sea by the N.C. Aquarium at Pine Knoll Shores. Anyone with questions should contact the Aquarium, 247-4004.

Nelson Bay Challenge Sprint Triathlon at Sea Level includes a 750-meter swim, 20K bike ride and 5K run in early April. Proceeds from the event support youth organizations. For more information call 728-8401 or 726-6902.

The North Carolina Maritime Museum's **Traditional Wooden Boat Show** is the first and largest gathering of wooden watercraft in the Southeast. Not a commercial show, it's an early-May weekend of scheduled demonstrations, talks and races that assembles people who share a well-honed interest in the art, craftsmanship and history particular to wooden boats. Call the museum for details at 728-7317.

The **Salter Path Clam and Scallop Festival** is a lot of fun with good local seafood and music in the heart of Salter Path, which is a hard place to miss. Or-

ganized by and benefiting the Salter Path Fire and Rescue Department and the Crystal Coast Pentecostal Holiness Church, the festival is always the first weekend in May. It begins with a clam chowder cookoff at the fire department on Friday night. Saturday's food and music, all local, is at the ball park on the sound side. For details, call 247-3260.

Emerald Isle Beach Music Festival features top beach music groups, a beauty pageant and other entertainment in mid-May. Benefits go to Children's Hospital of Eastern North Carolina and civic organizations. For additional information contact Holiday Trav-L-Park in Emerald Isle at 354-2872.

Blue Water Fishing Tournament is a mid-May fishing contest with a variety of categories. Proceeds from the tournament benefit local charities and civic or-

ganizations. Swansboro Rotary Club sponsors the event and may be reached at 326-5066.

Carteret County Arts and Crafts Coalition Spring Show is an outdoor exhibition and sale of arts and crafts by coalition members on Memorial Day weekend. Demonstrations, food and music enhance the festive atmosphere at the Beaufort Historic Site on the 100 block of Turner Street in Beaufort. For more information, call 728-7297.

June

Big Rock Blue Marlin Tournament is a week-long deep sea sportfishing tournament that includes a fish fry, parties and daily public weigh-ins. The early-June event benefits charities and nonprofit organizations. For more information

Santa arrives by sea to the towns of Beaufort and Swansboro during their annual Christmas boat flotillas.

Insiders' Tips

Chrome Domes Gather in Morehead

Baldheaded Men of America bare all during their annual convention held the second weekend of September

MOREhead, less hair — get it? Well, the Bald Headed Men of America got it and have been gathering for their annual September convention on the shores of the Crystal Coast for the last 21 years. This wacky, good-natured group of "chrome domes" has drawn national and international attention to the small coastal town of Morehead City.

Founder and local resident, John Capps, whose head is as slick as a peeled onion, has more one-liners than you can shake a stick at: "If you haven't got it, flaunt it"; "No drugs, plugs or rugs"; "God gave some men hair and others brains"; or "The convention is a hair-raising experience." And that's just for starters.

John and his wife Jane own and operate Capps Printing, located — where else — on Bald Drive in Morehead City. John formed the Bald Headed Men of America organization more than 20 years ago after being rejected for a job. He was in his mid-20s, and the employer who turned him down told him his baldness made him look too old for the position and that he didn't project the image the company wanted. Since then, John has changed the minds of thousands of people and has led a campaign focusing on baldness as both a humorous and painful issue.

Since the formation of the group, which now has a membership of more than 20,000 around the globe, John and some of its members have appeared on virtually every entertainment news magazine show on TV. They have been featured in hundreds of magazines and newspapers, both in the United States and in foreign countries. In 1993, a segment on the news show *20/20* featured bald John and his Bald Headed Men of America, and the BBC came to Morehead City that year to film a re-created Bald Headed Men of America annual convention for a documentary.

Attendance at the group's annual September convention varies but is never less than several hundred. Polished pate pals travel across the country to join the fun, and members from such far-flung locations as Australia, London and Ireland often travel to the States to attend the convention. The annual gathering includes family members too, and many couples load up the kids and make the jaunt a fall vacation.

The three-day affair includes activities such as cookouts, golf, boat cruises, picnics, a social and the official bald banquet, where contest winners of such challenging competitions as "the sexiest bald head," "the smallest bald spot," "most kissable" and "smoothest" carry away prizes.

The annual get-together does have a serious side, though, and offers self-help sessions for wives of bald men, workshops for those having trouble coming to terms with their baldness and a variety of open forums. The organization contributes annually to the Aleopecia Areata Research Foundation, which conducts research in baldness, especially hair loss in children.

This jovial group of jolly jousters jabs and jests about the bare facts of being bald. Their sense of humor is both infectious and inspirational. At the 1990 convention, Great Britain's Tim Hibbert showed up to write a feature story for the Daily Mail, a newspaper with a circulation of 4 million. Hibbert commented, "In England, people are too insular, too private, to ever get into a group like the Bald Headed Men of America. All these domes together, having a good time, would be unthinkable. At home, the thought of growing bald is traumatic, and the man suffers in private. But it's a silly thing to worry about. Here, believe it or not, they celebrate being bald. It's incredible. It would help if the English could be more like this."

Bald John eschews all the remedies on the market that are supposed to cure baldness. He labels them gimmicks and believes they instill false hopes among users and compound the stigma that bald is bad. Bald is just bald. Why is bald bad? Why isn't bald beautiful? To the Bald Headed Men of America, it is.

John's wife is as active in the group as her husband. In the office one day she fielded a call from anxious and despondent Jim in Poughkeepsie, N.Y. After listening and chatting for a few minutes she said with a wide smile, "Jim darlin', you need some humor in your life. Come on down to the convention and you'll see a whole new side of things." Jim came . . . and he left smiling.

about the Morehead City waterfront event call 247-3575.

Arts By the Sea, an arts and crafts festival, brings lots of music, food and people to the Swansboro waterfront in early June. Proceeds from the festival go to local civic organizations. For additional information call 326-5066.

The Carteret Arts Festival, sponsored by Carteret Arts Council and the Downtown Morehead City Business Associa-

tion in mid-June, brings artists and craftspeople and lots of art-related activities for youngsters to the Morehead City waterfront for a festive weekend. Music, refreshments, a beer garden and riverboat cruises are part of the fun. Most activities are free. Funds raised support area art programs. For more information call 726-9156.

Worthy Is The Lamb, an outdoor passion play, begins the summer season in mid-June. Plays are presented each Thursday, Friday and Saturday through September at Crystal Coast Amphitheater off Highway 58 in Peletier. Contact the theater, 393-8956 or (800) 662-5960. See our Attractions chapter for more information.

Annual Beaufort Old Homes Tour, always the last weekend in June, opens some of this country's oldest private homes and buildings for narrated tours. New restorations and those in progress keep the tour fresh and interesting each year. Crafts, music, demonstrations and re-enactments occur throughout the weekend at the Beaufort Historic Site, where the tour begins. For information, call the Beaufort Historical Association, 728-5225.

An **Antiques Show and Sale** is held in conjunction with the Beaufort Old Homes Tour at the Crystal Coast Civic Center in Morehead City in late June. The large show features around 40 dealers and repair and restoration specialists. For more information, call 728-5225.

July

Fourth of July fireworks and festivities, including a street dance, are held on the Morehead City waterfront to celebrate Independence Day. For information, consult the local newspaper before the weekend or call the town office at 726-6848.

Down East Fish Fry features fish, shrimp and other seafood, plus live entertainment on the fourth. Benefits help support the local rescue squad. For additional information call the Sea Level Rescue Squad at 225-7721.

Fourth of July Fireworks light up the Swansboro waterfront.

The **Sport Fishing Festival** is an indoor/outdoor sports exhibition featuring boat dealers, fishing tackle, equipment, arts and crafts and a fishing tournament in early July. Call the civic center, 247-3800, for more information.

Capt. Fannie's Billfish Tournament is a blue and white marlin catch and release tournament that leaves from Anchorage Marina, Atlantic Beach in early July. Trophies and cash purses are awarded. Call 726-4423 for this year's details.

Coastal Invitational Showcase spotlights artists and craftspeople from all over the southeastern United States who demonstrate and sell work during the weekend show at the Crystal Coast Civic Center in Morehead City in mid-July. The show is also conducted in December. Call 729-7001 for more information.

The annual **Historic Beaufort Road Race** includes a certified 10K, 5K and 1-mile walk and run in downtown Beaufort in mid-July. The popular race brings more participants yearly. For more information call St. Egbert's School, 726-3418.

The **Bogue Sound Watermelon Festival** in late July celebrates one of our most valuable summer resources, the best watermelon grown. The festival in Cape Carteret is new and growing, full of competitive fun with lots of focus on the honoree. Call 393-8123 for information.

The annual **Ladies King Mackerel Tournament** is a very popular event in Atlantic Beach in late July that involves only women anglers, although there are always lots of men involved in some capacity. They just can't stay out of it at this time of year. The tournament benefits local charities and nonprofit organizations. Call 726-3825 for information.

August

North Carolina Ducks Unlimited's

Photo: NC Travel & Tourism Division, Clay Nolen

The Old Homes Tour is held each June at Beaufort and features crafts, antiques, homes tour, bus tour and wooden boat races.

Band the Billfish Tournament tags and releases billfish. The early August event benefits state wetlands. For information contact Crystal Coast Civic Center in Morehead City or Sheraton Resort and Conference Center in Atlantic Beach at 726-1441.

Atlantis Lodge Sand Sculpture Contest began as one energetic family's pastime at a reunion and now draws some serious competition in early August for adults and children. Seeing is believing every year, and it's well worth the trip. The competition benefits the Outer Banks Wildlife Shelter. Contact the Atlantis Lodge in Pine Knoll Shores, 726-5168.

Strange Seafood Exhibition in mid-August offers a maximum of 700 people the opportunity to sample unusual recipes using sea urchins, eel, shark, periwinkles, squid and other seldom-eaten sea creatures. Demonstrations on cleaning, preparing and cooking are part of the activities. Contact the North Carolina Maritime Museum in Beaufort at 728-7317 for more information.

September

Carteret County Arts and Crafts Coalition Fall Show is an outdoor show and sale of excellent quality and original arts and crafts on Labor Day weekend. Food and music add to the festive atmosphere at Beaufort Historic Site, 100 block of Turner Street, Beaufort. Call 729-7297 for information.

Hardee's Annual Atlantic Beach King Mackerel Tournament is the nation's largest cash mackerel tournament. The tournament in mid-September benefits local nonprofit organizations and includes a memorable fish fry. Contact Sea Water Marina in Atlantic Beach, 247-2334 or (800) 545-3940, for more information.

Big Sweep is an annual statewide cleanup of waterways, beaches and roadsides by volunteers in mid-September. Locally, volunteers are organized by several interests including the Rachel Carson Reserve, 728-2170, and Carteret County's office of the North Carolina Cooperative Extension Service, 728-8421.

Bald Headed Men of America's Annual Convention includes self-help workshops, testimonials, golf games, picnics, contests for most kissable, and other activities in mid-September. Proceeds benefit Aleopecia Areata Research Foundation, which conducts research in baldness, especially in children. The organization was founded by Morehead City's John Capps. Call 726-1004 for more information.

October

North Carolina Seafood Festival brings thousands of people to the Morehead City waterfront during the first weekend in October. The two-day festival highlights an endless variety of seafood prepared in a multitude of ways. Crafts, exhibits, music, street dances, educational exhibits and programs, games and contests are also part of the activities. Proceeds from the event benefit numerous civic organizations. For information call 726-6273.

Beaufort Harvest Time provides living history re-enactments of daily family life in a coastal village in the 1700s. All activities take place at the Beaufort Historic Site in early October. The event benefits preservation of historic structures through the Beaufort Historical Association. Call 728-5225 for additional information.

The **Mullet Festival** in Swansboro has been celebrated for more than 40 years with a parade, a street carnival of bountiful mullet and seafood, arts and crafts on the Swansboro waterfront. The festive early-October Saturday event benefits local civic organizations. For information, call 326-5691.

Carolina Kite Fest fills the skies in Atlantic Beach with kite demonstrations,

competitions and night kite flying on the beach in late October. Kites Unlimited in Atlantic Station sponsors the event and can be reached at 247-7011.

The **Havelock Chili Festival** is a spicy competition that puts any lost heat back into late October. The sparks fly in Havelock City Park. Any smoldering issues concerning chili festival details can be resolved by calling 447-1101.

November

Mill Creek Oyster Festival is a family event in early November starring oysters. The Saturday festival co-stars other seafoods for the less adventurous and also includes music and crafts. The event benefits and is sponsored by the Mill Creek Fire Department, 726-0542.

Christmas Gallery Show is a two-week early-November show and sale of original juried artwork by members of the Carteret County Arts and Crafts Coalition. More than 40 local artists combine work to create a gallery show that opens in Morehead Plaza Shopping Center in Morehead City during the Thanksgiving holidays. Call 728-7297 for more information.

Festival of Trees is sponsored in late November by Hospice of Carteret County and features more than 60 decorated trees displayed at the Crystal Coast Civic Center, a breakfast with Santa, a fashion show, a luncheon and a festive preview party. Proceeds benefit the county hospice program. Call 247-2808 with questions.

Coastal Invitational Showcase brings numerous crafters and their wares to the Crystal Coast Civic Center, Morehead City, 729-7001, in late November.

Christmas Flotilla is an evening parade of decorated and lighted boats bringing Santa to the Swansboro waterfront during the weekend after Thanksgiving. For more information call 326-4152.

December

Core Sound Decoy Festival is held the first weekend in December at Harkers Island Elementary School, Harkers Island. The festival includes competitions in carving and painting decoys, exhibits and sales of old and new decoys, a loon calling contest, special competitions for children, educational exhibits and an auction. The event benefits Core Sound Waterfowl Museum. Call 728-1500 for additional information.

Christmas Open House takes place at the North Carolina Aquarium of Pine Knoll Shores and at the North Carolina Maritime Museum in Beaufort in mid-December. It's a good time to meet those involved in activities and programs, to hear of forthcoming plans and to volunteer to help. Call for dates: aquarium, 247-4004; museum, 728-7317.

Coastal Carolina Christmas Celebration opens historic homes and structures decorated for Christmas in traditional styles in mid-December. The celebration at Beaufort Historic Site benefits preservation of historic structures through the Beaufort Historical Association. Call 728-5225 for information.

Photo: Scott Taylor

A Crystal Coast moonlit ocean.

Crystal Coast
Nightlife

Most folks don't come to the Crystal Coast just for the nightlife. Many residents and visitors consider an after-dinner drink, a walk on the beach or the boardwalk about all the nightlife they want after a full day of watersports or exploring the sites. Others want to dance and socialize in a club.

Crystal Coast nightlife can be divided into two categories: outside or inside. For those who prefer to be outside (the area's mild climate allows that most of the year), there are harbor cruises, the beach and deck bars. For those who prefer to be inside, there are places for you too. Some nightspots offer both, with lounges inside and out.

You won't find the number of rockin' and rollin' places other beach areas offer, but there are a few dance spots and watering holes for those who want to mingle.

Shagging to beach music is very popular here, and many clubs on the beach cater to shaggers. The shag is a type of dance that was probably a derivative of the beach bop, although it is smoother and done to rhythm and blues or North Carolina's own beach music. The dance is basically an eight-step, alternate-step that has a definite rhythm and distinct appearance.

Most coastal nightlife takes place on or around the water. In addition to the many waterfront bars, several local boats offer sunset trips or dinner cruises. Check below as well as in the Fishing, Water Sports and Beach Access chapter of this book for more information about cruises.

We have listed the spots that cater primarily to nightlife seekers. If the business is located on Bogue Banks, we have used the milepost (MP) number for easy location. Many restaurants are considered nightspots because they feature live entertainment or have a bar, so check the Restaurant chapter for more information too. The local newspaper or any one of the weekly vacation guides might also help you in selecting a nightspot.

At the end of this section, we have included information about area liquor laws and ABC stores, which are the only places allowed to sell bottles of liquor.

Atlantic Beach

Atlantic Beach is home to a number of reputable nightspots that have stood the test of time and continue to offer quality entertainment. There are a few other spots that have been around for awhile, but we don't feel comfortable recommending them. New spots often open each spring. If you see a nightspot and we haven't listed it below, there may be several reasons — we would not recommend it to a friend, it just opened in the spring or we unintentionally overlooked it. Check a place out with another Insider before you venture out if you have any doubts. Here are a few suggestions.

ATLANTIC STATION CINEMA 4
MP 3   247-7016

This theater is only a few years old. At the west end of the Atlantic Station shopping center, it has four screens and is very clean and comfortable.

BEACH TAVERN

MP 2¹ᐟ²   247-4466

Beach Tavern has been around since 1972 and continues to attract a very diverse group of people who aren't looking for anything fancy. There are pool tables, darts, a jukebox and a wide-screen television. The grill serves burgers, hot dogs and good pizza. BT is open year round, seven days a week.

CAPT. STACY

Atlantic Beach Causeway   247-7501
                    (800)533-9417

The Capt. Stacy fleet is best known for its deep sea fishing, but it also offers moonlight cruises and harbor tours during the summer. Private party and dinner cruises can also be arranged.

CHANNEL MARKER

Atlantic Beach Causeway   247-2344

The Channel Marker offers a fun bar and waterfront atrium lounge. An outside deck overlooks Bogue Sound, and dock space is available for those arriving by boat. The bar has all ABC permits. This is a popular nightspot for all ages and opens at 4 PM.

NONAME
GRILL & LOUNGE

MP 3   240-2224

The bar at Chris' is separate from the dining area, and there is usually a crowd during the summer. Live music is often on tap, and there is a small dance floor. You'll find cold domestic and imported beer, wine and mixed drinks. Noname serves great Italian food along with seafood and steaks (see the Restaurant chapter).

COURTNEY'S BEACH & SHAG CLUB

Atlantic Beach Causeway   247-7766

Courtney's caters to shaggers and beach music fans. The club is open to members and guests and has all ABC permits. Courtney's also offers shag lessons.

W.B. KELLI'S

Atlantic Beach Causeway   247-1094

This bar is a favorite nightspot for the professional crowd on week nights is and for all ages on weekends. The lounge has all ABC permits. Patrons can sit at the bar, at inside tables or on the outside deck. There is dock space for those arriving by boat. For information about meals, see the Restaurant chapter.

JOLLY KNAVE
RESTAURANT & LOUNGE

Oceanfront, Atlantic Beach Circle   726-8222

The Jolly Knave, also called Harpers, is right on the beach and offers a great view of the ocean and happenings on the beach. The upstairs lounge provides a relaxed atmosphere for mingling. Downstairs, summertime guests will find a restaurant serving lunch and dinner for indoor or outdoor dining (see the Restaurant chapter). The lounge and restaurant have all ABC permits and serve beer and wine.

MARY LOU'S BEACH CLUB

MP 2   240-7424

Mary Lou's is another nightspot for those interested in beach music and shagging. The club is popular with beach music fans. A dance floor and lots of beach music are offered along with a little Top 40 and requests.

THE REEF RESTAURANT AND LOUNGE

Atlantic Beach Causeway   726-3500

The Reef's upstairs lounge is a very popular place after work and on the week-

ends. Guests can relax at indoor tables, on the deck or at the bar. Creative appetizers and island-style drinks are served along with beers, wines and mixed drinks. Live entertainment is provided during the summer. For information about The Reef Restaurant, see the Restaurant chapter of this book.

SHA-BOOM
Atlantic Beach Causeway   726-7000

Sha-Boom definitely caters to the younger, or those who think they are the younger, crowd. The club DJ spins Top 40 tunes and the dance floor is usually packed. If you're a fan of events such as bikini contests, lingerie shows and male burlesque shows you'll get 'em here. Sha-Boom has all ABC permits.

SKIPPER'S COVE
RESTAURANT AND NIGHTCLUB
MP 2   726-3023

Skipper's Cove is a popular nightspot for those seeking a dinner club or just some entertainment and dancing. The club's house band, a six-piece band that plays beach, country and Top 40, is popular. Live entertainment is included with your dinner, and the restaurant is famous for its extensive all-you-can-eat buffet. For those who would like to stop by later for a drink, some music and dancing, there is a small cover charge.

Pine Knoll Shores

CUTTY SARK LOUNGE
Ramada Inn, MP 8$^{1/4}$ 247-4155

This lounge is located in the Ramada Inn and is very popular. A disc jockey

Locals often travel to Kinston to watch the Kinston Indians play baseball. The Indians are a minor league professional team.

Insiders' Tips

entertains on various nights throughout the year, and there is often a piano player. The lounge is open weekdays and weekends.

WOODY'S ON THE BEACH
Sheraton Resort, MP 4³/⁴   *240-1155*

Woody's is an oceanfront club with all ABC permits. The club features a DJ and Top 40 music. This is a comfortable place to go with a crowd or to slip away with a special friend. The nightclub opens around 8 PM.

Indian Beach/Salter Path

FRANK AND CLARA'S RESTAURANT & LOUNGE
MP 11   *247-2788*

This upstairs lounge offers a variety of music from beach and shag to country and rock. There is no cover charge and no membership required, so this is the perfect spot if you are visiting the area.

Emerald Isle

EMERALD PLANTATION CINEMA 4
MP 20¹/⁴   *354-5012*

This movie theater is near the east end of the shopping center. Like the name indicates, it offers four screens.

RUCKER JOHN'S RESTAURANT AND MORE
143 Fairview Dr., MP 19¹/²   *354-2413*

This is a relaxing, upbeat nightspot that is very popular with the younger and middle-age sets. You'll find a nice bar area separate from the dining area. Rucker John's has all ABC permits and is just the right place to meet friends. See the Restaurant chapter for information.

Beaufort

BACK STREET PUB
429 Front St.   *728-7108*

This laid-back place is located in an alley behind Clawson's Restaurant and is called Back Bar by the regulars. It is small, and there is usually standing room only, although there is a nice outdoor courtyard. Domestic and imported beer, wine and wine coolers are served at the huge wooden bar. Upstairs is a "sailors' library" where folks can bring a book to swap or just sit down and read. Often there is live entertainment.

CRYSTAL QUEEN
600 Front St..   *728-2527*

This 82-foot coastal riverboat replica operates from the Morehead City waterfront and offers a variety of services. Guests can board for a sunset/moonlight cruise or a narrated daytime scenic tour. Private charters and catered events can also be accommodated. The vessel is licensed for 150 passengers.

DOCK HOUSE
500 Front St.   *728-4506*

Dock House has long been the traditional gathering place for locals and for those traveling along the Intracoastal Waterway. This is a popular summer nightspot in Beaufort for eating and entertainment. Live music is featured during the season, and you can sit on the boardwalk, on the upstairs deck or inside. Dock House offers a great selection of imported and domestic beers, mixed drinks, wines and wine coolers, and it serves lunch and dinner.

MYSTERY TOUR
Beaufort Waterfront   *726-6783*

Docked in Beaufort's Taylor's Creek,

the 65-foot double-decked *Mystery* tour boat cruises 18 miles of area waterways. See the writeup in our Attractions chapter for a complete description.

ROYAL JAMES CAFE
117 Turner St.   *728-4573*

Some consider the Royal James the best place in eastern North Carolina to shoot pool, and it is somewhat of a Beaufort tradition. You're likely to find guys there whose fathers also frequented the place. The jukebox belts out country and rock. Ice cold beer (domestic and imports), wine, wine coolers and soft drinks are available. The cafe also serves food (see the Restaurant chapter).

Morehead City

ANCHOR INN
RESTAURANT & LOUNGE
2806 Arendell St.   *726-2156*

The Anchor Inn is beside Best Western Buccaneer Motor Inn (see Accommodations). Patrons can sit at the bar or cozy up in comfortable chairs. This is really a nice place to go to wind down after work or wind up for weekend nightlife.

CAPT. RUSSELL'S LOUNGE
3004 Bridges St.   *726-3205*

Located beside Mrs. Willis' Restaurant (see the Restaurant chapter), Capt. Russell's serves munchies, sandwiches and your favorite beverages every day. The lounge opens at 5 PM and has all ABC permits. Inside, you can relax at the bar or at tables. There is a game area with darts and six pool tables.

CAROLINA PRINCESS
Eighth St.   726-5479, (800)682-3456

After unloading the anglers and their catches from a day of deep sea fishing, the *Carolina Princess* is cleaned and readied for a night of activity. The vessel offers cruises and is available for private charter.

CINEMA TRIPLE
Morehead Plaza Shopping Center
Bridges St.   726-2081

This theater is actually behind the shopping center. It offers three screens.

CONTINENTAL SHELF
513 Evans St.   726-7454, (800)426-7966

The *Continental Shelf* offers spring and summer evening cruises and a chance to see the surrounding area and wildlife by night. This 100-foot vessel is also available for private charter year round.

MOREHEAD TWIN
1400 Arendell St.   726-4710

Morehead Twin is located in the downtown section of Morehead City. The theater has two screens.

RAPSCALLIONS
715 Arendell St.   240-1213

Raps is a favorite gathering place among locals and is often packed during the summer. The downstairs bar area surrounds a huge oak bar and has tables and

plenty of floor space. Upstairs are two levels of dining areas.

Swansboro

In the past, if you were looking for nightlife in the Swansboro area, you could check out one of the roadside pubs or linger over your dinner at a restaurant. Things have improved in recent years, and there are a few more options now for folks who don't want to go straight home. The Flying Bridge Restaurant in Cedar Point and several restaurants on the Swansboro waterfront have lounges that offer pleasant surroundings and mixed drinks.

Liquor Laws and ABC Stores

Mixed drinks, beer and wine are available in establishments in every incorporated town (Beaufort, Morehead City, Atlantic Beach, Pine Knoll Shores, Indian Beach, Emerald Isle, Cape Carteret, Cedar Point and Swansboro) on the Crystal Coast except Newport. The community of Salter Path also has liquor by the drink. Mixed drinks are not allowed in the other unincorporated areas of Carteret County, which would include the Down East area. Most area restaurants offer a good selection of domestic and imported beers and wines. According to North Carolina law, a restaurant serving mixed drinks can not allow patrons to brown bag, or bring their own alcohol.

Grocery stores, convenience stores and specialty food shops throughout the area

Insiders' Tips

Sitting on the boardwalk in Beaufort is a great place to watch the sunset.

carry a variety of beers and wines. Liquor is only available through county-operated Alcohol Beverage Control, ABC, package stores, which can be found throughout the Crystal Coast. ABC stores are open Monday through Saturday. Hours vary depending on the season. Summer hours are generally from 10 AM to 9 PM, and winter hours, which usually begin in November and end around Easter, are from 10 AM to 7 PM.

Purchases at all of these ABC stores must be made with cash, MasterCard or VISA. No personal checks are accepted, and North Carolina law prohibits anyone younger than 21 years of age from entering the store or purchasing liquor.

There are six packages stores on the Crystal Coast:

BEAUFORT ABC STORE
Just north of Hwy. 70/Live Oak St. intersection
728-7924

MOREHEAD CITY ABC STORE
A&P Shopping Center, Hwy. 70   726-2160

ATLANTIC BEACH ABC STORE
MP 2 1/2   726-3221

EMERALD ISLE ABC STORE
MP 20 1/4   354-6000

CAPE CARTERET ABC STORE
Hwy. 24, beside police dept   393-2631

NEWPORT ABC STORE
Just east of Hwy. 70/Howard Blvd. intersection
223-4136

SWANSBORO ABC STORE
On Hwy. 24, between the bridges   326-4810

Carolina's Finest 30 MPH 100 Footer

CONTINENTAL SHELF

On the Waterfront in Morehead City
Year round Gulf Stream fishing

Deep Sea Fishing for Snappers, grouper, bass & more

Departs Daily
at 6:00 a.m.

*Half-day or Full-day
18 and 22 hour trips available*

We also offer
moonlight cruises and charters.

800-775-7450
919-726-7454

P.O. Box 3397 Morehead City, N.C. 28557

Crystal Coast
Fishing, Water Sports and Beach Access

The Crystal Coast is well known as the perfect place for a variety of water activities. Sports enthusiasts looking for ocean waves, calmer sound waters or something in between will find it here, and the area's generally mild climate allows folks to participate in their favorite sport year round.

In this section, we offer a look at the area piers, boat ramps, charter boats, fishing schools, marinas, boat and water sport equipment rentals and beach access areas. For businesses on Bogue Banks, we have given the milepost (MP) number to assist you in locating them.

Fishing

The Crystal Coast hosts numerous fishing tournaments, including one of the nation's largest king mackerel tournaments and one of the largest and oldest blue marlin tournaments. Details and dates of the fishing tournaments are listed in this book's Annual Events chapter.

Federal government studies show that chances of catching fish in North Carolina waters are unsurpassed along the entire East Coast. Of the 21 recorded catches of Atlantic Blue Marlin in excess of 1,000 pounds, five have been off the North Carolina coast. In fact, a 1,002-pounder is on display behind the Crystal Coast Visitors Center in Morehead City.

The Crystal Coast has unique opportunities for anglers. You can fish from the sandy beaches, piers, barrier islands

Scuba diving is a growing sport along the Crystal Coast.

or aboard a charter or head boat. No matter where you are, you're sure to catch your limit.

Fishing Reports

What's biting is as important to some people as the world news. Information about catches is available at most bait and tackle shops, marinas, piers or charter boat rental offices. Television station WCTI TV 12 offers a fish and game report during the sports segment of its news shows. *Coastal Carolina Fishing* is a very popular show, broadcast from WFXI TV 8 in Morehead City and from WYDO TV 14 in Greenville at 6:30 AM Monday through Friday and at 11 AM each Sunday. This is a syndicated exclusively saltwater show seen all the way to Myrtle Beach, South Carolina, and Norfolk, Virginia. Host Bill Hitchcock's main focus is on fishing, although he adds information about the weather, cooking and environmental issues.

Tackle Shops

Anglers can shop at any number of tackle shops on the Crystal Coast. You're sure to find the latest gear, plenty of supplies and bait and someone to give a bit of advice about what the fish are biting and where. We certainly can't list all the tackle shops in the area, but we will tell you about a few.

EJW Bike & Tackle, 2204 Arendell Street, Morehead City, 247-4725, has been in business for more than 50 years and continues to offer gear for a variety of sports including hunting, biking and archery. But, the main focus is on fishing. They offer rods and reels and all kinds of bait and clothing, and EJW will service rods and reels. The shop is owned by David Willis.

Freeman's Bait & Tackle, Atlantic Beach Causeway, 726-2607, is a complete saltwater tackle shop offering rods and reels, along with a repair and cleaning service. Freeman's also has bait, clothing and other supplies. The shop has nine wet slips, and owner Dolly Turney says they usually stay full.

Pete's Tackle Shop, 1704 Arendell Street, Morehead City, 726-8644, is a N.C. Official Weigh Station for the citation program. Pete Allred offers rods and reels and is most known for the repair and cleaning service his store provides. Pete's offers everything an angler needs for offshore and inshore fishing, including specialized clothing and bait. He has been in business since 1977.

Fishing Piers

Most of the fishing piers along the Crystal Coast are on Bogue Banks, offering access to the Atlantic Ocean. These piers are popular spots for fishing and looking during the spring, summer and fall, and some close in the winter. The majority are privately owned and a fee, usually between $3 and $5, is charged for

Insiders' Tips

One of the best ways to really get to know the Crystal Coast is to escape to Shackleford Banks and explore on your own. Take your own boat or catch one of the passenger ferries described in the Ferries chapter of this book.

Gulfstream Fishing!

**Winter Fishing Aboard
the Capt. Stacy IV
Friday, Saturday and Sunday**
- SPECIAL TRIPS -
36 Hr. Mixed Trip -
Tuna & Bottom Fishing

& Harbor Cruises

**Departing from the
CAPT. STACY FISHING CENTER, ATLANTIC BEACH, NC**

Capt. Stacy IV

takes you to the best deep sea fishing on
the Crystal Coast, departing at 6 am, returning at 5 pm.
Catch red and silver snapper, sea bass, grouper, etc.,
with everything you need to fish provided.

We offer Full Service: Marina with fuel, bait, ice & tackle - Charter
& headboat booking service for sports and bottom fishing

Call **1-800-533-9417** or **(919) 247-7501**

CAPT. STACY FISHING CENTER

Just over the bridge on the Atlantic Beach Causeway

a day/night of fishing. We've listed the piers on Bogue Banks first.

Triple S Fishing Pier, MP$^{1/2}$, 726-4170, is at the east end of Bogue Banks. Patrons are offered a lighted pier, tackle/snack shop and plenty of parking.

Sportsman's Pier, MP 1$^{1/4}$, 726-3176, has the slogan, "You should have been here yesterday." The pier has a tackle shop and a cafe that serves sandwiches, seafood, steaks and has all ABC permits.

Oceanana Fishing Pier, MP 1$^{1/2}$, 726-0863, is beside the Oceanana Resort Motel. The pier is lighted, with a tackle/snack shop and plenty of parking.

Iron Steamer Resort and Pier, MP 7$^{1/2}$, 247-4213, is beside the Iron Steamer Motor Inn. This 1,000-foot pier offers a tackle shop and rental fishing equipment.

Indian Beach Fishing Pier, MP 12, 247-3411, is about 1,200 feet long and offers a grill/tackle shop, efficiency apartments, a camping area and plenty of parking.

Emerald Isle Fishing Pier, MP 15, 354-3274, has a snack/tackle shop. The pier is lighted.

Bogue Inlet Fishing Pier, MP 19$^{1/2}$, 354-2919, offers patrons a lighted pier and a snack/tackle shop.

Causeway Pier, Morehead City-Beaufort Causeway, 726-7851, is at the east foot of the high-rise bridge. This lighted pier offers a snack and tackle shop.

Straits Fishing Pier, no phone, is on Harkers Island Road and is maintained by the Carteret County Parks and Recreation Department, 728-8401. The pier extends over Back Sound, and there is no fee.

Boat Ramps

The Crystal Coast is filled with boat ramps. Large or small, public or private, they are here. Below is a short list of just a few of the state-maintained public ramps. Because most ramps don't have names, we've listed them alphabetically according to location. There are private ramps in every part of the Crystal Coast area, and most marinas and campgrounds have boat ramps. Remember, this is only a list of the free state-maintained ramps, so call the closest marina and, chances are, you won't have to drive far.

BEAUFORT

A public ramp with four launching areas is available at the east end of **Front Street** near the tennis courts.

Two ramps and a dock are offered off **West Beaufort Road** beside Town Creek Marina. These are maintained by Carteret County Parks and Recreation Department.

MOREHEAD CITY

Municipal Park behind the Crystal Coast Visitors Center on Arendell Street, Highway 70, has several launching areas and a large parking area. The park is just east of Carteret Community College.

CEDAR ISLAND

A ramp is beyond the Cedar Island National Wildlife Refuge office on **Lola Road** at the south end of the island.

The refuge also maintains a ramp on the west side of (and almost below) the new high-rise bridge, **Highway 12**, just west of the island.

CEDAR POINT

A ramp maintained by the N.C. Wildlife Commission is located on the south side of **Highway 24** between Cape Carteret and Swansboro.

SEA LEVEL

A ramp is maintained on the east side of the high-rise bridge on **Highway 70** just before you get to the Down East community of Sea Level.

Head Boats and Charter Boats

The Crystal Coast is well known for the many excellent opportunities it offers to those interested in fishing. In addition to taking your own boat, there are several ways to get out to the big ones. Head boats are the large vessels with the ability to take more than 50 people out into the Gulf Stream for a day of fishing. The name came about because you pay by the head, or per person, for the trip. You don't hire the entire boat — just a spot on the deck. The crew provides the rods, reels and bait; you just take your personal belongings (maybe a cooler, some extra clothing, weather gear and sun protection).

Charter boats are the smaller vessels that are generally hired by a private party of four to six individuals for a half day or a full day of fishing in the Gulf Stream. If you don't have a full party, you might find a vessel with two or three interested individuals. Your group can join them to make a day of it.

Regardless of how you get there, once in the Gulf Stream, anglers will have a chance at red and silver snapper, king or Spanish mackerel, cobia, tuna, wahoo, blue fish, sailfish, dolphin, bass, grouper or other fish abundant in this area.

Space does not allow us to list all the fishing vessels available for hire, so we have tried to describe a few of the head boats — listing them in alphabetical order. We have also included a vessel that offers a chance to trawl for shrimp. The Crystal Coast is home to more than 50 charter boats ready to take you on a fishing adventure.

Most head and charter boats operate year round, with less frequent trips in the dead of winter. For more information about head and charter boats, we recommend you walk along the waterfront and marinas, talk with other avid anglers and contact the Crystal Coast Charter Boat Association, Morehead City, 729-1661.

CAPT. STACY FISHING CENTER

Atlantic Beach Causeway	247-7501
Atlantic Beach	(800) 533-9417

There are more than 14 vessels in the Capt. Stacy fleet, including everything from sportfishing boats to an 83-foot head boat and a 65-foot head boat. The head boats offer half- ($30) and full-day ($40 to $50) trips along with a 22-hour trip ($100) and a 36-hour trip ($130, winter; $150, summer). The fleet's charter boats can be hired for half- and full-day trips, and prices vary. The Capt. Stacy Center also offers moonlight cruises and harbor tours and can handle private parties.

CAROLINA PRINCESS

Eight St., Morehead City	726-5479
Waterfront	(800) 682-3456

Captain WooWoo Harker is one of

Photo: Scott Taylor

This silent sentinal stands watch.

the area's best-known captains. The 95-foot *Princess* offers a variety of ways to enjoy the area and the Gulf Stream. Full-day ($50 to $55) and 22-hour ($100) fishing trips are available year round, and half-day trips ($20 to $30) are offered each Wednesday. Full-day trips leave at 6 AM and return around 6 or 7 PM. The *Carolina Princess* can accommodate 100 people, but the average trip carries about 40 to 50 so it isn't too crowded. Group fishing trips, parties, receptions and weddings can also be arranged. The *Princess* also offers dinner cruises.

CONTINENTAL SHELF

513 Evans St.   726-7454
Morehead   City   (800)426-7966

The *Continental Shelf* is a 100-foot headboat that offers anglers full-day ($45 to $50), 18-hour ($75) and 22-hour ($100) trips. The boat docks on the Morehead City waterfront between the Sanitary Restaurant and Capt. Bill's Restaurant. Summer evening cruises aboard the boat offer guests a chance to see the surrounding area, islands and wildlife and enjoy a quiet, relaxing night. The *Continental Shelf* is available for private charter groups, fishing, evening cruising or daytime sightseeing.

MARY CATHERINE

700 Block Evans St.   726-8464
Morehead City   726-6519

This is a chance to have a new experience and fill your freezer with shrimp. The *Mary Catherine* is a 55-foot commercial trawler equipped with the latest fishing gear. Shrimp trawling is offered from May through mid-October. After a trip, you take home the catch. The boat is licensed for up to six passengers and operates every day during the season.

Fishing Schools

Most anglers come to the Crystal Coast ready and able, but a growing number want to know more about fishing in area waters or want to improve their chances of hooking the big one. For them, there are a few schools to attend. There is hope that the number of schools and workshops offered will grow in coming years.

Each fall the **N.C. Aquarium** at Pine Knoll Shores, 247-4004, puts on a two-day program about surf fishing that usually includes a trip to Core Banks and Cape Lookout. The 1995 workshop will be in November, although the cost and exact date have not been set. Those interested should call the N.C. Aquarium after June 1 and might also want to check if other workshops have been scheduled.

Morehead Marine Inc., 4971 Arendell Street, 247-6667, offers a free one-day, lecture-type workshop each year (usually in March). Speakers address a variety of subjects such as flounder and trout fishing, inshore bottom fishing, offshore trawling and live baiting. They also teach the all-important subject of how to throw a cast net. They are the local dealers for sales and service of Boston Whaler, Grady White and Evinrude outboards.

Water Sports And Rentals

Boating

Causeway Marina, Atlantic Beach, 726-6977, has several boats to rent and provides local navigation information and charts with each boat. **The Sailing Place**, Atlantic Beach Causeway, 726-5664, and **Water Sports Rental**, MP 12, 247-7303, rent motor boats.

Barrier Island Adventures, Beaufort, 728-4129, offers rental and charter boats for trips to Carrot Island, Shackleford Banks or Cape Lookout, as well as guided tours and fishing guide service. **Rose's Marina**, Harkers Island, 728-2868, rents motor boats from 16 to 30 feet in length.

Check the Ferries chapter of this book for information about local ferry services.

Jet Skis/Waverunners

AB Jet Ski Rentals, Atlantic Beach Causeway, 726-0047, rents jet skis and is beside Marsh's Surf Shop. **Waveriders Rentals**, MP 10$^{1/2}$, 247-3826, is across the street from Big Oak Drive In in Salter Path and rents Waverunners during the season. **Water Sports Rental**, MP 12 in Indian Beach, 247-7303, rents jet skis and other watersport equipment, offers lessons as well as half-day scenic guided Jet Ski tours. **Island Harbor Marina**, Old Ferry Road, in Emerald Isle, 354-3106, has jet skis for rent.

If you're Waverunner goes down, **Morehead Marine Inc.**, 4971 Arendell Street, 247-6667, will get you back into

the waves. Morehead Marine sells and services Waverunners.

Rowing

The **Beaufort Oars** is a rowing club headquartered at the N.C. Maritime Museum's Harvey Smith Watercraft Center on the Beaufort Waterfront. The group meets for fun and exercise, and new members are encouraged to join. For more information, call Dizy Brown at 728-3033.

Sailing

The **Sailing Place**, Atlantic Beach Causeway, 726-5664, offers rentals of sailboards, sunfish, daysailers, catamarans, power boats and canoes. The company also offers bareboat or captained charters of yachts from 19 to 45 feet, sailing lessons and sales of new and used sailboats. **Water Sports Rental**, MP 12, 247-7303, offers a variety of sailboats as well as sailing lessons. **Island Rigs**, MP 12, 247-7787, offers sunfish for rent and lessons.

If you want to go sailing and get a

Photo: NC Travel & Tourism Division, Clay Nolen

The Crystal Coast offers great pier fishing along Bogue Banks.

lesson in coastal ecology, call Captain Ron White, 247-3860, owner of the 42-foot sailboat *Good Fortune*. This custom-built craft is available for half-day, day- and 2-hour sojourns, educational trips, group and corporate charters and evening sails. Sunset excursions come complete with complimentary wine.

Scuba Diving and Snorkeling

The Crystal Coast is fast becoming a popular diving and snorkeling spot, and there are local businesses to meet the demand. Diving in this area is a year-round activity thanks to the nearby warm waters of the Gulf Stream, which lies about 35 miles off our shoreline. In summer, water temperatures range in the 80s, with visibility 75 to as much as 150 feet. Ide-ally, the best dive months are June through September when most tropical fish are present.

In a recent national scuba diving magazine a German submarine sunk off Cape Lookout in 1942 was selected as the fifth-favorite wreck dive. It was the only dive site on the list that is an actual wreck, not a man-made reef. Readers of Rodale's *Scuba Diving* magazine also voted Olympus Dive Center of Morehead City third in the United States in both the "favorite resort/operator" and the "day boat operator" categories. **Olympus Dive Center**, 726-9432, is located on the More-head City waterfront and is operated by Bobby Purifoy.

Discovery Diving Company, Beaufort, 728-2265, can teach you to scuba dive or snorkel. On the water at 414 Orange

Street, the company offers Professional Association of Diving Instructors (PADI) Open Water Diver training, rentals, repairs, service and dive trips.

Skiing

We are talking water skiing here. Is there any other kind? Most surf stores carry skis and information. Both **Water Sports Rental**, MP 12, 247-7303, and **The Sailing Place**, Atlantic Beach Causeway, 726-5664, can give you waterskiing lessons and then set you up in a boat for an hour or a day of practicing.

Surfing

Surfing is very popular along the Crystal Coast and always has been. There are plenty of places to catch the swell. Check with any area surf shop for information about wave conditions and surf contests. Most local surf shops offer surfboard and boogie board rentals.

BERT'S SURF SHOP
MP 2¹/², Atlantic Beach   726-1730

SURF ZONE BOARDS & BIKES
MP 4³/⁴, Atlantic Beach   247-1103

HOT WAX SURF SHOP
MP 20¹/⁴, Emerald Isle   354-6466

BERT'S SURF SHOP
MP 19¹/², Emerald Isle   354-2441

SWEET WILLY'S SURF SHOP
MP 19¹/², Emerald Isle   354-4611

77 DEGREE SURF SHOP
Belk of Morehead City   726-5121

Swimming

You can swim just about anywhere along the Crystal Coast, with the exception of a few posted areas. But even the most skilled pool swimmer may have difficulty dealing with ocean waves and undertows, so exercise caution and never swim alone. Some areas along Bogue Banks, such as the Atlantic Beach circle area and Fort Macon State Park, post lifeguards during the season. There are no public pools on the Crystal Coast, only those at hotels, condominiums, private communities and fitness centers.

Windsurfing (Sailboarding)

The popularity of this sport is growing quickly, and rental shops offering boards and lessons have come with that popularity.

The Sailing Place, Atlantic Beach Causeway, 726-5664, offers windsurfer rentals as well as individual or group lessons. **Island Rigs**, MP 12 in Indian Beach, 247-7787, offers sailboard rentals and lessons as well as rentals of kayaks, boogie boards, sunfish and skim boards. The shop at Island Rigs carries a complete line of accessories, beachwear, sportswear, car and bike racks, footwear and sunglasses. The outside deck overlooking Bogue Sound is a good place to have a cold drink and watch the action.

Beach Access Areas

As is true in many coastal areas, getting to the beach can be confusing. You aren't sure what is private property and what is public or where to park. The number of beach access areas is increasing, and that's a good sign. The areas listed here offer access to the water, and some offer parking and bathroom facilities and are handicapped accessible. Vehicle access is available for permitted vehicles at some access areas. Public Beach Access areas are usually marked with signs that feature blue letters and a sea gull flying in an orange circle. We have given the milepost (MP) number for those located on Bogue Banks. Some beach access areas have gates that open at first light and close at dusk.

Atlantic Beach

Atlantic Beach offers a pedestrian access area at the east end of the Sheraton Resort parking lot. A vehicular access area is provided at the south end of Raleigh Avenue.

SOUTH END OF
ATLANTIC BEACH CAUSEWAY

The character of The Circle changes from day to night, and it might not be the

Keep Your Eyes on the Sea for Dolphins

If you're walking along the beach and see fins gliding in and out of the water just offshore, don't be alarmed. Chances are you're being treated to a passing display of bottlenose dolphins. If you're really lucky, you'll see one catapult itself from the watery depths to leap above the horizon simply for the sheer fun of it.

These friendly, sleek, streamlined marine mammals are permanent residents in waters along the Crystal Coast. People often call them porpoises, but on the Eastern Seaboard, porpoise range only as far as New Jersey. What we have here are bottlenose dolphins.

Worldwide, there are about 80 species of whales and dolphins. Several species live and pass through offshore waters along our coast, including spotted, striped and common dolphins. Technically, dolphins are small-toothed whales, and because they give live birth and nurse their young, they are marine mammals. During summers, when calves are born, dolphins tend to concentrate in tidal rivers and estuaries along our coast. These areas provide plenty of food and shelter from large sharks. Still, many dolphins swim in and out the inlets and can be seen traveling in groups just beyond the breakers along shore.

Dolphins don't eat anything that can't be swallowed whole. In local waters, their main diet is crabs, mullet, menhaden, flounder and other small fish. Studies have shown that some dolphins are local residents, while others are seasonal, or migratory. Along the Crystal Coast, dolphins are commonly seen during the summer months in Back Sound, Core Sound, Bogue Sound, North River, Newport River, Nelson Bay, Straits and other estuary areas. Here they feed, mate and raise their young. Feeding activity can frequently be seen late on summer afternoons around the rock jetties off Radio Island and Fort Macon. In late fall, they leave the estuaries and head for open water, where they live and feed through April.

place where Insiders would recommend you let your kids roam free at night. But, it is improving and provides good access to the beach. A go-kart track and Ferris wheel have recently been added in the center of The Circle, giving it more of a family atmosphere. The beach has been rebuilt after storms washed lots of sand away and beachgoers will find beach volleyball nets and lots of beautiful beach.

WEST SIDE
OF ATLANTIC BEACH CIRCLE

On the west side of The Circle, this facility offers limited paved parking, a bathhouse with outdoor showers, a ramp over the dunes and gazebo/picnic areas. It is equipped for handicapped beachgoers.

LES AND SALLY MOORE
PUBLIC BEACH ACCESS
MP 1 1/2, Atlantic Beach

This access area offers toilet facilities,

Dolphins are air breathers. They have lungs, not gills, and must come to the surface to breathe. Rather than breathing through a nose like humans, dolphins breathe through a blowhole in the top of their heads. Boaters anchored in creeks, coves and bays often hear dolphins "blow" nearby. Exhibiting an unusual friendliness and perpetual smile, dolphins often follow alongside boats, sometimes swimming ahead or body surfing on the boat's wake.

The intelligence of dolphins is hard to determine, although there seems little question that their brains are highly developed. Marine parks have trained them to perform amazing stunts, and the military has been able to teach them to carry out rather complicated maneuvers. In the wild, however, they don't always display dolphin-perfect judgment. They sometimes wind up in places they're not supposed to be — like stuck in water that's too shallow. Similar to a sailboat that's run aground, they have to wait until the tide rises before they can float to freedom. Such a predicament poses a threat to these animals because they can become overheated in the sun and die.

Another perplexing behavior involves their eating habits. Stomach contents of dead dolphins have turned up cigarette lighters, fishing lures, rocks, camera lens caps and other foreign materials. Whether the dolphin ate them, or whether the dolphin ate a fish that ate them, is not known.

People often confuse the dolphin mammal with the dolphin fish. Believe us, when you see dolphin on a restaurant menu, you are not eating Flipper. The dolphin fish is now commonly listed on restaurant menus as mahi-mahi, dorado, or by other names to avoid confusion.

So, remember. When you are out on the beach, scan the area just past the breakers frequently and you'll be apt to see these graceful marine mammals surfacing and descending in a smooth flowing line as they feed, play and enjoy their watery world. Somehow just seeing them gives you the feeling that everything's OK.

outdoor showers, a covered gazebo and a boardwalk over the dunes to the beach. Once on the beach, the young and not so young will find swings, a climbing area and an old boat to hide in. This access is equipped for the handicapped.

FORT MACON STATE PARK
East End of Bogue Banks

Fort Macon State Park offers visitors miles and miles of sandy beaches to roam. The park has two popular access areas. The one at the west end of the park features a large bathhouse, outdoor showers, a seasonal refreshment stand, picnic shelters and outdoor grills. The other is near the fort and has a good deal of parking. The only amenity there is the restroom facility at the entrance to the fort. For more information about Fort Macon State Park, see the Attractions chapter.

Pine Knoll Shores

Town residents are provided access to the water at a few places, but there are no public access areas.

Indian Beach/Salter Path

SALTER PATH
REGIONAL PUBLIC BEACH ACCESS
MP 10¹/⁴, off Salter Path Rd.

This facility offers paved parking, a boardwalk over the dunes to the ocean, a picnic area and a comfort station with dressing area and outdoor showers. It is equipped for handicapped oceangoers as well.

PUBLIC BEACH ACCESS
MP 11, off Salter Path Rd.

This area, on the west side of Squatter's Restaurant, offers parking for cars and racks for bikes. The south end of the parking lot opens directly onto the beach to allow access to registered vehicles during the off season.

Emerald Isle

THIRD STREET PARK
MP 12¹/⁴, at Second St.

Visitors to this park actually turn on Second Street just west of the Indian Beach town line. A small gravel lot offers parking for a few cars and a bike rack. A ramp over the dunes takes oceangoers to the beach.

BESIDE EMERALD ISLE PIER
MP 15, off Salter Path Rd.

This is a large access area that offers parking for more than 100 cars on a gravel lot. The area is beside the Emerald Isle Pier, and visitors will have a short walk to the ocean beach.

OCEAN DRIVE
MP 15¹/⁴, off Salter Path Rd.

This area offers no parking spaces, only access to the beach for walkers or cyclists and vehicles with permits.

WHITEWATER DRIVE
MP 17¹/², off Salter Path Rd.

Beachgoers will find a wooden walkway to the beach at this site and two vehicle parking places for handicapped visitors.

BLACK SKIMMER ROAD
MP 19, off Salter Path Rd.

This access offers visitors a place to walk to the beach and access for vehicles. No parking is offered.

CEDAR STREET
MP 19¹/⁴, off Salter Path Rd.

This sound access has a small gravel parking lot and a short pier over the water.

Beaufort

NEWPORT RIVER PARK
Causeway, Hwy. 70

On the east side of Beaufort-Morehead City high-rise bridge, this facility offers a pier, sandy beach, picnic area, bath house and a launching ramp sufficient for small sailboats. The entrance to this park is directly across from Radio Island.

RADIO ISLAND
Causeway, Hwy. 70

Radio Island is the largest island between the Beaufort-Morehead City high-rise bridge and the drawbridge into Beaufort. The island is home to a variety of businesses — marinas, boat builders and a fuel terminal complete with large tanks. The beach access area is a favorite spot for locals because it fronts Beaufort Channel, offers few to no waves and provides an impressive view of Beaufort and the surrounding islands.

Crystal Coast
Marinas

North Carolina has the largest area of inland waters on the East Coast. The Outer Banks enclose several large inland sounds: Currituck, Albemarle, Pamlico, Core and Bogue, which are laced together north to south by 265 miles of the Intracoastal Waterway (ICW). This liquid highway of inland waters makes numerous coastal resorts and historical points of interest easily accessible by boat.

Of Carteret County's total 1,063 square miles, 531 miles are all water. The bountiful brine giving definition to the Crystal Coast challenges the greater portion of the populace and most annual visitors to see the area by water. The weather lures pleasure boaters and sailors almost all year. Even in the coldest months, you'll find a few days each week that are too inviting to stay ashore.

Because many boaters enjoy the shallow, protected waters along the Crystal Coast, numerous marinas are also available to serve the fleet of water traffic. There are more than 35 marinas, most located on or just off the ICW. And, via the ICW, boaters can sojourn to nearby Oriental and New Bern, where a number of marinas serve power and sailing vessels. See the New Bern Marinas chapter for listings.

Crystal Coast marinas vary in water depth, services available, amenities provided, transient accommodations and proximity to sights and services. Many condominium developments also provide owners the use of private docks. Here, we have provided a listing of Crystal Coast area marinas. Please call ahead or write to inquire about the specific services you'll need.

See our Fishing, Water Sports and Beach Access chapter for locations of boat ramps.

Atlantic Beach

TRIPLE S MARINA VILLAGE
E. Fort Macon Rd. MP$^{1/2}$ 247-4833

ANCHORAGE MARINA
517 E. Fort Macon Rd., MP 1$^{1/2}$ 726-4423

FORT MACON MARINA
E. Fort Macon Rd., MP 1$^{3/4}$ 726-2055

BAILEY'S MARINA
Atlantic Beach Causeway   247-4148

ANGLER INN AND MARINA
Atlantic Beach Causeway   726-0097

CAPTAIN STACY FISHING CENTER
Atlantic Beach Causeway   247-7501

Insiders' Tips

CROW'S NEST MARINA
Atlantic Beach Causeway   726-4048

SEA WATER MARINA
Atlantic Beach Causeway   726-1637

CAUSEWAY MARINA
Atlantic Beach Causeway   726-6977

Emerald Isle

ISLAND HARBOR MARINA
Old Ferry Rd. at the end of Mangrove Dr.
     354-3106

Beaufort

Boaters who arrive in Beaufort via Taylor's Creek may drop anchor in the designated anchorage and out of the main channel. A number of moorings are privately owned, and boaters are asked to respect waterway courtesies of space and anchorage. There is no charge for anchoring and no limit for length of stay. A public dinghy dock and restrooms are available. The dock master at the Dock House is available to answer questions. Town Creek on the north side of Beaufort is also a designated anchorage with dinghy landing.

BEAUFORT DOCKS
Taylor's Creek   728-2503

BEAUFORT GULF DOCK
Taylor's Creek (Fuel only)   728-6000

AIRPORT MARINA
West Beaufort Rd. on South Creek 728-2010

SEA GATE ASSOCIATION
Hwy. 101, 1 mile north of Core Creek Bridge on the ICW   728-4126

TOWN CREEK MARINA
W. Beaufort Rd.
North of the Beaufort drawbridge 728-6111

RADIO ISLAND MARINA
Morehead City-Beaufort Causeway   726-3773

Morehead City

DOCKSIDE MARINA AND SHIP'S STORE
301 Arendell St.   247-4890

PORTSIDE MARINA
209 Arendell St.   726-7678

MOREHEAD CITY YACHT BASIN
Calico Creek north of the
Morehead City high-rise bridge   726-6862

ISLAND MARINA
Morehead City-Beaufort Causeway
on Radio Island   726-5706

MOREHEAD SPORTS MARINA
Morehead City-Beaufort Causeway
202 Radio Island Rd.   726-5676

CORAL BAY MARINA
Hwy. 70 W. at Pelletier Creek   247-4231

70 WEST MARINA
On Pelletier Creek at 4401 Arendell St. 726-5171

HARBOR MASTER
Pelletier Creek at 4408 Central Dr.   726-2541

Insiders' Tips

For boaters transiting or weekending in the area, some marinas, especially those in Beaufort, offer courtesy vehicles for making necessary supply runs.

Photo: Scott Taylor

I thought YOU were reading the chart!

SPOONER'S CREEK YACHT HARBOR
Hwy. 24   726-2060

Western Carteret/Swansboro

Almost every home or business on the White Oak River or Bogue Sound has a dock, boat ramp or both. But the commercial docks, particularly the ones big enough and with channels dredged deep enough to accommodate a very large motor or sailing yacht, are few.

CASPER'S MARINE SERVICE
On the ICW south of town at 102 Broad St.
Swansboro   326-4462

THE FLYING BRIDGE
Off the ICW north of town on Hwy. 24
Swansboro   393-2416

DUDLEY'S MARINA
Off the ICW north of town on Hwy. 24
Swansboro   393-2204

Down East

BARBOUR'S HARBOR
Harkers Island   728-6181

CALICO JACK'S INN & MARINA
Harkers Island   728-3575

FISHERMAN'S INN
Harkers Island   728-5780

HARKERS ISLAND FISHING CENTER
Harkers Island   728-3907, (800)423-8739

MORRIS MARINA
1000 Morris Marina Rd.
Atlantic   225-4261

Crystal Coast
Sports, Fitness and Parks

The Crystal Coast has plenty to offer in the way of sports. Whether it be a run on the beach, basketball, beach volleyball, bicycling or windsurfing, the Crystal Coast's mild year-round climate makes it easier to do. And, if the weather just won't cooperate or you need some equipment, there are also a few fitness centers in the area.

This section will introduce you to a few of the area's most popular sports and, in most cases, give you a contact. Water sports are described in a separate chapter appropriately titled, Fishing, Water Sports and Beach Access. At the end of this chapter, we have listed some of the county and city parks on the Crystal Coast. Information about state and national parks is given in the Attractions section.

Sports

Like most areas, the Crystal Coast has its share of sports enthusiasts who participate in their favorite events casually or as part of an organized team. Here we have listed favorite sports and where to contact someone in the know.

Baseball and Little League

Teams for the little ones and big ones are sponsored by the Carteret County Parks and Recreation Department, 728-8401. The Kinston Indians, a minor league professional baseball team based in Kinston, provides great family entertainment. Games are played on week nights and weekends during the season, and you will find a newly renovated park with all the extras. Kinston is a 2-hour drive from Morehead City. For ticket information and a game schedule, call 527-9111 or (800) 334-5467.

Photo: Scott Taylor

Windsurfing in Bogue Sound is wonderful for beginners and experts alike.

Basketball

Most of the Crystal Coast parks have basketball courts, as do a few of the area fitness centers. The county Parks and Recreation Department, 728-8401, sponsors a basketball league.

Bicycling

Flat, coastal areas lend themselves to cycling, and it is as popular on the Crystal Coast as anywhere. Regardless of the type of bike (road or fat tire) you have, Salter Path Road (Highway 58) on Bogue Banks is one of the area's best riding roads. No road in the area has enough shoulder for cycling, but this one comes close. Emerald Isle's Coast Guard Road now has a bike path. If you just want to cruise around, there is a posted trail in and around Beaufort and maps are available at the Beaufort Historic Site on Turner Street. If you have an off-road bike and head for the beach.

Camping

The Crystal Coast offers a variety of camping opportunities, from rent-a-space RV camping with all the conveniences of home to tent camping with no conveniences at all. For more information see our Camping chapter.

Fitness Centers

EMERALD ISLE MUNICIPAL COMPLEX
Emerald Dr., MP 19
Emerald Isle   354-6350
Open to residents and nonresidents at a nominal fee, this facility offers a full-size gym for indoor tennis, basketball, volleyball, soccer and shuffleboard. Classes vary and often include aerobics, gymnastics and karate. There is also a weight room, a game room with pool and Ping-Pong tables, an exchange library and a fully equipped kitchen. Space for meetings and parties is also available. Outside you will find tennis courts, a basketball court and a children's play area.

HEALTHY CHOICE FITNESS CENTER
Hwy. 70 W.
Morehead City   247-1850
Healthy Choice offers just about everything you need in the way of fitness. The club has basketball and racquetball courts, weights and Nautilus equipment, batting cages, all the latest in fitness machines (stair climber, tread mills, etc.), tanning beds and aerobics classes. Take a tour to see all Healthy Choice offers.

MOREHEAD CITY RECREATION DEPARTMENT
1600 Fisher St.
Morehead City   726-5083
This is the area's most affordable fitness center. Members are offered use of a weight room with free weights and equipment, a gym with a full-size basketball court and a game room with pool and Ping-Pong tables. Membership is extremely reasonable, and the department offers aerobics, dance and karate classes, dog obedience classes and various youth sports programs such as basketball, T-ball and softball.

SPORTS CENTER
701 N. 35th St.
Morehead City   726-7070
Sports Center is the area's most complete fitness center. Members have access to a fully equipped weight room, Nautilus equipment, fitness equipment, an indoor swimming pool, racquetball courts, an indoor walking/running track and

Camp Bryan Rod & Gun Club,
A Living Legend

Most of what's left of the legendary hunt clubs of Carteret County that flourished between the turn of this century and the Depression years are legends and a few remains. Archival photographs preserve images of the often functional, sometimes grand, clubhouses built by fortunes that industry made. Of the grand old Pilentary Hunting Club on Core Banks, which hosted Franklin D. Roosevelt as Secretary of the Navy, only the cistern remains. Recalling the Harbor Island Club, where John Motley Morehead was a shareholder, are its ruins on the five-acre island between the Pamlico and Core sounds. The Carteret, and later, Core Banks, Gun & Rod Club, which brought the first telephone to Davis, eventually burned in 1970. A visual reminder of the opulent era is the Davis Island Hunting Club building, which is still maintained although it hasn't been used as a hunting club since the late 1930s. For the most part, the hunt clubs are obsolete remnants of their previous glory. But there's one exception deep in the Croatan National Forest.

The legacy of the Camp Bryan Rod & Gun Club is alive, well and, mostly, inherited or bought on rare occasions when the club extends a membership invitation. Its membership is small, including only 36 of the most prominent family names in North Carolina, counting two descendants of the original land owner, Confederate Maj. James Augustus Bryan.

The Camp Bryan legacy began in 1890 when Maj. Bryan extended use of his land, approximately 57,000 acres, and permission to build a clubhouse to a group of huntsmen, mostly affluent North Carolinians. Bryan's land holdings in Carteret, Craven and Jones counties included five lakes, a system of slave-dug canals for controlling lake water levels and his 1,000-acre farm, Lake Ellis Plantation. Although crops were planted on his fertile soil, the most bountiful crop was waterfowl. Mallards, wood ducks, teal, red heads and black ducks, geese, cormorants, herons and ospreys found all they needed on Maj. Bryan's land. And so did pesky local hunters. Perhaps offering the land for private hunting use solved the Major's problem with local hunters. But in retrospect, he may have foreseen that "if you build it, they will come."

There is no record of an original club charter, but the first president was George Nicoll, a wealthy Bostonian and avid hunter who had moved to New Bern for the climate. Nicoll enticed other affluent Northerners including Frank Stevens, "the concessions king" of many major league baseball parks and, perhaps the reason hot dogs are called "franks." (Steven's father actually invented the hot dog one cold day at a game. Ice cream wasn't selling, so he wrapped some German sausages he acquired in long rolls, shouted "Get them while they're hot!" and called them "dachshunds." A cartoonist later dubbed them "hot dogs," and as you may imagine, Frank Stevens reaped the family harvest of good sales and had plenty of time for hunting.)

During the nearly 40 years that Stevens hunted at Camp Bryan, he brought some of his friends from the baseball fields. Among them, Babe Ruth always caused the biggest stir. His appearance once caused schools to dismiss early in New Bern. Other ball players who came were Lou Gehrig, Charlie Keller, George Sugg and Christy Mathewson. Ed Barrow, general manager of the New York Yankees, also came. In the 1950s while involved in refresher training at Cherry Point during the Korean War, Ted Williams heeded the call of the wild and went to Camp Bryan for fishing.

In 1947, the trustees for the Camp Bryan Rod & Gun Club bought close to 11,000 acres from the heirs of Maj. Bryan. Since then, a new clubhouse has been built as well as individual member dwellings. A permanent caretaker and his wife maintain the camp and cook for member gatherings, as is traditional of the old hunt clubs.

classes of all kinds including karate, water and floor aerobics and swimming. The center also offers a full basketball/volleyball court, tanning salon, stair climbers, treadmills and NordicTrack. For relaxing, you'll find saunas, a whirlpool and a steam room. The center has a vitamin and clothing store, a snack bar and child-care services.

Fishing

The Crystal Coast has unique opportunities for anglers. You can fish from the sandy beaches, piers, barrier islands or aboard a charter or head boat. For more information see our Fishing, Water Sports and Beach Access chapter.

Flying

The Michael J. Smith Field in Beaufort offers services for private planes and private lessons. This airfield was named in memory of the pilot of space shuttle *Challenger*, which exploded January 28,

1986. A Beaufort native, Navy Capt. Michael Smith learned to fly at this airfield.

Golf

The Crystal Coast's championship courses await the golf enthusiast. For complete descriptions of area golf courses see our Golf chapter.

Horseback Riding

Eterna Riverview Stables, 726-8313, offers trail rides, lessons and boarding. The stables are off Country Club Road in Morehead City.

WhiteSand Trail Rides, 729-0911, hosts rides along the beach during the day, at sunset and in the moonlight. With stables on Cedar Island, WhiteSand also offers camping trips. WhiteSand provides the horses and you have the fun. They are open all year.

Zeigler Stables, 223-5110, is off Howard Boulevard in Newport. The stables offer riding lessons, boarding and a tack shop.

Hunting

Guide services have long been a popular means for duck and goose hunters to experience a new area. Using a guide familiar with the area cuts down on the chances of spending time in the wrong spot. The folks at The Driftwood Motel and Restaurant on Cedar Island, 225-4861, operate a guide service. Hunting dates depend on those set for the season but are usually mid-December through late January.

The Driftwood's hunting package includes guide service by a local and use of the boat, decoys and blinds, accommodations in the motel and hearty meals.

Blinds are scattered along 1,100 acres of marsh from Cedar Island to Portsmouth, in Core Sound and on Core Banks. Hunters can rent waders, have their kill cleaned, buy hunting accessories or get a hunting license at the Driftwood. Folks come to the Driftwood from all parts of the country each year to have a crack at the abundant redheads, pintails and other ducks and geese.

Jogging/Running/Walking

Lookout Rotary Spring Road Race kicks off the local race season on the last weekend in April with a flat 5K and 1-mile run/walk beginning and ending at the Sports Center, N. 35th Street in Morehead City. The race is sponsored by the

Lookout Rotary Club of Morehead City. For information call 726-7070.

The Carteret County Parks and Recreation Department, 728-8401, sponsors the **Beach Run Series,** which usually begins in late May. This low-key weekday series attracts lots of local runners and walkers. The 1-mile run/walk, 5K and 10K are on the beach and begin and end at the beach access area at the Atlantic Beach Circle. Dates vary depending on the tide.

The **Historic Beaufort Road Race** is the area's most popular race. Hundreds turn out in late July to tackle the 1-mile run/walk, 5K and 10K courses. The courses are flat and fast, but runners can be assured of plenty of heat and humidity. For information, call St. Egbert's School Track Club, 726-3418.

There aren't many choices with the **Twin Bridges Race.** You either run the 8K or stay on the porch. There aren't any hills at the coast, so race directors throw in two high-rise bridges. The race kicks off Saturday's events at the N.C. Seafood Festival, 726-6273, the first weekend in October on the Morehead City waterfront. The race begins at the drawbridge in Beaufort and ends on the Atlantic Beach Causeway.

Karate

Karate lessons are often offered by the Morehead Recreation Department, 726-5083, and several of the local fitness centers (see Fitness Centers entry in this chapter).

Soccer

There is a lot of action on the soccer fields across the area for children and adults. Carteret County Parks and Recreation Department, 728-8401, sponsors leagues for younger players and for women and men.

Softball

The county sponsors a men's and women's softball league each year. The teams are usually sponsored by local businesses and are very competitive. Call 728-8401 for information.

Summer Camps

The Crystal Coast is the site of a number of camps that offer summer programs and are available for group use year round. A few of the largest camps are listed here.

CAMP ALBEMARLE

1145 Hibbs Rd., Newport   726-4848

This Presbyterian camp operates year round and is open to the public. Summer camp sessions are divided into age groups, with weeks dedicated to campers from 3rd through 12th grades. Activities include swimming in the pool and sound, tennis, basketball, sailing and canoeing, along with other traditional camp activities. A sailing camp is also operated each summer. Overlooking Bogue Sound, the camp is on Highway 24 north of Morehead City.

CAMP MOREHEAD BY THE SEA

Hwy. 24, Morehead City   726-3960

Camp Morehead is for campers between the ages of 6 and 17. The camp opened in 1938 on Bogue Sound, 7 miles west of Morehead City. Programs center around the water, with sailing a key component. Campers also enjoy beach games, hikes, motor boating, fishing, crabbing,

clamming, canoeing and swimming, along with such activities as baseball, basketball, tennis, archery, riflery and golf.

CAMP SEAFARER AND CAMP SEA GULL
Rt. 65, Arapahoe   249-1212, 249-1111

The main campuses of these two camps are on the Neuse River in Arapahoe, which is about 27 miles north of Morehead City and 21 miles east of New Bern. The camps share an outpost and docks on the Morehead City waterfront. Camp Seafarer for girls opened in 1961, and Camp Sea Gull for boys has been in operation since 1948. Both are owned and operated by the capital area YMCA. Camp curriculum includes water activities such as swimming, motor boating, skiing, sailing, canoeing and cruising, with an additional land program that in-

cludes archery, golf, tennis, soccer, riflery and more. Both camps offer an Extended Season Program that includes family camping, group camping, youth retreats, environmental education programs serving schools throughout the state, corporate training and a conference center.

Tennis

The Crystal Coast is host to a number of tournaments each year (see Annual Events chapter). For more information, contact Spooner's Creek Racquet Club, 726-8560, or call Island Beach and Racquet Club, 726-2240. Public tennis courts are scattered throughout the area (see the parks listing at the end of this chapter).

Triathlons

The **Nelson Bay Challenge** is a popular sprint triathlon that takes place in Sea Level in early May. The race includes a 750-meter swim in Nelson Bay, a 20K bike ride and a 5K run. For many, the race is a warm-up for the triathlon season ahead. It is a well-organized race that offers spectators easy viewing of the transition area and a great post-race clambake. The funding sponsor is J.M. Davis Industries of Morehead City, 247-6902.

Volleyball

Beach volleyball is catching on. Tournament nets are located on the main beach on the Atlantic Beach Circle. An indoor volleyball league is sponsored by the Carteret County Parks and Recreation Department, 728-8401.

Parks

County Parks

The first seven parks listed below are managed by the Carteret County Parks and Recreation Department, 728-8401, and all offer a picnic area and comfort station. Other amenities are listed along with the location. Other area parks are included at the bottom of the list.

SALTER PATH BALL FIELD
Hwy. 58, Salter Path
This ball field is behind the community fire department.

FREEDOM PARK
Off Lennoxville Rd., Beaufort
Freedom Park is in a wooded area and has lighted regulation and youth fields, basketball courts and a picnic and play area.

NEWPORT RIVER PARK
East side of Beaufort-Morehead high-rise bridge
A short fishing pier and boat ramp sufficient for launching small sailboats are available at this park, along with a picnic area and restroom facilities. The park entrance is directly across from the entrance to Radio Island.

SWINSON PARK
Country Club Rd., Morehead City
Swinson Park is a popular spot for athletics. It offers lighted regulation and youth athletic fields, tennis and basketball courts and a picnic area.

WESTERN PARK
Off Hwy. 58, Cedar Point
This park offers a lighted youth softball/baseball field and a multipurpose field.

EASTERN PARK
Hwy. 70, Smyrna
This is a lighted park that features regulation and youth fields, basketball courts, tennis courts and a picnic area.

MARINER'S PARK
Off Hwy. 70, Sea Level
Across from the Sea Level Extended Care Facility, this park has lighted youth athletic fields and tennis courts.

Bogue Banks Parks

There are few parks on the island, so most residents and visitors use the beach access areas as picnic and play sites. For a listing of the access areas, see the Fishing, Water Sports and Beach Access chapter.

Emerald Isle Parks and Recreation Department, 354-6350, maintains two small public parks. The park behind the town hall, which is on Emerald Drive (Highway 58), MP 19, has a children's play area and picnic tables. **Merchant's Park** is on the south side of Emerald Drive at MP 19¹ᐟ² and offers parking, picnic tables, shelter and restroom facilities.

Beaufort Parks

The town's most popular park, **Freedom Park**, is maintained by the county (see County Parks above). It is about three blocks from Front Street on Leonda Drive. The town does maintain two others, Grayden Paul Jaycee Park and an unnamed park at the east end of Front Street

Grayden Paul Jaycee Park, Front Street is a small waterfront park at the south end of Pollock Street. The area offers a dock, swimming area, a small gazebo and a grassed picnic spot, although there is no beach. The park was named for Beaufort raconteur, the late Grayden Paul.

The unnamed park at the east end of Front Street is across from the boat ramp. You'll find a basketball court, two lighted tennis courts, bathroom facilities, a dock and waterfront picnic areas complete with grills.

Morehead City Parks

Morehead City Recreation Department, 726-5083, maintains several parks in town. Each offers residents and visitors different amenities. At 1600 Fisher Street, behind the recreation department, are two multipurpose fields used primarily for softball and baseball. Inside the facility, members are offered use of a

weight room loaded with free weights and machines, a gym with a full-size basketball court, and a game room with pool and Ping-Pong tables. Membership is very reasonable. The department also offers aerobics, dance and karate classes, dog obedience classes and youth sports programs (basketball, T-ball, softball, etc.) and more.

Catherine Davis Park, 600 Block, Arendell Street, is a grassy park used for concerts, festivals and other similar events and has no permanent facilities.

City Park, 1000 Block, Arendell Street, is a shady park that offers playground equipment and a few picnic tables.

Municipal Park, behind the visitors center, Arendell Street, offers plenty of parking, picnic areas and a boat ramp. The park borders Bogue Sound, just west of the Atlantic Beach high-rise bridge.

Piney Park, 2900 Block, Bridges Street, just east of Morehead Plaza, is tucked away in some trees and offers a quiet picnic spot.

Shevans Park, 1600 Block, Evans Street, has four tennis courts (two are lit), four basketball goals, a practice field and a fenced playground area.

Swansboro Parks

Bicentennial Park is at the base of the bridge into Swansboro on Highway 24. The park was dedicated in 1985 and contains a life-size statue of Otway Burns, Swansboro's favorite privateer from the War of 1812, and a memorial to Theophilus Weeks, founder of the town. The park is the perfect place to fish from the sea wall, play or simply sit and enjoy the beauty of the White Oak River.

Crystal Coast
Golf

The Crystal Coast's championship courses await the golf enthusiast. Many of the area's courses are ocean or soundfront and provide the perfect setting for your game. Most of the area's exceptional club courses are open to the public. Courses are busy year round, and many Insiders consider fall the most favorable time to play. It is best to call ahead, especially on weekends, for tee times. Several area hotels offer golf packages that include accommodations, meals, guaranteed starting times, greens fees and a few extras.

Below you will find the area courses open to the public. The slope ratings and course rating are given at the end of each course description. Two local driving ranges are listed at the end.

Courses

BRANDYWINE BAY
GOLF AND COUNTRY CLUB
Hwy. 24, Morehead City   247-2541

Located west of Morehead City, this 18-hole, par-71 championship course is set in dense woods and laced with streams and ponds. Originally designed by Bruce Devlin and redesigned by Ellis and Dan Maples, this coastal course plays 6,611 yards from the championship tees, 6,138 yards for regular men's and 5,196 yards for women's. Golfers will find a pro shop, snack bar, lessons by appointment and putting greens. Bill Howe is the resident golf pro. 119(72.7)

Photo: NC Travel & Tourism Division

Don't forget your clubs — the Crystal Coast has wonderful golf!

BOGUE BANKS
GOLF AND COUNTRY CLUB
Hwy. 58, MP 5, Pine Knoll Shores   726-1034

This is the only golf course on the island. The par-72 course is 6,100 yards with four holes overlooking Bogue Sound. Numerous lagoons and lakes meander throughout the narrow 419-Bermuda grass fairways leading to lush 328-Bermuda grass greens. Beautiful water oaks and lofty pine trees enhance the overall beauty of the course. From the blue tees it measures 6,100, from the white tees, 5,757, and from the red, 5,043. A pro shop, snack area, tennis courts, and daily and weekly rates are available. Golf and tennis lessons can be arranged. The course was recently renovated and now includes new cart paths. PGA Pro Coy Brown has been the golf pro here for 17 years. 116(68.8)

MOREHEAD CITY COUNTRY CLUB
Country Club Rd., Morehead City   726-4917

Located on the Newport River, this club offers a challenging 18-hole course and is Carteret County's oldest. The common Bermuda grass fairways and Bermuda greens are maintained beautifully year round by master professional Bob Henry and his staff. From the blue tees it measures 6,383, from the white, 6,060, and from the ladies' tees, 4,909. 113(70.4)

SILVER CREEK GOLF CLUB
Hwy. 58, Cape Carteret   393-8058

Located on Highway 58 just north of Cape Carteret, this par-72 championship course, with bentgrass greens and beautiful green Bermuda fairways and tees, was designed by Gene Hamm. The course plays 7,005 yards from Silver tees, 6,526 yards from blue, 6,030 yards from white tees and 4,962 yards from women's tees. A Southern-style clubhouse has a wide porch overlooking the course. Also located on the grounds are a snack bar, locker rooms, driving range, putting green, pro shop, tennis courts and swimming pool. 122(73.3)

STAR HILL GOLF AND COUNTRY CLUB
Club House Dr., Cape Carteret   393-8111

This is one of the area's finest 27-hole championship courses and measures more than 9,000 yards. Located at the junction of Highways 24 and 58, the course is nestled between the Intracoastal Waterway and Croatan National Forest and surrounds a 4,000-foot private airplane landing strip. Patrons will find a driving range, rental clubs, tennis courts, swimming pool and grill and snack area. You'll also find PGA Pro Phill Hunt on hand. First-Second 115(70.4), First-Third 118(70.8), Second-Third 113(70.1)

Driving Ranges

BOB'S GOLF RANGE
Hwy. 24, Morehead City   240-4653

Located outside Morehead City on Highway 24, Bob's Golf Range offers a 250-yard-deep driving range. Patrons can hit from T-mats or grass areas. The range is open throughout the year, although the winter hours vary.

GOLPHIN' DOLPHIN
Hwy. 58, Cape Carteret   393-8131

This business offers a 300-yard-deep driving range, an 18-hole miniature golf course with elevations up to 22 feet, a batting cage, a pro shop and a room for parties and meetings and more. The batting cage is for softball and baseball. Golf and baseball equipment is offered in the pro shop, and a separate room is available for parties or meetings. Golphin' Dolphin is behind Hardee's in Cape Carteret and is open everyday during the summer. Winter hours vary.

Crystal Coast
Ferries

A number of state-owned and privately owned ferries serve the Crystal Coast, offering visitors and residents a timesaving as well as enjoyable transportation alternative via the ICW. The state ferries operate under the administration of the North Carolina Department of Transportation (DOT) and are large, seaworthy vessels.

State Ferries

The **Cedar Island-Ocracoke Ferry** is the most popular state-operated ferry, carrying passengers and their vehicles between the Crystal Coast and Ocracoke. The Cedar Island terminal is a little more than 30 miles east of Beaufort, but allow at least an hour and a half for the trip. Reservations must be claimed 30 minutes before departure time, or they will be cancelled.

The **Cherry Branch-Minnesott** is essential for commuters from Oriental who must travel with their cars across the Neuse River to work in Havelock and surrounding areas. On the Crystal Coast side, the Cherry Branch terminal is well marked off Highway 101, about 5 miles south of Havelock. For visitors, this ferry will take you on an interesting exploration and is an especially nice route to Belhaven.

The small, "people only — no cars" ferry at **Hammocks Beach State Park** provides transportation from the park headquarters terminal to Bear Island. The ferry terminal is off Highway 24 about 2 miles west of Swansboro at the end of State Road 1511. The ferry operates daily from Memorial Day weekend through Labor Day and on an abbreviated Saturday and Sunday schedule in early May

Photo: Scott Taylor

Bottlenose dolphin are a frequent sight from North Carolina ferries.

and after Labor Day. If you are visiting Bear Island in season, get to the ferry landing early to avoid long waiting lines. Pets are not allowed on the ferry, and alcoholic beverages are prohibited in the park (see Attractions).

Regardless of the ferry you choose, you can almost always be assured of a calm crossing with plenty of time to look around. All ferry schedules and tolls are subject to change without notice, and ferries do not operate in rough weather. For more information about state-owned ferry crossings, contact the N.C. Department of Transportation Ferry Division, Maritime Building, Morehead City 28557, 726-6446 or 726-6413. Information about state ferries can also be obtained by tuning to New Bern's Radio 1610 AM. No reservations are required if you are traveling as a pedestrian or with a bicycle. Following is a list of state-operated ferry schedules and fares.

Cedar Island - Ocracoke Toll Ferry

2¼ HOURS CROSSING - 50 CAR LIMIT
RESERVATIONS RECOMMENDED

Depart Cedar Island	Depart Ocracoke
Summer Schedule (May 24 - Oct. 3)	
7:00 AM	7:00 AM
8:15 AM	9:30 AM
9:30 AM	10:45 AM
12 Noon	12 Noon
1:15 PM	3:00 PM
3:00 PM	4:15 PM
6:00 PM	6:00 PM
8:30 PM	8:30 PM

Winter Schedule (Oct. 31 - May 9)	
7:00 AM	7:00 AM
10:00 AM	10:00 AM
1:00 PM	1:00 PM
4:00 PM	4:00 PM

| *May 10 - May 23* | |
Oct. 4 - Oct. 30	
7:00 AM	7:00 AM
9:30 AM	9:30 AM
12 Noon	12 Noon
3:00 PM	3:00 PM
6:00 PM	6:00 PM
8:30 PM	8:30 PM

Fares (One Way)	
Pedestrian	$1
Bicycle Rider	$2
Motorcycles	$10
Vehicle and/or combination less than 20 feet	$10
Vehicle and/or combination 20 feet to 40 feet	$20
Vehicle and/or combination up to 55 feet	$30

Call Cedar Island, 225-3551, or Ocracoke, 928-3841, for reservations and to verify times.

Ocracoke - Swan Quarter Toll Ferry

2½ HOURS CROSSING - 28 CAR LIMIT
RESERVATIONS TAKEN/
YEAR-ROUND SCHEDULE

Depart Ocracoke	Depart Swan Quarter
6:30 AM	9:30 AM
12:30 PM	4:00 PM

Fares are the same as those for the Cedar Island - Ocracoke Toll Ferry. For departures from Ocracoke, call 928-3841; from Swan Quarter, call 926-1111.

To catch the Cedar Island Ferry to Ocracoke with your vehicle, you *must* be in line half an hour before departure time or your reservation will be cancelled. No exceptions!

Insiders' Tips

Ocracoke - Hatteras Inlet Free Ferry

40 MINUTE CROSSING - 30 CAR LIMIT
NO RESERVATIONS TAKEN

Depart Ocracoke	Depart Hatteras

Summer Schedule (May 1 - Oct.31)

5:00 AM	5:00 AM
6:00 AM	6:00 AM
7:00 AM	7:00 AM
8:00 AM	
8:30 AM-6:30 PM	7:30 AM-6:30 PM
Every 30 minutes	Every 30 minutes
7:00 PM	7:00 PM
9:00 PM	8:00 PM
10:00 PM	9:00 PM
11:00 PM	10:00 PM
12 midnight	12 midnight

Winter Schedule (Nov. 1 - April 30)
Leaves Ocracoke every hour from 5 AM through 11 PM.
Leaves Hatteras every hour from 5 AM through 10 PM and 12 midnight.

Cherry Branch - Minnesott Beach Free Ferry

20 MINUTE CROSSING - 30 CAR LIMIT
YEAR-ROUND SCHEDULE/
NO RESERVATIONS TAKEN

Dep. Cherry Branch	Dep. Minnesott Beach
5:45 AM-12:15 PM	6:15 AM -12:15 PM
Every half-hour	Every half-hour
1:15 PM-5:45 PM	1:15 PM-6:15 PM
Every 30 minutes	Every 30 minutes
6:45 PM-12:45 AM	6:15 PM-1:15 AM
Every hour	Every hour

Hammocks Beach State Park Ferry

25-MINUTE CROSSING - NO VEHICLES
NO RESERVATIONS TAKEN
OPERATES JUNE 1 - LABOR DAY

Monday - Tuesday Schedule

Departs Mainland	Departs Island
9:30 AM	10:00 AM
Every hour	Every hour
Until 5:30 PM	Until 6 PM

Wednesday - Sunday Schedule

Departs Mainland	Departs Island
9:30 AM	10:00 AM
Every half-hour	Every half-hour
Until 5:30 PM	Until 5:30 PM

Fares (Round trip)	
Adult	$2
Child	$1
Younger than 4	Free

Call Hammocks Beach, 326-4881, to verify times.

Private Ferries

A number of privately owned vessels also stand ready to carry passengers to just about any destination along the Crystal Coast. Of course, you always have the option of hiring a luxurious sailboat complete with crew and catered meals as well as the option of simply renting a small motorboat to do your own navigating. Whatever your choice, there is lots to explore.

Along with state-owned ferries and privately owned vessels, the National Park Service (NPS) authorizes specified concessionaires to operate under NPS guidelines and take passengers and/or vehicles to uninhabited Cape Lookout National Seashore (see our Attractions chapter). The seashore is a 56-mile stretch of barrier islands made up of North Core Banks, home of Portsmouth Village; South Core Banks, home of Cape Lookout Lighthouse; and Shackleford Banks, home to wild ponies.

The NPS allows two privately owned ferries to carry passengers and vehicles to North and South Core Banks and Portsmouth Village. Both operate out of Down East communities and don't have all the extras you will find on the state ferries. What you will find is a medium-size, seaworthy vessel, equipped to carry one or two vehicles, a few passengers and some equipment. They normally operate between April and November, although schedules and fees vary. Most concessionaires require reservations, so it is best to call ahead to see what schedule the ferry is operating on. Check current fares, and see if there is room aboard for you. Each concessionaire can provide information on cabins and camping (see Camping). Federal regulations prohibit pets on any of these ferries.

Alger Willis Fishing Camps, Inc., operating out of the Down East community of Davis on Highway 70, 729-2791, carries passengers, vehicles and ATVs (all terrain vehicles) to the northern end of South Core Banks. Again, costs vary according to the season but usually are $12 round trip per person and about $60 round trip for a standard-size vehicle. Cabins, delivered supplies (ice, groceries, bait, etc.) and ground transportation can be arranged at the office.

Morris Marina, Kabin Kamps and Ferry Service, Inc., operating out of the Down East community of Atlantic on Highway 70, 225-4261, transports passengers, vehicles and ATVs from the community of Atlantic to Portsmouth or to the south end of North Core Banks. Transportation costs vary according to the season but usually are $12 round trip per person and around $60 round trip for a vehicle. Owners Katie and Don Morris can also arrange island transportation as well as cabins and supplies (ice, groceries, etc.).

If you are on Ocracoke and wish to visit Portsmouth Village, Rudy Austin, 928-4361 or 928-4281, or Dave McLawhorn, 928-5921, can get you there. The captains don't start their boats for less than $40, so round-trip fares are $40 for one or two passengers (if two are going, split the expense at $20 each) and $15 for each additional passenger. Group rates are $15 per person. The service runs on demand only, so call to make arrangements.

A few other passenger ferries are permitted by the NPS to transport island hoppers to Core Banks, Portsmouth Village and Shackleford Banks. Most of these can also be hired for service to other areas or just for a cruise around the harbor. Charter and rental boats are available for getting around the area's waterways (see Water Sports Rentals). The concessionaires with the NPS, in alphabetical order, are listed below. Keep in mind, however, that there are other privately run services.

BARRIER ISLAND TRANSPORTATION CO., INC.

P.O. Box 400
Harkers Island 28530   728-3575, 728-3907

Barrier Island provides passenger ferry service to Shackleford Banks and the Cape Lookout Lighthouse area. This is a passenger ferry only; no vehicles are allowed. Fares are $12 round trip per person, $6 for passengers ages 5 to 11, and free for children 4 and younger. Once on shore, visitors can either walk the quarter

---

The gulls that follow the Cedar Island Ferry always expect a handout. They'll almost eat from your hand. (Ferry officials ask that you only feed them off the back of the ferry.)

Insiders' Tips

mile to the ocean or hitch a ride on the jitney at a cost of $3 to the beach or $6 to Cape Point. On a hot July day, the jitney is definitely worth the money. The ferry leaves from Calico Jack's Marina on Harkers Island. Call for reservations and departure times.

OUTER BANKS FERRY SERVICE
328 Front St., Beaufort   *728-4129*

Part of Barrier Island Adventures, the Outer Banks Ferry Service is owned and operated by Perry Barrow and offers transportation to Carrot Island, Shackleford Banks and Cape Lookout. The service runs on demand year round from 9 AM to 5 PM. The ferry office is located in the Atlantic Coast Realty office on Front Street. Group rates are available.

SANDDOLLAR TRANSPORTATION
Harkers Island   *728-3533, 728-6181*

This ferry service provides transportation to Shackleford Banks and the Cape Lookout Lighthouse area. It departs from Barbour's Harbor Marina in Harkers Island. Call for rates, reservations and departure times.

ISLAND FERRY SERVICE
300 Front St.
Beaufort   *728-5247, 728-6888*

This ferry provides service to Shackleford Banks and Carrot Island. It is docked at the west end of Front Street behind Harpoon Willie's and departs each day in season at 10 AM and 1 PM. Beginning the end of October, it operates by reservation only.

Crystal Coast
Arts

The state of the arts on the Crystal Coast is active, visible and valued. Our most treasured annual events reflect the value of the arts to our communities. And as art often imitates life on the coast, the arts enjoy an important place in the museums and reflect the relationship of coastal people with the sea.

The active community of artists on the Crystal Coast is involved in an eclectic array of artistic production. Many artists find the pace of coastal living conducive to developing their talents and move here for that purpose. It's not unusual to meet professionals from other locations earning a living here painting, writing, or making pottery. Arts organizations actively support artists' endeavors and welcome new members and volunteers.

Theater

CARTERET COMMUNITY THEATER
Greta Boshamer   726-9069

This group of amateur actors and actresses puts on a series of plays each year

Photo: Alice Martin

The Mattie King Davis Art Gallery on the Beaufort Restoration Grounds is a great place to pick up works by local artists.

Simka Simkhovitch and the Post Office Murals

If you visit the Beaufort Post Office on a daily basis, they become easy to ignore. Most Beaufort residents barely give them a glance. But the three murals on the post office's upper walls are now treasures from the Great Depression's hungry years when the United States Government commissioned these now-famous murals for its newly built, small-town post office buildings under its Federal Arts Program.

The murals are signed "Simka Simkhovitch, 1940," hardly a local name, but it brings us to an interesting story of how and why that can be fully explored in files from the National Archives available at the Carteret County Public Library on Turner Street in Beaufort.

Born in 1893 in Chernigov, Russia, near Kiev, Simka Simkhovitch attended the Art School of Odessa and the Royal Academy of Petrograd. In 1918, a year after the Russian Revolution, he was awarded first prize by

the First Soviet Government, and his paintings were purchased for the Museum of the Winter Palace and the Museum of Art in Leningrad. The Cracow Museum in Poland also acquired his work. He taught art and flourished in Russia until 1924 when the government's attitude toward art

changed. In an effort to solidify its position through traditional values, the Soviet government established that "radicalism" was out and "social realism" was in. Simka must have decided he was out, because he became a United States citizen in 1924.

At home in Greenwich, Connecticut, Simka was doing well. He had his first one-artist show in New York in 1927 followed by several years full of portrait commissions, critical praise and prizes. His paintings were collected by the Whitney Museum of American Art and the Chicago Art Institute as well as by many private collectors. His art, wrote one critic, shows "the rare merit of sound craftsmanship that so few of the moderns possess." Then came the Great Depression. In 1933, he was awarded recognition by the Worcester Art Museum, after which his files show no more achievements until his 1939 commission to paint the Beaufort Post Office murals.

During the decade between 1934 and 1944, the Treasury Department's Section of Fine Arts chose 600 artists through open competitions to create 1,000 post office murals, with the government's stylistic guidance aimed at reminding the people of small towns that hardships are made to be overcome.

Simka arrived in Beaufort in early March 1939 and must have gone straight to work, because by mid-April he submitted a portfolio to Washington that would bring smiles to any New Dealer's face.

The place of honor over the postmaster's door was given to the mural portraying the wreck of the *Crissie Wright* on January 11, 1886. This wreck has lived vividly in the local folklore because it happened within sight of town, and many locals tried valiantly to save the crew. All hands were lost, and some of the victims lie in the Old Burying Grounds on Ann Street. "A startling morning light illuminates the scene," Simka's file says of the mural, "reminiscent of the blazing bonfires which had been built on the shore the night before to buoy up the spirits of the shipwrecked men."

Things aren't stormy all the time, Simka and the Treasury Department remind us in the remaining two murals. Fair skies and "Sir Walter Raleigh sand ponies," as Simka called them, symbolize freedom, "a right of legend they have had since the day of Sir Walter Raleigh." And over the postal clerks' stations, the abundance mural showing Canada geese and fishing nets reminds us that, indeed, we are provided for on the Crystal Coast.

Washington was only a bit critical of the "emphasis on the telephone poles" in two of the murals. The Treasury Department was obviously unfamiliar with range markers used in the waterways.

The murals, as it turns out, were painted on canvas in Simka's Greenwich studio and are very well hung on the post office walls to disguise that fact. Stop in to see them. They're quite a lift.

that we greatly appreciate. The theater also stages an occasional dinner theater performance. The group regularly stages plays for the county's youngsters. Always receptive to talented newcomers, the community theater welcomes everyone at tryouts and widely advertises cast calls.

Music

The Crystal Coast is home to several choral groups that perform frequently and occasionally audition new prospects. We are fortunate to host some extraordinary concert series and a wonderful music festival weekend in the spring. There are also a number of jazz fans in our midst, and an active jazz society has formed to support and promote one of America's most innovative music styles.

CARTERET CHORALE
Laurence Stith 726-6193

This group of more than 30 extremely talented vocalists has worked together to create a chorale known widely for its top-notch performances. The chorale performs regularly in Carteret County and has taken its talent as far as the Soviet Union, and it annually performs at the National Cathedral in Washington, D.C. Director Laurence Stith, who performed professionally as a pianist and vocalist before coming to Carteret County, is also a composer. The group regularly performs songs Stith has written.

CRYSTAL COAST CHORAL SOCIETY
Finley Woolston 347-6371

Originally formed in the mid-'80s in Swansboro to perform at the town's bicentennial celebration, the group has continued to appear in concert every year since and includes vocalists from Onslow and Carteret counties. Several members are retired professional musicians, and others are extremely talented amateurs.

CARTERET COUNTY CHAPTER OF N.C. SYMPHONY

Tom Dale   *247-6499*

The Carteret County chapter of the N.C. Symphony brings our superb state symphony to the area to perform three annual concerts. A well-supported annual fund drive provides for an additional three concerts for elementary and middle school students at no cost to the children. Volunteers are always welcome.

AMERICAN MUSIC FESTIVAL

808-ARTS

An exquisite chamber music series, the American Music Festival is composed of five extraordinary concerts performed in the acoustically complementary North Carolina Maritime Museum auditorium in Beaufort. Membership support makes the series possible, and in case you missed the series ticket opportunity, the $10 admission at the door is money well spent. The series has gathered some of the most recognized of North Carolina's musicians including classical and jazz pianist Paul Tardiff and composer Stephen Jaffe.

COASTAL JAZZ SOCIETY

Marjorie Hoachlander   *247-7778*

The society's primary mission is jazz education for all ages. The organization also aims to increase awareness and enjoyment of jazz within coastal areas of the state. The Coastal Jazz Society presents well-known musical groups in concert at its annual Jazz Fest By The Sea in June, hosts a popular series called Jazz At Homes and arranges lectures on the history of jazz. The Coastal Jazz Society welcomes the membership of anyone who enjoys listening to or playing jazz.

LA MUSIQUE CLUB OF CARTERET COUNTY

Rachel Mundine   *223-4538*

This music club is open to performers and music lovers. Members meet at 11 AM on the first Monday of each month at Webb Civic Center, 812 Evans Street, Morehead City. The group performs a number of concerts each year, including Civil War music at Fort Macon.

BEAUFORT BY-THE-SEA MUSIC FESTIVAL

This beautifully organized annual spring weekend is jam-packed with a complete range of music, all performed in downtown Beaufort. The Beaufort Business and Professional Association sponsors and schedules the festival. (See our Annual Events chapter for more information.)

Dance

The Crystal Coast has several dance studios, where everyone from toddlers to adults learn ballet and modern dance. Each performs recitals and often participates in area festivals, group functions and parades. Some of the studios also offer gymnastics, baton, tap and jazz. Following are a few of the studios in the area.

Carolina Strut Performing Arts and Fitness Center, Morehead City, 726-0431; Crystal Coast Gymnastics and Sports Academy, Morehead City, 726-7020; Dance Arts Studio, Morehead City, 726-1720; and Swansboro Dance Studio, Cedar Point, 393-6159.

Square and round dance classes for adults are held regularly at the Carteret County Senior Citizens Center, 1600 Fisher Street. Call 726-4648 or 728-4219 for more information.

Ballroom dancing and shagging (see the Nightlife chapter for a description of shag dancing) are very popular in this area. Classes are often offered at private studios or at beach clubs, so watch for announcements in the newspaper, or ask another Insider about opportunities.

Arts Organizations

CARTERET ARTS COUNCIL
704 Arendell St., Morehead City   726-9156

This nonprofit organization, partially funded by the North Carolina Arts Council, is a distributing agent that funds arts events, promotes arts organizations and sponsors workshops and lectures. Every February it sponsors the Arts From The Heart Exhibition, which involves artists from three surrounding counties. The council also sponsors the Carteret Arts Festival, a June weekend of music and

exhibits by selected artists. Both events take place in Morehead City.

CARTERET COUNTY ARTS AND CRAFTS COALITION
Pat Pitts   728-7297

What began in the late '70s as a small group of professionally oriented artists seeking an outlet for their work has grown into a juried, professional art group of almost 75 members. The coalition conducts three major shows each year: one on Memorial Day weekend, another on Labor Day weekend and a two-week Christmas gallery show during Thanksgiving. New members are welcome, and jurying of new work takes place twice each year.

Commercial Galleries

To our great advantage, some coastal artists have also become involved in the business of commercial galleries that showcase their works. Some galleries represent local and regional artists; others bring art works from much farther afield. Discover many of our treasured local artists at the following galleries.

Handscapes Gallery in Somerset Square, Front Street in Beaufort, 728-6805, represents local and regional artists in silver, pottery, and varied media. Down East Gallery, 519 Front Street in Beaufort, 728-4410, represents the paintings of local artist, Alan Cheek, and publishes prints of his work. The Mattie King Davis Gallery, on the Beaufort Historic Site,

728-5225, displays the varied works of many local artists from Memorial Day through Labor Day.

In Morehead City, **Carteret Contemporary Art** exhibits an extraordinary selection paintings and sculpture by regional, national and local artists at 1106 Arendell Street, 726-4071. **Windward Gallery**, 508 Evans Street on the Morehead waterfront, 726-6393, represents the paintings of local artist, Alexander Kaszas. The **Painted Pelican Art Gallery**, 4645 Arendell Street, 247-5051, represents work in stained glass, carvings and paintings of several local artists/owners.

In Atlantic Beach on Salter Path Road, **The Laughing Gull Gallery**, 726-2362, exhibits a nice collection of local and regional artists, as does Swansboro's **White Oak Gallery**, 137 Front Street, 326-3600.

In addition to these commercial galleries, the following museums and public buildings offer changing exhibits of local and regional artists.

The **N.C. Maritime Museum**, 315 Front Street, Beaufort, 728-7317, always exhibits the finest work by state and local artists complementing the museum's maritime focus. Monthly exhibits are sponsored by the Arts for the Hospital committee, and are shown at **Carteret General Hospital**, 3500 Arendell Street, Morehead City, 726-1616. The **Carteret County Museum of History and Art**, 100 Wallace Drive, Morehead City, 247-7533, features at least one local artist a month.

The county's three public libraries sponsor artists in revolving displays that change monthly.

Carteret Community College, 3505 Arendell Street, Morehead City, 247-6000, displays work by students in the school's arts and crafts courses in the college library, as well as work by local and regional artists. The college Upstairs Gallery also features student work and work by other local and regional artists. And just east of the school in Harkers Island, the **Core Sound Waterfowl Museum**, 728-1500, exhibits the best of hand-carved decoys and wildlife art.

Art Lessons

The Continuing Education Department of Carteret Community College offers courses in specific visual arts techniques each quarter. For county residents age 65 or older, there is no tuition charge, only the cost of materials. Call 247-6000 for further information.

Writers' Organizations

CARTERET WRITERS

Julia Phillips   726-5541

This active group of professional writers and aspirants gathers monthly on the third Thursday for lunch and a scheduled speaker at Mrs. Willis' Restaurant in Morehead City. Carteret Writers sponsors workshops, seminars and competitions throughout the year as well as an ongoing outreach program in the public schools.

Crystal Coast
Places of Worship

The Crystal Coast offers visitors and newcomers hundreds of worship centers to choose from. Whether you're interested in attending a service, admiring architecture or learning about history, Crystal Coast churches have something to offer.

There seems to be a church around every corner, but that's not unusual in the southern Bible Belt. Even the smallest of communities may have two or three churches.

Many of the area's oldest churches are in Beaufort. These wooden structures, for the most part, have been preserved just as they were years ago. Other area churches are modern, beautiful structures or weathered and vine-covered. Each has its own legends and stories held dear to members of their congregations.

It would be impractical to list the hundreds of worship centers scattered around the Crystal Coast. We have described a few of the area's most noted churches, whether that be because of the building's age, size of the congregation or convenient location.

For more information about other churches in the area, you can check the Yellow Pages.

EMERALD ISLE CHAPEL BY THE SEA
6712 Emerald Dr., Emerald Isle   354-3210

This interdenominational church sprung out of the Bogue Banks Resort Ministerial Association, which was formed in 1968. The association was asked to assign a minister to Emerald Isle for the summer months, and services began in the town hall beginning in May 1969. In 1971 plans were made for the church to become independent of the association and to have services during the winter. Ground was broken for the chapel in 1972, and the first meeting was held on Easter Sunday 1973. Today the church is attended by locals along with visitors from across the state and country.

ANN STREET
UNITED METHODIST CHURCH
Ann and Craven Sts., Beaufort   728-4279

Built around 1854, the church features curved wooden pews and beautiful stained-glass windows. An unusual feature of the church is its hand-carved rosettes in the ceiling. The steeple of the church, stretching high above the houses on the low coastal land, was shown on old mariners' charts as a point of reference, a beacon to aid those at sea. It is one of three churches surrounding the Old Burying Ground. The church's modern educational building stands across the street and is used for community events.

PURVIS CHAPEL AME ZION CHURCH
217 Craven St., Beaufort   728-5503

Purvis Chapel was built in 1820 and is Beaufort's oldest continuous use church. It stands in the same block as Ann Street United Methodist Church. Originally built by the Methodist Episcopal Church, it was later deeded to the AME Zion congregation and is still owned and operated by that group. The bell in the church was cast in Glasgow,

Scotland, in 1797. The building is listed on the National Registry of Historic Places.

ST. PAUL'S EPISCOPAL CHURCH
209 Ann St., Beaufort   728-3324

St. Paul's Episcopal Church, c. 1857, is the area's oldest Episcopal church. The church building was built in two years by local shipbuilders. Visitors will notice that the interior of the sanctuary bears a striking resemblance to an upside-down ark. It is reported to be one of the 10 most acoustically perfect buildings in North Carolina. Holy Eucharist is on Sunday and a midweek Eucharist is conducted each Wednesday.

ST. STEPHEN'S CONGREGATIONAL CHURCH
Craven and Cedar Sts., Beaufort   No phone

St. Stephen's Congregational Church was built in 1867 along with the neighboring two-story school building that housed the Washburn Seminary. Records show the lot was purchased for $100 in 1867, and the seminary served as a school for many years.

FIRST BAPTIST CHURCH
Ninth and Bridges Sts.
Morehead City   726-4142

Morehead City's First Baptist Church is one of the town's oldest churches. The congregation originally shared a small building near the waterfront with the town's Methodists. After the War Between the States, the congregation built the current new structure.

FIRST UNITED METHODIST CHURCH
Ninth and Arendell Sts., Morehead City 726-7102

Standing on the corner of Ninth and Arendell streets, this church is home to one of the oldest Methodist congregations in eastern North Carolina. The church congregation's roots go back to Shepard's Point in 1797. The original chapel was built in 1952 and later was converted to a bakery by the Union Army. Today's sanctuary was dedicated in 1952.

ST. EGBERT'S CATHOLIC CHURCH
1612 Evans St., Morehead City   726-3559

St. Egbert's parish had its start in Morehead City in the early 1920s. The church now has its own school for students from kindergarten through 6th grade. In late 1991 it completed extensive renovations and additions to the church and parish house. Community service is emphasized, with support groups regularly meeting in church facilities. Parish services are offered Saturday and Sunday, and Mass is held on various weekdays.

ST. ANDREW'S EPISCOPAL CHURCH
2005 Arendell St., Morehead City   247-6909

St. Andrew's is a beautiful church of unique design. The church was constructed in 1957. Parking is provided behind the church on Evans Street. The church has a large active congregation and offers three Sunday services and one Wednesday morning service.

Crystal Coast
Service Directory

This service directory offers an abbreviated listing of some useful information about services on the Crystal Coast. Most of the businesses we recommend are tried and true establishments. We realize this list is only a sampling, so we suggest you check the local phone directory for additional service providers.

Emergency Phone Numbers

COAST GUARD

Information	247-4598
Search and Rescue Emergencies	247-4545
Swansboro Lifeboat Station in Emerald Isle	
	354-2719

CARTERET OR ONSLOW COUNTY SHERIFF

Emergency	911
Business number	728-3772

FIRE DEPARTMENT OR RESCUE SQUAD

For an emergency call in any township in Carteret County, dial **911**.

POLICE DEPARTMENTS

For emergency calls, regardless of your location, dial **911**.

For business calls, dial the appropriate number below. If a number isn't listed in your community, use the sheriff's office business number.

Atlantic Beach	726-4040
Beaufort	728-4561
Cape Carteret	393-2183
Emerald Isle	354-2021
Indian Beach	726-3772
Newport	223-5111
Morehead City	726-3131
Pine Knoll Shores	247-4353
Swansboro	326-5151

Photo: Scott Taylor

Wild horses on Carrot Island in Beaufort.

OTHER NUMBERS

Crime Stoppers	726-INFO
Crisis Helpline	247-3023
Magistrates	728-8516
State Highway Patrol	726-5766
Carteret General Hospital	247-1616
Neuse Center for Mental Health	726-6515
Alcoholics Anonymous	726-8540
American Red Cross	247-6000
Carteret County Health Department	728-8550
Carteret County Department of Social Services	728-3181

Animal Services

There are leash laws in the towns and on the beaches. Many towns have registration requirements, so check at the town hall. Strayed or lost pets can be reported to the **Carteret County Humane Society's** animal shelter, 247-7744, or the **Crystal Coast Animal Protection League**, 247-3341.

If your pet becomes ill or injured, you might try one of the following veterinarians.

BEAUFORT

Dr. Guy Jaconis	728-7600

MOREHEAD CITY

Dr. David Bird	726-0181
Dr. David Hall or	
Dr. Roxanne Taylor	726-4033

CAPE CARTERET AND CEDAR POINT

Dr. John Puette	393-6581

NEWPORT

Dr. Walter Westbrook	223-5115

Kennels

MITCHELL VILLAGE ANIMAL HOSPITAL
5007 Arendell St.

Morehead City	726-4033

NELSON'S KENNELS
4008 Arendell St.

Morehead City	247-2026

HADNOT CREEK KENNELS
Hwy. 58

Cape Carteret	393-2855

CRYSTAL COAST KENNELS INC.
Sam Garner Rd.

Newport	223-3007

LAKE ROAD BOARDING KENNEL
Lake Rd.

Newport	223-4183

Wildlife

If you see or find an injured, sick or orphaned wild animal, call **Outer Banks Wildlife Shelter** (OWLS), 240-1200. You can either take the creature to the facility on Highway 70 at the junction of Highway 24 beside Lowe's, or you can have a trained volunteer pick up the animal. This local organization was established to counteract the adverse pressure of development on the wildlife of the Crystal Coast. OWLS works to rehabilitate and release wildlife. It relies on donations and volunteers.

Bus and Taxi Service

BUS STATION OF MOREHEAD CITY
1212 Arendell St. (Hwy. 70)   726-3029

A-1 YELLOW CAB CO.
Service to Atlantic Beach, Beaufort and Morehead City   728-3483

CRYSTAL COAST CAB
Service to Atlantic Beach, Beaufort, Down East, Morehead City, Newport   728-5365

YELLOW CAB CO.
Service to Atlantic Beach, Beaufort and Morehead City   726-3125

SWANSBORO CAB CO.
Service to Swansboro, Emerald Isle and Cape
Carteret   326-5300

PRESIDENTIAL LIMOUSINE
Service anywhere in the tri-county area
                                      726-8019

Car Rentals

Arrangements for rental cars should
probably be made in New Bern or a larger
area. In Carteret County, call Michael J.
Smith Airfield, Beaufort Airport, 728-
1777.

Government Offices

Town Halls

ATLANTIC BEACH
MP 2¹/², W. Fort Macon Rd.   726-2121

BEAUFORT
217 Pollock St.   728-2141

CAPE CARTERET
204 W.B. McLean Dr.   393-8483

CEDAR POINT
Lois Ln.   393-7898

EMERALD ISLE
7500 Emerald Dr., MP 19   354-3424

INDIAN BEACH
Salter Path Rd., MP 11   247-3344

MOREHEAD CITY
706 Arendell St. (Hwy. 70)   726-6848

NEWPORT
402 Howard Blvd.   223-4749

PINE KNOLL SHORES
100 Municipal Cr., MP 7   247-4353

SWANSBORO
Corner of Church and Webb Sts.   326-4428

Libraries

The three public libraries on the Crystal Coast are part of a multi-county system. Therefore, if a book is not on the
shelf at one library, ask and it might be in
another and available to be loaned to your
library. Most libraries offer special programs for children and adults. A traveling bookmobile service is offered throughout the county.

BOGUE BANKS LIBARY
320 Salter Path Rd., MP 7
Pine Knoll Shores   247-4660

CARTERET COUNTY PUBLIC LIBRARY
210 Turner St., Beaufort   728-2050

NEWPORT PUBLIC LIBRARY
431 Howard Blvd., Newport   223-5108

ONSLOW COUNTY
PUBLIC LIBRARY BRANCH
Hwy. 24, Swansboro   326-4888

WEBB MEMORIAL LIBRARY
812 Evans St., Morehead City   726-3012

In one form or another, the Crystal Coast offers just about
any service that a big city would. Of course, you might have
to look a little harder, but the casual lifestyle here makes it
well worth it.

Insiders' Tips

Media Information

Newspapers

CARTERET COUNTY NEWS-TIMES
4034 Arendell St.
Morehead City   *726-7081*

Carteret County has no daily newspaper, but is well-covered with the *Carteret County News-Times*, which is published Wednesday and Friday afternoons and Sunday mornings. A comprehensive county publication, the paper covers all area activities. The paper includes news and features on the Crystal Coast and surrounding areas. State and national sports are included. *Carteret County News-Times* is published by Carteret Publishing Company, Morehead City.

TIDELAND NEWS
101-2 Church St.
Swansboro   *326-5066*

Tideland News is published each Wednesday from its office in Swansboro. Owned by Carteret Publishing Company of Morehead City, the paper covers activities in the western part of the county — Swansboro, Cape Carteret, Cedar Point and Emerald Isle.

JACKSONVILLE DAILY NEWS
Bell Fork Rd., Jacksonville   *353-1171*

The *Jacksonville Daily News*, a morning paper published each day, includes state and national coverage and primarily covers Onslow County and the U.S. Marine Base at Camp Lejeune. The paper also covers Carteret County activities, particularly those concerning countywide issues.

THE MAILBOAT
P.O. Box 3
Harkers Island 28531   *728-4644*

The Mailboat, published on Harkers Island, is a quarterly publication that includes anecdotes, recollections and stories about life as it used to be in Carteret County's Down East communities. Each publication is a treasured addition to local libraries. In addition to the quarterly publication, *The Mailboat* puts out an annual booklet of Christmas recollections, which is included in the subscription price or may be purchased from area book stores.

Televison Stations

VISION CABLE CHANNEL 10
Hwy. 70, Newport   *223-5011*

Vision Cable Channel 10 supplies cable television to most areas of Carteret County. The station airs a variety of programming. Show subjects vary from school and health issues to sports talk shows. Studio manager Marty Feurer focuses on community events and works hard to disseminate information about community projects and community service activities. "Coastal Headline News" is shown twice an hour and "Do What?," a guide of local events for visitors and residents, is scheduled at various times.

WFXI-FOX
Hwy. 70, Morehead City   *240-0888*

Television Channel 8 shows the Fox programming. "Coastal Carolina Fishing" is a popular show aired each morning at 6 (at 6:30 in the winter). This show focuses on what's happening in area waters.

WCTI
225 Glenburnie Dr.
New Bern   638-1212
Television Channel 12, the local ABC affiliate, prides itself on its comprehensive local coverage as well as ABC programming. It gives the most complete Carteret County coverage of any network television station in the area. A fish and game forecast is given during the news sports segment.

WITN
Hwy. 17, Chocowinity   946-3131
Television Channel 7, the local NBC affiliate, has its studios in Chocowinity. Along with NBC programming, the station has area news coverage, including high school and college sportscasts.

WNCT
3221 S. Evans St., Greenville   355-8500
Television Channel 9, the local CBS affiliate, includes a morning local talk show and local news and sports shows along with its network programming.

Radio Stations

WTKF, 107.3 FM
Hwy. 70, Newport   247-6343
North Carolina's first talk FM, WTKF carries news, talk, sports and NASCAR. Listen to the nation's hottest talk hosts with the nation's hottest talk topics. Rush Limbaugh, Alan Colmes and Bruce Williams entertain and inform while area hosts feature local news and newsmakers. The station also features a dozen local daily newscasts plus TV-12 weather twice an hour.

WBTB, 1400 AM
209 Ocean St., Beaufort   728-1635
WBTB features Christian talk from the Moody Bible Network. It has nondenominational programming with a Christian perspective on issues of the day. Call-in shows, news programs and children's programming make WBTB a well rounded source for news and family entertainment.

WKQT, 103.3 FM
Hwy. 70, Newport   247-1033
Classy 103.3 offers a variety of adult contemporary music that appeals to all ages. The station offers news and weather 5 minutes before the hour and sports at 25 minutes after. During the spring, summer and fall, listeners can hear fishing and surf reports. The station provides ski reports in the winter. Classy 103.3 is the flagship station for East Carolina University athletics. The station carries all football and basketball games with pre- and post-game coverage.

WMBL, 740 AM
Little Nine Rd.
Morehead City   240-0740
WMBL combines a talk format with

Many Insiders keep a stash of "hurricane food" in their kitchen cabinet. That might include unopened peanut butter, canned meats and fruits, crackers, jellies and instant breakfast mixes. It's also a good idea to have plenty of matches, candles and batteries on hand during hurricane season.

Insiders' Tips

the easy listening sounds of the 1940s, '50s and '60s. Jay Cobb's talk shows are a magnet for community projects and volunteer leaders. Big Band music is featured each Sunday morning, and the station airs the University of North Carolina at Chapel Hill basketball and football games. This station shares facilities with WRHT.

WRHT, 96.3 FM

Little Nine Rd.
Morehead City   *247-2002*

WRHT, Sunny 96.3 FM, offers listeners Top 40 and contemporary hits. It features beach music each Sunday evening and takes requests anytime; call 726-9600.

WTEB, 89.3 FM

College Court
New Bern   *638-3434*

This public broadcasting station offers *Morning Edition* news weekday mornings and the evening newscast *All Things Considered.* Jazz music is featured on Friday, Saturday and Sunday nights. The *Choral Tradition* features the best in choral music Sunday afternoon, and Big Band sounds can be heard Saturday evening.

WRNS, 95.1 FM / 96 AM

Kinston   *522-4141*

Based in Kinston, this station plays the latest and hottest country music. The station always has a contest going and offers all kinds of prizes including concert tickets and trips. The station also features Paul Harvey. The request line number is (800) 682-WRNS.

Rental Services

If you couldn't bring it with you or just plain forgot it, there are places ready to rent it to you whether you're a visitor or resident in need of a few extra things. If you are looking for vacation-type rentals (linens, cribs, high chairs), check the Vacation Rental chapter of this book. The Water Sports chapter has information about water sports equipment rentals.

Country Aire Rental and U-Haul Inc., Highway 70 in Morehead City, 247-4938, and Highway 70 in Beaufort, 728-2955, rents a little bit of everything — beds, baby furniture, tools, equipment (tillers, mowers, sanders, tractors, paint sprayers, etc.) and wedding and catering supplies.

General Rental, on Highway 24 just east of Cape Carteret, 393-2220, rents a wide variety of items: beds, baby furniture, car seats, all kinds of home repair tools (saws, drills, sanders), vacuums, carpet cleaners, party tents, mowers, tillers and midsize construction equipment.

PR Rentals and Sales, 4803 Arendell Street (Highway 70), 247-9411, offers furniture, appliances, vacuums and electronics rentals.

Sparkle Fresh Cleaning & Linen, Emerald Isle, 354-7031, rents bed sheets, bath towels, cribs and high chairs.

Walston's True Value Hardware, Cedar Point, 393-6111, rents carpet cleaners and all types of tools from a half-inch drill to a ditchwitch. They also have ladders, tillers and mowers.

Storm and Hurricane Information

Carteret County Emergency Management Office can be reached by calling 728-8470.

Hurricane season runs from June 1 through November 30. Each time a storm threatens, residents and visitors are urged to heed warnings and take precautions.

Evacuation routes are marked on the area's main roads to guide people away from the dangerous coastline in case of a storm. While some people may find a storm exhilarating, the resulting damage of minor storms lets those of us on the coast know that it is prudent to be informed and take precautions.

Residents of Bogue Banks, the barrier island strip from Atlantic Beach to Emerald Isle, are required to obtain re-entry passes from their respective town halls before a hurricane hits. While nonresidents are prohibited, residents can use the pass to return to the island after an evacuation.

Improved communications greatly increase the chance for escape before a storm hits. But, in order for the warnings to be effective, they must be heeded. The following definitions are used in announcing the condition of an approaching hurricane:

A hurricane **WATCH** means it is possible that, within 36 hours, hurricane conditions may exist in a specific area.

A hurricane **WARNING** is announced when it is possible that hurricane conditions may be 24 hours or less away from a particular location.

In low-lying areas or places such as Carteret County's barrier islands and parts of the Down East area, emergency management officials may decide to evacuate an area in preparation for what appears to be a rapidly approaching storm. In these cases, shelters open at announced sites, usually schools, to provide a place for residents to wait. If you go to a shelter, it is recommended that you take important personal papers, food, water, clothing, medicines, blankets, baby foods, diapers, formula and other specialized items required for a wait of hours or days. Battery-powered radios and flashlights are useful also. Pets are not allowed in the shelters.

When a hurricane makes landfall, both wind and water damage are sure to create mayhem with property and will likely take human lives, if the people have not taken cover when advised to do so. In the center of the high winds is the **EYE** of the hurricane. Should the eye pass over, it will allow a temporary calm, but this is not a signal that the storm has ended. After a brief respite, when the eye is overhead, the winds and rains will resume with at least as much force and violence as before.

Strong winds pounding waves onto the shore, heavy rains and abnormally low pressure within the hurricane produce what is called a **STORM SURGE**. In addition to being extremely forceful, a surge may raise water levels as much as 20 feet above normal. The storm surge of Hurricane Hugo was measured at 17 feet. It is essential that you avoid being trapped in your car, mobile home or other structure in a low area. **LEAVE IN TIME** if an evacuation is ordered.

Tax Rates

The Carteret County 1994-1995 tax rate and municipal rates are based on a $100 valuation.

Carteret County	46¢
Atlantic Beach	45¢
Beaufort	40.5¢
Cape Carteret	35¢
Cedar Point	5¢
Emerald Isle	21.5¢
Indian Beach	19¢
Morehead City	45¢
Newport	46¢
Pine Knoll Shores	20.5¢

The 1994-1995 Onslow County tax

rate and Swansboro rate are also based on a $100 valuation.

Onslow County	*57.5¢*
Swansboro	*50¢*

In addition to property taxes, North Carolina residents pay a 7 percent state income tax. Call the N.C. Deptartment of Revenue at 726-7910 for more specifics. The office is only open on Mondays.

Utility Services

Utility services on the Crystal Coast vary from area to area. Regardless of whether you are buying or renting, you can usually expect to have the gas, electricity, water and sewer services turned on within 24 hours. Telephone service could take three to four days to be connected, and cable TV service could take a week.

Deposits or connection fees vary from service provider to service provider, some depend on whether you have had service with that company before. Some are refunded if you are in good standing with that company after a year.

Utility service for each area is listed separately below. If you have questions about the service provider you need to contact, ask a real estate agent, the town hall, county office staff or the previous resident.

Electricity

Carolina Power & Light (CP&L), 3504 Bridges Street, Morehead City, 726-7031, offers electricity to the majority of residents and businesses. The amount of the deposit required depends on the size of your house or apartment, the service area and your credit. This deposit is refundable after one year if good credit is established. CP&L provides electricity to about 22,000 customers in Carteret County and in the Havelock area of Craven County.

Carteret-Craven Electric Membership Cooperative, Highway 24 west of Morehead City, 247-3107, provides electrical service to much of western Carteret County. A deposit is required when making application. This member-owned corporation has about 25,000 members and services all residents of Bogue Banks except those living in Atlantic Beach; all residents in Cape Carteret, Cedar Point and along Highway 58 to Maysville; residents along Highway 24 toward Morehead City and down Nine-Foot Road and Lake Road to Havelock; residents along Highway 70 from Morehead City to the old residential district in Newport; and all Morehead City residents in the Country Club and Crab Point areas.

Harkers Island Electric Membership, 849 Island Road, 728-3769, provides electricity to residents of Harkers Island. This is an electric distribution cooperative owned by those it serves. The co-op was formed in 1939 and continues to provide electric utility service to residential property owners and commercial accounts on the island.

Carolina Power & Light in Jacksonville, 1099 Gum Branch Road, 455-1375, can arrange for electrical service in Swansboro.

Gas

Propane gas is provided through any number of private area businesses. Check the Yellow Pages for a list of bottled gas providers.

Carteret-Craven Electric Cooperative

Locally owned and locally controlled by 25,000 member-owners

♦

**Serving
Morehead City
Havelock
Salter Path**

A vital part of growth in Carteret and Craven Counties for over 53 years

Telephone

Apply for service by calling **Carolina Telephone**, 903 Arendell Street, Morehead City, 726-8152. Depending on your previous record, you may be asked to pay a deposit. That deposit usually is refunded after a year. Connection could take three or four working days, longer if there has not been telephone connection at that address before.

Sprint Carolina Telephone in Jacksonville, 300 New Bridge Street, 633-9011 (toll free), can arrange for service in Swansboro.

Water and Sewer

The number you call to get water and sewer connection depends on where you live. If you live in a town, apply to the water and sewer department at the town hall. If you live outside town limits, chances are you will rely on a well and septic tank. Check with the county office; some rural areas are served by a water supplier. If you get service from your town or a provider, you will be required to pay a hookup fee, which varies from system to system.

West Carteret Water Corporation, 247-5561, is a private membership-owned cooperative with offices at Pender Park in Broad Creek on Highway 24. The company provides water to areas in the western part of the county, not including Bogue Banks. The service area mainly focuses on Highway 24 from Gull Harbor to Cedar Point, the many sideroads along that stretch and north along Highway 58 for several miles. The company expects to continue expanding across the western portion of the county. They deal with water only; there is no sewer system serving the western part of the county. Instead, people have septic tanks.

Carolina Water Service, 247-4216, provides water to residents of Pine Knoll Shores and Brandywine Bay. Brandywine Bay has sewage service.

Bogue Banks Water Company, 7412 Emerald Drive, 354-3307, provides water to residents of Bogue Banks from Salter Path to Emerald Isle. They offer no septic tank service.

Trash/Recycling

Trash is picked up within town limits on varying days. Special arrangements can be made for picking up large trash items, lawn trimmings and limbs. Recycling programs have been started in most towns, but not in rural areas of the county. For information, contact your town hall (see listings in this section), or call the county office at 728-8450. Green box sites (dumps) are located throughout the county.

Zip Codes

Atlantic	28511
Atlantic Beach	28512
Beaufort	28516
Cape Carteret	28584
Cedar Island	28520
Cedar Point	28584
Davis	28524
Emerald Isle	28594
Gloucester	28528
Harkers Island	28531
Marshallberg	28553
Morehead City	28557
Newport	28570
Oriental	28571
Salter Path	28575
Sea Level	28577
Smyrna	28579
Stacy	28581
Stella	28582
Swansboro	28584
Williston	28589

Crystal Coast
Real Estate
and Neighborhoods

This is the section for those of you seriously considering purchasing property or relocating to the Crystal Coast. And, we might add, you are making a wonderful decision.

Welcome! But be ready for a change in lifestyle, maybe even culture shock, and definitely be prepared to gear your speed down to "low" if not "idle."

This chapter is designed to introduce you, first, to the neighborhoods that make up the expansive Crystal Coast and then to acquaint you with some of the area's real estate companies and builders. The lists are by no means complete but will familiarize you with the area and help you locate businesses and services.

The chapter begins with neighborhoods at the beach, which is actually the island of Bogue Banks including the townships of Atlantic Beach, Pine Knoll Shores, Indian Beach, Salter Path and Emerald Isle. From there we move to delightfully different Beaufort, then to the central town of Morehead City, westward to Swansboro and finally to the Down East reaches of the county.

Like everywhere else, homes on the Crystal Coast vary tremendously in price, and location is everything. Here, good locations include being on the water, in historic districts, on or near golf courses and in upscale subdivisions. While you may find very comfortable living quarters in the $50,000-to-$70,000 range, you can also spend hundreds of thousands for a large, plush home in an exclusive waterfront neighborhood with a slip for your boat. A great deal of recent development has taken place away from the water, and a wide range of housing is available.

A note on zoning: If the property you are considering is not in an incorporated city or subdivision, ask your real estate agent or the county planning office what uses are permitted in that area. Large portions of the Crystal Coast are unzoned and may permit certain uses you have not bargained for. Then again, some folks are looking for that kind of freedom. Ask questions so you'll know before you commit.

The agencies and businesses suggested throughout this section are listed alphabetically. These are not the only companies of their type. There are many other fine and reputable firms, but we simply couldn't list them all. *The Insiders' Guide* is revised annually, and we welcome your input concerning additions or omissions in the next edition.

Like most beach resorts, the Crystal Coast has a large number of condominium developments. We've mentioned a few here; however, for a more complete list of what is available, check with your real estate agent. Also, for information on timeshare and fractional ownership possibilities, check the Vacation Rentals chapter of this book.

There is no specific relocation service on the Crystal Coast; however, rest assured that most agents will move heaven and earth to ensure that your move is smooth. After all, they are in the business of sharing with newcomers what we Insiders have already learned — this is a great place to be!

Neighborhoods

Bogue Banks — The Beaches

Many newcomers to the Crystal Coast move here for one reason — to live on the beach. In Atlantic Beach, Indian Beach and Salter Path, there are a number of older homes, sometimes selling for less than what could be considered market value because of the age of the house or its lack of modern amenities. Newer homes, condominiums and townhouses have been built in recent years.

Emerald Isle and Pine Knoll Shores are the more recently established towns. Both have many new structures and home sites in a variety of price ranges; so, whatever you want, you can probably find it.

ATLANTIC BEACH

Atlantic Beach has a nostalgic air about it — a throwback to the 1950s when beach houses were built to be functional and rambling, when small cottages nudged right up next to ponderous two-story clapboards on narrow streets running parallel to the ocean. Today, some see Atlantic Beach as a bit ramshackle and hodgepodge. Others reminisce about red convertibles, Sandra Dee and beach blankets. But changes are afoot. Plans to revitalize "the Circle," where most beach entertainment businesses are centered, are under way.

Today, private homes and vacation rentals are mixed throughout the small oceanfront town and, over the years, building has extended several blocks back from the water to N.C. 58, or Salter Path Road. Most all living accommodations in Atlantic Beach are within walking distance of the ocean, and the majority of new homes are concentrated on the eastern end of the island, along Fort Macon Road. Here, too, are a number of condo and townhouse developments, such as Seaspray, A Place At the Beach, Southwinds, Sands Villa Resort, Island Quay and others.

The residential area known as Hoop Hole Creek on Bogue Sound, a few miles from the downtown center, is a beautifully forested area with a few lots remaining. Condos and townhouses such as Dunescape Villas, Island Beach and Racquet Club, Coral Bay East and West and others are also in this section.

PINE KNOLL SHORES

The developers of Pine Knoll Shores deserve lots of credit for being farsighted. Built in a maritime forest, the development has done an admirable job of minimally impacting the environment. Drive through and you will see what we mean — there are trees everywhere. Restrictive covenants require a complete survey of all trees larger than three inches on each lot. Before you can get a permit to build, you have to prove you will save as many trees as possible and disturb the land as little as possible. The process can be tedious, but the result is worth it, as most all residents will agree.

The area is nearly 75 percent developed, and both large and small homes come on the market fairly regularly. Lot prices start at $35,000 and homes range from the low $100,000s to the mid $200,000s, depending on the proximity to canals, open water or the area's 18-

Photo: Irving Hooper

You can find old homes with wonderful detail on the Crystal Coast — but don't forget your paint scraper.

hole golf course. Within the central portion of the town, a good many homes are built on canals, with the option of private docks.

Pine Knoll Townes, Bogue Shores Club and Beachwalk at Pine Knoll Shores are townhouse and condominium developments between MP 6 and MP 7 on Highway 58. All are on the ocean and in a lovely maritime forest setting. Design features include courtyards, sun porches, gourmet kitchens, private balconies and other upscale luxuries. Prices range from $80,000 to as much as $300,000 for plush living accommodations.

Beacon's Reach, MP $8^{1/2}$ to MP $9^{1/4}$, is a large development in a maritime forest on land once owned by the Roosevelt family. It includes both multifamily and single-family dwellings. Each "village" is carefully planned, and residents have access to lighted tennis courts, swimming pools and parks on the ocean and the sound, as well as a marina. Villages include Ocean Grove, with three- and four-bedroom units; Westport, with one- two- and three-bedroom units and both soundfront and fresh water lagoon-front units; the Breakers, with oceanfront condominiums; Fiddlers' Walk with soundside condominium units; and Maritime West, with oceanfront units.

Condominiums and single-family homes range from $99,000 to $600,000 plus on the ocean. Soundside and oceanside lots range from $35,000 to just more than $200,000.

SALTER PATH/INDIAN BEACH

Many of the longtime residents in these two small communities are descended from fishermen, and many still make their living from the sea. Some homes are low, rambling structures on the soundside, nestled under windswept live oaks bent from prevailing winds. If you are lucky enough to find one of these cottages on the market, you will have a piece of paradise.

The Summerwinds condominium complex is a large, oceanfront development offering spacious living quarters with prices starting at just more than $100,000. Recreational facilities include an indoor, heated swimming pool, whirlpool, saunas, exercise rooms, a spa and racquetball courts. Outside are three oceanfront pools with sundecks and a boardwalk. Units at the oceanfront Windward Dunes in Indian Beach range between $90,000 and $149,500 with pools, saunas and tennis courts.

EMERALD ISLE

The western end of the island is family oriented, and not until a few years ago did a substantial number of residents become "year rounders." Originally, the only access to Emerald Island was by boat and, later, by ferry. It wasn't until the 1970s that the B. Cameron Langston high-rise bridge opened the area to tourists and newcomers. Emerald Isle is the fastest growing area of the county. Areas along Coast Guard Road, off Highway 58, have seen an astounding amount of

development in recent years. Some of the nicer subdivisions are here.

You'll find many of the town's recently built residences quite impressive. Homes and cottages come in all styles, but most are multi-storied, with wide porches and decks, so residents can take advantage of the beach view and sea breezes. Although some developers have bulldozed dunes and cleared much of the natural vegetation, others have left stands of maritime forest. There are a number of condominium and townhouse developments as well, such as Pebble Beach, Queens Court, Sound of the Sea and others in the price range between $59,900 and $139,000.

Lands End is an exclusive planned residential community on Coast Guard Road off Highway 58 near the Point in Emerald Isle. Ownership includes use of a spacious clubhouse, a pool, four lighted tennis courts, stocked freshwater lakes and a lighted boardwalk to the beach. All roads are private, and utilities are underground. Homes range from $149,000 to $2.1 million. Lots start at around $45,000.

Emerald Plantation is a relatively new soundside subdivision that extends from Highway 58 to Bogue Sound. A mixed-use development with single-family homes, townhouses and patio homes, amenities include a clubhouse, pool, boat launch, boat ramp, tennis courts and a security gate. Lot prices range from $18,000 to $135,000, and homes range from $110,000 to $300,000. The Wyndtree subdivision is a large tract near Emerald Isle Point that has restrictive covenants as to sizes of houses but offers a wide diversity of sites from oceanfront to ocean view. Lot prices range from $35,000 to about $49,000, and single-family homes from $110,00 to $400,000.

The Point on Coast Guard Road off Highway 58 at the westward tip of the island is one of the most established areas and has a wonderfully wide beach. Homes range from $162,500 for new constructions to $400,000.

Deerhorn Dunes, Sea Dunes and Ocean Oaks are three well-planned subdivisions and are almost indistinguishable from one another. On Coast Guard Road off Highway 58, all are relatively new and were built at about the same time. They are made up primarily of single-family homes, nicely landscaped on spacious lots. Lot prices begin at $35,000, with ocean view lots less than $70,000. Single-family homes range between $110,000 and $200,000, with oceanfront homes climbing to as much as $400,000.

Windfall is one of the newer subdivisions in Emerald Isle off Highway 58. It is a small development made up of about 24 lots that are second, third and fourth row locations away from the ocean. Lot prices range from $70,000 to $96,000, with homes from $175,000 to $250,000.

Cape Emerald off Highway 58 on the soundside of Coast Guard Road is a subdivision of primarily permanent residents. Amenities include a clubhouse, heated pool and spa and two tennis courts. It also has a security entrance and community sewage system. Lots range from $20,000 to $95,000, and homes from $100,000 to $350,000. Royall Oaks, Dolphin Ridge and Pointe Bogue are three new, beautifully landscaped developments that offer peace and privacy in a verdant, spacious wooded setting. Off Coast Guard Road, lots vary from 75-feet wide to 30-feet wide on ocean and roadfronts. Interior lots also vary in size due to efforts to preserve the area's wetlands. Lot prices begin at $50,000. Pointe Bogue

Photo: Curtis Krueger

Inland creeks are wonderful places to see wildlife.

and Royall Oaks have soundfront sites, and Dolphin Ridge has oceanfront sites.

Beaufort

Beaufort's geographic design lends itself to small residential areas built around roads and water. Most new development is east of Beaufort along U.S. 70 or north along N.C. 101. This small port town is a haven for boaters and is a hub of activity during the summer months. Many of its historic homes have been restored as residences or bed and breakfasts. Its lovely waterfront is a natural setting for music and socializing at outdoor cafes. Wild ponies can be seen across Taylor's Creek on Carrot Island. The town's many shops, restaurants and tourist attractions give Front Street a festive air. Joggers, strollers, exercise walkers and bike riders flow constantly along the main Front Street thoroughfare, and the Historic District can easily be covered on foot.

Beaufort's Historic District is the oldest residential area in town, covering about 15 square blocks. Homes here date back to the 1700s, and exterior characteristics are governed by guidelines of the Beaufort Historic Preservation Commission. Charged with assuring the integrity of the area, the commission reviews all proposals for exterior changes such as paint color, siding, window treatments, redesign and other building changes.

Businesses and signage in the historic district are also regulated. The historic commission was not formed until the 1980s, so you will see a few things that do not meet their standards. Property prices vary greatly in the historic district, depending on distance from the water, size and age of the house or building and its condition. You could be looking at a $425,000 waterfront home, a $90,000 residence a couple of blocks away from the water or a home at the far end of Ann Street for somewhere in the $60,000s.

Beaufort homes outside the historic district also carry a variety of price tags, again depending on the distance from the water as well as size, age and condition. Deerfield Shores, Gibb's Landing, Howland Rock, Jones Village, Tiffany Woods and Sea Gate are examples of subdivisions north of the downtown area. Taylor's Creek is the newest development on the east end of Taylor's Creek on the Beaufort waterfront.

Deerfield Shores, off Highway 101, is in an attractive area on the Newport River and Intracoastal Waterway. Central to the development is the Carolina Marlin Club, a private boating (sail and motor) club complete with a 73-slip marina, clubhouse and swimming pool. Slip owners own the marina and clubhouse, which is also used by the Morehead-Beaufort Yacht Club. Interior lots in Deerfield range from $12,000 to $35,000; marinafront lots begin at about $40,000 and riverfront lots sell for about $75,000 to $100,000.

Gibb's Landing is a small subdivision on North River, reached by following Highway 70 east and turning right on

Steep Point Road. Subdivision amenities include a community dock, pool and gazebo. Large lots range from $70,000 on the waterfront to $25,000 for lots across the street from the waterfront.

Howland Rock might be considered one of Beaufort's most prestigious neighborhoods. The entrance is on Highway 70, just across from the Trading Post. This older subdivision offers residents such amenities as a boat ramp, recreational area and homeowners' association. Most of the homes were custom built with attention to detail. Price tags start at about $135,000 and go up to $350,000. Some lots are still available, including a few on the waterfront that can go for as much as $175,000.

Jones Village is in Beaufort town limits and is one of the area's oldest subdivisions. There are several entrances from Live Oak Street (Highway 70) to the subdivision, which wraps around behind Jones Village Shopping Center. The development is a quiet, well-settled area that seems to attract a pleasant mix of people. You'll find retirees living alongside young couples. Homes sell for $70,000 to $125,000.

Tiffany Woods is a new development about 4 miles east of Beaufort on Highway 70. Developers are offering large wooded lots for about $16,000 and up. Several cul-de-sacs run off the lighted main road, giving the neighborhood a feeling of privacy. This is one of the nicer new neighborhoods in the area. Sea Gate is a waterside resort community 7 miles from Beaufort on Highway 101 at Core Creek. The development is on the Intracoastal Waterway with a deep-water marina, ships' store, gas and diesel fuel, clubhouse, playground, swimming pool, tennis court, boat ramp and security entrance. Homes range from $60,000 to $250,000. Waterfront lots range from $27,000 to $45,000.

The Taylor's Creek development at the east end of Lennoxville Road is a pricey new development of only 10 gorgeous building sites at the east end of Taylor's Creek. Lots are offered from near $70,000 to $200,000 and include pool and dock use.

Morehead City

Morehead City is the area's largest city, so you'd expect it to have the most neighborhoods, and you're right. Most early communities began at the water's edge because that's where the work was. Today, people continue to live by the water, but not so much for the work as for the beauty of the views and the breeze.

The city's earliest inhabitants lived near what is now the N.C. State Port, bounded by Bogue Sound, the Newport River and Calico Creek. As the area filled up, homes were built farther west.

Although Morehead City's downtown has not seen as much restoration activity as Beaufort's, it is happening. Between Arendell Street and Bogue Sound, from about Ninth to 14th street, is a neighborhood of small, woodsided homes of active fishermen known as the Promise' Land. Some of these houses were moved to the mainland by sailing skiffs at the turn of the century when severe storms almost destroyed the once-flourishing fishing village of Diamond City on Shackleford Banks. Homes were dragged out of the water and rolled on logs to their new foundation. It is said that one spectator commented on the sight, "It looks like the Children of Israel coming to the Promise' Land." Hence, the name stuck.

The town has expanded as its population has grown. Now, with improved access and all-weather bridges, more and more developments are popping up along the outskirts of town, many in the direction of Crab Point via N. 20th Street, Country Club Road and Barbour Road. Once an isolated farm community, Crab Point is one of Morehead City's oldest subdivisions and also the site of some of the newest developments, so prices vary greatly. Clustered within each development are houses of a broad range of prices, mainly because of the high prices demanded by houses on the water.

Joslyn Trace is a relatively new subdivision on North 20th Street at the junction of Country Club Road. Homes here are both one and two story, and lots range from $14,500 to $16,500. Creek Pointe and Mandy Farms are two neighborhoods just off Country Club Road, with homes ranging from $75,500 to $115,000.

South Shores is a new, private waterfront community on the Newport River. It offers members of its homeowners' association lighted streets, curb and gutter, swimming pool and tennis courts. Lots begin at about $20,000 and go up to $45,000.

Country Club Road is a main thoroughfare along the backside of Morehead City. West Carteret High School is at the western end and the Morehead City Country Club toward the eastern end. In between lies mostly long-settled neighborhoods, although a few new developments have gone up in recent years. In most areas the lovely old trees have been left in place, and some homes are suitable for retirees or as "first homes." An equal number are huge and obviously expensive. Generally speaking, the closer you get to the Morehead City Country Club, the more expensive the real estate becomes. In the more exclusive areas, there are very few lots left, but homes are being resold here as in all areas of the Crystal Coast.

Country Club East is a newer development across from and fronting the golf course. Here, two- and three-storied homes are the norm. Prices vary, depending on the size and features. Established homes with amenities such as a fireplace

and two-car garage can sell for $134,500. A four-bedroom, two-story home with partially finished attic can sell for up to $250,000.

River Heights lies to the east of the country club and is one of the older suburbs. Homes here are rarely on the market, and when they are, they are sold at premium prices.

Hedrick Estates on the west side of Country Club Road features nice one-and two-story homes, with well-landscaped yards. Lots are available, and established homes range from about $73,000 to $100,000. Adjacent to Hedrick Estates is Westhaven Village, made up of one- and two-story homes on large wooded lots. Homes here range from around $90,000 to $130,000.

West-Car Meadows off Country Club Boulevard is a well-established development, backed by Swinson Park and close to the new primary school, the high school and shopping areas. This is a good location for young families with children. Northwoods is a fairly new development off Country Club Road, with single-family dwellings on large tree-covered lots. A three-bedroom, two-bath home with formal dining room and living room, screened-in porch, deck and garage can sell for between $100,000 and $160,000.

Bonham Heights, Mansfield Park and Mitchell Village are older, spacious and well-established neighborhoods along the sound off Highway 70. Homes vary from modest bungalows to two- and three-story residences. Most residents have lived in these areas for a number of years; however, homes do occasionally go on the market. Prices can vary from $85,000 several blocks away from the water to $350,000 for soundfront. Many waterfront homes have deep water access at their back doors. It's worth a drive through these areas to see what is available.

The Bluffs is a condominium development at the end of Mansfield Parkway, overlooking Bogue Sound. Units are individually owned townhouses or condominiums, with a sound view from most units. A three-bedroom, two-bath condominium can sell for around $110,000; a four-bedroom, four-bath unit will sell for around $189,000.

Western Carteret County

As the county's population increases, development in the western part of Carteret County continues, especially in response to the incoming personnel needs at Cherry Point. This area has some long-established neighborhoods, but many new ones are springing up along Highway 24 between Morehead City and Cape Carteret and along Highway 70 between Morehead City and Havelock.

Spooner's Creek and Spooner's Creek East are long-standing neighborhoods, built around the marina at the mouth of Spooner's Creek and along Bogue Sound. The area features large homes, many with their own private docks. Homes are within walking distance of Spooner's Creek Marina, which has rental dockage and enough deep water for large yachts. Spooner's Creek Racquet Club has lighted tennis courts. Homes here are affordable to those in the upper income brackets.

Brandywine Bay is an exclusive planned subdivision, stretching from Bogue Sound to Highway 70. Begun in 1972, the project was built around the Earle Webb estate. The Webb Mansion, an impressive brick structure surrounded by lumbering live oaks high on a bluff overlooking Bogue Sound, is now a private home. The waterfront portion of Brandywine Bay consists of a noncommercial marina with a community boat launch ramp surrounded by residential building lots. Marina slips are individually owned. Three separate townhouse projects surround the harbor with space available for future construction. There are single-family residences and lots available on either side of the townhouses and harbor. Across Highway 24 is the main residential section of Brandywine, which surrounds a beautiful 18-hole championship golf course. While some homes here were built in the 1970s, there is usually a nice selection of resales of both houses and lots. A new section, The Honors, recently opened. Golf & Shore Properties, 240-5000, has an office on site and handles most sales of new lots. A number of real estate companies handle resales.

Gull Harbor, Soundview, Ho-Ho Village and Barnesfield are all established developments along Bogue Sound on Highway 24. While some homes are quite large and elaborate, others are moderate

in size and style. Many have deep-water docks, and a few lots may still be available. Homes range from around $150,000 and up.

Somerset Plantation is one of the newest developments off Highway 24 and features a swimming pool, tennis courts, boat ramp, residential day dock, boat slips and a secured entrance. Lot prices range from $33,000 to $145,900, depending on proximity to the water. Houses can range from $100,000 to $229,000, depending on size and water proximity.

In the Broad and Gales Creek areas are Bluewater Banks, Fox Lair and Rollingwood Acres. These are new subdivisions close to Broad Creek Middle School. Bluewater Banks is a soundfront development, and Rollingwood Acres is on Broad Creek. Home prices vary

greatly, depending on location and water access. In Fox Lair, a nonwaterfront development, homes range from $90,000 to $140,000, whereas in Bluewater Banks prices range from $124,000 up.

Farther up Highway 24 are Pearson Subdivision, Bogue Sound Yacht Club, Blue Heron Bay and Hickory Shores. Again, some of these developments are longer settled than others. Homes vary from spacious and elaborate to small and practical. A few select lots remain for sale at Bogue Sound Yacht Club, beginning at about $40,000 and going up to $150,000. Blue Heron Bay is one of the newest developments, with lots ranging from $21,000 to $115,000 and homes from $100,00 to $350,000. Hickory Shores has interior lots, beginning at $17,500, and going up to $75,000 for waterfront.

Swansboro

Swansboro offers a variety of housing opportunities, including historic houses near the business district, mobile homes on the outskirts of town and charming new homes on unbelievably beautiful lots overlooking the water.

The Swansboro Heights Extension area is a 34-lot, fully built development with homes reselling in the $70,000 range. In the town itself, there are basically three types of homes. In the oldest part of town are the historic homes, some rehabilitated and restored and others in need of attention. Around the fringes of the business district and extending several blocks in all directions are houses that were built about 50 years ago. They, like the older homes, are a mix of beautifully restored and maintained residences, with some that would be on the market as "fixer-uppers." Closer to the city limits are homes built within the past 25 or 30 years. Most are still in good condition but not terribly distinctive in design.

In recent years, newer developments have been opening, bringing a totally new look to Swansboro's housing picture. The River Reach development is perhaps the most dramatic change in Swansboro's real estate market and is almost fully settled. However, a few lots remain on the White Oak River and Stevens Creek, selling for around $60,000. Homes sell in the $150,000 to $200,000 range.

Plantation Estates is another waterfront subdivision on the White Oak River, with homes ranging from $125,000 to $150,000. Hurst Harbour is an exclusive new subdivision near the ferry landing at Hammocks Beach State Park. Prices begin in the $135,000 range, with interior lots around $55,000. Oyster Bay offers moderately priced homes and lots and is being settled by the area's young professionals. Prices average from $100,000 up to $150,000. Walnut Landing was designed for more economical residences, with costs averaging between $70,000 and $80,000.

Port West Townhouses are beside Swansboro Primary School and are made up of 13 buildings with four units each. Most units are rentals; however, some are owner occupied. The townhouses feature one, two or three bedrooms and range from the mid $40,000s to mid $50,000s.

Down East

Traditionally, the Down East communities themselves have made up the majority of neighborhoods. They string along the highway and the waterfronts and revolve around the church, or the volunteer fire/rescue department. You should keep in mind that living Down East isn't for everyone. Newcomers must be ready to forfeit the conveniences of town living and be able to entertain themselves with the simple pleasures of day-to-day life. If you are ready to make those trade-offs, then you may have found your little piece of paradise.

Many of the county's traditional fishermen and boatbuilders live Down East, an area along Highway 70 that merges into Highway 12 and extends from Bettie to Cedar Island. As you cross the area's many bridges, it is not unusual to see clammers hip-deep in water with an inner tube in tow, harvesting the mud-sucking mollusks from the sound bottom. Boat sheds are more common than garages, and the whir of saws and smell of wood chips are sure signs of happy boatbuilders. Fishing and shrimp boats ply the waters

year round, and egrets, herons, ospreys and other shorebirds live in the marshes and wetlands along the highway.

Like many people who hold on to land settled by their ancestors and look to Mother Nature for their livelihoods, the indigenous people who make up these communities are reserved and self-sufficient. They are fiercely independent and expect others to be the same. But in times of trouble or crisis, you will find none more kind or gracious than those living in the little fishing villages that make up the area known as Down East.

As more people move to Carteret County, its eastern sector has seen the development of a few subdivisions outside the fishing communities. Homes and acreage are also available from time to

time. If you want to get away from it all, this is the place to do it.

Harbor Point in Straits has two sections and was established several years ago. Home sites are on a secluded peninsula, and the development offers a park area and boat ramp. Interior lots sell for around $17,000, with waterfront lots at about $45,000. Osprey Isle in Smyrna has homes and lots on the water and paved streets. Nassau Heights is a new development in Williston, with lots ranging from $18,900 to $24,900. Ward's Creek Plantation and Tranquility Estates in Otway are both new developments. Ward's Creek offers waterfront, water view and water access lots, with prices starting at $12,500. Tranquility Estates is a waterfront and interior lot subdivision on Ward's Creek, with lots ranging from

$13,500 to $62,000. Owner financing is available.

Real Estate Companies

Like most coastal areas, the Crystal Coast has plenty of real estate companies and agents to serve you. There are many good real estate firms in the area, and here we have listed, in geographical and alphabetical order, some of those that are most active. Most all are members of the Multiple Listing Service (MLS) and can show you any listing in the area; however, most companies and agents specialize in a certain geographic area — usually the town or community where their office is located and the adjacent communities. It's always a good idea to ask agents what areas they specialize in and whether they will show you property that other companies have listed.

In the past, North Carolina law authorized real estate companies to work for sellers because agents are paid by the sellers. Today, a new procedure also allows companies to operate as a buyer's agency, meaning they can negotiate price and terms in the best interest of the buyer. This procedure can be advantageous to those interested in purchasing a home or property. Ask if your agent offers this service.

In 1994, the North Carolina General Assembly was considering a residential property disclosure, titled House Bill 1032. A study commission has recommended reintroducing the bill in the 1995 session. If passed, the bill would require each property owner to disclose any defects that they have actual knowledge of when attempting to market their property or to sign a disclaimer stating that they make no representations or warranties as to the condition of the property. Many real estate companies routinely offer such disclosure information, but you may want to request it from your real estate agent.

The Morehead City-Carteret County Board of Realtors, 247-2323, can answer questions you have about companies that operate in the area.

Atlantic Beach

AL WILLIAMS PROPERTIES
119 Morehead Ave. 726-8800
Atlantic Beach Causeway *(800) 849-1888*

Offices for this real estate sales and development business are in the Causeway Shopping Center. Listings often include exclusive condominium properties and waterfront homes on the beach and in Morehead City as well as building lots and acreage. Three Realtors are available to show you any of them.

ALAN SHELOR REALTY
Crow's Nest Shopping Center 247-7700
Atlantic Beach Causeway *(800) 849-2767*

This company offers listings in every area of the Crystal Coast. Six Realtors are on staff to assist clients in sales of residential, resort and commercial properties, acreage and building lots. The com-

---

pany also offers a selection of resort rentals, 240-7368. Alan Shelor Realty has been in business more than 20 years.

CANNON & GRUBER, REALTORS
509 Morehead Ave.   726-6600
Atlantic Beach Causeway   (800) 317-2866

Formed in 1995 and combining more than 20 years of experience in local real estate, Cannon & Gruber, Realtors offers many enviable listings not often on the market as well as beach and soundfront condominiums. Carolyn Wilson Cannon and Harriet Broughton Gruber are happy to show you these or any currently listed properties.

CENTURY 21 COASTAL PROPERTIES
Atlantic Beach Causeway   726-4700
                                (800) 637-1162

This full-service agency handles both sales and rentals, with 20 agents on staff. It deals in properties throughout the county, including the western sector and Down East. Properties include condominiums, single-family homes, acreage, exclusive building lots and commercial sites. Other services include a building department that offers home design and construction services.

COLDWELL BANKER
SPECTRUM PROPERTIES
Atlantic Beach Causeway   247-5848
                                (800) 334-6390

The Coldwell Banker firm is a full-service agency in Atlantic Beach newly combining services with Spectrum Resort Properties in Emerald Isle (see Emerald Isle section). The two offices each offer about 14 agents who specialize in properties throughout the county. It handles condominiums, homes, home sites and commercial property, as well as long-term and seasonal rentals, 247-5366, and professional property management services.

GULL ISLE REALTY
135 Morehead Ave.,   726-0427
Atlantic Beach Causeway   (800) 682-6863

This agency has six staff members who handle the sales of condominiums, homes, building lots and investment properties on Bogue Banks and the mainland. Gull Isle Realty also offers a number of resort rentals, 726-7679. The firm has been in business for more than 20 years and has a state-licensed appraiser.

OMNI REAL ESTATE
513 Morehead Ave., Atlantic Beach Causeway
                      247-3101, (800) 334-2727

Omni, a Tetterton Management Group Company, specializes in condominiums and homes for sale on the beach and in Morehead City including the new nine-unit condominium development on the Atlantic Beach Causeway, Marlin Harbor. The full-service company also offers property listings county wide and manages rentals for investment buyers. A vacation guide is published by Omni each year showing vacation rental properties. Its onsite rental office can lead you to the vacation location that fits your needs.

NATIONAL
SOUND N' SEA REAL ESTATE
205 Morehead Ave., Atlantic Beach Causeway
                      247-7355, (800) 682-7368

Owned and managed by Demus and Ellen Thompson, Sound N' Sea is a full-service company, specializing in the sale of homes, condos and commercial properties both on the island and mainland as well as vacation rentals, 247-RENT. The company is the oldest continuously owned and operated full-service real estate firm in the Atlantic Beach-Pine Knoll Shores area.

THE SELLING TEAM,
WILLIAMS & COMPANY

513 Atlantic Beach Causeway   726-1300
(800) 334-2727

Representing properties listed by Omni Real Estate (see earlier listing), the Selling Team works as a partnership on behalf of their clients. They offer the properties best suited to their client's specifications by combining their experience in and knowledge of the local market. And clients' schedules are of utmost concern; you tell them when, and they'll show you current selections that match your wish list. The Selling Team is Llew Ramsey and Elaine Main.

Pine Knoll Shores

SUNNY SHORES

320 Salter Path Rd.   726-7616
(800) 726-1409

Newly formed this year by a couple of veteran Pine Knoll Shores Realtors, Sunny Shores is a full-service company offering sales, vacation rentals, property management and maintenance. Robert Lewis handles sales; Carol Piner handles rentals and property management. All listings may be previewed on video tape, and the house specialty is meeting special rental requirements.

WILLIAMS AND COMPANY

Hwy. 58   247-7347, (800) 624-8978

Owner Stewart Orgain operates a full-service company with two offices to handle residential sales, property management and vacation rentals, (800) 626-3113. The main office, across from the Ramada Inn on Salter Path Road, handles sales of Beacon's Reach building lots and condominiums as well as properties in Pine Knoll Shores, Emerald Isle and Morehead City. The firm also operates a

property maintenance company and manages condominium homeowners' associations.

EMERALD ISLE

BLUEWATER ASSOCIATES
BETTER HOMES AND GARDENS

200 Mangrove Dr.   354-2128, (800) 326-3826

Across from the K&V Plaza, this full-service firm offers condominium and home sales on the beach and mainland with emphasis on sales of new constructions, building lots and resales in Emerald Isle and Cape Carteret. The company has its own construction arm that builds or finishes to client specifications and represents properties in such new developments as Magens Bay in Cape Carteret. Its rental department handles vacation and long-term rentals. Thirteen agents and other staff serve clients in Emerald Isle.

CENTURY 21
COASTLAND REALTY INC.

7603 Emerald Dr.   354-2131
(800) 822-2121

The first realty franchise on the beach, this full-service company has been in business since 1980. It offers many completed homes, both new and previously owned, in some of Emerald Isle's most exclusive locations. It also sells building lots, constructions in progress and acreage on Bogue Banks and the mainland. Condominium resales and pre-construction sales are also their specialty, including the newest development with occupancy in summer 1995, Pier Pointe. The staff includes 11 sales agents and a rental department handling vacation properties.

EMERALD ISLE REALTY
7501 Emerald Dr.   354-4060, (800) 849-3315

This agency has been a tradition on the coast for 31 years and hosts thousands of vacationing families each year. This family-owned property management, rental and sales firm is now in its new headquarters offering nearly 600 vacation rental properties, an on-line rental reservations system and in-house maintenance and housekeeping departments. Rentals can be arranged by calling 354-3315. The company's sales team is equally strong, handling resales of homes and condo-miniums, commercial properties and building sites.

EMERALD PROPERTIES
9100 Emerald Dr.   354-4488, (800) 398-8612

This agency is a small real estate firm that specializes in property sales in Cape Carteret and Emerald Isle. It offers residential and commercial properties, building lots and condominium resales. It also coordinates sales of remaining building lots in the Windfall and Wyndtree developments and the spectacular Tanglewood Ridge one-acre oceanfront lots.

ERA CARTERET PROPERTIES

7801 Emerald Dr.   354-3289, (800) 448-2951

This full-service agency handles all types of properties both on the island and the mainland and has been in business since 1969. It is also very prominent in the property management field, with some 100 available rentals, 354-3005. Five agents conduct commercial and residential sales of new and established homes and offer business opportunities as well as lots and acreage. In addition, the firm offers warranties and other services that can be advantageous to clients, and it can help with custom construction and design.

KETTERER REALTY

Hwy. 58 at Mangrove Dr.   354-2704
(800) 849-2704

This agency has a solid reputation earned through 21 years of service to home buyers on the Crystal Coast. The firm employs six agents who offer both new and resale homes in Emerald Isle and the western sector of the county as well as commercial sites, building lots and acreage. As exclusive agents for Dolphin Ridge, Royall Oaks and Pointe Bogue developments, Ketterer Realty's services extend to house plan designs and construction details as well.

LOOK REALTY

9101 Coast Guard Rd.   354-4444
(800) 849-0055

A full-service real estate operation with 10 sales agents and a rental and property management staff, LOOK Realty offers a variety of properties in the Emerald Isle/Cape Carteret area including resales, building lots, waterfront acreage and commercial properties. It handles sales for the proposed community, Crystal Shores, in Cedar Point and, if you are in the market for new construction, the company offers on-site contractor and home design services.

COLDWELL BANKER
SPECTRUM PROPERTIES

7413 Emerald Dr.   354-3070, (800)682-3423

A full-service agency with offices also in Atlantic Beach, this company offers an extensive inventory of homes, condominiums and building lots in Emerald Isle and Cape Carteret with 14 knowledgeable agents to match new homeowners with affordable property in the right locations. The Emerald Isle office also has a good reputation for its vacation and annual rental department, 354-3040, (800) 367-3381, and property management details.

REALTY WORLD-CLARK REALTY

8101 Emerald Dr.   354-2523, (800) 982-4166

Clark Realty, established 24 years, is one of the oldest real estate companies in Emerald Isle. "If it's for sale in Carteret County, we will be able to help you," they say. Six agents are available to show clients any MLS listing or those among the company's inventory of resales and building lots in the Emerald Isle/Cape Carteret area, especially Star Hill. The company also offers condominiums, mobile home lots and commercial property and represents the Sea Crest oceanfront development proposed in Emerald Isle.

SUN-SURF REALTY

7701 Emerald Dr.   354-2958, (800) 849-2958

This company is a full-service agency that receives very high marks from other Realtors in the area. It has its own construction firm, Staebler Homes Inc., for custom-built homes and offers a variety of vacation homes, building lots and condominiums on the island. It also has a very successful, professionally operated

vacation rental program, 354-2658. Like other real estate firms, it represents sellers. Unlike other firms, it is also a buyer's agency, meaning it negotiates price and terms in the best interest of the buyer. A free brochure explaining the firm's buyer's agency policy is available.

WATSON-MATTHEWS REAL ESTATE
9102 Coast Guard Rd. 354-2872
(800) 654-6112

Originally Rouse-Watson Realty, this business has been active since 1979 with sales of condominiums, single-family dwellings and duplexes, as well as investment and commercial property. Watson-Matthews offers building sites in Lands End and other developments and pre-construction packages. The firm's agents will work with you in finding the perfect buy, whether it is a second home or a primary residence.

Beaufort

ATLANTIC COAST REAL ESTATE SERVICE
328 Front St 728-6793, (800) 645-9379

On the Beaufort waterfront across the street from the N.C. Maritime Museum, this full-service company offers commercial and residential properties, rentals, investments and property management.

BEAUFORT REALTY COMPANY
325 Front St. 728-5462, (800) 548-2961

This company specializes in residential and commercial property in the Beaufort historic district and handles some of the most handsome historic properties offered for sale. The company also offers sales of properties in Beaufort subdivisions, Down East, in Morehead City and on the beach. The company does appraisals and also offers annual and vacation rentals.

CENTURY 21 DOWN EAST REALTY
415 Front St.   728-5274, (800) 849-5795

As the name implies, Century 21 Down East Realty specializes in property in Beaufort and Down East, including Harkers Island. It also handles property in Morehead City and is affiliated with the Morehead City office, Century 21 Newsom-Ball. The firm handles residential and commercial sales, as well as appraisals. It is Beaufort's oldest full-service real estate company, and its agents are knowledgeable and helpful.

HOMEPORT REAL ESTATE
400 Front St.   728-7900, (800) 948-5859

Realtors and brokers Pat Kindell and Candy Rogers have lived in the area and operated businesses for more than 21 years. Upstairs in the Somerset Square building just off the Beaufort boardwalk, the company specializes in historic and resort properties as well as retirement and relocation along the Crystal Coast. Agents also work as buyers' brokers for clients. The company handles commercial and residential properties on the beach, mainland and Down East and also offers rental services.

Morehead City

BROWN AND SWAIN REAL ESTATE
4659 Arendell St.   247-0055

From Beaufort to Brandywine Bay, from points Down East to Cherry Point, Betty Brown Swain always has interesting listings. She offers a range to interest any client from mobile home lots to Beaufort waterfront homes and always has a good buy in a fixer-upper. She handles sales of building lots in many area subdivisions as well as commercial property and acreage.

CENTURY 21 NEWSOM-BALL REALTY
4644 Arendell St. 240-2100, (800) 849-5794

Ken Newsom and Ben Ball own both the Morehead City business and the Century 21 office in Beaufort. Both Realtor/brokers and the 14 sales associates working with them in the Morehead City office have well-rounded knowledge of the area. The company offers complete services, emphasizing the sale of homes, businesses and acreage. It also provides appraisal and property management services.

CHALK & GIBBS REALTY
1006 Arendell St.   726-3167

This Better Homes and Gardens agency has been in operation since 1925. It handles sales of single-family dwellings, townhouses and condos, as well as building lots and acreage. The company also offers property management and annual rental services for Morehead City and Beaufort, as well as certified appraisals. In addition to real estate, Chalk & Gibbs has a complete insurance branch.

CHOICE SEACOAST PROPERTIES
1512 Arendell St. 247-6683, (800) 444-6454

This real estate firm is owned and operated by Trish and Tom Dale who, along with two other agents working with them, represent a variety of properties and innovative services. "Mailmost" increases exposure of homes listed through weekly mailings to qualified buyers, and "Netmost" enables buyers and sellers to save money through lower commissions. Choice lists residential and commercial properties, lots, acreage, condos and townhouses and offers property management services.

GOLF & SHORE PROPERTIES
Brandywine Bay, Hwy. 70   *240-5000*
(800) 523-4612

In the Brandywine Bay complex on Highway 70, Golf & Shore Properties specializes in properties in Brandywine Bay but also represents properties throughout the county. Mary Poineau and Katie Porter are both experienced agents who can help you select lots, single-family homes and townhomes.

HOME FINDERS
ROBINSON AND ASSOCIATES
4644-A Arendell St.   *240-7653*

Alan and Sharon Robinson own and operate this family business, with the assistance of an additional agent. Mr. Robinson has been in the real estate business since 1979, and his wife joined him in 1988. The company handles single-family homes in the Morehead City to Newport area plus lots and acreage. It also offers property management services and works with several builders in the area to offer building plans and construction.

LAWRENCE REALTY

5087 U.S. 70   726-0804, 726-1711

With 21 years of real estate experience on the Crystal Coast, Annette Lawrence can show you the current listings in either residential or commercial properties in the neighborhood of your interest. A Certified Residential Specialist, Annette offers full coverage, including annual rentals as well as sales, throughout Carteret County.

PUTNAM REAL ESTATE COMPANY

3800 Arendell St.   726-2826

Putnam Realty is one of those companies that other real estate agencies recommend. It is a full-service agency that specializes in the sale of new and established homes throughout the county, as well as building lots and constructions in progress in fast-growing Newport developments. Its eight agents also handle commercial properties, townhouses and mobile homes. The company offers full appraisal services and property management.

RE/MAX MASTERS REALTY

4459 Arendell St.   247-3629
(800) 849-1144

In Colony Square on Highway 70, this agency offers new homes and resales as well as townhouses, lots, acreage, condos and commercial property throughout the county. In addition, the firm assists clients in selecting and modifying house plans to meet their needs in Newport's recently developed Deer Park. The agency also offers commercial buildings and business opportunities as well as buyer's agent services.

SAUNDERS REAL ESTATE COMPANY

28th and Arendell Sts.   247-7444

In the center of Morehead City, this company offers a great variety of properties from homes in some of the area's most exclusive residential districts to fixer-uppers with investment potential. The company offers lots and acreage and specializes in commercial business opportunities. The firm employs five agents and can provide appraisals and property management services.

Western Carteret and Swansboro

BALLARD REALTY

Hwy. 24 at Nine Foot Rd.
Broad Creek   240-2121, (800) COAST-NC

Broker/owner Brenda Ballard specializes in the western section of the county and especially in the subdivisions off Highway 24 such as Fox Lair, Bluewater Banks, Soundview Park, Rollingwood Acres, Silver Creek and others. Ballard Realty also markets properties in Newport and Swansboro and manages long-term rental properties.

SHACKLEFORD REALTY

415 W.B. McLean Dr.
Cape Carteret   393-2111, (800) 752-3543

With more than 20 years of service, Shackleford Realty is well known in the county for its market expertise in and around Cape Carteret, Swansboro, Cedar Point and Emerald Isle, as well as in subdivisions along Highway 24. The agency handles many of the sales in the Star Hill and Hunting Bay housing divisions and also offers farms, town houses, lots and acreage. Ethel Shackleford operates the business, and the agency is recommended by other realtors around the county.

CENTURY 21 WATERWAY REALTY

Hwy. 24, Swansboro   326-4152

This agency, one of the oldest in

Swansboro, sells building lots, new homes and resales in the Swansboro/Cape Carteret/Emerald Isle area. Most of the company's agents are longtime residents of the area and can give you the real scoop about where the best buys are and about the best financing. The company also handles commercial properties, lots and acreage along the White Oak River and the ICW.

Down East

Most real estate agencies in Beaufort and Morehead City handle property east of Beaufort, and there are only a few real estate companies with offices actually in the Down East area. We suggest you contact your favorite realtor if you are interested in property in the eastern sector of the county. Chances are he or she will be able to help you.

EASTERN GATEWAY REALTY
Hwy. 70
Bettie   728-7790, (800) 205-5465

It's impossible to go to or come from the Down East parts without passing the Eastern Gateway office in Bettie. Specializing in properties from Beaufort to Cedar Island, this company always offers an enviable number of waterfront listings, lots and acreage. Owner Mary Hill and the firm's two other agents are all experienced and knowledgeable in Down East property, and best of all, they're right there.

Builders/Contractors

Building costs vary on the Crystal Coast, but in general you can expect to pay between $50 and $65 per square foot to build your home. There are many reputable builders, but the important thing is

to find the right one for you. Where you own property may dictate what you can build and how you can remodel. Before beginning, check with the Carteret County Building Inspector's Office, 728-8545, or the town building inspector to see what permits may be required.

The following is a guide to a few of the residential builders and contractors on the Crystal Coast. It is by no means a complete list, but will give you an idea of some of those who come highly recommended. The list is arranged in alphabetical order, with no recommendations for one builder over another. Most contractors and builders work throughout the area.

For additional builders, contact the Carteret County Home Builders Association, 223-5527. This organization is a membership group of builders that includes real estate companies, contractors and banks as associate members. For specialized work, such as tile or custom cabinets, any of the builders listed below can refer you to a reliable company or tradesperson. At the end of this section, we have briefly listed a few of the area's best building supply stores.

Mack Baker Construction in Crow's Nest Shopping Center, Atlantic Beach, 247-6444 has been in business 14 years and builds residential custom homes throughout the county.

S.F. Ballou in Morehead City, 726-0780, specializes in custom-built homes across the county with emphasis on Morehead City, Atlantic Beach and Pine Knoll Shores. This company is recommended by many area Realtors.

Creative Carpentry, Atlantic Beach, 726-2578, is operated by Joe Tarascio who does general contracting and specializes in custom homes, remodeling and home maintenance. This business has been in Atlantic Beach more than 20 years.

Frontier Home Builders, Stella, 393-6674, constructs custom homes in both Onslow and Carteret counties and also does remodeling, additions and renovations.

Edwin Holt General Contractor, Inc., Cape Carteret, 393-8875, has established a reputation for well-built homes, remodelings, renovations and additions. The company also builds custom pools and spas.

Mark Hannula Construction, Inc., Morehead City, 240-1980, has a broad range of experience in custom homes, renovations, remodeling and light commercial construction. This company stresses affordable quality in building.

R.L. Kelly Construction, Emerald Isle, 354-6766, has been in business 10 years specializing in residential, commercial and multifamily construction on the mainland and in Emerald Isle. The firm works closely with several area Realtors.

Jerry Lawrence General Contractor, Inc., Beaufort, 728-3625, has been in the building business for more than 30 years. His company builds residential homes and commercial buildings and also does remodeling.

S.M. Marshall Construction & Realty, Inc., Emerald Isle, 354-3684, has been in business nine years and is licensed for all construction but specializes in residential homes, especially in Emerald Isle.

McMillan Builders Inc., Atlantic Beach, 247-3833, is an experienced company with an established reputation for sound construction at reasonable prices. The company offers custom-built homes from your plans or theirs.

Gerry Sadler Construction Company, Gerry Sadler Construction Co., Beaufort, 728-2908, specializes in new construction, renovations and remodeling and has excellent recommendations for restoration work on some of the oldest homes in Beaufort.

Thomas Simpson Construction Company, Morehead City, 247-4401, has been in business since 1978 and specializes in residential construction. The company also builds docks and seawalls.

Staebler Homes, Inc., Emerald Isle, 354-3784, is highly recommended for custom residential home construction, and many examples are visible in Emerald Isle. The company will build from homeowner's plans or provide other choices. It specializes in Timberpeg post-and-beam constructed homes.

Superior Structures, Beaufort, 728-4170, builds, remodels and repairs residential and commercial buildings. The company also specializes in high quality restoration of historic homes. Much of its work is visible in Beaufort.

Paul R. Taylor and Sons, Newport, 726-5024, has been in business since 1972 and has a good reputation for well-built homes. The firm specializes in residential construction and does some remodeling.

Tyson Building and Design, Emerald Isle, 354-2483, builds primarily residential custom homes and has built extensively in Emerald Isle's Sea Dunes and Ocean Oaks subdivisions. In business since 1977, the company has a good reputation.

Valente Construction Company, Emerald Isle, 354-3515, builds residential homes in all price ranges and has earned a good reputation for quality workmanship.

Clayton White Remodeling and Repair, Morehead City, 726-1821, has been in the building business for 18 years and has a good reputation for residential and commercial remodeling, custom renovations, historic restorations, deck construction and additions.

Building Supplies

There are a number of area businesses that provide building supplies. Here is a very brief list of those carrying the most complete lines of materials.

COMMUNITY LUMBER AND SUPPLY
Hwy. 24 W., Swansboro   (910)326-5051

GUY C. LEE BUILDING MATERIALS
Hwy. 70 W., Morehead City   726-0114

HUNTLEY'S BUILDING SUPPLY
Junction of Hwy. 70 E. and 101
Beaufort   728-3111

LOWE'S
Hwy. 70 W. at Hwy. 24
Morehead City   247-2223

MOREHEAD BUILDERS SUPPLY
2514 Bridges St., Morehead City   726-6877

SAFRIT'S BUILDING SUPPLY
1308 Mulberry St., Beaufort   728-3843

WICKES LUMBER
Hwy. 70 W., Morehead City   726-6901

Photo: Tabbie Nance

A youngster learns the art of painting decoys at the Core Sound Decoy Festival.

Crystal Coast
Schools and Child Care

Educational opportunities in Carteret County include public and private schools. This section is designed to give you information about schools and child-care facilities on the Crystal Coast. This book's Higher Education and Research chapter contains information about the local community college.

The county's public school system is the largest provider of education in the county. About 8,100 students attend pre-kindergarten through 12th grade in the county's 14 public schools. Each is accredited by both the N.C. Department of Public Instruction and the Southern Association of Colleges and Schools. The local school system employs about 910 people. Carteret County public schools are governed by an elected five-member board of education. Members serve four-year terms and are chosen in county-wide, nonpartisan elections. School board members meet in open session each month.

Elementary school students follow a basic state curriculum that features reading/language arts, math, science, social studies, health, physical education, music and art. The middle school concept is used in the three middle schools and to varying degrees in grades 6 through 8 at

other schools. This approach groups teams of students and educators to work together creating consistency for each.

The county's two high schools and three middle schools offer a comprehensive management program. This program emphasizes high expectations in the areas of discipline and class attendance. Extended day classes are part of this program. Students needing remediation are required to attend the after-school classes, and other students voluntarily attend for enrichment opportunities.

Each high school offers a handbook listing specific course offerings. Vocational education is offered in several areas: agriculture, home economics, distributive education, health occupations, business, occupational exploration and introduction to trade and industry.

Carteret County offers a year-round school for those living in the district who choose to attend. An alternative school for grades 8 through 12 offers innovative teaching methods for students having difficulty with traditional methods.

Student services include guidance counselors, psychologists, social workers and nurses. Bus transportation is provided to and from school for students who live at least 1.5 miles from the school. Lunch

East and West Carteret High Schools put on wonderful theater productions throughout the year. Don't miss them.

Insiders' Tips

is served at each school, and breakfast is served at several schools. Free or reduced-rate meals are available to those who qualify.

New students should register at the appropriate school prior to school opening. Kindergarten and first grade must present immunization records and have a physical examination.

Each school has an advisory council that meets monthly to discuss issues. The councils report to the board of education. Most schools have a Parent-Teacher Organization (PTO) as well as booster organizations.

If you have questions about the school system, contact the Carteret County Schools Central Office (Board of Education), P.O. Box 600, Beaufort 28516, 728-4583. Information booklets are available.

Schools

Public Schools

BEAUFORT

Two schools are located within the Town of Beaufort, and one school is on the outskirts. Beaufort Elementary School, 801 Mulberry Street, 728-3316, serves about 550 students in pre-kindergarten through the 5th grade. Once students have completed 5th grade, they attend Beaufort Middle School, 100 Carraway Street, 728-4520. The middle school has an enrollment of about 360 students in the 6th, 7th and 8th grades. Once students have completed 8th grade, they attend East Carteret High School, which is on Highway 70 E. just outside town. About 790 students in grades 9 through 12 attend East Carteret, 728-3514. The school offers students 20 clubs/organizations and 16 areas of athletic

competition, and the band is well known for outstanding performances. Students who complete 8th grade at Atlantic, Smyrna, Beaufort Middle or Harkers Island schools attend East Carteret High School.

MOREHEAD CITY

In the Morehead City area, children in the public school system follow a path from primary to elementary to middle to high school. While you should check with your new neighbors or call the county school board office, 728-4583, here is the basic rule: If you live in Morehead City or down Bogue Banks as far as Indian Beach, your child will attend a Morehead City school. If you live at the west end of the county or Bogue Banks, your child will start school at White Oak Elementary School, then advance to Broad Creek Middle School. From there your child will go to West Carteret High School, along with students from Morehead City Middle School. Older students who live in the county west of the Newport River attend West Carteret High School.

Morehead City Primary, 4409 Country Club Road, 247-2448, opened last fall and serves more than 780 students in pre-kindergarten through 3rd grade. Morehead City Elementary School at Camp Glenn, 3312 Arendell Street, 726-1131, serves students in 4th and 5th grade. The school building was renovated last year and serves about 450 students.

Morehead City Middle School, 400 Barbour Road, 726-1126, is the third school in the progression for students in the Morehead City area. It serves almost 650 students in 6th, 7th and 8th grades. Upon completion of 8th grade, students advance to West Carteret High School, Country Club Boulevard, 276-1176. With an enrollment of about 1,550 students,

West Carteret is the largest of the county's two high schools. A new addition houses 17 classrooms, and renovations are under way in the media center, computer lab and guidance and administrative offices. The school offers students about 25 clubs/organizations and 18 areas of athletic competition, and the band and choral departments are award winners.

Cape Lookout High School, 1108 Bridges Street, 726-1601, is the county's new alternative school. Class sizes are limited to ensure a lower student-teacher ratio.

SWANSBORO

The four schools in Swansboro fall under the jurisdiction of the Onslow County Board of Education, Jacksonville, 455-2211. Swansboro Primary School, 118 School Road, 326-4574, offers curriculum for students in kindergarten through 2nd grade. The school is located one block off Highway 24. Swansboro Elementary School, 119 Norris Road, 326-5350, includes 3rd, 4th and 5th grades and is located just off Highway 24. Swansboro Middle School, 112 W. Corvett Avenue, 326-3601, is attended by students in grades 6, 7 and 8. Swansboro High School, 201 Queen's Creek Road, 326-4300, serves about 640 students in grades 9 through 12. The school is just off Highway 24.

DOWN EAST

Three schools are located in the Down East area of Carteret County. Each of these schools is named for its community, and each serves students through the 8th grade. Upon completion of 8th grade, students from these three schools attend East Carteret High School.

Atlantic Elementary School, 550 School Drive, 225-3961, has an enrollment of about 190 students in grades pre-kindergarten through 8th. Harkers Island Elementary School, Island Road, 728-3755, serves about 180 students from kindergarten through 8th grade, and it is the smallest school in the county system. Smyrna Elementary School, Marshallberg Road, 729-2301, has an estimated 380 students attending pre-kindergarten through 8th grade.

WESTERN CARTERET COUNTY

Three schools are located in the western part of the county. White Oak Elementary School, Cape Carteret, 393-8354, offers curriculum to about 570 students in kindergarten through 5th grade. Newport Elementary School, 34 Chatham Street, 223-4201, has about 930 pre-kindergarten through 5th grade students. After completion of the 5th grade, students from White Oak and Newport attend Broad Creek Middle School, Highway 24, 247-3135. The middle school provides instruction to about 770 students in 6th, 7th and 8th grades. After completing 8th grade, students attend West Carteret High School.

Educational programs for children are offered at the N.C. Maritime Museum year round.

Insiders' Tips

Private Schools

There are a few private schools in the county serving students in kindergarten through 12th grade. There is also a small group of home-school participants. For information about home schools, contact the Carteret County Schools Central Office, 728-4583.

Beaufort Christian Academy, Highway 70 E., Beaufort, 728-3165, is a ministry of Beaufort Free Will Baptist Church and enrolls students from kindergarten through 12th grade. **Grace Christian School**, Country Club Road, Morehead City, 726-1044, shares a facility with Grace Fundamental Baptist Church and serves 5 year olds through 12th graders. **The Tiller School**, 1950 Highway 70, Beaufort, 728-1995, is in its second year and serves students in kindergarten through 6th grade. The Tiller School is not church affiliated.

St. Egbert's Catholic School, 1705 Evans Street, Morehead City, 726-3418, is affiliated with St. Egbert's Roman Catholic Church and provides instruction to students in kindergarten through 5th grade.

Gramercy Christian School, Highway 70, Newport, 223-4384, provides instruction for students in kindergarten through 9th grade. The school plans to expand to include 10th grade this fall and continue expanding by one grade level each year until it offers a full curriculum toward graduation. **White Oak Christian Academy**, Highway 24, near Cape Carteret, 393-6165, is affiliated with the White Oak Church of God and serves students from 3 years old through 12th grade.

Child and Family Learning Center, 909 Arendell Street, Morehead City, 240-

1770, offers testing and supplemental instruction in all subject areas for students from pre-K through adult. All of their teachers are North Carolina certified, and this organization gets good results by specializing in individual and small group instruction. They have an additional center located in Jacksonville, (910) 353-4440.

Newport Development Center, Church Street, Newport, 223-4574, specializes in training for handicapped children and adults who need more than regular classrooms can offer.

Child Care

Reliable sitters for children and the elderly are available on the Crystal Coast. **Nancy's Nannies**, Morehead City, 726-6575, is used widely and offers responsible adult sitters for children and the elderly for a day, night, weekend or longer. A few day-care centers offer extended hours on weekends. Often hotel front desk clerks can recommend a sitter.

Fees for day-care services vary and are often based on the age of the child, the number of hours the child spends at the facility and the number of siblings attending the facility. Generally, the cost per week is between $30 and $50. Many facilities provide children with transportation to and from school if needed, and most provide summer programs. There are also a number of qualified, caring nannies who will provide care for your child in your home or theirs.

Beaufort

Beaufort has several child-care facilities. **Ann Street United Methodist Church**, 500 Ann Street, 728-5411, provides preschool care, day care and after-school care for students from the age of 3 through elementary school. **Beaufort Christian Academy,** Highway 70 E., 728-3165, offers day-care services during the week for children ages 2 through 5 and after-school care for older students. **Colony Day Care Center,** 103 Fairview Drive, 728-2223, offers care for children from 4 weeks to 12 years of age. Colony offers day care, preschool and before- and after-school care.

Morehead City has several child-care facilities. **My School,** 105 Eaton Drive, 247-2276, serves youngsters from 8 weeks of age through elementary school age with preschool and before- and after-school programs. **Colony Day Care Center,** 700 N. 35th Street, 247-4831, recently expanded and offers child care for kids from 1 to 5 years of age.

ABC Day Care, Mandy Plaza N. 35th Street, 240-2222, opened last fall and serves children from 6 weeks to 5 years old. Before- and after-school care is also offered. **Miss Nancy's Early Learning Center,** 204 N. 18th Street, 247-2006, serves children from 6 weeks to 12 years of age with preschool, day care and after-school care. **Kids Kampus,** 600 N. 35th Street, 247-1866, is designed for children from 5 to 12 years old in need of before- and after-school care.

Swansboro

Swansboro area residents can utilize services at several centers. **Coastal Kiddie College,** Highway 24, 326-3386, serves children from 6 weeks to 12 years of age with day care and before- and after-school care. **Hug A Bear Day Care,** Mount Pleasant Road, 326-7002, cares for children from infancy to age 12. **Swansboro United Methodist Child Care and Preschool,** Highway 24, 326-3711, accepts children from 4 weeks to 10 years of age and offers preschool and before-and-after-school programs.

Western Carteret County

Western Carteret County residents will find the larger child care facilities in the community of Newport. **Miss Pat's Learning Center and Child Care,** 100 Fort Benjamin Road, 223-3432, serves children from age 3 to 12 with preschool and before-and-after-school programs. **Newport Child Care Center,** 51 Chatham Street, 223-3500, serves children from 6 weeks to school age with a preschool program. **Newport Kids, Inc.,** 30 E. Chatham Street, 223-4303, offers before- and after-school care for school-age children as well as a summer program. **St. James Day Care and Preschool Center,** 1011 Orange Street, 223-3191, offers day care for children from 6 weeks through kindergarten. Before- and after-school programs for older children are provided.

Strolling on the beach is a favorite pastime on the Crystal Coast.

Crystal Coast
Retirement and
Senior Services

Our mild year-round climate and relatively low property taxes attract great numbers of retirees to North Carolina each year. The Crystal Coast is one of the areas frequently chosen for retirement years because there is much more bang for the retirement buck here. Property values on or near the water are still, relative to anywhere else, very low. The Crystal Coast enjoys a fast-growing population of highly educated, well traveled, active, retired senior citizens.

As our number of older residents increases, the county and its various towns are developing more activities directed toward suiting the needs and interests of the senior set. With the variety of sports, hobbies, volunteer opportunities and entertainment available, most retirees can stay as busy as they like.

Housing requirements can change quickly during the retirement years. Many townhouse and condominium developments are perfect for retirees who also decide to retire from house and lawn maintenance. All real estate companies can guide you toward more simplified living arrangements in beautiful locations.

Housing exclusively for older citizens on the Crystal Coast is available in a variety of settings, from federally subsidized accommodations for the elderly and handicapped to exclusive retirement complexes where you buy the unit and pay a monthly maintenance fee, which includes taxes, meals, laundry and around-the-clock security service. In addition, there are several nursing homes, rest homes and family care centers for those who need extra attention.

If you are shopping for one of these alternatives, it is very important to make several visits to the places you are considering. Information about all nearby facilities is available at the Department of Social Services, 2822 Neuse Boulevard in New Bern, 637-1703 or, of course, at the facilities.

Housing Options and Facilities

HARBORVIEW TOWERS
812 Shepard St., Morehead City   726-0453

Harborview Towers is in a downtown residential neighborhood on the Morehead City waterfront overlooking Bogue Sound. The modern 10-story, 50-apartment complex is adjacent to the

The Carteret County Museum of History houses a fascinating collection of artifacts and historical documents and is a great source for genealogical research.

Insiders' Tips

Harborview Health Care Center, which includes a nursing home and family care facilities. Units are sold to residents, and a monthly fee includes maintenance, housekeeping, laundry, emergency and scheduled transportation, one meal a day in the dining room, all property expenses except telephone, property taxes and homeowner's policy on apartment contents. There are efficiency apartments, as well as one- and two-bedroom units. All but the smallest units have balconies providing views of either Newport River or Bogue Sound. There is outdoor parking, with some covered parking on the building's ground floor. The facility has an activities director, full-time security, and a live-in administrator, Doris Jernigan, who is also the owner.

EKKLESIA APARTMENTS

Ekklesia Dr., Morehead City   726-0076

Ekklesia Apartments is a HUD subsidized retirement complex in a quiet part of town on Barbour Road. The complex was built by four area churches, which retain much of the management authority. About two blocks from Morehead Plaza Shopping Center, Ekklesia includes 74 one-bedroom units and six two-bedroom units, all arranged in one-story clusters around the community center, which houses laundry facilities, a mail room and a large meeting room complete with kitchen. The site manager and activities director offices are also in the community center. Regular activities include monthly birthday parties, special holiday parties, bingo, club meetings, a support group for the visually handicapped and such special events as the annual Watermelon Festival.

AMERICARE OF EARTERN CAROLINA

3020 Market St.
Newport   223-2600, (800) 948-4333

Newly opened in November 1994, Americare offers 16 beautifully furnished two-bedroom apartments, each accommodating four residents who are able to live independently with some assistance. Assistance included three nutritious meals a day with special diet considerations served in the dining room, laundry, and housekeeping services, medication monitoring and administering, scheduled transportation and a variety of social, recreational and educational opportunities. The community within a community complex is designed around an exterior courtyard with a gazebo-style bandstand for special performances and events or a village green for community gatherings. Each apartment has a courtyard patio. Monthly rental includes all services and an enthusiastic staff that is available at all times.

SAILORS' SNUG HARBOR

Hwy. 70 E., Sea Level   225-4411

Sailors' Snug Harbor is a totally unique retirement facility built specifically for retired Merchant Marines and operated by one of the oldest charitable trusts in this country. The facility is more than 160 years old although the building and location in Sea Level is less than 20 years old. The trust was penned by Alexander Hamilton in the late 1700s for his friend Capt. Robert Richard Randall who wanted to build a "marine hospital for aged, decrepit, and worn out seamen" to be called "The Sailor's Snug Harbor." Properties of the trust included a small tract of land on Manhatten Island, now called Greenwich Village. The mariners, as Capt. Randall specified the resident retired Merchant Mariners should be called,

enjoy a lovely facility in a beautiful setting.

Nursing Homes

Nursing homes, by law, must provide registered nurses on duty at least 8 hours a day, seven days a week, with licensed nurses on duty around the clock under the supervision of the director of nursing. These facilities provide both short- and long-term care. Generally, physical therapy and speech therapy are provided, according to doctors' orders. The homes provide planned activities, regular classes

and worship programs for the ambulatory.

CRYSTAL COAST
REHABILITATION CENTER
Penny Ln., Morehead City   726-0031

Morehead Nursing Center is a facility that provides skilled nursing care for 92 patients who require intermediate or acute care. On-site staff members can provide speech, physical and occupational therapy, and a full-time activities director keeps ambulatory patients active and alert. Center activities include current events, ceramics, painting, church activities, parties and other social functions. The center accepts Hospice patients, and 11 Medicare beds are available.

HARBORVIEW HEALTH CARE CENTER
812 Shepard St., Morehead City   726-6855

Harborview Health Care Center has an in-house therapy department and includes a nursing home for 125 patients who require skilled and intermediate nursing care. The center provides three nutritional meals daily, and both second and third floors have two large glassed-in solariums that overlook Bogue Sound and Morehead City. It is certified for Medicare and Medicaid and is a member of the N.C. Health Care Facilities Association and the American Health Care Association. A staff activity director plans programs, and volunteers also conduct a variety of events for residents. Church services, Bible study, communion services, music therapy and other interactive functions are offered.

Rest Homes

Rest homes provide custodial care, not nursing care, and have a doctor on call but only registered nurses on staff. There are trained nurses' aides on duty at all times under the direction of trained supervisors. While some residents use the facility for short-term care, most residents· make use of the home on a long-term basis.

BROMAN REST HOME
478 Howard Blvd., Newport   223-4554

Broman Rest Home is housed in a 26-year-old, homey brick facility and is the only establishment of its kind in the county west of Carteret General Hospital in Morehead City. It is licensed for 61 residents and accepts Medicare and Medicaid patients. Wheelchair and walker

residents receive assistance with daily functions, and specialized therapists can be provided when needed. An activities coordinator visits weekly, and residents are offered regular outings and in-house activities.

CARTERET CARE REST HOME
Professional Park
Morehead City   726-0401

Carteret Care Rest Home is three blocks from Carteret General Hospital in Professional Park. The care facility is licensed for 60 patients, and residents are involved in programs aimed at keeping them active and interested. Twenty-four hour care is provided, and an in-house facility-maintained physician's office is available to an assigned physician who visits once a month. Nurse assistants and medication assistants are on staff, as is an activities director. The facility provides transportation for residents, and volunteers conduct church-related programs and activities. Local garden club members maintain gardens and bird feeders.

SEA LEVEL EXTENDED CARE FACILITY
Hwy. 70 E., Sea Level   225-4611

This extended care facility is housed in the former Sea Level Hospital building and provides acute and intermediate nursing home care, plus a home for the aged. It also offers a unique guest care service for those whose caregivers need a respite (see our Accommodations chapter).

Family Care Centers

Family care centers provide a home-like atmosphere for those who need some care but can basically live independently. Residents must be ambulatory and perform some light housekeeping duties. They usually have kitchen privileges.

They generally live in semiprivate bedrooms with a shared bath, have meals together and use the living room or other facilities jointly with other residents. There is a resident supervisor who does the heavy housework and cooking and, in general, looks after the residents. Transportation for medical attention, worship and shopping is provided. Medicine is under lock and key and is dispensed by the supervisor according to the doctors' directions.

HARRIS FAMILY CARE CENTER AND WADIN' CREEK FAMILY CARE CENTER
Hwy. 101, Beaufort   *728-7490*

These are two separate care facilities in a country setting north of Beaufort. They are owned and operated by George and Millie Harris. Each house is licensed for six residents. The Harris house has only women residents, and the Wadin Creek house can accommodate men or women. Each has three double bedrooms and two large bathrooms. Some outings and activities are planned. The live-in manager cooks, dispenses medicine and does heavy cleaning.

Organizations

The **American Association of Retired Persons (AARP)** has two active chapters on the Crystal Coast. The Morehead City chapter meets on the third Monday of each month for lunch at 11:30 AM at the Ramada Inn, MP 8¾, in Pine Knoll Shores. A speaker is scheduled for each meeting, and a newsletter is published to keep members apprised of goings-on of interest. To join the membership for lunch, reservations are taken in advance at either 240-3908 or 354-3078. Lunch is $6 per person. The White Oak Chapter of the AARP meets for lunch at Pirate's Landing in Cape Carteret on the second Monday of each month. Reservations for this chapter meeting are taken at 393-8378.

Agencies and Services

The **Senior Center**, 1610 Fisher Street, Morehead City, 247-2626, provides a variety of programs for those older than 60. Classes, trips, workshops and entertainment events are planned for senior citizens, and facilities are also used for a variety of community activities, including lively lessons in line dancing and square dancing, billiards, table tennis, club meetings and the like. A hot lunch is available, but arrangements need to be made at the center. The center also serves as headquarters for the SHARE food co-op. Each fall the center holds a Volunteer Opportunity Fair with representatives present from dozens of institutions in the county to share information on volunteer opportunities in the area. The center is open weekdays from 8 AM until 5 PM.

The **Senior Health Insurance Information Program**, 247-4366, is a service of the Retired Seniors Volunteer Program (RSVP) that refers senior citizens' health insurance questions to trained volunteers. The volunteers help compare the benefits and disadvantages of various policies so seniors can make an educated buying decision. They also help file insurance and medicare claims and find solutions to insurance problems.

The **Lifeline Program**, 247-1530, operates out of the emergency room at Carteret General Hospital and was set up to help older or chronically ill persons live independently. The subscriber has a special machine attached to his or her home telephone and wears a small device at all times. In case of sudden illness, a fall or other emergency, the subscriber simply depresses the button on the portable unit, which activates an alarm in the hospital emergency room where a staff member will respond. Newer devices include the capability of transmitting voice messages to and from the subscriber. If there is no answer or if the answer indicates an emergency, help is sent right away.

The area's **Meals-On-Wheels** program provides home delivery of hot meals, usually one a day, five to seven days a week. The program is designed to help the elderly, shut-ins, those recuperating from surgery and handicapped persons. Some systems require full payment for meals, some seek contributions and others operate entirely on donations. Volunteers deliver the meals. Meals-on-Wheels operates out of Beaufort, 728-3356; Morehead City, 354-3130; Newport and Broad Creek, 223-4534; and the White Oak River area, 326-5333.

Carteret County has its own **Senior Games** program for residents 55 and older. Local games are held each May, and a year-round program leads up to the annual games in July. Games also include Silver Arts competition in painting, sculpture, literature, heritage crafts and instrumental and vocal music. For information, contact the Senior Center, 247-2626.

Another special senior activity is **Week At Camp**, a week-long camping experience in August at a 4-H camp in the foothills outside Reidsville, North Carolina. Participants come from all over North Carolina and other states through both managing agencies, the Carteret County Parks and Recreation Department, 728-8401, and the Dare County Cooperative Extension Service, 473-1101. For a fee of about $200 per person, campers get transportation, insurance, room and board, nonstop entertainment, workshops and other extras. In addition, for those seeking a little more challenge, the High Adventure option takes participants white water rafting and outdoor camping for two days out of the week. The camp has a swimming pool for exercise and a freshwater lake for paddleboating and canoeing and fishing. Classes and workshops are scheduled daily, and there's entertainment each evening. Meals are served family style.

Veterans' Groups

Because of the proximity of several military bases and military hospitals, many people retiring to Carteret County are veterans. There are numerous veterans' organizations in the area, and all welcome new members. And, for the veteran with a problem, there's the Veterans' Service Office in Beaufort, 728-8440.

The **American Legion, Post 46**, Morehead City, 726-4674, meets the third Thursday evening of each month at Webb Civic Center, Ninth and Evans streets, Morehead City.

The **Disabled American Veterans, Chapter 41**, Morehead City, 726-2712, meets the first and third Sunday of each month at 3 PM at Webb Civic Center, Ninth and Evans Streets, Morehead City.

The Ladies Auxiliary meets at the same time and place.

The **Veterans of Foreign Wars, Post 2401**, Beaufort, 728-4390, meets the first and third Monday of each month at the post home just off Highway 101 at Airport Road. The Ladies' Auxiliary meets the second and fourth Monday at the same place.

The **Veterans of Foreign Wars, Post 9960**, Swansboro, 393-8053, meets the second and fourth Thursday of each month at the post home on VFW Road off Highway 58 just outside Cape Carteret. The Ladies Auxiliary meets the first and third Monday each month.

The **Veterans of Foreign Wars, Post 8986**, Newport, 726-8806, meets the first and third Tuesday at the post home on Hibbs Road between Highways 24 and 70. The Ladies Auxiliary meets the second Tuesday of each month.

Photo: Scott Taylor

Whoooo could ever guess that the Outer Banks Wildlife Shelter needs volunteers?

Crystal Coast
Volunteer Opportunities

Countless organizations on the Crystal Coast rely on volunteers of all ages to render their time, talents and services. Through varied volunteer opportunities, residents are involved directly in nurturing herbs, narrating historical tours, directing tourists, preparing shark souffle, building houses, assisting hospital patients and orchestrating and delivering food and presents to families who really appreciate help at Christmas. Volunteers add varied levels of interest to their lives on the Crystal Coast through their activities and meet other people with common interests while sharing their time and skills.

People who like history, meeting the public, answering stray questions on a narrated beach walk or showing tourists around interesting historical restorations will enjoy channelling some spare time in the direction of the aquarium, museums and historic sites. If you'd enjoy lending a hand and hammer, you will be welcomed into the fold at Habitat For Humanity, and Hammocks Beach State Park will be equally glad to see you helping with repairs. All the public libraries employ volunteer help in children's programs, one-on-one assistance for patrons and outreach programs. Volunteers preferring the company of animals will be delighted with the opportunities at the Outer Banks Wildlife Shelter or at the Humane Society's animal shelter. The Hospital Auxiliary places volunteers in every area at Carteret General Hospital. Meals-on-Wheels and Hospice both de-

pend on volunteered kindness to deliver meals or offer relief to caregivers. The Domestic Violence and Rape Crisis programs train volunteers who are interested in offering specific care in crisis situations. Help Line, the crisis telephone line, is fully staffed by trained volunteers who are available to lend an ear and offer referral information. The Retired Senior Volunteer Program (RSVP) is very active and recognized for its matchmaking of retired volunteer expertise with appropriate recipients.

Whether or not you are new to the area, if you have some time to share, the range of interesting possibilities through volunteer efforts will open new doors. Consider the following list of organizations that are always welcoming and training new volunteers. You can learn something new or teach others something you do well. Your call will be welcomed and your experience broadened.

Public Sites and Parks

CORE SOUND WATERFOWL MUSEUM
Harkers Island   728-1500

BEAUFORT HISTORICAL ASSOCIATION
138 Turner St., Beaufort   728-5225

CARTERET COUNTY HISTORICAL SOCIETY
100 Wallace Dr., Morehead City   247-7533

N.C. MARITIME MUSEUM
315 Front St., Beaufort   728-7317

N.C. Aquarium at Pine Knoll Shores
Salter Path Rd., Hwy. 58   247-4004

Fort Macon State Park
E. Fort Macon Rd., Hwy. 58
Atlantic Beach   726-3775

Hammocks Beach State Park
1572 Hammocks Beach Rd.
Swansboro   326-4881

Carteret County Public Library
210 Turner St., Beaufort   728-2050

Bogue Banks Public Library
Pine Knoll Village, Pine Knoll Shores   247-4660

Newport Public Library
Howard Blvd., Newport   223-5180

Animal Care Services

Outer Banks Wildlife Shelter
5810 Arendell St., Morehead City   240-1200

Humane Society of Carteret County
Hibbs Rd., Morehead City   247-7744

Human Care Services

Big Brothers/Big Sisters
727 Arendell St., Morehead City   240-1024

Carteret County Habitat For Humanity
312 Live Oak St., Beaufort   728-5216

Carteret County Domestic Violence Program
402 Turner St., Beaufort   728-3788

Guardian Ad Litem
514-4701

Newport Developmental Center
Church St., Newport   223-4574

Retired Senior Volunteer Program (RSVP)
17th and Fisher Sts., Morehead City   247-4366

Foster Grandparent Program
17th and Fisher Sts., Morehead City   726-5219

Senior Games
17th and Fisher Sts.
Morehead City   247-2626, 728-8401

Hospice of Carteret County
Webb Memorial Library and Civic Center
Ninth and Evans Sts.
Morehead City   247-2808

Martha's Mission Cupboard
901 Bay St., Morehead City   726-1717

Meals-on-Wheels
Morehead City   726-5834
Beaufort   728-3356
Newport   223-4534

Carteret Literacy Council
Carteret County Public Library
210 Turner St., Beaufort   728-2050

Project Christmas Cheer
Daisy Hilbert   726-5970

Carteret County Hospital Auxiliary
Carteret General Hospital
Morehead City   247-1532

Help Line
Beaufort   247-3023

Environmental Services

Big Sweep
N.C. Cooperative Extension Service
Carteret County   728-8421
Rachael Carson Reserve   728-2170

N. C. Coastal Federation
3233-4 Hwy. 58, Swansboro   393-8185

Crystal Coast
Hospitals and Medical Care

Routine and specialized medical care, diagnostic procedures, treatment and surgery are available and practiced routinely on the Crystal Coast. In cases requiring equipment or specializations not presently available here, referrals are usually to New Bern or Greenville, which are no more than 2 hours away. In cases of emergency, residents and visitors are offered medical attention on a walk-in basis at several locations around the county during weekday business hours. At other times, Carteret General Hospital's emergency room may be the best bet.

In almost every town or community throughout the county, there are clinics or specialized practices with one to a half-dozen doctors. It is not unusual, however, for routine appointments to be scheduled months in advance, although sickness and emergency cases are generally worked in. When moving to the Crystal Coast, it's best to arrive with a referral from your most recent doctor. Otherwise, as there is no medical referral service in Carteret County, ask a few Insiders for their recommendations and take the consensus.

Hospitals

CARTERET GENERAL HOSPITAL
3500 Arendell St.

Emergency room	247-1540
Morehead City	247-1616

Carteret County's only hospital is Carteret General Hospital. The hospital of-fers 24-hour-a-day emergency services, oncology, chemotherapy, ambulatory surgery, CT scanning and many other specialties. Continual additions of facilities and equipment are making giant strides in keeping the hospital abreast of the latest developments in medical diagnosis and treatment. The hospital recently completed a major addition, adding 28,000 square feet of space to its operating room facilities and doubling the capacity of its day surgery area. A new surgical services facility includes an operating room, endoscopy, a recovery room and day surgery and waiting room areas. The hospital recently refurbished its second, third and fourth floor nurse station areas.

If other facilities are needed, the hospital makes arrangements to air-evacuate patients to Pitt County Memorial Hospital in Greenville or to other larger city hospitals. This is sometimes necessary in the event of an extremely premature birth, severe burn or major head injury.

CRAVEN REGIONAL MEDICAL CENTER
2300 Neuse Blvd., New Bern   633-8111

This major medical facility includes 24-hour-a-day emergency room service, outpatient surgery, diagnostic services, critical care units, cardiac care services offering diagnostic catheterization and open heart surgery and radiation oncology. Magnetic resonance imaging (MRI), CT scanning, home care, long-term care for older adults, speech and language therapy, rehabilitation, adult psychiatric services and women's health services are also offered. For more information, see the New Bern Medical Care chapter.

BRYNN MARR BEHAVIORAL HEALTHCARE SYSTEM

192 Village Dr., Jacksonville (910) 577-1400
Helpline counselor (800) 822-9507

Brynn Marr Hospital extends comprehensive services throughout eastern North Carolina in treatment of emotional and behavioral problems, mental illness, substance abuse and chemical dependencies for individuals of all ages. Designed to offer the least restrictive level of care needed by clients, Brynn Marr's Behavioral Healthcare System offers outpatient care, day treatment programs or full hospitalization for critical care needs. Brynn Marr's Helpline is a free crisis and referral service that offers round-the-clock telephone assistance with confidentiality in identifying needs and recommending an appropriate next step toward problem solution. One may see a counselor at Helpline offices in the Crystal Coast area in Jacksonville or Hampstead for a no-cost evaluation. For senior citizens, the hospital's New Beginnings day treatment programs address the specific mental health issues of elderly adults. Brynn Marr also offers numerous support services and outreach programs to the community, including no-cost professional workshops on mental health topics and free community education programs.

ONSLOW MEMORIAL HOSPITAL

317 Western Blvd., Jacksonville 577-2345

This hospital is used by some residents of western Carteret County because Jacksonville is only about 20 miles from Swansboro. The facility offers 24-hour emergency service and admissions and in-and-out treatment for minor illnesses, injuries or emergencies. The hospital houses its own poison control unit and has physicians on staff with a wide variety of specialties.

PITT COUNTY MEMORIAL HOSPITAL

Stantonsburg Rd., Greenville 551-4100

This large facility is affiliated with the East Carolina University School of Medicine and East Carolina Children's Hospital. It offers a wide spectrum of treatment, specialized staff and facilities that range from its well-known emergency room to a neonatal nursery used by smaller hospitals across the region. The hospital also has an orthoscopic surgery clinic, and the new Leo W. Jenkins Comprehensive Cancer Center provides radiation therapy, chemotherapy and oncologic surgery.

NAVAL HOSPITALS

Camp Lejeune 451-1113
Cherry Point 466-5751

For active duty and retired military and their families, there is the Naval Regional Medical Center at Camp Lejeune, the U.S. Marine Corps Base at Jacksonville and the completely new Cherry Point

---

Naval Hospital at the U.S. Marine Corps Air Station at Cherry Point, Havelock.

Urgent Care

WESTERN CARTERET MEDICAL CENTER
Hwy. 58, Cape Carteret   *393-6543*

The Western Carteret Medical Center, a subsidiary of Carteret General Hospital, is located in the Cape Carteret shopping center. The clinic has physician staffing and offers care for minor emergencies and walk-ins, physicals, blood pressure clinics, diabetic counseling and scheduled appointments. It is open weekdays from 8:30 AM until 5 PM.

EASTERN CARTERET MEDICAL CENTER
Hwy. 70, Sea Level   *225-1134*

Eastern Carteret Medical Center offers the same services as the Western Carteret Medical Center in Cape Carteret. It was established to serve the eastern part of the county and is open from 8:30 AM until 5 PM weekdays.

MED CENTER ONE
Atlantic Beach Causeway
Atlantic Beach   *247-2464*

Med Center One is on the Atlantic Beach Causeway, not far from the base of the high-rise bridge between Morehead City and Atlantic Beach. This privately owned facility has in-house X-ray services and a pharmacy and provides emergency and other services on a walk-in basis. Hours are from 8 AM until 6 PM Monday through Friday, 9 AM to 6 PM Saturday and noon to 5 PM on Sunday. In addition to minor emergencies, the clinic schedules appointments and sees walk-in patients for general medical care.

NEWPORT FAMILY PRACTICE CENTER
Howard Blvd., Newport   *223-5054*

With the nearest emergency room and hospital facilities in Morehead City or New Bern, Newport Family Practice Center offers a needed service in the Newport community. This privately owned clinic is open from 8 AM to 5 PM weekdays, and from 9 AM to noon on Saturday. Appointments are preferred, but in an emergency, walk-ins are accepted.

Support Groups and Services

In Carteret County there are a number of active support groups with concerns related to children and family difficulties, mental and physical health, lifestyle changes or challenges and alcohol and drug abuse. Most support groups meet at the Neuse Center, Carteret General Hospital or at area churches, but that certainly doesn't cover all of them. Following are samples of the many groups meeting regularly in Crystal Coast. For further information, call the contact numbers listed. If you don't find a group listed related to your concern, contact the Neuse Center for Mental Health, 726-0515 or Helpline, 247-3023.

AIDS Support Group for Patients and Families	*223-5851*
Alzheimer's Group	*726-0031*
Autism Society	*223-4108*
Battered Women Support Group	*726-3362*
Bereavement/Grief Support Groups	*726-5580, 726-3151*
Better Breathers Support Group	*247-6000*
Breast Cancer Support Group	*393-7293*
Cancer Support Group	*247-4338*

Morehead General Medicine

500 N. 30th Street · Morehead City

726-2282

Charles Goodno, M.D., Ph.D.

DIPLOMATE. AMERICAN BOARD OF INTERNAL MEDICINE
Internal Medicine · General Medicine
Minor Injury · Same Day Care
New Patients Welcome - 2.5 miles from Atlantic Beach Bridge

Children of Divorced/
Divorcing Parents — 247-2202

Codependents
Anonymous — 726-1757, 728-1730

Diabetes Support Group for Patients and Families — 726-7990

Growing Through Divorce — 726-4840

Hospice of Carteret County — 247-2808

Lesbian Support Group — 726-6202

Lifeline — 247-1530
Provides a direct, electronic link between Carteret General Hospital and people needing emergency care

Multiple Sclerosis Support Group — 726-0515

Nervous Disorders Support Group — 728-5460

Nuese Center for Mental Health
Morehead City — 726-0515
New Bern — 633-4171

Overeaters Anonymous (no contact number)
Meets at 8 PM Wednesdays at the Webb Center, Evans St., Morehead City.

PAC: Positive Alternatives and Choices — 728-4096
Tutoring for dropout prevention

Post-traumatic Stress Disorder Support Group — 728-4930

Stop Smoking Support Group — 247-1616

Toughlove Parent Support Group — 726-3556

Unpaid Family Caregivers Support Group — 728-8430
Victims of Sexual Assault and Abuse — 728-4460

Widows' and Widowers' Support Group — 247-6664

Private Medical Practices

Family Medicine

CARTERET FAMILY PRACTICE CLINIC
2 Medical Park Ct., Morehead City — 247-5177

CAS CADER, M.D.
5 Medical Park, Morehead City — 726-8414

JAMES CROSSWELL, M.D.
97 Campen Rd., Beaufort — 728-3875

MOREHEAD GENERAL MEDICINE
500 N. 35th St., Morehead City — 726-2282

SEASIDE FAMILY PRACTICE
Hwy. 70E., Bettie   728-7176

Internal Medicine

**CARTERET INTERNAL MEDICINE
AND CARDIOLOGY CENTER**
212 Penny Ln., Morehead City   247-5426

DOWNEAST MEDICAL ASSOCIATES
3610 Medical Park Ct.
Morehead City   247-2013

EASTERN CAROLINA INTERNAL MEDICINE
532 Webb Blvd., Havelock   447-7088

MOREHEAD GENERAL MEDICINE
Dr. Chales Goodno   500 N. 35th St.
Morehead City   726-2282

Neurology

COASTAL NEUROLOGICAL ASSOCIATES
3110 Arendell St., Morehead City 240-1574

Obstetrics and Gynecology

CARTERET OB-GYN ASSOCIATES
302 Medical Park, Morehead City 247-4297

CARTERET WOMEN'S HEALTH CENTER
302 Penny Ln., Morehead City   726-8016

Ophthalmology

COASTAL EYE CLINIC
3110-6 Arendell St.
Morehead City   726-1064
802 McCarthy Blvd., New Bern   633-4183

Otolaryngology

**COASTAL EAR, NOSE AND
THROAT AND FACIAL PLASTIC SURGERY**
3601 Bridges St., Morehead City   247-3257

J.M. ESPOSITO, M.D.
208 Professional Cr., Morehead City   247-3016

Pediatrics

**CARTERET CLINIC FOR
ADOLESCENTS AND CHILDREN**
221 Professional Cr., Morehead City 726-0511
Cape Carteret   393-2134

COASTAL CHILDREN'S CLINIC
315 E. Main St., Havelock   447-8100

COASTAL PEDIATRIC CARE
212 N. 35th St., Morehead City   247-5212

Surgery

CARTERET SURGICAL ASSOCIATES
306 Medical Park Ct.
Morehead City   247-2101

WAY SURGICAL ASSOCIATES
3 Medical Park, Morehead City   247-4769

Crystal Coast
Higher Education and Research

The Crystal Coast offers several options for students interested in pursuing additional education and the area is well known as a home for research laboratories.

Higher Education

Carteret Community College (CCC), 247-6000, 3505 Arendell Street, Morehead City, is part of North Carolina's 58-campus community college system. The college has programs for the traditional college student or the trade student seeking to upgrade skills. The college offers associate degrees in a number of programs as well as courses in adult basic education and high school completion. Through East Carolina University in Greenville, the college has transferable general education courses. Vocational courses, such as heating and cooling systems, auto mechanics, welding, computers, boat building and photography, are offered. CCC provides educational support and customized skills training to area businesses and industries. Day and evening classes are available, and there are several off-campus class sites throughout the county.

Coastal Carolina Community College, (910)455-1221, is also part of the state's community college system. Based in Jacksonville, it provides many of the same programs as Carteret Community College.

Research Facilities

The Crystal Coast is home to numerous research facilities, most of which have something to do with the surrounding

The Cape Hatteras *is a research vessel based at the Duke University Marine Lab in Beaufort.*

water and resources. These facilities offer research, product development and personnel training for corporations around the world.

Area laboratories have been involved in developing many exciting products. Contract research has included work with companies such as Strohs Brewery, W.R. Grace, Hercules Chemical, Biosponge Aquaculture Products, International Paint, Allied Chemical, Sunshine Makers, Aquanautics, Mann Bait Company, 3M Corporation and General Dynamics.

Duke University Marine Laboratory was set up by Duke University on Piver's Island near Beaufort in 1938. This interdepartmental facility has two objectives — research and teaching. The laboratory's large resident academic staff and innumerable visiting professors and researchers from throughout the United States and abroad have contributed to its worldwide reputation. The laboratory maintains a campus and two research vessels. The largest is the *R/V Cape Hatteras*, a 131-foot ship owned by the National Science Foundation. The ship is designed to carry out basic and applied research and education as required to meet national, state and private needs.

Also located on Piver's Island is **Duke University Marine Biomedical Center**, which is supported by the National Institute of Health. The center focuses research on marine organisms and their relationship to human and environmental health. This is one of four such centers in the nation.

The **University of North Carolina Institute of Marine Sciences** has a facility in Morehead City with activities directed toward understanding basic aspects of the marine sciences. Established in 1947, this is the oldest state-supported marine research laboratory in North Carolina.

The **National Oceanic and Atmospheric Administration** (NOAA) operates the Southeast Fisheries Center on Piver's Island near Beaufort. Here, research focuses on fish important to recreational and commercial fishing groups. This Beaufort lab is one of six labs operated as part of the Southeast Fisheries Center.

NOAA operates a weather forecast center near Newport. The **NOAA National Weather Service Center** provides state-of-the-art weather tracking and forecasting and includes a Doppler weather radar system with advanced weather capabilities.

The North Carolina Division of Marine Fisheries has a large facility in Morehead City. Charged with stewardship of marine and estuarine resources in coastal creeks, bays, rivers, sounds and the ocean within 3 miles of land, this state agency is often in the midst of conflict between lawmakers, environmentalists and fishermen.

The Rachel Carson component of the **North Carolina National Estuarine Research Reserve** is just across Taylor's Creek from Beaufort. It may look like just a series of islands, but this system is an active research and classroom area. Pub-

CARTERET COMMUNITY COLLEGE
3505 Arendell Street, Morehead City, North Carolina 28557-2989

COLLEGE TRANSFER PROGRAM (Through a contract with East Carolina University)
TWO-YEAR ASSOCIATE DEGREE PROGRAMS   ONE-YEAR DIPLOMA PROGRAMS
CERTIFICATE PROGRAMS

For more information call (919) 247-6000
An Equal Employment Opportunity Educational Institution Serving the Community Without
Regard to Race, Creed, Sex, National Origin, or Disability

lic educational trips to the island are frequently offered. The reserve system was created by Congress in order to maintain undisturbed estuaries for research and education on the natural and human processes that affect the coast. The other three components that make up the state Research Reserve are Masonboro Island, Zeke's Island and Currituck Banks. For more information about the Rachel Carson component, call Joyce Atkinson at 728-2170 and see our Attractions chapter.

Dear Carteret County Visitor,

Thank you for your interest in Carteret County. I hope you have an opportunity to visit the county and enjoy our unspoiled beaches, our rich tradition of art, architecture and folklore, and our fresh and varied seafood offerings. In addition to its wonderful quality of life, Carteret County offers many business advantages for large companies looking to relocate or expand, as well as small companies desiring to locate in a beautiful natural area.

The state-owned and operated port in Morehead City is one of the deepest and most accessible ports on the east coast. Access to the Morehead City Port from the Intracoastal Waterway provides unique opportunities for water-oriented commerce. Texasgulf and Weyerhaeuser are examples of companies which ship substantial cargoes through the Morehead City Port.

Carteret County excels in education at the elementary, secondary, community college and post-graduate levels. Carteret Community College offers prospective employers customized training programs at no cost to the company. The marine science laboratories of Duke University, the University of North Carolina-Chapel Hill and the National Marine Fisheries Service have established Carteret County as a world-renowned research center, with excellent opportunities for business research and development.

Carteret County offers an abundant and proud labor force at non-union wage scales, supplemented with skilled labor from nearby military facilities at Cherry Point and Camp Lejeune. Developed acreage tracts are available for industrial, commercial and resort development opportunities. Carteret County Economic Development Council is available to assist you with confidential site information, local permit assistance and labor needs. I hope that you will consider business opportunities in Carteret County, *"Where Business Is A Pleasure."*

Sincerely,

Donald A. Kirkman
Executive Director

Crystal Coast
Commerce and Industry

Tourism and fishing play the lead roles in the county's economic picture, but there are a number of domestic and international companies that call Carteret County home. The Carteret County Economic Development Council, Inc., 726-7822 or (800)462-4252, and the Carteret County Chamber Of Commerce, 726-6350, can provide detailed information about area industry and business. Below is a brief look at a few of the area's major businesses.

The **North Carolina Port** at Morehead City is the most visible industry in the county. Situated on the east end of Morehead City, the 116-acre main facility offers a foreign trade zone and one of the deepest channels and turning basins of any East Coast port. This is one of two state-owned ports; the other is in Wilmington.

The large piles of wood chips along the highway at the port are brought to Morehead City on trucks and train cars by **Weyerhaeuser and Canal Wood Corporation**. The chips, which are used for the production of fine quality paper, are exported via ships to Japan.

Texasgulf exports phosphate-based materials throughout the world and utilizes the Intracoastal Waterway to barge these materials from the company's Aurora mine to the port.

The Port at Morehead City facility is the port of embarkation and debarkation for the Second Division of the **U.S. Marine Corps** at Camp Lejeune, North Carolina. The port includes much of the land on Radio Island, which is the body of land on the southeast side of the Morehead City-Beaufort high-rise bridge.

Atlantic Veneer Corporation in Beaufort is the largest manufacturer of hardwood veneers in North America. With manufacturing facilities on three continents, the company also produces lumber, plywood and edgebanding. It exports about half of its products. With about 700 people, this corporation is the county's largest manufacturing employer.

Several apparel companies have their headquarter on the Crystal Coast, including **Cross Creek Apparel**, makers of Cross Creek Apparel and Russell Athletic Wear, and **Down East Togs**, makers of a variety of sportswear and apparel for the Tom Togs label.

Of Carteret County's 90,000 acres of farm land, 44,000 make up **Open Grounds Farm**. The farm is the largest east of the Mississippi River and produces corn, soybeans, beef cattle, wheat and cotton. Owned by the Ferruzzi Group, one of Italy's largest companies, the farm stretches from the Merrimon Road outside Beaufort east to Highway 70 near Sea Level. Individuals can get a look at the farm by stopping at the main gate to check in. Permission most often is granted, although visits are not recommended on Sundays or during busy planting or harvesting times.

Beaufort Fisheries at the east end of Front Street opened in 1934 and is called the oldest existing industry in the area — and the most fascinating. Where there

were once many, this is the only menhaden plant now operating in the state. Menhaden, an oily, high protein fish, is caught by company vessels and brought to the docks along Taylor's Creek to be processed into fish meal, oil and solubles. Fish meal is used as a protein component in many animal feeds. Fish oil is used primarily in margarine, cosmetics and paints. Fish solubles are high protein liquid by-products also used in the feed market. During the processing, and depending on wind direction, a unique smell can travel through the seaside town. While some newcomers find the smell offensive, locals, particularly the older folks who remember when fish plants were the biggest businesses in town, call it "the smell of money." Annual production is estimated at 10,000 tons of meal and 300,000 to 450,000 gallons of oil.

Parker Marine Enterprises specializes in the construction of fiberglass fishing and pleasure boats. The company plant is on Highway 101 outside Beaufort. Boats are sold through authorized dealers.

Aquaculture and mariculture are exciting new forms of agriculture being promoted by the state. This production provides a dependable, year-round supply of seafood for wholesale and retail markets. **Carolina Cultured Shellfish** is one of the region's largest aquaculture operations and has facilities on Harkers Island.

There are also a number of large seafood dealers in the area. Two of the largest are **Luther Smith & Son Seafood** and **Clayton Fulcher Seafood**. These two family-owned and -operated businesses work from fish houses in the Down East community of Atlantic. Smith operates several steel-hulled trawlers in waters up and down the East Coast and has a second fish house in Beaufort. Fulcher buys seafood directly from independent commercial fishermen and has a second fish house on Harkers Island.

Crystal Coast
Military

The Crystal Coast is surrounded by military bases and training facilities, but that hasn't spoiled the beauty. It has just added a few more people. There often is a bit of controversy over noise and extra traffic, but for the most part, things are calm.

Here is a brief description of a few of the closest military establishments. For more information about Cherry Point, see our Havelock chapter.

MARINE CORPS
AUXILIARY LANDING FIELD
Bogue Field, off Hwy. 24　　　*393-2027*

This 875-acre fronts Bogue Sound. The field primarily is used for field carrier landing practice, and many of these landings are performed at night to simulate landing on an aircraft carrier.

ATLANTIC OUTLYING FIELD
AND PINEY ISLAND (MARINES)

These two facilities are in the Down East area. Atlantic Outlying Field is a 1,514-acre facility in the community of Atlantic. Piney Island, or BT-11 as the military refers to it, is a 10,000-or-so-acre electronic practice range at the eastern tip of Carteret County. As part of the Mid-Atlantic Electronic Warfare Range (MAEWR), Piney Island is used by various military groups, including active duty personnel and reservists. While planes actually do fly over the area, bombing simulations are recorded and scored electronically via computers to lessen the environmental impact.

COAST GUARD BASE FORT MACON
Fort Macon Rd.
Atlantic Beach　　　*247-4598*

Coast Guard Base Fort Macon is at the east end of Bogue Banks and is the home port of several large cutters and smaller vessels. The base is charged with patrolling the area from Drum Inlet on Core Banks south to the North Carolina-South Carolina border. Coast Guard missions include search and rescue and law enforcement.

COAST GUARD
STATION SWANSBORO
Station St.
Emerald Isle　　　*354-2462*

This station is at the west end of Bogue Banks in Emerald Isle. When the station was first established, Emerald Isle was not a town, so it was named after Swansboro, the town to the north. The name never changed. This station's four vessels patrol an area from Marker 21 in Bogue Sound, which is in the area of Gales Creek community, south to the Surf City swing bridge in Pender County.

Inside
New Bern

To really understand the New Bern of today, it's important to know about its past. This river town maintains its heritage by standing guard over its colonial, Georgian, Federal, Greek Revival and Victorian architectural styles. And, its citizens still maintain an attitude of friendliness and Southern gentility.

The town's Swiss look comes honestly. It was settled in 1710 by Swiss and German immigrants who named it after the Swiss capital of Bern. Officially founded by Swiss Baron Christoph von Graffenried, New Bern is distinguished by its red-brick clock tower above city hall just like any Swiss city. The town emblem, as in Old Bern, is a black bear and that symbol appears frequently throughout the city.

New Bern has been fought over by Indians, Swiss, British, Colonials, Yankees and Rebels. After each skirmish, it pulled itself up by its boot straps and plodded onward. The result is a panoply of American history draped along tree-lined streets with just the slightest look of old Switzerland — an odd mix that makes the town quite picturesque.

Historic markers point out the houses where the first elected assembly in the colonies met in defiance of the crown in 1774, where a signer of the U.S. Constitution lived and where George Washington slept — twice. Markers also show you where noted jurist William Gaston, the first chief justice of the state Supreme Court and composer of the state song, had his office.

The second-oldest city in North Carolina, New Bern is the site of many firsts. It was in New Bern that the first state printing press was set up and the first book

Photo: NC Travel & Tourism Division, William Russ

The New Bern Academy is part of the Tryon Palace Restoration Complex and serves as a museum. The original school was built in 1766.

Photo: Kenny Barrow

The National Cemetery is a great place for an evening walk.

and newspaper were published. The state's first public school opened here. The first official celebration of George Washington's birthday was held in New Bern, and it was here that the world's first practical torpedo was assembled and detonated. In the 1890s, C.D. Bradham, a local pharmacist, invented Brad's Drink in New Bern. The drink later became known as Pepsi-Cola.

Without question, New Bern's centerpiece is Tryon Palace, the lavish Georgian brick mansion named after William Tryon, the British colonial governor who had it built in 1770. It is a sumptuous showplace, inside and out. Twin rows of oaks leading up to the entrance provide a stately introduction, and the scenic backdrop is the wide and lovely Trent River. The palace is where delegates gathered for the first State Legislature meeting in 1777.

But even before all that, before the palace, the school and the white man's voice, the site captured the interest of the Tuscarora Indians. It is believed the Indians may have had hunting camps and villages here for thousands of years. Who could blame them?

Downtown New Bern sits on a point of land at the confluence of the Neuse and Trent rivers. Once the main hub, its downtown fell into great disrepair in the early 1970s due to the development of shopping malls and suburban housing outside the business district.

That all changed, however, in 1979 when local government gave Swiss Bear, Inc., a nonprofit corporation composed of civic leaders, the authority and responsibility to revitalize the downtown area. Today, art galleries, specialty shops, antique stores, restaurants and other businesses have resurrected downtown, turning it into a bustling hub of activity. Progressive, exciting changes are continuous and, in 1995, involve a small downtown park on Pollock Street planned by Swiss Bear, Inc., two residential and retail developments in progress on Middle Street and a new home for the Craven Convention and Visitors Bureau at the corner of Middle Street and Tryon Palace Drive. The Swiss Bear downtown revitalization project is very visibly successful.

Just a few miles upstream from down-

New Bern

HISTORICAL DISTRICT

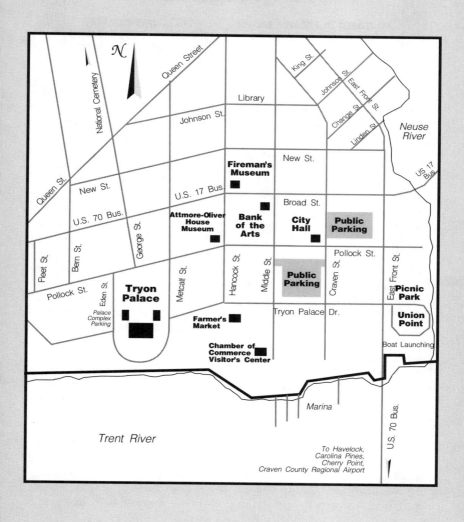

town, the Neuse River slows and quickly broadens into a mile-wide concourse. Joined by the Trent, the Neuse takes a lumbering left turn and widens within sight to 4 miles across, making it the widest river in the United States. The two rivers converge at downtown's Union Point Park. Sitting on a park bench by the docks, you can look downriver for what seems like forever.

This inviting link to the broad, shallow Pamlico Sound and the Atlantic Ocean helped shape New Bern's destiny. The town long thrived on the richness of its rivers and the fertile soil surrounding them. In Colonial times, West Indian and European vessels would dock here to trade cargos of merchandise. The river led to pitch, tar and tobacco from inland and, of course, to local hospitality. Now the rivers serve as the focus of the area's recreational activities: water skiing, sailing and fishing. Hotel-based marinas for modern day skippers edge toward the Trent River channel from both banks between Union Point Park and the railroad trestle and also front the Neuse.

New Bern's southeastern boundary is only a few miles from the Croatan National Forest, a 157,000-acre preserve that shelters deer, bears, alligators and Venus' flytraps. Canada geese and osprey are common sights along the rivers, as are the resident great blue herons. Given the right weather conditions and salt water intrusion, the Neuse River has been known to hide eight- and ten-foot sharks.

New Bern has three historic districts with homes, stores and churches dating back to the early 18th century. Within easy walking distance of the waterfront are more than 200 homes and buildings listed on the National Register of Historic Places. Several bed and breakfasts, most of the area's best restaurants, banks, antique and specialty shops, Tryon Palace, city and county government complexes and many of the town's 2,000 crape myrtles are also nearby.

The crape myrtle is New Bern's official flower. And no wonder. On those hot summer days when you feel like drooping, the crape myrtle seems to laugh as it bursts forth in a profusion of blossoms. New Bern does its gardening quietly. Led by the example of the professionally pampered Tryon Palace gardens, the town's residents have a yen to make things grow.

During the spring explosion of dogwoods and azaleas, a ride through the DeGraffenried neighborhood, about a mile from downtown, is breathtaking.

Gardens, both public and private, extend throughout the city and its suburbs. Summertime brings day lilies, dahlias, zinnias, black-eyed Susans and petunias. Home gardens produce tomatoes, chives, squash, corn and other favorites. In fall, it seems everyone goes ga-ga for chrysanthemums. Flowering cabbage and pansies brighten the winter.

Besides the downtown historic district, New Bern also has the Ghent and Riverside neighborhoods, both of which carry official historic neighborhood designations. Ghent, across Trent Road from the DeGraffenried neighborhood, was the town's first suburb, and the dogwood-planted median on Spencer Avenue was once the bed of a trolley. The neighborhood displays an eclectic collection of architectural styles.

Riverside, developed at the turn of this century and across town from Ghent, runs between the Norfolk Southern railroad tracks and the Neuse River to Jack Smith Creek. It has a sort of baron-and-worker feel to it, with imposing mansions along National Avenue, giving way to the less sumptuous residences on neighboring streets.

Tucked between New Bern and the Trent River is Trent Woods, the third wealthiest incorporated town in North Carolina. Here is the New Bern Golf and Country Club, the Eastern Carolina Yacht Club and some of the priciest real estate around. Trent Woods' pine-shaded roads have company in New Bern's housing market. About 5 miles south of town off Highway 17 is River Bend, which was begun as a planned development and has now incorporated. Like Trent Woods, it

has its own country club, golf course, tennis club, marina and waterfront acreage along the Trent River and canals that lead to it.

Both River Bend and Fairfield Harbour, another planned community about 8 miles east of New Bern on the Neuse River, have attracted retirees primarily from the Northeast. Fairfield Harbour's amenities include a couple of golf courses, two swimming pools, tennis courts, marinas, restaurants, a lounge, miniature golf, horseshoes and walking and riding paths.

If all this sounds boringly nice, take heart. Insiders' brows furrow when they talk about the town's traffic lights and its lack of nightlife.

First the traffic lights. For those motoring along Highway 17 — no, there's no bypass, and Highway 17 isn't four-laned all the way through North Carolina yet — the traffic lights offer a major break in the flow of your trip. In the downtown area, small Colonial-size city blocks, widely varying levels of traffic and ill-timed traffic lights give you a chance to stop and read the historic markers, whether you want to or not. If you're headed south, you can expect another bottleneck around the road's intersection with Highway 70.

New Bern's nightlife is limited. There are a few lounges, some live music, a few movie theaters and a bowling alley, but those with a hankering for more may not hit town at the right time. There are good professional and amateur acting groups in town, a professional dance company and a subscription performance season.

The town also has festivals and shows — the Wildlife and Sportsman's Show and the Chrysanthemum Festival are among the most popular. Twice a year, residents gather at the Trent River waterfront — on July 4, for the fireworks and in early December for the Christmas flotilla. But much of the town's social life takes place in private homes and social clubs and at various civic and charity functions that are staged on an annual basis.

To really get to know New Bern, you have to take it as it is. Think of the river city as a slow treasure hunt where gems are revealed as you walk its streets. It's there that you will discover the real New Bern. Visit its museums — the Bank of the Arts, Tryon Palace Historic Sites and Gardens, the New Bern Academy Museum, the Fireman's Museum and the Civil War Museum. Take time to read the historic markers and talk to the people in their gardens and on their porches.

You're likely to find a sailor from California, a cyclist from New Zealand, a waif from New York or a retired shop owner from Honolulu sharing your bench. Ask them why they chose to live here. New Bernians like to talk about their town.

New Bern is a gentle place, a place where a person can still enjoy the passing scene, where people know how to appreciate a pretty day. It's just that kind of town.

Photo: Bill Scroggins/The Sun News

From seafood to salad, buffets offer something for everyone.

New Bern
Restaurants

New Bern offers residents and guests alike a variety of dining options. Restaurants feature a diversity of culinary fare from around the world. You'll find everything from traditional Southern home cooking to fine European cuisine.

If you're looking for good seafood, you'll love dining out in New Bern. In fact, you would be hard-pressed to find many restaurants that do not offer some type of shellfish and other seafood.

The following guide highlights some of the better known restaurants. We've listed them in alphabetical order and, because of space, had to leave out a number of the other restaurants all over town. We also did not list the chain and fast food restaurants with which you are probably familiar. Our list will give you a look into the variety of restaurants you'll find in New Bern. We encourage you also to ask locals for recommendations, and to call ahead for hours of operation.

The following codes reflect the price of an average dinner for two, consisting of appetizers, entrees, desserts and coffee. Prices are subject to change. The majority of these establishments accept most major credit cards.

Less than $20	$
$21 to $35	$$
$36 to $50	$$$
$51 and more	$$$$

Annabelle's Restaurant & Pub
Twin Rivers Mall 633-6401
$-$$

Annabelle's offers a variety of foods in a relaxed atmosphere. The same menu is presented for lunch and dinner, and it includes something for everyone. Choose from a variety of beef, ribs, chicken and seafood entrees. The restaurant also has international selections, including Mexican fare. Annabelle's has a children's menu and early-bird specials Monday through Thursday. The hot fudge cake is a favorite dessert. The bar serves beer and wine and has all ABC permits.

Anneliese's Surf & Turf
N.C. 55 E. 633-5828
$$

For German food at its best, it's Anneliese's. The restaurant is just a stone's throw from downtown. Don't let the outside fool you; inside you will find the best German food around, along with seafood and steaks. Try the sauerbraten or the bratwurst, bockwurst, kielbasa, weinerschnitzel or the rouladen — roast beef filled with bacon, onions and carrots and served with gravy. German entrees are served with potato dumplings, red cabbage and German-style cold salad, or with hot German potato salad and sauerkraut. Seafood can be fried or broiled; the fisherman's platter offers shrimp, clam strips, flounder, scallops and crab. You'll also find soft shell crabs, sea trout and a number of sauteed items. Filet mignon and rib eye top the steak menu, and there are also surf and turf options. End your meal on a sweet note with Black Forest cherry cake or apple strudel. Anneliese's offers imported beers and wines.

THE BAGEL COTTAGE
712 Pollock St.   636-1775
$

Originally begun as a take-out bagel shop a few years ago, this snacks-and-lunches-only restaurant is behind an old home across from Tryon Palace. The shop offers a dozen varieties of fresh baked bagels and almost as many homemade spreads, chicken salad, shrimp salad and homemade soups. There are special salads, quiches and muffins each day, along with tempting desserts and bagel chips for snacking. You can eat inside the small shop or take advantage of the outside tables overlooking the Tryon Palace Cutting Gardens. There are also a few rocking chairs on the porch where you can make yourself comfortable.

THE BERNE RESTAURANT
2900 Neuse Blvd.   638-5296
$

For hearty country-style cooking and seafood, the Berne Restaurant is the place to go. On the corner of one of New Bern's busiest intersections, this large establishment bears the tell-tale sign of good food to be found within: The parking lot is always full at meal times. A traditional country breakfast is featured everyday, and a breakfast buffet is offered Saturday and Sunday. Home-style dinners are featured, from the regional specialty of pork barbecue to a rib eye steak dinner. The Berne also has a large selection of seafood and shellfish including trout, flounder, oysters (in season), shrimp and more fried or broiled. There is a children's menu and banquet facilities that can accommodate more than 200 people.

BILLY'S HAM AND EGGS
1300 Glenburnie Rd.   633-5498
$

Open 24-hours a day, Billy's Ham and Eggs serves more than just that. Everything on the menu is home cookin' just like grandma used to make. Try ham and eggs, country-style fried potatoes, a Belgian waffle or a pork chop along with grits, pancakes or homemade biscuits. For hamburgers the way you remember them — before fast-food days — try Billy's Big Beef Burger, a hefty helping of ground beef cooked to order and served on a sesame seed bun with all the fixins'. There are lots of home-style veggies on the menu. Seafood specialties include trout, shrimp, oysters, clam strips and crab cakes. Other selections include ham, chicken, meat loaf, hamburger steak, roast beef, spaghetti and pork chops. There is also a children's menu and, of course, there are plenty of homemade cakes and pies.

CHARBURGER
1906 Clarendon Blvd.   633-4067
$

The Charburger is a good place to find a real hamburger served with hot — not greasy — fries, in a no-nonsense setting. Before you place your order at the counter, check out the daily specials. Then take a seat in a booth and enjoy. Fried chicken, hot dogs, hamburgers, shrimp, trout and steak sandwiches are among the specialties. Also, try the chicken and the sandwiches. For dessert, try the apple turnover or an ice cream sundae. Charburger serves lunch and dinner.

THE CHELSEA — A
RESTAURANT & PUBLICK HOUSE
Broad and Middle Sts.   637-5469
$$-$$$

Dining at The Chelsea is a bit of a history lesson. Constructed in 1912, the building was first used as a drugstore by Caleb Bradham, the inventor of Pepsi-

Photo: Scott Taylor

This boat may be bringing in tonight's fresh seafood special.

Cola. A colorful wall mural tells the story of the founding of this popular soft drink, once simply called "Brad's Drink." The Chelsea has full lunch and dinner menus. Lunch choices include sandwiches, several cold plates and salads and could feature crab cakes, fish and chips, liver and onions and quiche of the day. Dinner entrees include a variety of beef, chicken and seafood dishes, and there are always chalkboard specials. You might try the London broil or the sauteed seafood fillets or the mixed grill. We love the shrimp and crawfish special. Entrees are served with a healthy house salad, vegetable, a choice of potato or rice pilaf and freshly baked bread. The large bar offers mixed drinks, domestic or imported beer and wine to complement your meal. This is a popular nightly gathering place (see New Bern Nightlife), and there is often live entertainment.

CLANCY O'HARA'S RESTAURANT AND LOUNGE

2000 S. Glenburnie Rd.   637-2206
$$

Clancy O'Hara's interior features rough-hewn timbers salvaged from old homes and Victorian decor. Clancy's enormous salad bar is a local favorite and includes vegetables and condiments, along with meatballs, seafood, cheeses, fruits, various breads and desserts. Lunch might include an assortment of burgers, sandwiches and specials. There are sandwiches made with prime rib or shrimp, a triple-decker club and baby-back ribs. For dinner, try prime rib, charbroiled steaks, ribs, pasta and seafood. Clancy O'Hara's lounge has full ABC privileges, so you can have a pre-dinner drink at the bar, or enjoy your favorite wine or beer with dinner. The restaurant has banquet facilities

with a private bar and seating for as many as 50 guests.

DIXON'S SODA SHOP

Middle and Pollock Sts.   633-3389
$

Dixon's is a favorite gathering place among New Bernians for breakfast and lunch. Breakfast selections of eggs and bacon with grits or hash browns are the norm, but you must try the homemade muffins. The lunch menu offers a variety of sandwiches and great burgers, plus homemade chicken and tuna salad and calorie counter specials. Dixon's is well known for its real milk shake, malts, fresh-squeezed lemonade and orangeade. Diners can eat at the counter or in an old-fashioned booth. There is an interesting collection of old Pepsi bottles and cans in the diner.

SONNY'S EL MEX RESTAURANT

235 Craven St.   637-9000
$

El Mex is a favorite spot for lunch and dinner where the focus has been on Mexican and American creations that include steak, chicken or shrimp fajitas, burritos and enchiladas. A chicken and rice dish, Pollo Magnifico, is a house specialty, and the baby back rib entree, prepared with a special barbecue sauce, is another favorite. Sonny's has expanded its 1995 menu to include lots of shrimp dishes, crab cakes and grilled fish. Its new flowering onion and crab dip are great ways to start off your meal. The bar serves mixed drinks, wine and beer, including Mexican imports, carafes of Sangria, pitchers of Margaritas and many wines.

THE FLAME

2303 Neuse Blvd.   633-0262
$$-$$$

The unique Victorian decor, elegant

Little Did Caleb Bradham Know...

Could a would-be pharmacist ever have believed that a drink concocted in the back room of a drugstore in the 1890s would, more than 100 years later, be advertised by legendary crooner Ray Charles, singing, "You got the right one, baby, uh-huh"?

Probably not.

Today, Caleb Bradham's syrupy concoction is known around the world as Pepsi-Cola. The building where the original mix was first brewed still stands at the corner of Middle and Pollock streets in downtown New Bern.

Caleb Bradham had aspirations to be a pharmacist, but was forced to leave school and return home when his father's business failed. In his drugstore, sometime during the 1890s, he concocted a new soda fountain drink he called Brad's Drink. He advertised it as "exhilarating, invigorating and aids digestion." By 1898, young Bradham had given the new carbonate the name Pepsi-Cola.

Bradham began his cola operation on an organized basis in 1903. The company, headquartered in the back room of the drugstore, packaged the syrup for sale to other soda fountains. The bottling process was on the rise but still in second place to "over the counter" sales at soda fountains.

It wasn't long before the business outgrew its back-room location, and Bradham moved his Pepsi-Cola operation into rented quarters. Soon after, the young inventor bought the Bishop Factory for $5,000 and equipped it for bottling. He began bottling in 1904 and almost immediately offered franchises. By 1906, there were 15 bottling plants in North and South Carolina, Virginia and West Virginia.

Business boomed until right after the war years, 1917-18, when sugar jumped from 5.5¢ a pound to 22.5¢ a pound. For Pepsi-Cola, which was retailing at a nickel per bottle, it spelled disaster.

After collapsing into bankruptcy, the company changed hands four times before winding up in 1931 as a subsidiary of Loft, the parent of the internationally known Pepsi of today.

meals and irreproachable service make dinner at The Flame a memorable event. For a special occasion, try The Flame's steak and lobster. You'll want to add one of the specialties of the house: the Flame's stuffed baked potato. Other specialties include grilled shrimp and teriyaki chicken. And don't pass up a trip to the gourmet salad and soup bar. Evening specials are offered on some weekdays and could include steak-and-lobster-for-two combos or a second steak at a fraction of the cost of the first. The restaurant has all ABC permits and specializes in fine wines.

FRED AND CLAIRE'S
247 Craven St.   638-5426
$

This cozy little establishment in the downtown historic district offers a variety of intriguing and delicious dishes, all prepared fresh daily. Dishes include cheese and broccoli casserole, shepherd's pie or crab quiche served with fresh fruit, a muffin and sherbet. Lasagne, salads, soups, breads and desserts are all featured. Specialty sandwiches include spicy sausage subs, fillet of flounder on a French roll and homemade pimento cheese. You'll also find burgers and hot dogs. Fred and Claire's also offers wonderful dinner omelettes, seafood, and chicken livers and onions. Your favorite domestic or imported beer and wine are available to complement your meal.

FRIDAY'S 1890 SEAFOOD
2307 Neuse Blvd.   637-2276
$-$$

The decor of Friday's gives you the feeling of being below the deck of one of the many pirate and merchant ships that frequented the North Carolina coast in the 1800s. It's rustic, and the tables are tucked away for privacy. Friday's offers a varied menu that includes the all-time seafood favorites of shrimp, flounder, trout, lobster and crab legs served with all the traditional fixings. Landlubbers' favorites include pork barbecue, rib eye, hamburger steaks and chicken. Dinners include potato, hush puppies, coleslaw and a cup of clam chowder or a trip to the salad bar.

THE HARVEY MANSION
221 Tryon Palace Dr.   638-3205
$-$$$

This restaurant and lounge are in a restored building constructed by John Harvey in the 1790s. Through the years, the building served as a home, mercantile establishment, boarding house, military academy and even the early home of Craven Community College.

The restaurant opened in 1979, and Chef Beat Zuttel has a devoted following. Diners at the Harvey Mansion will find quite a selection — including a continental lunch, pasta buffet and gourmet dinner. Dinner might start with an appetizer of duck with pear and ginger compote or sauteed escargot. For your entree, consider the chef's Berner Roesti mit Kalbsgeschnetzel and Champignons (veal morsels, mushroom sauce and Swiss potato) or try Scallops à la Menthe or Shrimp Provencale. The menu is seasonal to ensure freshness and availability of seafoods. Seafoods are featured each night and can be grilled, poached or sauteed. Homemade desserts include Key lime and berry tartlettes, banana nut chocolate torte and yogurt moosecake.

Downstairs Harvey's Cellar Lounge offers an intimate atmosphere and a unique copper bar (see our Nightlife chapter). The Harvey Mansion offers private dining areas and functions as an art gallery. Guests can enjoy an extensive selection of wines, champagne by the bottle or glass, mixed drinks and domestic and imported beers.

HENDERSON HOUSE RESTAURANT
216 Pollock St.   637-4784
$$$

This award-winning restaurant is in a restored, historic New Bern home and features a collection of original art work. Henderson House offers elegant candlelight atmosphere for dinner. The menu includes dishes created with veal, duck, lamb and pheasant. Entrees offered might include tornadoes of beef with Bearnaise sauce, veal chop with chantrelles, pheasant in port wine, shrimp almondine or a delicious seafood casserole. There is an extensive wine list that favors the French vintages but also includes wines from the world over. You can order mixed drinks to go with your dinner. Lunch or dinner at the Henderson House is recommended and will certainly be a time to remember.

LATITUDE 35

I Bicentennial Park
Sheraton Hotel & Marina 638-3585
$$

Although the elegant decor and menu at this hotel restaurant suggest strictly fine dining, don't be put off if you've just jumped off your boat. You can come as you are and enjoy the cuisine and the panoramic view of the Neuse River and hotel marina. Latitude 35's breakfast buffet is a favorite of hotel guests and locals alike. Guests can feast on egg dishes, grits, breakfast meats, French toast, waffles, muffins, wonderful biscuits, fresh fruit and cereals. Weekday lunches offer sandwiches, soups and creative salads along with lite plates featuring pasta, salad, seafood or meat. Attention turns to seafood in the evening. You'll find all types of fish and shellfish that can be broiled, baked, fried, grilled, peppered or blackened. The salad bar is included with each entree. For land lubbers, Latitude 35 offers pasta, chicken and beef, and there is an extensive children's menu.

MOORE'S BARBECUE

U.S. 17 S. 638-3937
$

Moore's specializes in eastern North Carolina chopped barbecued pork, but offers more. Whether you eat in or take out, the food at Moore's is good, homestyle cooking. Guests can get a meal of pork or chicken barbecue, served with coleslaw, french fries and hush puppies, or a seafood plate — shrimp, flounder and trout. Moore's features both meals and bulk orders as take-outs. But before you decide what you want, check on specials. In addition, Moore's can cater small, large or huge events or put on a North Carolina-style pig pickin'.

MUSTARD'S LAST STAND

Tryon Palace Dr. and Hwy. 70 638-1937
$

Mustard's Last Stand is a movable concession stand that offers the very best in hot dogs and Polish sausages on fresh baked rolls. The hot dogs are better than those at the ball park, and you don't have to fight for a parking space. The stand is next to the Exxon station at the corner of Tryon Palace Drive and Highway 70. Mustard's also offers drinks, chips and more.

POLLOCK STREET DELICATESSEN AND RESTAURANT

208 Pollock St. 637-2480
$-$$

In an old house in New Bern's downtown historic district, this restaurant serves wonderful New York-style cuisine. Pollock Street serves breakfast, lunch and dinner. Diners can eat downstairs, upstairs or on the patio and can choose something as simple as a bagel with cream cheese, a homemade salad or a full meal with cheese-stuffed pasta shells, veal, chicken or sea scallops with pasta. The delicatessen offers an assortment of hot or cold sandwiches and sandwich platters. Daily specials are usually offered for lunch and dinner. Try the quiche or soup of the day served with fruit, a sub or a reuben. Dinner entrees feature chicken, seafood, pasta, veal, stuffed shells and steaks. And, you can enjoy beer or wine. Homemade desserts include Key lime pie, cheesecake and chocolate mousse. Salads, deli-sliced meats and sandwiches can be ordered to go. Live music is often offered, and the restaurant can accommodate special events. The Deli offers full-service catering.

RAMADA STEAK HOUSE

101 Howell Rd.   *636-3637*
$-$$

If you're looking for a steak, try the certified Angus beef served at the Ramada. Each cut of meat is aged for tenderness and prepared with care by either slow roasting or cooking on a real hickory wood grill. You can order rib eye, New York strips, tenderloin and prime rib. The Ramada offers Steak Oscar and beef tips. Although the specialty is Angus beef, the Ramada also serves a variety of poultry and seafood selections. You'll find crab cakes prepared with jumbo lump crabmeat, shrimp and grilled catch of the day. The Ramada overlooks the Neuse River and Ramada Inn marina, and you can eat indoors or out on the deck. They are open for breakfast and dinner. The Sunday brunch buffet offers a wonderful selection of breakfast items, plus made-to-order omelettes. Sinbad's Lounge in the Ramada offers more seafood.

SANDPIPER RESTAURANT

2403 Neuse Blvd.   *633-0888*
$

If you are looking for seafood at a reasonable price, consider the Sandpiper. The restaurant offers lunch and dinner from one menu and specializes in oyster stew and clam chowder, shrimp and oyster cocktails, and steaks. Full meals include fried seafood platters with fish, shrimp, oysters, deviled crab and scallops. A typical house special might include fried trout fillets, fried shrimp, French fries and a healthy serving of coleslaw. One of the nice things about the Sandpiper is that each meal is preceded with hot hushpuppies and butter.

SCALZO'S

415 Broad St.   *633-9898*
$$

For outstanding authentic Southern Italian creations, dine at Scalzo's. Founded by Chef Mario Scalzo, the restaurant's word in food and ingredients is fresh. For starters, try the sauteed shrimp or calamari, lamb meatballs, antipasto, roasted peppers or Italian bean salad. The variety of different pasta dishes is enormous, with 18-plus sauces that can be matched with a variety of pastas. The pasta selection includes meat or cheese ravioli, gnocchi and capellini. The sauces range from the familiar marinara to an unusual black olives and capers creation. There is a mixed seafood sauce, red or white clam sauce and several vegetable or meat sauces. Create your own meal with pasta, sauce and veal, eggplant, beef or chicken. Veal Gorgonzola, a house specialty prepared with cheese, white wine and fresh tomatoes, is a favorite with Scalzo's loyal patrons. For dessert, choose from among several delicious Italian confections. Scalzo's has an extensive international wine list of red and white Burgundies and Bordeaux.

Photo: Scott Taylor

There is nothing like a lazy afternoon sail.

New Bern
Accommodations

Overnight lodgings are increasing in New Bern, and the river city now has several major hotels silhouetting its skyline. There are also a number of excellent bed and breakfasts, at least one of which is said to be inhabited by a friendly spirit. However, those seeking less spiritual digs have a number of other options to choose from.

Hotels positioned along the city's picturesque waterfront offer lovely views of the Trent and Neuse rivers, and a number of economy and budget motels are near the downtown area. Cozy and architecturally interesting bed and breakfasts are sprinkled throughout the historic district.

The listing here is alphabetical and not intended to recommend one place over another. Room prices fluctuate with the seasons, but for the purpose of reflecting rate information, we have shown high season rates for double occupancy. Winter rates may be substantially lower. Rates are subject to change, therefore we urge you to verify rate information when making your reservations. All hotels and bed and breakfasts accept most major credit cards. The following scale is used to represent rate ranges.

$25 to $52	$
$53 to $75	$$
$76 to $99	$$$
More than $100	$$$$

THE AERIE

509 Pollock St.　　　　　　636-5553
$$$　　　　　　　　(800) 849-5553

Just one block from Tryon Palace, this bed and breakfast is housed in a Victorian-style home built in the 1880s. It is furnished with fine antiques and reproductions, and a player piano graces a downstairs sitting room. Each of the seven guest rooms comes with either twin, queen or king beds, a private bath and cable television. The inn provides complimentary wine, beer, soft drinks and light refreshments, as well as a wealth of games, reading material and books on local lore. A full-gourmet breakfast is served each morning in the dining room.

The Tea Room at The Aerie is open Wednesday through Saturday serving teas, coffees and cocoa, scones with cream and jam, tarts and an assortment of tea cakes. Even if you're not staying the night, you're invited to enjoy afternoon tea at The Aerie.

Avoid Neuse Boulevard during commuter hours and take Glenburnie or Simmons streets to reach either end of town.

Insiders' Tips

COMFORT SUITES AND MARINA

218 E. Front St.   636-0022
$-$$$ (800) 638-7322

This new hotel has a Colonial look and a warm, friendly atmosphere. It features 100 suites, many with waterfront balconies, that offer beautiful views of the mile-wide Neuse River. All suites have refrigerators, microwaves and coffee makers; whirlpool suites are also available. Other amenities include free local calls, complimentary continental breakfasts, weeknight evening receptions, an outdoor pool with waterfront courtyard, an outdoor heated whirlpool, a fitness center, a guest laundry, a board room and meeting facilities. Room service is available and prepared in the kitchen of the Harvey Mansion. Vouchers for golf privileges are available, and special golf packages can be arranged. The hotel's new 24-slip marina accommodates boats up to 120 feet. Slips can be rented by the day, week, month or long-term. Boat and jet ski rentals by Shorebird are available right at the marina. The hotel is within walking distance of New Bern's downtown area and historic sites.

DAYS INN

925 Broad St.   636-0150
$$ (800) 329-7466

Recently refurbished, New Bern's 110-room Days Inn offers guests tastefully appointed units, an outside pool and a deluxe continental breakfast. Conveniently onsite is the delightful restaurant and lounge, the Broad Street Bar & Grille. The inn is only two blocks from Tryon Palace and New Bern's historic downtown district. A large banquet room can accommodate 300 guests, and smaller conference facilities are available to accommodate conventions, workshops or family functions of any size. Laundry service and free local calls are offered to guests, and historic walking tours and golf packages can be arranged.

FAIRFIELD HARBOUR

750 Broad Creek Rd.   638-8011
Variable rates

Any of Fairfield Harbour's 237 time-share units is available for rent. Units range in size from a small condominium for two to a two- or three-story house that can accommodate eight guests. Units can be reserved on a weekly basis through area real estate offices or on a month-long basis at the onsite Fairfield Realty office. Renting guests are offered a full range of recreational amenities. Fairfield Harbour features two golf courses, a country club with an outdoor pool, nine tennis courts, a recreation center with an indoor and outdoor pool, an exercise room, a game room, video rental and miniature golf. For those activities requiring a fee, Fairfield guests receive a reduced rate.

HAMPTON INN

200 Hotel Dr.   637-2111
$-$$ (800) 448-8288

Off U.S. 17 at the U.S. 70 bypass, this new, modern, 101-room hotel opened in May 1993. Tastefully furnished like other hotels in its chain, it is equipped with a pool and Jacuzzi, an exercise room and meeting facilities. It also offers free local calls and free in-room movies; 75 percent of its rooms are designated for nonsmoking guests. Guests on the go are offered a free continental breakfast or may dine at one of many nearby restaurants. Twin Rivers Shopping Mall is just across the highway. Golf packages can be arranged, and tour packages of New Bern's historic district, which is about 3 miles from the hotel, can be arranged by the hotel staff. Government discount rates are offered, and the hotel has a special third-and-fourth-adults-stay-free plan. Children stay free with their parents.

HARMONY HOUSE INN

215 Pollock St.	*636-3810*
$$-$$$	*(800) 636-3113*

The rocking chairs and swing on the long front porch and the two front doors (you'll see what we mean) distinguish this Greek Revival-style bed and breakfast in the downtown historic district from all others. The original part of the house was built sometime before 1809. Additions and porches were added and, around the turn of this century, the house was sawed in half and the west side was moved nine feet to accommodate a new hallway and staircase. The inn now has nine guest rooms and one romantic suite, all furnished with antiques and reproductions. All rooms have private baths and decorative fireplaces. A full breakfast, which may include house specialties such as orange French toast, stuffed pancakes, egg and bacon casserole and fresh-baked coffeecake, is served each morning in the dining room. A social hour is hosted each evening offering guests a selection of beverages, and before bed, a glass of sherry or port wine is available.

KING'S ARMS INN

212 Pollock St.   *638-4409*
$$$ *(800) 872-9306*

Built in 1847, the King's Arms Inn was a private residence until 1980 when it was established as Colonial Inn, New Bern's first bed and breakfast. Named for a New Bern tavern said to have hosted members of the First Continental Congress, King's Arms has nine guest rooms, each with television, telephone, private bath and furnished with antiques and reproductions. Breakfast is served in-room and includes cinnamon coffee, specialty teas or juice and home-baked breads, muffins and fresh fruit. Complimentary soft drinks and home-baked treats are always on hand, and the hosts happily make arrangements and reservations for their guests to enjoy the best of New Bern.

THE MAGNOLIA HOUSE

315 George St.   *633-9488*
$$$

Formerly the Margaret M. Hanff House, c. 1870-1889, the Charleston-pink bed and breakfast inn is just a stone's throw from Tryon Palace and within walking distance of the town's center and waterfront. Hosts Don and Kim Trudo offer three cozy guest rooms, each with its own decor including one room decorated with pieces from the East Lake period when the house was built. Rooms are fully heated and cooled and have private baths. House furnishings include family treasures, locally gathered antiques, estate pieces and local art. An onsite gift shop makes antique finds available to guests or anyone who catches the antique bug while in New Bern. Guests are welcomed into each morning with fresh-baked breads and muffins, seasonal fruits and fresh-ground coffees. Afternoon tea with scones, tarts and finger sandwiches is served at 4 PM.

NEW BERNE HOUSE INN

709 Broad St.   *636-2250*
$$ *(800) 842-7688*

This Colonial Revival-style bed and breakfast is about a block from the Tryon Palace Complex. Among the furnishings in the seven guest rooms is a notorious brass bed said to have been rescued from a burning brothel in 1897. All rooms are air-conditioned and have private baths and telephones. Rooms accommodate two people and are furnished with either twin, queen or king beds. Lounging is encouraged in the front porch swing. Refreshments and beverages are served, and guests are treated to a full, home-cooked breakfast. The house library is always open, and a tandem bicycle is available for those who enjoy leisurely cycling around town. The inn also conducts monthly mystery weekends, which have proven to be great fun for both the innkeepers and their guests.

PALACE MOTEL

Hwy. 17 S.   *638-1151*
$

Long a mainstay for New Bern travelers, the 66-room economy Palace Motel has a pool and full-service restaurant that features homestyle Southern cook-

ing. All rooms have telephones, and televisions are cable- and HBO-equipped. Guests here will need transportation to see area attractions.

RAMADA INN WATERFRONT AND MARINA

101 Howell Rd.   636-3637
$-$$ (800) 228-2828

One of the newer hotels in New Bern, the 112-room Ramada is across the Trent River from the city's downtown area. All rooms offer water views, have in-room coffee makers and complimentary fruit baskets. The Ramada also offers four suites with Jacuzzis. The Ramada Steakhouse specializes in certified Angus beef, and Sinbad's Bar and Grill lounge has an expansive, covered, outdoor deck patio. Both eateries provide lovely waterfront views. The hotel has a swimming pool. For boaters, a 150-slip floating dock

marina comes complete with showers, phone hookups, electricity, lock boxes, cable and HBO hookups. Dockage is offered for transients, as well as for longer stays of a week, month or even a year.

THE SHERATON GRAND NEW BERN HOTEL AND MARINA

1 Bicentennial Park   638-3585
$$-$$$ (800) 326-3745

One of the attractions of this downtown riverside hotel on the Trent River is that all rooms are waterfront. One hundred guest rooms are all appointed in the Sheraton tradition and overlook the Trent River and the hotel's marina. A new addition recently added 72 guest rooms, suites and mini-suites in the style of grand Southern inns. The inn is attached to the hotel via a covered walkway and offers guests both waterfront and city-side views.

The inn addition has an executive level made up entirely of suites. To serve the hotel and inn, two restaurants and two lounges offer dining and relaxing. Latitude 35 overlooks the marina and features full breakfast, lunch and dinner menus spotlighting the chef's signature entrees. The City Side Cafe offers casual dining and a lighter menu and features live entertainment. The Pro Sail Lounge is a great place for a relaxed day's end, and the Quarterdeck Gazebo & Bar extends the night under the stars with outdoor entertainment. The Sheraton has ample meeting facilities, a swimming pool an exercise room and boat and bike rentals. Golf and tennis privileges at area clubs can be included in your stay. Group rates are available.

VACATION RESORTS INTERNATIONAL
Broad Creek Rd.   *633-1151*
Variable rates

A professional management company since 1964, Vacation Resorts International is new to the Fairfield Harbour community this year (see earlier writeup in this chapter) and offers fully furnished one- to three-bedroom condominiums on a daily, weekly or monthly basis. All units at Fairfield Harbour will accommodate six to eight people, and all units are on one of the two 18-hole golf courses in the development. Guests are extended all development amenities including the 300-slip marina, rental boats, country club with restaurant, three swimming pools and two golf courses. For rentals on a daily basis, a minimum of three days is required.

ZIEGLER MOTEL
1914 Trent Blvd.   *637-4498*
$

Set amid a virtual forest of dogwoods and azaleas one block off U.S. 17 S., this neat, clean, 11-room, family-run motel offers modest accommodations. Two cottages are also available. It is in a primarily residential section of town, and transportation will be necessary to visit area attractions.

New Bern
Camping

If you enjoy communing with nature, you can rough it or do it with some flair in the New Bern area. Just north of New Bern on U.S. 17 is a commercial campground that welcomes your stay and will help entertain you. East of town off U.S. 70 is Croatan National Forest, which has several camping areas and an additional campground farther down the highway close to Cape Carteret off N.C. 58. Primitive camping is allowed anywhere in the national forest except in picnic areas and parking lots.

The forest service camping facilities have been recently upgraded, and most can now accommodate any size recreational vehicle. For a more complete discussion of the Croatan National Forest, see our Crystal Coast Attractions chapter. For camping information, call forest headquarters, 638-5628, or stop in and pick up a camping areas map at the ranger station on Fisher Avenue 9 miles south of New Bern off Highway 70 E.

NEUSE RIVER CAMPGROUND
Hwy. 17 N., Bridgeton   638-2556

This campground, about 3 miles north of New Bern, is the kind of place you can't miss. Small rustic cabins, a miniature golf course and colorful animal creations all but pull you off the highway. The back side of the park, which has about 80 spaces for visitors, is on the Neuse River. Some camp sites are specially designed for tents, while others have full RV hookups. The campground provides a comfort station, laundry, dump station, outdoor theater, pizza and sub shop, indoor arcade, dance floor and jukebox, boat ramp and swimming pool. A man-made swimming lake, surrounded

Photo: Scott Taylor

Lazy summer days seem to last forever.

by a white sandy beach and filled with treated water, awaits your leisure. It is open year round with fees ranging from $15 to $17.50 per night. The busiest months are April, July and October.

FISHERS LANDING

Croatan National Forest
Hwy. 70 E., Riverdale   638-5628

Perched on a bluff above the Neuse River about 8 miles south of New Bern, Fishers Landing can be reached by turning left across U.S. 70 E. at the Riverdale Mini-Mart. This recreation area offers only the barest of man-made amenities, but what it lacks in creature comforts is more than compensated for by the chance to be among some unusual creatures. Take an early morning walk along the crescent-shaped sandy beach, which is accessible by wooden stairs set into the cliff, and you'll see ospreys, egrets, sea gulls and herons. Between the small parking lot and the bluff is a wide, grassy area, backed by a row of trees. The river is swimmable, but shoes are suggested for protection against rocks and tree stumps on the bottom. The site offers unimproved walk-in camping and picnicking, non-flush toilets, grills, drinking water and picnic tables. It is open year round, and there are nondeveloped trails for exploring the thick surrounding forest.

NEUSE RIVER
CROATAN NATIONAL FOREST

Hwy. 70 E.   638-5628

Locally known as Flanner's Beach, this area is 10 miles south of New Bern on secondary N.C. Highway 1107, Flanner's Beach Road. Twenty-four camp sites are available plus picnicking facilities, a bathhouse, swimming, hiking, fishing, flush toilets and a dump station. Fees are $8 per site per night. The area is normally open April through October; however, that is subject to change at the beginning and end of each specified season. This recreation area is a favorite of locals.

CEDAR POINT

Croatan National Forest
Cape Carteret   638-5628

On the White Oak River a mile north of Cape Carteret (follow signs from N.C. 58), this area is a bit of a drive from New Bern. But, it is a good stopover if you want to experience a coastal marsh and maritime forest in their truest forms. The site offers 41 camp units, picnicking, drinking water, toilets, electric hookups, a shower building and an unimproved boat ramp. It is well suited for group camping and has an interpretive nature trail nearby that winds through hardwood and pine forests. Boardwalks cross marshes and open water, and viewing blinds are set up for bird watching. Camp fees are $15 per night. Formerly open year round, this camping area now closes for the winter and is open April through October.

NEUSIOK TRAIL

Croatan National Forest   638-5628

This area is strictly for those who enjoy roughing it. There are no camping

---

Insiders' Tips

Camping in boat ramp areas is discouraged by the park service in an effort to keep these areas easily accessible to launch for day fishing and boating. Please camp outside the parking areas.

facilities along the trail, but you may primitive camp if you pack out your garbage. You will need to bring along drinking water and wear boots to cross wet areas. The trail begins on the Newport River and ends on the Neuse River at Pinecliff Recreation Area. It passes through pine and hardwood forests and interesting areas of pocosin and dense titi brush. The total length of the trail is approximately 21 miles, and it crosses several paved and non-paved roads. Because of biting, stinging and zinging insects, fall, winter and early spring are best for camping and hiking.

Catfish Lake and Great Lake allow additional primitive camping. Boat ramps are available at Brice's Creek, Cahooque Creek and Haywood Landing. These popular areas are favored for their natural beauty and handy access to water; however, insects can be prolific in the summer months. For directions to these areas, call forest headquarters or stop in and pick up a map at the ranger station on Fisher Avenue.

Discover New Bern

© Janet Francoeur
P.O. Box 3544, New Bern, NC 28564

Hearne's Jewelers
The Store That Combines Courtesy With Integrety

Fine Jewelry & Watches · 14K Gold Jewelry
Jewelry & Watch Repair · Remounting
22 Years Of Service

Mike Hearne   Jimmy Hearne
Rivertowne Square, New Bern, North Carolina
(919) 637-2784

A fine art & fibers studio/gallery
Your made in North Carolina Gift Headquarters
Owned & operated by 5 New Bern artists & craftspeople

226 Middle Street - Downtown New Bern - 919-633-4369

Featuring Original Art and
Souvenirs worth framing
Also Stained Glass, Weaving,
Stenciling, Specialty Foods
and Hand Thrown Pottery.

Hours - Monday - Saturday 10-5:30 - Sunday 11-3

Drawing © Janet Francoeur - Artist in Residence

New Bern
Shopping

New Bern offers a variety of shopping opportunities from large department stores to unique shops and boutiques.

Twin Rivers Mall has about 55 stores, making it the largest collection of stores under one roof in town. At the junction of U.S. 17 and U.S. 70, the mall is anchored by Belk, JCPenney and Kmart. Nearby is **Rivertowne Square** with Wal-Mart and Brendles as anchors, and **Berne Square** with Roses and Kerr Drug as anchors.

As downtown New Bern continues to develop and grow, so do the shopping opportunities. Looking at the downtown shops today, it is hard to imagine that in the mid-1970s stores were vacant.

Scattered along Pollock Street near Tryon Palace and through downtown, a selection of shops exists that should make anyone's must-shop list. The experience is known as The Governor's Walk. We've highlighted just a few of the shops on the walk and a few others in the area. These shops are certainly not the totality of the New Bern shopping experience. But they'll whet your shopping appetite. Antique shops are featured at the end of this section.

ELUSIVE TREASURES
301 Pollock St.   *633-1556*

Elusive Treasures is the place for custom-crafted gemstone jewelry. Patrons will find an intriguing collection of jewelry as well as home and office decorations created from earth's natural treasures: minerals, fossils, geodes and collector gemstones. The shop craftsmen can create custom jewelry in sterling silver, gold (10, 14, 18, 22 or 24 karat) and platinum and can wire-wrap jewelry, crystal or glass jewelry. Stop by to have that special piece designed and crafted. The shop also has "Jewelry Hospital" with on-premises services such as ring sizing, polishing and cleaning, prong repair, remounts, chain repairs, stone replacement, and bead or pearl restringing.

CAROLINA CREATIONS
226 Middle St.   *633-4369*

Carolina Creations is a combination of many things and is the favorite store of many Insiders. It is a weaving studio, knit shop, art studio and gallery. Weavers, spinners and knitters will find looms and spinning wheels as well as a wonderful selection of fibers, including silk, cotton, linen, rayon and wool. There is also plenty of spun yarn ready for use and cross-stitch supplies and patterns. North Carolina pottery is featured along with beautiful stained glass creations. Ink drawings and watercolor pieces depict New Bern and other areas. The shop offers some classes.

HEARNE'S JEWELERS
256 Middle St.
and Rivertowne Sq.   *637-4590, 637-2784*

Hearne's Jewelers offers quality men's and women's jewelry and is a trusted, well-established company. Founded in 1972 by father Mickey Hearne, the business combines courtesy with integrity. Hearne's offers exquisite rings, earrings, necklaces and bracelets, as well as a fine line of watches including those made by Seiko and Citizen. This is also the place to go for jewelry repairs, remounts and watch repairs. Stop by one of Hearne's two locations before you make your next jewelry selection, and let the friendly staff members assist you.

SAINTS' CREATIONS
809 Pollock St.   *638-6775*

This shop is in the beautiful old All Saints Chapel and is run and staffed by volunteers from the New Bern Historical Society. The shop features original handcrafted gifts by area artisans. There are paintings, prints, note cards, gifts and sometimes a decoy or two.

TRYON PALACE
GIFT AND GARDEN SHOPS
613 Pollock St.   *638-1560*

With two separate stores, one featuring New Bern and Colonial memorabilia and gift items, and the other devoted totally to garden things, the Palace Shops shouldn't be missed. The gift shop faces Pollock Street, and the garden shop is on the palace grounds. Insider gardeners visit the Garden Shop every spring to get old-time plants and herbs that are hard to find elsewhere.

CRAFTER'S EMPORIUM
210 Craven Street   *514-9400*

This shop offers a collection of work by area artists and craftsmen. Although the shop appears small from the outside, one step inside reveals otherwise. Shoppers will find ceramics, wood crafts, needlework, paintings, nautical items, notecards, baskets, clothing items, jewelry and many supplies.

TRENT RIVER COFFEE COMPANY
208 Craven Street   *514-2030*

For coffee, tea and espresso, this is

the place. Come sit down, relax and enjoy a hot cup of fresh brew. There are also Italian sodas, gifts, fresh coffee beans and more.

HILL'S
219 Middle St.   *633-3773,633-3774*

Hill's was established in 1910 and is a quality men's haberdashery and ladies' specialty shop. Hill's offers the finest in men's and ladies' styling from the traditional to the unique. They're open from 9 AM to 5:30 PM Monday through Saturday.

THE FOUR C'S
252 Middle St.   *636-3285*

The Four C's is a trail and nature shop offering active outdoor wear for women and men and gifts. They carry Patagonia and Atlantis clothing as well as Teva Sandals. You'll find New Bern T-shirts, books, cards, kites, jewelry, and a nice selection of duffle bags and totes. For imaginative gifts of all sorts, make sure you drop by for a look.

CAPTAIN RATTY'S GEAR & GIFTS
202 Middle St.   *633-2088*

If you're looking for a particularly memorable gift for a friend who is into sailing, stop at Captain Ratty's. They have marvelous seagoing gifts, unusual souvenirs from New Bern, Weems and Plath marine clocks, lanterns and instruments, antique charts and prints. Captain Ratty's also carries High Seas and Henry Lloyd foul-weather gear. This is also the place to shop for your Sunday morning, out-of-town newspapers.

BRYANT-McLEOD LTD.
321 Pollock St.   *638-2333*

Long a fixture of downtown New Bern, this fine men's store features haberdashery for gentlemen. Mono-

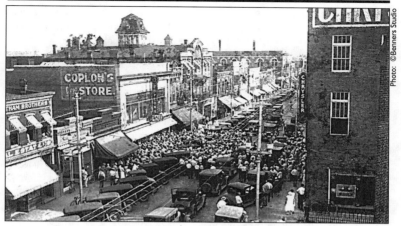

Photo: ©Benners Studio

Every so often one of the stores in New Bern would hold a sale no one wanted to miss.

gramming, tailoring and free gift wrapping are all offered to customers.

BRANCH'S OF NEW BERN
309 Pollock St.   *638-5171*

Branch's is really much more than the office supply store it appears to be. Among the fine gift items on display are David Winter cottages, Baldwin brass and Tom Clark figurines. There is also a wonderful selection of bird feeders and lawn and garden ornaments. Branch's has a sister store in Morehead City.

BERN BEAR GIFTS
303 Pollock St.   *637-2300*

New Bern is the only officially- designated daughter city of the mother, city Bern, Switzerland. This store reflects that relationship. The store carries Swiss, German, Austrian, North Carolina and New Bern imports, gifts and novelties. There are also flags from New Bern and the state, Swiss music boxes, German clocks and steins and Swiss Army knives. Patrons will also find Swiss chocolates.

FAVORITE GIFTS & THINGS
220 Craven St.   *633-5254*

In the old City Hall building, this shop features unique gifts and decorative accessories. Patrons will discover lovely lawn and garden accessories, bird feeders and supplies, children's items, educational books, gourmet food items and tasteful seasonal decorations.

MITCHELL HARDWARE
—SINCE 1898
215 Craven St.   *638-4261*

You have to experience this place. The window display is like a historical showing of farm and garden equipment. Step inside to find an eclectic offering of traditional hardware items in a turn-of-the-century setting. Mitchell's carries a complete line of hardware, garden and yard equipment, practical gifts, cast iron and enamel ware, garden seeds and bulbs. There is also a large country store section with everything from country hams to crockery and pottery.

BACKYARD BEARS
718 Pollock St.   637-7122

This is the perfect shop for a teddy bear lover. Inside you will find teddy bears for all ages along with limited editions, collectibles and gifts. Plus, the gourmet country fudge is sure to please everyone. The shop also features 3-D windsocks, unique greeting cards and more.

FARMER'S MARKET
421 Tryon Palace Dr.

Housed in a new building, the Farmer's Market is the place to go for fresh vegetables and fruits, seafood, flowers and crafts. The market is located between Middle Street and Tryon Palace.

COOKS & CONNOISSEURS
3310 Trent Rd.   633-2665 (COOK)

This is a wonderful specialty food store that offers gourmet and international foods from around the world. Visitors will find a variety of coffees, 40+ varieties of cheese, unique and necessary cooking tools and an extensive selection of wines and beers. Gift baskets can be prepared for that special friend, and fresh bread, croissants, muffins and cookies are prepared daily. A cooking school is also offered.

NEW BERN NET & CRAFT SUPPLIES
2703 Hwy. 70 E.   633-2226

New Bern Net & Craft Supplies offers a variety of items. Shoppers will find basket weaving supplies, a full line of craft supplies along with handcrafted Indian jewelry and Indian craft supplies. New Bern Net also sells gill nets ready to fish and tackle and sport fishing supplies.

TURNER TOLSEN
3302 Clarendon Blvd.   638-2121

Turner Tolsen offers fine furnishings for the home or office as well as outdoor furniture, accessories and a gift gallery. Let the designers consult with you to create that special look.

Antiques

New Bern offers plenty of antique shops to nose around in and discover lost treasures. We've included just a few to whet your appetite. The New Bern Preservation Foundation hosts an antique show each year, usually in May, that features invited dealers. For more information, contact the Foundation, P.O. Box 207, New Bern 28563, 633-6448.

POLLOCK GALLERY
250 Middle Street   637-7232

Pollock Gallery specializes in American and English antiques and gifts of distinction. Shoppers will find china, porcelain, silver, linens and art.

SEAPORT ANTIQUE MARKET OF NEW BERN
504 Tryon Palace Dr.   637-5050

This is a multi-dealer shop specializing in quality antiques and collectibles. The antique market is a great place to browse and look at all the treasures.

WILL GORGES ANTIQUES & CIVIL WAR ITEMS
308 Simmons St.   636-3039

Run by Will Gorges, a Civil War buff himself, this shop has just about everything in the way of memorabilia and collectibles from the Civil War. There are all kinds of authentic Civil War memorabilia, including muskets, pistols, uniforms, books and other items. Will Gorges also operates the Civil War Museum on Metcalf Street.

MIDDLE STREET FLEA MARKET
329 Middle St.   *638-1685*

Visit Middle Street Flea Market and you'll find dealers that offer a lot of good stuff. The market features antiques, collectibles, furniture, silver, china, some jewelry and lots more. The market also buys items.

OLDE VARIETY FLEA MARKET
Hwy. 70 E.   *633-5558*

This market is beside the Trent Olds-Cadillac dealership east of town on Highway 70. Inside, shoppers will find booths filled with the wares of about 20 dealers. There are antiques and collectibles, reproduction furniture, household accessories, clocks, jewelry, paintings, sports cards and country collectibles. The shop also buys items.

POOR CHARLIE'S
FLEA MARKET & ANTIQUES
206 Hancock St.   *638-2798*

Poor Charlie's features 17 dealers with booths offering just about everything a shopper could imagine. An old warehouse houses the booths and gives shoppers a feeling of an old-style market. Patrons will find reproduction furniture, household accessories and lots of nostalgic items.

TOM'S COINS AND ANTIQUES
244 Middle St.   *633-0615*

As the name implies, Tom's offers coins and antiques of all types, and much more. The shop has beautiful antique and reproduction furniture, estate jewelry, stamps and sports cards. There are lots of nostalgic items and collectibles.

THE ANTIQUE DEPOT
626 Hancock St.   *636-5322*

The Antique Depot offers household items, antique and reproduction furniture, old jewelry, china and glassware on consignment.

NEARLY OLDE SHOPPE
501 Tryon Palace Dr.   *No phone*

The Nearly Olde Shoppe is filled with antiques, almost antiques and those unique items that you only see once in a long while. The shop also buys items.

Photo: Kenny Barrow

This ancient fire engine can be seen at the Fireman's Museum.

New Bern
Attractions

The importance of history to New Bern cannot be overemphasized. What exists today is attributable to a history that predates the founding of America by Europeans.

Shortly after its settlement in 1710, New Bern was nearly wiped out by Tuscarora Indians. Gradually the Indians were forced to move inland and New Bern, with its ideal location at the confluence of the Neuse and Trent rivers, began to flourish as a farming and shipping community.

The city soon became an important port, exporting naval stores and later tobacco and cotton. The captains of the ships that hauled these high-demand products used the spires of New Bern's churches to guide them up the Neuse River, which at the time had few navigational aids or other landmarks. Several of the older homes have "widows' walks" projecting above the roofs, where wives would watch for their husbands' ships returning from long sea voyages.

Pirates also found the dark coves and creeks along the rivers ideal for subversive activities and, of course, for hiding treasures. Blackbeard is supposed to have stayed in a huge house by the Neuse, where he planned his raids on oceangoing ships carrying rich cargo between the American colonies, England and the West Indies.

New Bern can credit its gentility to the once-thriving area plantations that produced exportable products to be shipped around the world. The planta-

tions themselves often became small cities, but today little remains of the beautiful estates that depended on the dark waters of the Neuse and Trent rivers for livelihoods. What does remain are the moss-hung oak and cypress trees guarding the many creeks and slews along the winding Trent and broad Neuse. Like other cities, New Bern endured the pangs of growth and change, eventually developing a character all its own. It did not, however, forget its past.

History taught New Bern many hard lessons, one of which was to value its heritage. To that end, a great number of old homes and churches have been restored, and, in cases of potential loss, relocated, thanks to groups such as the New Bern Preservation Foundation. Salvaged structures now number more than 150, and restoration efforts are ongoing.

While the historical museums, homes and buildings are the focal point of New Bern, there are additional attractions in the river city and surrounding area. A growing community of reputable artists grace New Bern with their work, which is often exhibited at the Bank of the Arts, the public library, ART Gallery Ltd., Carolina Creations, City Art Works and in the town's public buildings.

Because of its cultural activities, New Bern was known as "the Athens of North Carolina" in the first quarter of this century, a title it is working to regain today. Fine antique and art shops have opened in recent years, and browsers are always welcome. Not listed in any of the guidebooks (except this one) but known to New Bernians are its churches, each distinctive and worthy of a sightseeing visit. For a listing of historic churches and other houses of worship, see our New Bern Places of Worship chapter.

Of the area's seven historic houses of worship, it is perhaps Christ Episcopal Church on Pollock Street that has the most interesting lore. Included in the church's regalia is a silver communion service donated by King George II. The service survived two fires and reconstruction but, according to local history, was stolen in the 1960s or '70s. The thief, so goes the tale, fenced it with a man who recognized it for what it was and returned it to the church.

In addition to the official sights of New Bern, walking tours of the historic district are very popular. Sites open to the public center on the town's history; however, many of the historic homes are private residences and are closed to the public. Nonetheless, walking the streets and viewing the architecture and landscapes of these grand old homes will truly give you the feel of the city's Colonial heritage.

Most attractions are within walking distance of each other, and we have listed a number of the sites here. For a detailed walking map and description of the more than 100 historic locations, let your first stop be the **Craven County Convention and Visitors Bureau**, 219 Pollock Street, or call 637-9400 or (800) 437-5767. Everyone there is very helpful with orienting you to their town. Hours are 8 AM to 5 PM Monday through Friday; 10 AM to 5 PM, Saturday; and 1 to 4 PM, Sunday.

For those who enjoy the woodlands as well as the city, nearby **Croatan National Forest** provides a close-up look at coastal marshes, estuaries and maritime forests. The 157,000-acre preserve is home to insectivorous plants, unique wildflowers, marsh and shorebirds and a variety of forest animals such as black bear, alligators, deer and wild turkey. Forest hiking trails and overnight campsites are popular with nature lovers. For a detailed discussion, see our Crystal Coast Attractions chapter.

TRYON PALACE
HISTORIC SITES AND GARDENS
Pollock and George Sts.   638-1560

Tryon Palace, built in 1770 by Colonial Gov. William Tryon, was known at the time as one of the most beautiful buildings in America. The elegant, Georgian-style mansion is mostly a reconstruction of the original building that stood at the same site. After its use both as a colonial and state capitol, the palace fell into grave disrepair. At the time the reconstruction was undertaken in the 1950s, only one wing — the stables — remained standing. The palace now houses an outstanding collection of antiques and art, and the grounds are devoted to extensive landscaping, ranging from English formal gardens and a kitchen garden to wilderness garden areas.

Included as part of the main palace complex are the John Wright Stanly House (1783) on George Street and the Dixon-Stevenson House (1828) on Pollock Street. The Stanly home, which was originally on New Street and moved to its present location in the early 1960s, was built by a Revolutionary War patriot who entertained George Washington on two occasions. The Dixon-Stevenson House is a prominent Federal-style home noted for its rare neoclassical antiques. The palace also has dominion of the New Bern Academy Museum at New and Hancock streets.

Historical re-enactments supplement the daily palace and garden tours during special times in the summer months. Annual events include the colorful Christmas Celebration tours in December, Decorative Arts Symposium in March, Gardener's Weekend during New Bern's Spring Historic Homes and Gardens Tour in April, King George III's Birthday and Festival of Colonial Life in June, Independence Day Celebration, the Chrysanthemum Festival in October and monthly Garden Workshops offered year round. Cooking, blacksmithing and weaving are among regular craft demonstrations. The palace gift shop in the Daves House and the crafts and garden shop behind the palace east wing are open daily. An audiovisual orientation program is shown at the visitor center for all guests.

The palace is open year round from 9:30 AM to 4 PM Monday through Saturday and from 1:30 to 4 PM on Sunday. The last tour begins at 4 PM. A number of tour options are available including two-day and annual passes, and group discounts are extended to prearranged groups of 20 or more. For current price information or group reservations, call (800) 767-1560 or 514-4900. The historic sites and gardens are partially equipped for handicapped visitors.

John Wright Stanly House
307 George St.   *638-1560*

On his Southern tour in 1791, President George Washington dined and danced at Tryon Palace, but his two nights in New Bern were spent at the nearby home of John Wright Stanly. Washington described his overnight accommodation as "exceeding good lodgings."

During the Revolutionary War, Stanly's merchant ships plied the waters as privateers, capturing British ships to aid the American cause. The elegance of Stanly's house, built in the early 1780s, reflects the wealth of its owner. Distinctive American furniture of the period complements the elegant interior woodwork, and Stanly family history provides a fascinating chronicle of father and son, epidemic and duel, war and wealth. Admission is charged as part of the Tryon Palace Complex admission.

Dixon-Stevenson House
609 Pollock St.   *638-1560*

Erected in 1828 on a lot that was originally a part of Tryon Palace's garden, the Dixon-Stevenson House epitomizes New Bern's lifestyle in the first half of the 19th century when the town was a prosperous port and one of the state's largest cities.

The house, built for a New Bern mayor, is a fine example of neoclassical architecture. Its furnishings, reflecting the Federal period, reveal the changing tastes of early America. At the rear of the house is a garden with seasonal flowers, all in white. When Union troops occupied New Bern during the Civil War, the house was converted to a regimental hospital. Admission is charged as part of the Tryon Palace Complex admission.

The Attmore-Oliver House
511 Broad St.   *638-8558*
Parking entrance on Pollock St.

Built in 1790 by prominent New Bernian Samuel Chapman, the Attmore-Oliver House today is the home of the New Bern Historical Society. It was enlarged to its present size in 1834 and houses 18th- and 19th-century antiques, a doll collection and Civil War memorabilia. Of particular interest is the fine Greek Revival portico and two-story porches at the rear of the house. It is open seasonally Tuesday through Saturday from 1 to 4:30 PM and at other times by appointment. It closes from mid-December through the end of March. The house may be reserved for private functions and is not handicapped accessible.

WALKING TOUR ATTRACTIONS

As mentioned earlier, a number of New Bern's historic homes are private residences; however, a leisurely stroll along river walks through the historic district will allow you to observe the landscapes, architecture and gardens of these vintage homes. Walking will give you a real sense of the many Old World customs that characterize this Colonial town. Self-guiding brochures are available at the Visitors Bureau at 219 Pollock Street. Guided walking tours, organized by New Bern Tours, 637-7316, for six or more people, depart from the Commission House across from the Tryon Palace gate. A few of the more noted residences and buildings are listed here.

The **John Horner Hill House**, 713 Pollock Street, is a Georgian period dwelling built between 1770 and 1780. It is noted for its rare nine-over-nine sash at the first-floor windows.

The **Henry H. Harris House**, 718 Pollock Street, was built in 1800 and is a well-preserved example of vernacular Federal period architecture.

The **Anne Green Lane House**, 804 Pollock Street, is a transitional late Georgian-early Federal period house built between 1790 and 1800. It was remodeled during the Victorian period.

The **All Saints Chapel**, 809 Pollock Street, is a good example of Gothic-style architecture. It was built c. 1895 as a mission chapel by Christ Episcopal Church.

The **John H. Jones House**, 819 Pollock Street, is a small Federal-period house with an unusual central chimney. Its original separate kitchen remains at the rear.

The **White House** at 422 Johnson Street is a simple sidehall Federal house built c.1820-1830. It is noted for its two end chimneys with a small closet in between.

The **Cutting-Allen House**, 518 New Street, is a transitional late Georgian-early Federal period sidehall house built in 1793. It is considered unusual because of its flanking wings and large rear ballroom. It was saved from demolition in 1980 and moved to its present location.

The **Hawks House** at New Street at Metcalf offers a side-by-side comparison of styles. Dating from the 1760s, the western part of the house is Georgian, and the eastern section is Federal, added by Francis Hawks, son of John Hawks, architect of Tryon Palace.

The **Clark-Taylor House**, 419 Metcalf Street, was built between 1795 and 1804. It is one of several gambrel-roofed houses in the historic district.

The **Attmore-Wadsworth House**, 515 Broad Street, is an unusual one-story Italianate-style house built c. 1855. Several Italianate-style homes are part of the city's historic architecture.

The **McLin-Hancock House**, 507 Middle Street, is unique for its strict symmetry and diminutive scale.

The **W.B. Blades House**, 602 Middle Street, was built in 1903 and is noted for its elaborate Queen Ann design.

The **Jerkins-Duffy House**, 301 Johnson Street, was built c. 1830 and is unusual because of its exterior Federal design and interior Greek Revival elements. It is also noted for its captain's walk and exposed-face chimneys.

The **George Slover House**, 209 Johnson Street, was built c. 1890 and is an eclectic combination of Queen Anne and shingle-style architectures.

The **Charles Slover House**, 201 Johnson Street, is a stately brick townhouse built in 1847 and was selected as headquarters by Gen. Ambrose Burnside during the Civil War. It was purchased in 1908 by C. D. Bradham, inventor of "Brad's Drink," now known as Pepsi-Cola.

The **Eli Smallwood House**, 524 E. Front Street, is one of the finest of New Bern's Federal-period brick sidehall houses, built c. 1810. It is noted for its handsome portico and elegant interior woodwork.

The **Dawson-Clarke House**, 519 E. Front Street, was built c. 1808 and is one of several historic homes exhibiting the use of double porches, a popular style in the coastal region.

The **Coor-Gaston House**, 421 Craven Street, is a Georgian home c. 1770 built by architect, builder and patriot-statesman James Coor. It was purchased in 1818 by Judge William Gaston and was the scene of the founding of St. Paul's Roman Catholic Church. Gaston was a brilliant orator, lawyer, member of Congress, State Justice and author of the state song.

The **David F. Jarvis House**, 220 Pollock Street, is good example of Neoclassical Revival architecture.

The **Edward R. Stanly House and Dependency**, 502 Pollock Street, was built c. 1849 in Renaissance Revival style. The cast-iron grills over its windows are unique in New Bern.

The **Wade House**, 214 Tryon Palace Drive, was built in 1843 and remodeled before 1885 in the Second Empire style. The cast iron crest on the mansard roof and the iron fence are notable surviving features.

THE NEW BERN ACADEMY MUSEUM
New and Hancock Sts.   *638-1560*

New Bern Academy, founded in 1764, is the oldest public school in North Carolina and one of the oldest in America. It was used as a school recently enough to still be remembered by a number of residents.

After it closed, it sat vacant for several decades. In the 1980s, it was purchased and renovated by Tryon Palace and today houses exhibits focusing on early education, architecture and the story of New Bern as a Union-occupied city in the midst of the Confederacy.

The Academy Museum is open daily. Admission is charged as part of the Tryon Palace Complex admission.

BELLAIR PLANTATION AND RESTORATION
1100 Washington Post Rd., Hwy. 43 N. 637-3913

The last and largest brick plantation country house of the 18th century in North Carolina, the Bellair Plantation (c. 1734) is a majestic three-story brick building approached from Highway 43 N. by two long driveways, one lined by lavish old cedars. Georgian handcrafted wood-

---

You haven't seen New Bern until you've meandered the residential streets in the historic district and along the waterfront.

Insiders' Tips

work greets visitors at the imposing eight-panelled door and continues through the main rooms. Original family furnishings are still in the house, probably because Bellair was specifically guarded from harm during the occupation of Federal Forces during the Civil War by order of Gen. Ambrose Burnside. The written order, dated March 20, 1862, still hangs on the wall at Bellair. The basement holds the cooking fireplaces with crane, tools and ironworks of the period. One-hour tours of the historical site are offered hourly from 1 to 5 PM Saturdays and Sundays. The last tour each day begins at 5 PM.

THE CIVIL WAR MUSEUM
301 Metcalf St.   *633-2818*

Opened in 1990, the New Bern Civil War Museum houses one of the finest in-depth private collections of Civil War memorabilia and weapons in the United States. Included are rare uniforms, battlefield artifacts and other items. Articles from the museum have been featured in Time-Life Books, *Mid-Atlantic* magazine and numerous other periodicals. In 1992, a display from the museum won Best in Show at the Old North State Civil War Exhibition. History buffs and Civil War scholars say it is a site not to be missed.

Less than a block from Tryon Palace, the museum is open from April 1 to September 30 from 10 AM to 4 PM Tuesday through Saturday. From October 1 to March 31, it is open weekends only from 11 AM to 4 PM. Admission is $2.50 for adults and $1.50 for students. The museum has a gift shop and access for people with handicaps.

BANK OF THE ARTS
317 Middle St.   *638-2787*

A former bank built in 1912, the interesting granite structure now serves as headquarters for the Craven Arts Council and Gallery. The classical facade of the building features Ionic columns leading into the open, two-story gallery. Detailed pilasters and Corinthian columns have been highlighted by colors in the Beaux-Arts motif. Changing exhibits of various media — painting, sculpture, photography, pottery, fiber art and other art forms — showcase the work of local and Southeastern regional artists. Many special events, such as concerts, lectures and receptions, are offered throughout the year.

Visitors are welcome to browse free at the Bank of the Arts, open Monday through Saturday from 10 AM to 5 PM. The arts building is handicapped accessible.

FARMER'S MARKET
421 Tryon Palace Dr.   *633-0043*

Bringing fresh local produce to downtown New Bern throughout the year, the Farmer's Market is a town treasure operated by the Cooperative Extension Service. From fruits to flowers and through the range of baked, canned and prepared goods, the Farmer's Market is a favorite stop, but you have to keep the days and hours in mind. From June 15 through September 15, days of operation are Tuesday, Thursday and Saturday from 6 AM to 1 PM. After September 15 and before June 15, the Farmer's Market is open Saturdays only, 6 AM to 1 PM.

THE FIREMAN'S MUSEUM
410 Hancock St.   *636-4087*

The New Bern fire company is one of the oldest in the country operating under its original charter. It is just behind the fire department's Broad Street headquarters and houses steam pumpers and an extensive collection of other early fire-fighting equipment. Also on exhibit are rare photos, Civil War relics and even the mounted head of faithful old fire horse, Fred, who died in his tracks while answering an alarm.

Museum hours are Tuesday through Saturday from 9:30 AM to noon and 1 to 5 PM, and on Sunday from 1 to 5 PM. The museum is open year round, except for a week around the Fourth of July and a week around Christmas. Admission is $2 for adults and $1 for children. The museum is handicapped accessible.

CEDAR GROVE CEMETERY
Queen and George Sts.

If you're one of those people who loves wandering through old graveyards, this is one you'll not want to miss. Statuary and monuments beneath Spanish moss-draped trees mark burial traditions from the earliest days of our nation. One smallish obelisk lists the names of nine children in one family who all died within a two-year time span. Although the causes of their deaths are not known, a disease of some sort is most probable. The city's monument to its Confederate dead and the graves of 70 soldiers are also here. The cemetery's main gate features a shell motif, with an accompanying legend that says if water drips on you as you enter, you will be the next to die.

BELLE OF NEW BERN
I Bicentennial Park   638-8800

Docked behind the Sheraton Hotel at Bicentennial Park, this authentic 150-passenger, 125-foot paddlewheel riverboat is quite a lady. The *Belle* cruises the Trent and Neuse rivers and is air-conditioned, heated and enclosed for year-round comfort. The paddlewheeler offers historical, dinner and private charter cruises, and

group rates are available. Reservations are required and must be confirmed by full payment of cash, check or credit card. Tickets are nonrefundable. The *Belle* sails on its historic cruises Tuesday through Sunday, departing the dock at 1 PM and returning at 2:30. Boarding begins at 12:30, and a snack bar on board offers sandwiches, sodas, beer and cocktails. Tickets are $7.95 plus tax for adults and $4.95 plus tax for kids younger than 12. Dinner cruises, which include entertainment and dancing, occur Thursday through Saturday. Departure is at 7 PM, and return time is about 10 PM. Dinner includes salad, entree, vegetables, dessert, coffee, tea and milk. A cash bar offers cocktails, beer and wine. Prepaid dinner reservations are required by 1 PM on cruise day and are nonrefundable. Tickets are $31.50 plus tax and gratuity. A Sunday buffet cruise for $19.95 departs at 1:30 PM for 2 hours. The *Belle's* office is in the lobby of the Sheraton Hotel and is open from 9 AM to 5 PM Tuesday through Saturday and by appointment on Sunday.

NEW BERN TROLLEY TOURS
Tryon Palace   637-7316
Pollock St.   (800) 849-7316

Touring the town by trolley is a comfortable and interesting alternative to a walking tour if you've arrived without your sneakers. Narrated 1½-hour tours depart Tryon Palace between April 1 and December 31 at 11 AM and 2 PM on most weekdays and at 2 PM on Sundays. Tours or charters for special groups or occasions may also be arranged. Professional guides narrate the tours with attention to historical and architectural interests and spice the narrative with folklore and local knowledge. Trolley tours are $10 for adults and $5 for children 12 and younger. For reservations and further information, call 637-7316 or (800)849-7316.

UNION POINT PARK

Tryon and E. Front Sts. 636-4660

This lovely waterfront park is often the site of outdoor activities and offers a welcome respite for weary visitors who want to take a load off their feet. Music is sometimes featured here. It is an excellent place to simply sit and watch the world float by. There are lovely river views, and the site is particularly pleasant for late evening sunset viewing. On-site facilities accommodate picnicking, boat launching and creature comforts.

CROATAN NATIONAL FOREST

141 E. Fisher Ave. 638-5628

Croatan National Forest is an expansive nature preserve bordered by New Bern, Morehead City and Cape Carteret. It is headquartered on Fisher Avenue, which is approximately 9 miles south of New Bern just off Highway 70 E. Well-placed road signs make the office easy to find.

Within the forest's boundaries are endangered animals and rare plants. Black bear, otter, deer, raptors and other forest creatures live in this coastal woodland. Insectivorous plants such as the Venus's-flytrap, butterworts, pitcher plants, sundews and bladderworts find the forest an ideal habitat and are protected by law. The forest is also well-known for its beautiful wildflowers. Pamphlets on the wildflowers and insectivorous plants are available at the Fisher Avenue headquarters. Because of the forest's coastal location, many unique features can be found here. Some of the ecosystems present include pocosins, longleaf and loblolly pine, bottomland and upland hardwoods. Sprinkled throughout the Croatan are 40 miles of streams and 4,300 acres of wild lakes.

The forest areas are excellent for hiking, swimming, boating, hunting, fishing and picnicking. Miles and miles of unpaved roads lace through the woodland, providing easy if sometimes roundabout access to its wilderness. Recreation areas are available for a day's outing or for longer visits. Camp fees vary, so call headquarters, 638-5628, for season rates.

Because the Croatan is so expansive and undeveloped, it is best to stop in at headquarters on Fisher Avenue and pick up a forest map before heading out. The best times for venturing into coastal woodlands are fall, winter or early spring. Summer can be very hot and buggy, so prepare yourself with insect repellent. Some forest areas are closed November through March. For more information on the Croatan National Forest, see the Crystal Coast Attractions chapter.

New Bern
Kidstuff

New Bern has always been a magical place. Maybe it's the confluence of rivers, or the climate, but it has held powerful attractions for Indians, explorers and pirates — and probably still does. It is only the most chosen of small towns that has a real palace where the townspeople keep up the shine and polish and make the gardens grow. So in such a town, it is not surprising that the children are also well nurtured and are offered much to learn and enjoy.

It is the magic of New Bern and the townsfolk that have given all the kids Kidsville, a wonderful fort and imaginative playground, and the udderly moovelous Cow Cafe. One of the best ways to see New Bern is as a child, or, at least, with one.

CHILDREN'S PERFORMING ARTS SERIES
Craven Arts Council
317 Middle St., New Bern   638-2577

This delightful, annually scheduled series is sponsored by the Craven Arts Council (see our New Bern Arts chapter), which stages whimsical dramas, puppetry and musicals especially to entertain, inform and involve children throughout the year. Call or write for particulars.

THE COW CAFE
301 Ave. C, New Bern   638-1131

Treat yourself, and take a kid, to the Cow Cafe at the Maola Milk and Ice Cream Company's processing plant. Inside is a window on the world of milk processing. You'll see everything a cow can be, from the cafe seats to the toilets, and through the imaginable range of gifts, snacks and lunches, which do *not* include

Kids love nothing more than dipping a net in the ocean and seeing what they can come up with.

Photo: NC Aquarium at Pine Knoll Shores

burgers, but do include hot dogs. It's hard to ignore the milk shakes and malts, but if you're limited to only one selection, take the Death By Chocolate. It's our choice of execution.

THE FIREMAN'S MUSEUM
410 Hancock St., New Bern   636-4087

Located behind the New Bern Fire Department's headquarters on Broad Street, the Fireman's Museum houses steam pumpers and other early fire-fighting equipment used by this fire department, which is one of the country's oldest. Rare photos, Civil War relics and the mounted head of Fred, the faithful fire horse who died while answering an alarm, are part of the collection. The museum is open Tuesday through Saturday from 9:30 AM to 5 PM and Sunday from 1 to 5 PM. See our New Bern Attractions chapter for further information.

KIDSVILLE PLAYGROUND
1225 Pine Tree Dr.   636-4061

Kidsville is a beautifully planned and constructed, active and interactive fort-like play environment that captivates both kids and adults. Next to the West New Bern Recreation Center on Pine Tree Drive near the intersection of U.S. 70 and N.C. 17, Kidsville is the product of the fund-raising efforts of two mothers and a town with enough heart to contribute all that was needed to make it real. Efforts in 1994 raised $100,000 for the necessary materials. All the labor and the location were contributed. With or without a kid, Kidsville merits a visit. If you choose to slide, climb or clamber through its interesting maze or spend your time taking note of the plaques naming the many contributors, Kidsville will wow you. You may arrange for large group visits by contacting the New Bern Parks and Recreation Department.

New Bern
Annual Events and Festivals

"The Athens of North Carolina" has been New Bern's fond and familiar epithet since Colonial times, and living up to it, the town does an Olympian job of entertaining and educating throughout the year. Tryon Palace hosts a variety of special events, and the Craven Arts Council and Gallery sponsors art exhibitions, music and dance performances year round. Sailing regattas take place all year. And, the city is known to throw itself a party at the drop of a hat.

Each year, New Bern hosts the Craven Concerts Series including an annual concert by the North Carolina Symphony, solo artists and dancers. Performance dates change with each year's calendar. The New Bern Civic Theater schedules a variety of dramatic presentations year round, as do neighborhood dramatic groups. Numerous musical and art organizations annually schedule shows and perform at city functions and festivities. The New Bern Farmer's Market hosts dance bands for the public at various times during the year, and the Downtown Business & Professional Association offers an inviting day's end function every month, and interesting things are always brewing at Tryon Palace. Current calendar information may be obtained through the Craven Arts Council, 638-2577.

January

Because of the area's mild climate, Tryon Palace tries to accommodate local green thumbs with monthly **garden workshops** beginning in mid-January. The workshops combine a historical perspective on the art of gardening with practical advice on timely topics throughout the year such as winter gardens, spring

Each year Tryon Palace boasts beautiful, manicured gradens.

Photo: Tryon Palace

bulbs, gardening with herbs, container gardening, heirloom vegetables, dried flower wreaths, holiday decorating and Christmas confections. The horticultural workshops are conducted in the Tryon Palace Visitor Center. Admission is by purchase of a $4 garden ticket or annual pass. No advance reservations are necessary. For information about any of these popular workshops, phone 514-4900 or (800) 767-1560.

The Downtown Business & Professional Association's **Alive at Five Happenings** take place on the fourth Thursday of each month throughout 1995 at 5 PM in various downtown locations. Monthly Happenings in 1995 will include celebrations of the Craven Arts Council and Gallery's 20th year in May, the Red, White and Blueberry Festival in June, Swissfest in July, School Daze in August and the Halloween parade in October. Alive at Five begins in late January and continues each month of the year in downtown New Bern. Contact Mary Conover, 638-6817, for full details.

The **Shrine Convention** occurs annually during the third week of January bringing Shriners to New Bern from all over North Carolina. Numerous nobles put on the most colorful parade possible on Saturday of convention week in downtown New Bern.

February

The town goes cosmopolitan in early February for two performances of some of the finest jazz you'll hear anywhere. The shows, sponsored by the Craven Arts Council and Gallery, take place at the Sheraton Grand Hotel. The **Sunday Jazz Showcase** performances are always a sell-out, and reservations are a must. Perfor-

mances are at 1:30 and 7:30 PM. For information, call 638-2577.

Antiques also take the stage in mid-February when the New Bern Preservation Foundation sponsors its annual two-day **Antique Show and Sale** at the Sudan Temple on East Front Street. The show hosts as many as 30 dealers who exhibit 18th- and 19th-century American antiques for sale. Proceeds benefit the Preservation Foundation. Tickets are $3.50 in advance and $4 at the door. For information, call 633-6448.

March

Besides their gardens, New Bernians are also proud of the authenticity of their vintage belongings. Here again, Tryon Palace fills the bill with its annual **Decorative Arts Symposium** in mid-March, illustrating regional styles in decorations. The event often includes nationally recognized speakers as well as meals, social events and special tours. A registration fee is required, and a brochure is printed each year outlining the events. For information, call 514-4900 or (800) 767-1560.

The outdoor **North Carolina In-Water Boat Show** in late March is staged at the Sheraton Hotel and Marina, 1 Bicentennial Park. The boat show features an estimated 50 boat dealers and manufacturers from up and down the East Coast and surrounding states. According to show organizer Smitty Gray, the event exhibits some of the newest boat styles on the market. As many as 200 boats in all sizes are displayed both in the water and on land. Numerous exhibit booths show electronic equipment, fishing tackle, safety equipment and other marine related gear. For information, call Smitty at 469-1071.

During the boat show weekend in late

March, decoys, carvings and wildlife paintings are among the wares displayed and sold at the **North Carolina Wildlife and Sportsman's Show**, which is held at various locations in downtown New Bern. The show features decoy carving demonstrations, custom-made knives and guns and carvings, paintings and limited-edition prints. For information, call the New Bern Area Chamber of Commerce, 637-3111.

The **Coors Light-Ramada Regatta** opens the sailing season each year in late March. Hosted by the Ramada Inn since 1991, the regatta is open to several classes of sailboats. For information, call 636-3637.

April

What started out to be a simple fundraiser for the New Bern Historical Society is now attracting busloads of people in early April for the two-day **New Bern Spring Homes and Gardens Tour**. The event is now cosponsored by the Historical Society and the New Bern Preservation Foundation, and the town puts on its prettiest face to welcome visitors. The tour includes private homes, gardens and churches in the historic district, with guides and location maps provided. The tour can best be enjoyed on foot and is an ideal opportunity to explore selected homes and landmarks in the river city. During the two-day event, Tryon Palace opens its gardens free and offers palace tour tickets at a discount to tour ticket holders. Tour tickets may be purchased on tour days at the headquarters for both sponsoring organizations — Attmore-Oliver House, 510 Pollock Street, 638-8558. Tickets can also be ordered by mail in advance.

The New Bern Historic Homes and Gardens Tour weekend is **Gardeners' Weekend** at Tryon Palace. Palace gardens and New Bern Academy Museum are open free throughout the weekend, and walking tours of the gardens are guided by horticultural staff members on Sunday. Thousands of gloriously colored tulips are in bloom, along with expansive plantings of blazing daffodils and pansies. For specific information, call 514-4900 or (800) 767-1560.

If golf is your game, sign on for the annual **Two-Man Classic Invitational Tournament** in early April. Sponsored by the New Bern Area Chamber of Commerce and the Greater Havelock Chamber of Commerce, tournament play is held simultaneously at The Emerald Golf Club and at Carolina Pines. For information, call the New Bern Chamber at 637-3111.

May

In early May, the Craven Arts Council stages a one-day **Cinco de Mayo Fiesta** from 11 AM to 5 PM behind El Mex Restaurant on Craven Street. The free festival is in celebration of Mexico's Independence Day and features arts of the Hispanic culture including music, food,

On the corner of Pollock and Middle streets is a cannon buried muzzle down. The cannon was taken from the Revolutionary British ship-of-war *Lady Blessington* following an engagement with a privateer owned by New Bern patriot, John Wright Stanley.

Insiders' Tips

crafts, pinatas, dancing and other entertainment. For information, call 638-ARTS.

In late May, the Neuse River Foundation sponsors **Neuse River Day**, a Saturday festival to celebrate and save a valuable natural resource. The day's activities take place at Union Point on the Trent and Neuse rivers and include boat rides, a ski show, a yacht parade, a fish fry, food booths, sail races, amusement rides and informational exhibits and demonstrations that increase awareness of the impact we have on the delicate balance of river ecology. Proceeds from the event help to fund a full-time river keeper position. For further information, contact the Neuse River Foundation, 637-7972.

Beginning the last weekend in May are **Tryon Palace's Drama Tours**, which are daily living history presentations by characters who enact a typical day in the palace in the year 1771. The tours continue through mid-August. For information, call the palace at 514-4900 or (800) 767-1560.

June

Visitors are invited to a Colonial America celebration of **King George III's Birthday: Festival of Colonial Life** in mid-June at Tryon Palace. The palace grounds and gardens buzz with activity of 18th-century life including a regimental encampment, entertainment, craft demonstrations and activities for all ages. Interior and Drama Tours of the palace historic sites are offered at the regular fee. For information, call 514-4900 or (800) 767-1560.

July

As one of America's first towns to have a **Fourth of July** celebration, New Bern still enjoys a well-turned-out celebration full of traditional hot dogs and fireworks. Previously, fireworks were set off at the Ramada Inn, but live cinders fell on nearby sailboats, so the practice was quickly snuffed out. Now the fireworks display takes place at Lawson Creek Park on First Street near downtown. Spectators can watch the sky light up at Lawson Creek, or from even better vantage points at either Union Point Park or Bicentennial Park. Military bands have traditionally performed patriotic music to complement the event. Additional holiday activities take place at Tryon Palace, where gardens are open free to the public and entertainment and activities occur throughout the historic sites.

September

Sailors from all over the Southeast converge on New Bern for the annual **Michelob Cup Regatta** each Labor Day weekend. A leisurely, fun sailing competition for cruising class boats, the regatta has tried several courses and gone back to its original Oriental-to-New Bern run, a distance of about 12 miles by river. Festivities begin on the eve of the race in Oriental and continue at the Sheraton Marina following the competition. The New Bern Rotary Club sponsors the event, and everyone can join the fun that usually involves dances and seafood feasts. For information, call 633-9463.

October

Kicking off the festivities on New Bern's schedule in early October is **Oktoberfest**. The early Saturday evening event gathers New Bernians with European roots to an oom-pah-pah get-down at the Farmer's Market on Tryon Palace Drive in downtown New Bern where they polka and schnitzel the evening away. For information call 636-1640.

Swiss Bear Downtown Revitalization group, in cooperation with Tryon Palace and the city of New Bern, hosts one of eastern North Carolina's major annual events, the **Chrysanthemum Festival**, in early October. The colorful three-day weekend festival is a celebration of gorgeous autumn weather, colorful flowers and an inviting downtown full of interesting activities. Spread along the downtown streets and waterfront area are booths of food, crafts, paintings and antiques, an antique car show and performances both in the street and on stages in various locations. Festival activities include sporting events and a Bass fishing tournament, traditional and changing events for the entire family each year. Tryon Palace grounds, highlighted with thousands of mums in bloom, are open free, and military encampments provide interest on the wide back lawn. Craft demonstrations, entertainment and other activities attract a grand turnout year after year. For festival information call Swiss Bear at 638-5781. For palace activities, call 514-4900 or (800) 767-1560.

In late October, the New Bern Historical Society conducts its **New Bern at Night Ghost Walk** with just a hint of ghouls and goblins. Walking tours take place from 5 to 9 PM on two weekend nights and feature historic homes and the Cedar Grove Cemetery, complete with funeral music and mourning memorabilia at area churches. Banners, T-shirts and books are available as souvenirs of a truly chilling experience. For information, call 638-8558.

November

Residents and visitors from surrounding counties look forward to Tryon Palace's two-part **Decorating for the Holidays** workshop in mid-November. The workshops teach participants how to make innovative and natural holiday decorations. Subjects covered often include wreaths and wreath-making, garland-making, the use of Christmas greenery, kissing balls and spectacular centerpieces using fresh fruits and natural greenery. Admission to the workshops is by purchase of a $4 garden ticket or advance purchase of a Christmas Celebration Tour ticket. Workshop times and locations vary. For information, call 638-1560.

December

It's traditional in New Bern that the city's **Coastal Christmas Celebration** begins the first weekend in December when a festive flotilla brings Santa to Bicentennial Park. Now in its 10th year, the **Coastal Christmas Flotilla** is truly a water-land celebration bringing Santa to town aboard a Hatteras yacht. The flotilla proceeds down the Trent River and passes Union Point, allowing spectators long, lingering looks at boats festooned with sparkling lights, diving dolphins and red-nosed reindeer.

Staff and volunteers prepare for weeks for the **Tryon Palace Christmas Celebration,** and by early December the palace looks much as it did during the holidays in 1770, when Governor William Tryon hosted a "very grand and noble Entertainment and Ball" to celebrate the grand opening of his sumptuous home and the Royal capitol. The palace is lighted and adorned with fresh fruit and fragrant greenery. Cooks are busy in the kitchen, preparing confections and delicacies, and the air is filled with holiday aromas. **Christmas Insider Tours** take place through mid-December focusing on decorations and food in Tryon Palace and other historic sites from the 18th to 20th centuries. Through mid-December, palace horticulture staffers lead visitors on **Winter Garden Tours** focused on evergreens and exterior decorations. Two weekends are reserved for evening **Christmas Candlelight Tours** featuring 800 candles burning throughout the palace. Carolers, dancers and musical entertainment are continuous during the spectacular evening tours. For information, call 514-4900 or (800) 767-1560.

Other events in downtown New Bern's Coastal Christmas Celebration include a community and North Carolina Symphony performance of Handel's *Messiah* at Centenary United Methodist Church. A living nativity, community caroling along the waterfront and lighting of the community Christmas tree in the yard of Christ Episcopal Church at Pollock and Middle streets each December will soften any Scrooge. You will definitely catch the spirit of the season in New Bern.

New Bern
Nightlife

New Bern offers a nice variety of nightlife, although it isn't overrun with entertainment spots. That's refreshing for a riverfront city. Nightlife here revolves around smaller gathering places where friends meet to mix and mingle. Several lounges are on the waterfront so guests can relax inside or outside and watch the sunset over the river.

Information about laws regulating liquor sales and stores selling liquor is included at the end of this chapter.

New Bern is home to a professional acting group, a professional dance troupe and a community theater organization. These groups stage a number of performances throughout the year, and there are several performances for children. The **Craven Arts Council**, 638-ARTS, has information about these groups. See our New Bern Arts chapter for more information.

Nightlife takes various forms here in New Bern. There's a six-screen movie theater at **Southgate Cinema 6** on Trent Road, 638-1820. You'll find three screens at **Cinema Triple** on Neuse Boulevard, 633-4620. **B&R Lanes** at 1309 Tatum Drive, 633-3424, is a popular bowling alley.

As for the wander-in, sit-down-and-enjoy-yourself type of nightlife, New Bern has that to offer too. Although there are others, among the more popular nightspots are those that follow.

THE CITY SIDE CAFE
Sheraton Hotel and Marina   638-3585

City Side is one of New Bern's most exciting gathering places. The atmosphere is lively and upbeat for those nights when you might want to party late. Entertainment varies and includes jazz, comedians and live bands playing beach, classic rock and Top 40. The City Side Cafe serves international food and international-style beers, coffees and has all ABC permits. Favorite menu items include the top-your-own pizzas and burgers.

OAR HOUSE LOUNGE
I Marina Rd. in River Bend   633-2006

If you're looking to party and have lots of fun, head to the Oar House. On the Trent River in River Bend, the Oar House can be reached by car or boat — just dock at a slip beside the lounge. Inside you'll find a large dance floor, a bar serving mixed drinks, bar snacks and

---

According to North Carolina law, a person is legally impaired when his or her blood alcohol level is .08 or higher.

Insiders' Tips

plenty of fun. Sunday afternoons are for beach music and the T-Bird Shag Party. (The shag is the indigenous dance of the coastal Carolinas and is danced to a type of music called beach music.) Other nights you'll find a jukebox or a DJ entertaining.

SINBAD'S GRILL & BAR
101 Howell Rd.
Ramada Inn   636-3637

This is a spot that might be comfortably peaceful one night and buzzing with activity the next. Attracting a mixture of locals and visitors, the lounge offers guests lots of windows from which to view the river, the marina and downtown New Bern. Live entertainment is offered on most weekends; a DJ spins tunes on weeknights; karaoke is featured on Wednesday and Saturday; and there is a jukebox.

PRO SAIL CLUB
1 Bicentennial Park
Sheraton Hotel and Marina   638-3585

Named after a professional sailing competition series, the Pro Sail is the place to enjoy casual relaxation in a sailor's haven. The club features a long, irregular-shaped bar, comfortable seating and lots of windows overlooking the harbor. There is also an outside deck. Live entertainment is offered on most weekends, and there is a large-screen television.

THE CHELSEA
335 Middle St.   637-5469

The Chelsea is a favorite downtown gathering place for those interested in mixing and mingling with friends or soon-to-be friends. The bar is in the restaurant area (see the New Bern Restaurants chapter) and serves mixed drinks, beers and wine. The building and the decor are interesting in themselves. Built in

the early 1900s, the building initially was a drugstore/soda shop where Caleb Bradham invented what would later be known as Pepsi. The Chelsea often features live entertainment, so call ahead to see what's happening.

HARVEY'S CELLAR LOUNGE
221 Tryon Palace Dr.   638-3205

As the name implies, this lounge is in the cellar of the Harvey Mansion, which offers patrons an upstairs restaurant serving lunch and dinner (see the New Bern Restaurants chapter). This intimate lounge features a small, unique copper bar and offers a bar menu and mixed drinks. Call ahead; there is often live entertainment that might include music or scenes from a play.

ANNABELLE'S PUB
U.S. 17
Twin Rivers Mall   633-6401

Annabelle's Pub is part of the restaurant and offers a casual, relaxing atmosphere. The bar serves beer, wine and mixed drinks and features at least one drink special each day. For information about the restaurant, see the New Bern Restaurants chapter.

CLANCY O'HARA'S LOUNGE
2000 S. Glenburnie Rd.   637-2206

Come relax at this popular lounge and restaurant. The lounge has full ABC privileges and also serves wine and beer. More information about Clancy O'Hara's Restaurant is in our New Bern Restaurants chapter.

Liquor Laws And ABC Stores

Craven County voters were among the first in North Carolina to take advantage of local-option mixed-drink sales. A 1980 referendum to settle the issue passed by a slim 50 votes.

ABC stores are the only establishments in the state allowed to sell liquor. Beer and wine are sold in grocery and convenience stores and in specialty food shops throughout the area. All ABC stores are open Monday through Saturday, but the hours vary. Purchases must be made with cash, MasterCard or VISA. No personal checks are taken, and only those 21 years old or older are allowed in the stores.

ABC STORE NO. 1

318 Tryon Palace Dr.   637-3623

ABC STORE NO. 4

1407 Neuse Blvd.   637-9744

ABC STORE NO. 5

2005 Glenburnie Rd.   638-4847

New Bern
Fishing and Water Sports

Because of New Bern's location, it's not surprising that New Bernians take to the water like, well, ducks. The weather is mild enough year round to entice the locals into sailing, skiing, fishing or relaxing nearby.

Some rental boats are available at Northwest Creek Marina, 638-4133 or (800) 443-9129, and Shorebird Boat Rentals on Tryon Palace Drive, 638-7075, can power, jet or sail you on the river on your own terms. Whether aboard your own or a rented vessel, you will enjoy a number of annual events on the water. But those who are the most serious about spending every free day in the river are out there for the fishing.

Expect to hook bass, bream and flounder in local waters. Bass fishing tournaments are popular competitions often scheduled during the year as fund-raising events by area organizations. Swiss Bear, Inc., usually schedules a bass fishing competition during the Chrysanthemum Festival each October. The Neuse River is also home to many crabs, the catching of which provides tasty and profitable rewards for many locals.

Nearby Croatan National Forest permits fresh and saltwater fishing; however, fishing in the forest's freshwater lakes is poor because of the acidity of the water. But along its river shoreline, oystering, crabbing and flounder gigging can be worthwhile efforts. For the best spots, talk to a ranger at the headquarters office on Fisher Avenue, 9 miles south of New Bern just off U.S. 70 E. If you just like to cruise the backwoods, several forest locations have boat ramps or launch sites, including Brices Creek, Cahooque Creek, Catfish Lake, Great Lake and Haywood Landing. Some of these sites are deep in the forest, so it is best to check with a ranger for specific directions, or better yet, stop by headquarters and pick up a forest map.

For skiing enthusiasts, the spot of choice is along the Trent River from Lawson Creek Park to Trent Woods. Smaller than the Neuse, the Trent is more protected from prevailing winds and usually has calm water. A number of area skiers enjoy the twists and curves of Brices Creek, although skiing there becomes more and more limited with increased land development and the imposition of speed limits.

For sailors, the premiere events are the annual Michelob Cup and Coors Light-Ramada Regatta, both of which are detailed in our Annual Events chapter. Other sailing competitions can be enjoyed during the Blackbeard Sailing Club's Winter Series, held from November to February. To compete in the series or for information, call the sailing club, 633-3990, or On The Wind Sailing School and Service at Fairfield Harbour, 633-0032.

Several yacht clubs are active in the New Bern area including Eastern Carolina Yacht Club, which meets in Trent Woods at 4005 Trent Pines Drive and the New Bern Yacht Club, which meets at the Sheraton Grand Hotel and Marina downtown.

New Bern
Marinas and the
Intracoastal Waterway

Boaters visiting the New Bern area have two waterways to explore: the expansive Neuse River, which flows into Pamlico Sound, or the slow, meandering Trent River, which flows into the Neuse.

The Neuse River is ideal for cruising by sail or power, with miles of sandy beaches, clearly marked channels, easy access via the Intracoastal Waterway (ICW) and Pamlico Sound and many marinas and protected anchorages. The Trent River is deep, has a marked channel and is navigable by small boat. Its lower reaches are fine for uncrowded water skiing. Brices Creek, a tributary of the Trent, winds far into the forest and offers excellent fishing and wildlife observation.

Rotating bridges at New Bern open on demand daily except from 6:30 AM to 7:30 AM and 4:30 PM to 5:30 PM. On weekends and holidays between May 24 and September 8, the bridges are closed between 2 PM and 7 PM, with openings at 4 PM and 6 PM. The remainder of the year, the daily schedule is in effect seven days a week. The bridge tender monitors channel 13 VHF. The railroad bridges upriver from New Bern are always open except when in use. National Oceanic and Atmospheric Administration (NOAA) stations in the area are New Bern, WX-2 (162.475 MHz), and Beaufort and Hatteras, WX-3 (162.40 MHz).

A clearly marked channel up the Neuse from the ICW will bring you into historic New Bern. The natural channel depths generally run between eight and 12 feet, with little noticeable tidal effect. A strong easterly or northerly wind will raise the level, while a sustained westerly breeze, say 25 knots, can lower this level by as much as two feet. Also noteworthy to boaters are sapling net stakes dotting the river, strung with nets in the early spring and late fall. The nets are usually buoyed by corks or plastic bottles, or marked by white flags.

The Neuse is a very wide river, which invites day and night sailing in addition to motor cruising and water skiing. The many wandering tributaries promise scenic canoeing and exciting fishing.

Boats of all sizes can find berthing space in downtown New Bern and nearby marinas. Whether you're cruising the area or wish to launch your boat at one of the many local ramps, most locations have similar facilities. In the downtown area, especially, it is not unusual for leisure yachters or sailors to arrive for what they thought would be a short visit only to find themselves staying weeks, sometimes months, even years, living aboard their vessels.

Much of the Nuese River's shoreline south of New Bern forms a boundary of the vast 157,000-acre Croatan National Forest. Here locals and visitors enjoy public recreation areas, with swimming and picnic facilities near the Minnesott ferry terminal and at Flanner's Beach south of New Bern.

Nearby marinas at Clubfoot Creek, Minnesott Beach and Oriental, all on the Neuse River, make for enjoyable day sails or cruising trips from New Bern. In addition, there are many marinas along the Crystal Coast, which is easily accessible from New Bern via the Neuse River and the ICW. See our Crystal Coast Marina chapter for listings.

If you're traveling to New Bern from some distance away, it is wise to call ahead to assure docking space availability, especially during the warmer months.

The **Comfort Suites and Marina**, 218 E. Front Street, 636-0022, is in the historic district at the Riverfront Park on the Neuse River. Offering year-round services, the 24-slip marina has six transient slips and accommodates power or sailing vessels up to 120 feet. Its marked entry channel has a controlling depth of 20 feet; dockside depth is 10 feet. Marina facilities offer some groceries, ice, a laundromat and other amenities of the Comfort Suites including an outdoor heated whirlpool and swimming pool.

The **Sheraton Marina**, 1 Bicentennial Park, 638-3585, is part of the Sheraton Hotel complex. It is on the Trent River and has a floating breakwater/dock that can serve larger yachts. The marina is open year round, docks sail and power vessels up to 300 feet, has 200 slips, 25 of which are transient berths, a marked entry channel, an approach and dockside depth of 12 feet, gas and diesel fuel,

pump-out station, ice, electricity, showers and a restaurant. All floating docks and finger piers have recently been rebuilt. Telephone service is available, and cable TV is free.

Ramada Marina, 101 Howell Road, 636-2888, is across the Trent River from the Sheraton Marina. It is open year round and serves sail and power vessels up to 110 feet. It has 150 concrete floating slips, 10 of which are transient berths, a marked entry channel with 12-foot approach depth, dockside depth of 16 feet, pump out station, ice, electricity, showers, laundromat, restaurant and snack bar. The marina has recently added a patio and grills for boaters' convenience. Phone and cable TV hookups are also available.

The **River Bend Yacht Club**, 1 Marina Drive, 633-2006, is reached by boat via entry channel south of the Trent River bridge. It is about 5 miles upstream from downtown New Bern. A private club, the marina is open year round and serves sail and power vessels up to 40 feet. It has 75 slips, six of which are transient berths, a marked entry channel, launching ramp, gas, electricity and an approach and dockside depth of six feet. It offers propeller and hull repair services and stocks marine supplies, groceries and ice. In addition to dock space, which can be rented short- or long-term, guest memberships to the town's golf course, tennis courts and swimming pool can also be purchased. The Oar House restaurant and lounge is available for food and libations.

Northwest Creek Marina, Fairfield

Harbour, 638-4133 or (800) 443-9129, has become the center of action for this resort development. It is on the north side of the Neuse River, is open year round, and serves sail and power vessels up to 70 feet. It has 235 slips, 15 of which are transient berths, a marked entry channel with seven feet of water depth, dockside depth of 12 feet, gas and diesel fuel, a pump out station, a launching ramp, electricity, showers, a weight and sauna room and a laundromat. The Marina Market can help provision your boat for the day or an extended cruise with groceries, supplies, clothing and fishing gear. Marina patrons have full use of the resort's two 18-hole golf courses, indoor and outdoor pools and lighted tennis courts. For dining, the Creek Cafe at dockside features an upstairs bar and lounge and full-course dining downstairs in the restaurant, including take-out pizzas and sub sandwiches. Transportation will be needed to visit New Bern's attractions.

Duck Creek Marina, Sandy Point Road, Bridgeton, 638-1702, is at the head of Duck Creek on the north side of the Neuse across from the Ramada Marina. It is open year round and serves sail and power vessels up to 46 feet. It has 55 slips, a marked entry channel with approach depth of six feet, dockside depth of eight feet, railway and 35-ton lift, storage yard for repair work, marine supplies, electricity and showers. Because the marina is across the river from New Bern, you will need transportation for shopping, or to visit the city's attractions.

Union Point Park, Tryon and E. Front streets, 636-4060, serves as a city park and public docks. Boaters often anchor here to orient themselves to the area and locate more permanent mooring. The park features a boat ramp and public facilities; however, a city ordinance prohibits its overnight dockage.

Tidewater Marina Co., Inc., 300 Madame Moore Lane, 637-3347, is on the Trent River. It is open year round and serves sail and power vessels up to 40 feet. It has 16 slips, three transient slips, a marked entry channel with controlling depth of 21 feet, 15 feet at dockside, railway and lift, a launching ramp, gas and diesel fuel, supplies and electricity. It also offers repairs on propellers and hulls. Because it is away from New Bern's hub,

Photo: Scott Taylor

A calm mid-summer's afternoon.

you will need transportation to see the sights.

Nearby Marinas

For the convenience of boaters, we are including an alphabetical list of some of the marinas near New Bern that you can call on as you make your way up and down the Neuse River or toward Pamlico Sound.

Clubfoot Creek on the south side of the river near Havelock provides anchorage for water traffic, and the riverside community of **Minnesott Beach** on the north side of the Neuse also offers safe mooring. The quaint village of Oriental, on the ICW on the north bank of the Neuse, is called "the sailing capital of North Carolina," but many power and

pleasure vessels find safe harbor at area docks as well.

Matthews Point Marina, RFD 1, Havelock, 444-1805, is off the beaten track on Clubfoot Creek on the south side of the Neuse River, 10 miles east of Cherry Point. Nestled comfortably in a safe harbor, the marina is open year round and serves sail and power vessels up to 45 feet. It has 106 slips, six of which are transient berths, a marked entry channel, approach depth of seven feet, dockside depth of six feet, gas and diesel fuel, a launching ramp, electricity, a pump-out station, showers and ice. A clubhouse, cookout area and upper deck lounge are also available to boaters.

If you're looking for a boat or need one serviced, stop by **Walsh Marine** in Havelock, 213 U.S. 70 W., 447-2266. Let

Danny Walsh and his crew show you the latest in boats, motors and trailers or service the one you have. Walsh has been the No. 1 Suzuki dealer in the district for the last nine years, and this dealership carries many other lines.

Minnesott Beach Yacht Basin, Minnesott Beach, Arapahoe, 249-1424, is on the north side of the Neuse River. It is open year round and serves sail and power vessels up to 50 feet. It has 150 slips, five of which are transient berths, a marked entry channel, approach depth of 8.5 feet, dockside depth of 10 feet, gas and diesel fuel, a 60-ton lift, electricity, a pump out station, supplies, ice, limited groceries, showers, a laundromat and a pool. Propeller and hull repairs are available for both gas and diesel vessels. The marina has a lounge with a TV and fireplace and is close to the country club golf course. Transportation to a nearby restaurant can also be arranged.

Oriental Marina, Hodges Street, Oriental, 249-1818, is just off the ICW. It is open year round and serves sail and power vessels of up to 80 feet. It has 15 slips, 10 of which are transient, an eight-foot deep entry channel, dockside depth of six feet, gas and diesel fuel, electricity, groceries, ice, showers, a laundromat, a restaurant and an 18-room motel. Gas and diesel fuel is available as are some repairs.

Sea Harbour Marina, Harbour Way, Oriental, 249-0808, is on Pierce Creek about a mile from town. It is open year round, has 90 slips, serves sail and power vessels up to 45 feet, has gas and diesel fuel, a pump-out station, electricity, water hookups, a pool and rest rooms.

Whittaker Creek Yacht Harbor, Whittaker Point Road, Oriental, 249-0666 or 249-1020, is about a half-mile from town on Whittaker Creek. It is open year round, has 150 slips including 20 transient slips, serves power and sailing vessels of up to 120 feet and has a marked entry channel with eight feet of water on approach and at dockside. Gas and diesel fuel are available as are a pump-out station, electricity, supplies, a ship's store, ice, a laundromat and restrooms. It offers repairs and a courtesy car. A pool and restaurant are on-site.

New Bern
Sports, Parks and Fitness

New Bern is a sporting and recreational center surrounded by water and an abundance of parks. There are numerous places for adults and children to exercise and take part in sporting programs. Walking is one favorite form of exercise in New Bern. We call it strolling and use that time to check on the progress of neighbors, their children or area businesses.

For those who are seeking a more tiring pursuit, New Bern and Craven County both offer active recreation programs and public areas for tennis, power walking, jogging, baseball/softball and soccer. Both the city and county also maintain public boat ramps.

Sports and Recreation

New Bern
Recreation Department
636-4060

New Bern Recreation Department operates the bulk of its programs from two centers — the Stanley White Center on Chapman Street, 636-4061, and the West New Bern Recreation Center, 1225 Pine Tree Drive, 636-4061. The programs vary at each center and with each season. Programming includes youth lessons in swimming and tennis, summer day camps, youth ceramic classes and football. T-ball, minor and major baseball is offered to youth between the ages of 6 and 12. Babe Ruth baseball is played by youths 13 through 18. Every spring, a coed volleyball match takes place each

Tuesday night at the West New Bern Recreation Center. It is open to everyone, so stop by.

Craven County
Recreation & Parks
636-6606

Craven County's recreation facilities are connected to schools. Facilities offered to the public include tennis courts and ballfields. Youth programs include karate, gymnastics, T-ball, soccer leagues and camps, baseball, swimming and a six-week summer day camp. Adults can take part in numerous programs including softball, basketball, exercise and line dance classes. A special feature of the county system is the fitness trail at Brinson Elementary School on Old Cherry Point Road. The county recreation department also sponsors the area's Senior Games and Special Olympics. Craven Community College has a number of lighted tennis courts available for public use.

Twin Rivers YMCA
100 YMCA Ln.   638-8799

At the intersection of Fifth and Sixth Streets is a 45,000-square-foot athletic facility that houses a 25-yard, six-lane heated indoor swimming pool, a regulation-size gymnasium with an upstairs track, a gym, a youth activity center, racquetball courts, a free weight room and a wellness center with power steps, a treadmill and bicycles. Patrons can be analyzed and have a personalized activity program developed. There is a CAM II Center with

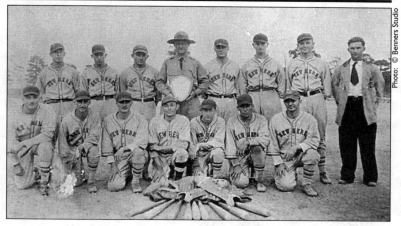

Photo: © Benners Studio

New Bern has a long history of being a sports-loving town.

Nautilus equipment and a fitness center with sauna and whirlpool. Classes are taught regularly in swimming, gymnastics, aqua aerobics, arthritis aquatics, water safety instructor training, junior lifesaving, basic lifeguard training, scuba and cardiopulmonary resuscitation. There are programs in aerobics, fitness for people older than 40, racquetball, volleyball, Jazzercise and weights. Competitions are conducted in a variety of activities. Youth programs are offered in gymnastics, basketball, volleyball, softball and T-ball, and transportation is provided from several schools for after-school programs. The Y sponsors day camps during Easter and Christmas vacations. Babysitting services are available, and the Y can host children's birthday parties.

COURTS PLUS
2911 Brunswick Ave.   *633-2221*
Courts Plus of New Bern is a membership racquetball facility with four indoor courts. The facility also offers swimming and aqua aerobics in its five-lane indoor pool and outdoor pool. The facil-

ity offers Nautilus workout equipment, karate, basketball, volleyball and aerobics. There are saunas and whirlpool for soothing relaxation, plus a whirlpool and steam room. Locker and towel facilities are also available, as are tanning booths. The pro shop offers apparel, equipment and accessories for your fitness needs. Courts Plus has several racquetball leagues and serves as site host for a number of regional racquetball tournaments. The lounge offers refreshments and light snacks. Child care and special programs for children are also offered.

Parks
New Bern's public parks and their offerings are listed below:

GLENBURNIE PARK
In the Glenburnie Gardens residential area off Oaks Road, this park has a boat landing and picnic and recreation areas, all shaded by a grove of old pine trees. There are several picnic shelters with tables and grills at the park.

GEORGE STREET BALLFIELD

Next to the United Senior Services building, this area includes basketball courts and other play areas.

KAFER PARK

Adjoining the George Street area, this ballpark was once home to New Bern's professional baseball team.

LAWSON CREEK PARK

Off Pembroke Road and fronting the Trent River, this is the major boat launching area for water enthusiasts. The park also has two soccer fields, a nature trail and Jack's Island, a picnic area. The nature walk meanders through the marsh land that makes up much of the park area.

UNION POINT PARK

Another boat launching and picnic area, this park is downtown where the Trent River joins the Neuse. It is a great place to sit and watch the river traffic. The park includes a stage, where Sunday summer afternoon concerts are often performed.

FORT TOTTEN PARK

At the intersection of Trent Road and Fort Totten Drive, this small park has a ballfield and children's play area.

New Bern
Golf

The New Bern area is filled with golf courses that have won acclaim from amateurs and professionals alike and host a number of large golf tournaments. Golfing residents and visitors are fortunate: Popular courses are easily accessible, and the usually mild climate allows for year-round play.

Here is a list of the courses in the immediate vicinity. For information about other golf courses nearby, see our Crystal Coast Golf chapter, which includes information on the Morehead City Golf and Country Club, Bogue Banks Country Club in Pine Knoll Shores, Star Hill Golf and Country Club in Cape Carteret, Brandywine Bay Golf Club, near Morehead City and Silver Creek Golf Club, on Highway 58 near Cape Carteret.

THE EMERALD
6001 Clubhouse Dr.   *633-4440*

The Emerald was designed by Rees Jones, and the 7,000-yard course was created to be a challenge to golfers at all levels of skill. Various grasses are used to give each hole a totally different feel and appearance. The 18-hole course is sculptured to create variety. Most holes have four or five pin locations. The fourth tee, for example, features four locations that hit across the water and one high land route. Carts are available. While only residents of The Emerald community can be permanent members of the golf club, there are social memberships that entitle members to tennis, swimming pool and club facilities as well as golfing privileges.

The Emerald is home to the Curtis Strange Golf Classic, played annually to raise money for the Shriners' Hospitals. Golfers can take advantage of a fully stocked pro shop, a driving range and lessons by pro Jerry Briele.

FAIRFIELD HARBOR
750 Broad Creek Rd., Bridgeton   *638-5338*

Fairfield Harbour is a resort community, with timeshare accommodations plus several large residential developments. To get there, cross the Neuse River on Highway 17. Turn right on Highway 55, and continue about a mile to Broad Creek Road. Signs will direct you from there. Fairfield Harbour has two golf courses and 36 holes. Fairfield Harbour Country Club is a private links-style course with 18 holes and a par of 72. You may want to take your camera out on this enjoyable nearly 6,000-yard course because it affords lovely views of Broad Creek. The course is open to property owners, including those who own a week or more in the timeshare facilities. David Cook is the golf pro here.

RIVER BEND
GOLF AND COUNTRY CLUB
94 Shoreline Dr., River Bend   *638-2819*

River Bend Golf and Country Club, an 18-hole course with a 71 par, is a semi-private course allowing greens fee play. The course is open everyday. All you need to do is call and set your tee time. Ron Anderson is a PGA professional. River Bend offers a well-stocked pro shop, tennis courts and an Olympic-size swimming pool. This is truly one of the area's nicest courses.

NEW BERN
GOLF AND COUNTRY CLUB

4200 Country Club Rd.
Trent Woods   *637-2413*

This golf course is open to members and their guests. If you are new to the area and are interested in belonging to the country club, don't delay because there is generally a waiting list. Tennis courts are adjacent to the lovely clubhouse, which overlooks the Trent River with its overhanging hardwood trees laced with Spanish moss. Members and guests will also find a swimming pool, tennis shop and pro shop.

CAROLINA PINES
GOLF AND COUNTRY CLUB

Carolina Pines Blvd.   *444-1000*

On the Neuse River just west of Havelock, this is a challenging 18-hole, par-72 course with a pro shop, driving range and target greens. Tim Dupre is the club pro. Golfers will also find tennis courts, a pool, and a club house with a lounge and patio overlooking freshwater lakes and golf links.

New Bern
Arts

For about the first three decades of the 20th century, New Bern was known as the "Athens of North Carolina" because of its many artistic and educational endeavors. While the Great Depression put a halt to much of the activity, a rebirth occurred in the 1970s, and locals enjoy performances and exhibits from an increasing number of area and touring artists.

The **Craven Arts Council and Gallery** on Middle Street, 638-2577, supports and features all art disciplines and is a ticket outlet and information center for almost any art event taking place in Craven County. The council sponsors the popular New Bern Sunday Jazz Showcase, the Children's Performing Arts series and many other visual and performing arts events throughout the year.

The **New Bern-Craven County Public Library** at the corner of Johnson and Middle streets, 638-7800, selects an artist of the month and displays his or her work in its recently expanded buildings. Photographers and other visual artists have been the most popular.

One artist who has exhibited at the library and is perhaps the most popular of the area's visual artists is painter Willie Taglieri. Taglieri decided to come south and create his works when he retired from the New York City Police Department. Each year he chooses one of his paintings to be reproduced as Christmas cards. Another popular visual artist is Janet Francoeur. Her pen and ink drawings are favorites of both locals and visitors. Works by either of these artists can be seen in public and private collections throughout New Bern.

New Bern is also home to an active community theater group — the **New Bern Civic Theater**, which has its own performing hall, the Saax Bradbury Playhouse, a former movie theater on Pollock Street. The group stages a number of productions annually. Also active in town are numerous musical groups, historical dancers and a series of performances by professional touring dancers, **Atlantic Dance Theater**, which gives a number of performances throughout each year in the public schools. Following we've described our arts organizations. If a group doesn't have a street address or regular office, we have given the contact person's name and phone number.

CRAVEN ARTS COUNCIL AND GALLERY
317 Middle St.   *638-2577*

Besides nurturing local artists, this organization provides exhibition space for local, regional and national artists in the Bank of the Arts, a reclaimed 1912 bank building that also houses the arts council's administrative offices. The large, open main gallery is the staging area for nine exhibits each year. Popular traveling exhibits are often featured, and overall works include a variety of media, ranging from traditional to contemporary. At Christmas, the gallery becomes a huge gift shop for the sale of art works, cards, fine crafts and other original creations. As part of its continuous support of the arts, the council organizes and runs Arts in the Schools, an outreach program of performances and artists' presentations designed to increase art awareness in youngsters. The council also publishes the monthly newsletter, *Luminary*. Classes in oil, watercolors and other art forms are often taught and conducted in the Bank of the Arts.

NEW BERN CIVIC THEATER

414 Pollock St. 633-0567

A community group, the civic theater relies on a bevy of part-time performers and behind-the-scenes technicians and assistants to produce a variety of performances at the Saax Bradbury Playhouse. The group's theatrical productions range from serious drama to lively musicals, including original works. On this year's schedule is Neil Simon's *Brighton Beach Memoirs* and *Hello Dolly*. Their children's performing group, StageHands, stages entirely unique performances simultaneously in sign and spoken language.

ATLANTIC DANCE THEATER

Elizabeth Pope 636-1760

A professional touring dance troupe, the company's dancers come from across the United States to put together dance programs targeted toward public schools. For school performances, the company performs traditional ballet as well as other dance styles to give young audiences a broad view of dance as an art form.

CRAVEN HISTORICAL DANCERS

Page Bauguess 636-0476

Now totaling about 15 members of all ages, this unique dance troupe performs 18th-century social dances in costume. Their dances include reels, country dances, minuets, cotillions and jigs. They entertain at holiday and fund-raising madrigal dinners, where they perform dances from the 1500s. Craven Historical Dancers are often included in Tryon Palace's holiday festivities. They have danced at the Hope Plantation in Edenton and traveled as far as New York to dance at a Baroque music festival. The group meets weekly, and new members do not need previous dance experience to join.

CRAVEN COMMUNITY BAND

Jack Bircher 638-8321

This group of lively musicians averages about 35 members from New Bern and surrounding counties. The band performs all styles of music, ranging from swing and Big Band to pop and novelty arrangements. It is featured at many civic functions, such as the Chrysanthemum Festival and Christmas Flotilla. Concerts are frequently performed at Craven Community College, Union Point Park and other area venues. To get involved, prospective members are invited to bring their instrument and sit in on rehearsals each Monday at 7:30 PM at Grover C. Fields Middle School on Clarendon Boulevard.

**When it's
too important
to trust to
anyone else...**

Benners Studio

"Where Photography is an Art"
206 Middle Street, New Bern, NC 28563
(919) 636-2373

Now in our 48th year of serving
Eastern North Carolina

FAIRFIELD HARBOUR CHORUS

Pat Rivett   638-8470

This chorus began with 24 enthusiastic members in 1984. Today, membership totals approximately 60 vocalists. The group performs about 15 concerts each year, featuring all types of music, including show tunes, gospel, Broadway hits, holiday arrangements, pop and contemporary. It has given numerous performances in area churches, rest homes and retirement homes and has combined its talents to perform with other choruses at Cherry Point and Craven Community College. Members must be residents of Fairfield Harbour. Rehearsals are conducted on Monday evenings at 7 at the Fairfield Community Center. Rehearsals begin the first Monday after Labor Day and continue until mid-May. The group is subsidized by a grassroots grant from the Craven Arts Council.

CRAVEN CONCERTS

Karen Harrison   633-5862

This organization schedules five musical concerts each year, staged at Grover C. Fields Middle School auditorium on Clarendon Boulevard. Attendance is by subscription membership only, with membership fees of $30 for adults and $5 for students. Productions include a wide variety of performances and always include one concert by the North Carolina Symphony. The 1995-96 calendar includes performances by jazz pianist Judy Carmichael, New York Theater Ballet and Banjomania. A membership campaign is conducted each spring, and membership forms and information are available at the Craven Arts Council and Gallery on Middle Street.

CRAVEN COMMUNITY CHORUS

Phillip Evancho   638-7357

This large choral group has 70 members and performs locally, as well as in surrounding counties and out of state. There are no auditions, and membership is open to anyone who can carry a tune and enjoys singing. The group likes to include musicians whenever possible and usually plans its shows around a theme. Performances have featured Dixieland standards, Old West favorites, Big Band hits and classic '50s rock 'n' roll. The singers also perform folk songs, patriotic compositions, spirituals, swing, pop, some classical works and holiday favorites. During Christmas of 1994, they were invited to the Biltmore Estate in Asheville to take part in a dramatic holiday production, and for 1995 they have been invited to sing at the National Cathedral in Washington, D.C.

TWIN RIVERS ART ASSOCIATION

Kathy Pickett   636-3422

The Twin Rivers Art Association sponsors two shows each year. Work is limited to two-dimensional paintings in any medium, including multimedia. Group shows are staged in the spring and late fall; however, members exhibit paintings throughout the year at various locations in New Bern and surrounding coun-

In the early months of the year, Craven Arts Council's annual Children's Performing Arts Series brings professional touring performers to the Craven Community College's Orringer Auditorium for delightful events for preschool and school-age children.

Insiders' Tips

ties. Membership is $15 per year; show fees are $15 per show. Meetings are held at 7:30 PM on the first Wednesday of each month, except in July and August, at PJR Studio on Shoreline Drive in River Bend. The group exhibits its work at River Bend Town Hall, Bank of the Arts and Twin Rivers Mall.

ART GALLERY, LTD.
502 Pollock St.   *636-2120*

In the case of this gallery, ART is an acronym for A Regional Tradition of excellence. Representing some of North Carolina's most recognized fine contemporary artists, the gallery offers original paintings and limited edition prints, works in glass and sculpture in a variety of media, jewelry, stoneware, porcelain and tapestry. On the second floor of the Edward Stanly House, the gallery's hours are 11 AM to 5 PM Tuesday through Saturday or by appointment.

CITY ART WORKS, INC.
225 Middle St.   *636-3434*

City Art Works gallery and studios represents the work of fine contemporary artists of the southeastern United States and offers professional assistance in making selections. Original paintings in watercolors, oils and pastels are featured as well as jewelry, pottery and sculpture. Gallery hours are 10 AM to 4 PM Monday through Friday, 10 AM to 1 PM on Saturday or by scheduled appointment.

New Bern
Places of Worship

New Bern has a number of historic churches that are open to residents and visitors who would like to tour or attend services. In addition to the distinctive architectural styles seen in many of the downtown churches, unique features include the pipe organ at First Presbyterian Church on New Street, the stained-glass windows in Centenary United Methodist Church at Middle and New streets, the gifts from King George II displayed at Christ Episcopal Church on Pollock Street and the graceful white arches in First Baptist Church on Middle Street. All these churches are within three blocks of one another.

In New Bern, church-sponsored events attract community-wide interest. During the Christmas celebration in New Bern, many churches conduct special concerts. Another staple of the town's Christmas celebration is a full performance at Centenary United Methodist Church of Handel's *Messiah* by a combined church choir of hundreds of voices and soloists. Musicians for the performance are members of the North Carolina Symphony.

All the major Protestant religions as well as Catholics and Jews have long-established churches in New Bern. We have highlighted a few of the downtown historic churches and listed just a few of the many others. This list is by no means inclusive of the places of worship in New Bern. You might want to look in the Yellow Pages for a complete list of other options.

CHRIST EPISCOPAL CHURCH
320 Pollock St.   *633-2109*

Having celebrated its 250th anniversary in 1991, the parish of Christ Episcopal Church is the oldest in New Bern and one of the oldest in North Carolina. This is actually the third church building to stand in this area. The first was completed in 1750 and was later destroyed by fire. The foundation of that first church is on the current church grounds. The second church was completed in 1824 and destroyed by fire in 1871. The current Gothic Revival building incorporates surviving walls of that second church and was completed in 1875. The church steeple, with its four-faced clock, is one of the identifying marks of the downtown skyline. Among the treasures on display are a 1752 *Book of Common Prayer*, a huge 1717 Bible and a five-piece silver communion service given to Christ Church by King George II. Each bear the royal coat-of-arms. Today, the church has about 900 members. Those interested in touring the building should enter the side door.

CENTENARY UNITED METHODIST CHURCH
309 New St.   *637- 4181*

First organized as a congregation in 1772, the current Centenary church was designed by Herbert Woodley Simpson and completed in 1904. Its rounded walls and turrets have an almost Moorish look. Standing at the corner of New and Middle

Streets, Centenary has about 800 members. Visitors can tour the building.

FIRST BAPTIST CHURCH
239 Middle St.   *638-5691*
Organized in 1809, the narrow Gothic Revival church was built in 1847. The church property adjoins McClellans and O. Mark Square. The main sanctuary is strikingly simple and peaceful in its design. The Sunday service is televised by WCTI-TV 12.

FIRST PRESBYTERIAN CHURCH
418 New St.   *637-3270*
The oldest continually used church building in New Bern, First Presbyterian was built in 1819-1822 by local architect and builder Uriah Sandy. The congregation was established in 1817. The Federal-style church is similar to many built about the same time in New England but is unusual for North Carolina. Like that of Christ Church, the steeple on First Presbyterian is a point of reference on the skyline. The church was used as a Union hospital and lookout post during the Civil War, and the initials of soldiers on duty in the belfry can still be seen carved in the walls. The church has about 1,200 members today.

ST. PAUL'S CATHOLIC CHURCH
3005 Country Club Rd.   *638-1984*
With its new church constructed about 10 years ago, St. Paul's is the oldest Catholic parish in North Carolina. Members built their first New Bern church on Middle Street in 1840. That building is open to the public during daylight hours. The new church features strikingly modern architecture and is in a large, park-like setting. Sharing the land is St. Paul's School, a private school.

TEMPLE B'NAI SHOLEM SYNAGOGUE
505 Middle St.   *633-9818*
To look at the stucco, Neoclassical Revival synagogue from the outside, you might think it housed a specialized art museum, a library or a performing arts hall. A Herbert Woodley Simpson-designed structure, the synagogue was built in 1908 by the congregation organized about 1824.

Photo: Scott Taylor

Every year boats much larger than this are lost due to bad weather.

New Bern
Service Directory

This section offers useful information about New Bern services and businesses. We suggest you consult the local phone directory for additional service providers or ask locals. In all cases, it is best to call ahead to verify services offered and prices. All the phone numbers are in the 919 area code.

Information Numbers

Emergency: Police, Sheriff, Fire and Rescue	911
New Bern Police Department	633-4010
New Bern Fire Department	636-4066
New Bern Rescue Squad	633-2717
Craven County Sheriff's Office	636-6620
Crisis Line	638-5995

Animal Services

Need a place for Spot to spend the night? Does Fifi need her nails clipped or hair coiffed? Let's hope it's not anything more serious. Should your pet need grooming or medical care, a number of local businesses and veterinarians can handle your needs.

Craven Animal Hospital	637-4541
Pampered Pooch	633-5822
The Pet Spa	633-3933
Neuse Veterinary Clinic	637-7128
Ridgeway Animal Clinic	633-1204

Automotive Services

Whether your vehicle needs routine maintenance or something more intensive, a number of New Bern dealers, service stations and specialized shops can help you out. There are many domestic and foreign automobile manufacturers in the area, so check the Yellow Pages for listings.

A few automotive service outlets that can handle most anything are listed here in no particular order.

70 EAST FOREIGN AUTO SERVICE
U.S. 70 E.   633-0960

BALDREE'S
2200 Trent Blvd.   637-5552

DARNELL'S GULF SERVICE CENTER
502 Broad St.   633-3177

NEUSE STARTER AND GENERATOR SERVICE
2503 Alabama St.   633-0719

WHITE'S TIRE SERVICE
2813 Neuse Blvd.   633-1170

LESTER GASKINS AUTO SERVICE
2206 Neuse Blvd.   637-4461

WESTERN AUTO
3705 U.S. 17 S.   633-2114

Bus and Taxi Service

New Bern is served by **Carolina Trailways**, which has a station at 504 Guion Street. Call 633-3100 for schedule and fare information. The bus station is open limited hours.

Taxis are franchise operations in New Bern and operate 24-hours a day from the dispatcher at **Safeway Taxi Co.**, 633-2828.

Car Rental

You will need a car if you plan to see more of the area than downtown New Bern. If taxis are not your thing, a few car rental businesses are based at the airport.

AVIS RENT A CAR
Craven Regional Airport   637-2130

HERTZ RENT A CAR
Craven Regional Airport   637-3021

NATIONAL CAR RENTAL
Craven Regional Airport   637-5241

Local Government Offices

NEW BERN CITY HALL
300 Pollock St.   636-4000

**NEW BERN CITY
WATER & SEWER DEPARTMENT**
2825 Nuese Blvd.   636-4056

**CRAVEN COUNTY
BOARD OF COMMISSIONERS**
406 Craven St.   636-6601

CRAVEN COUNTY MANAGER
406 Craven St.   636-6600

**CRAVEN COUNTY
WATER & SEWER DEPARTMENT**
412 Craven St.   636-6615

Libraries

The **New Bern-Craven County Public Library**, 638-7800, 400 Johnson Street, has more than 87,000 books, numerous periodicals, magazines and newspapers, a children's library and theater, audiovisual equipment and an auditorium. A contribution for the expansion came from the Kellenberger Foundation, begun by the same family that spearheaded the restoration of Tryon Palace. The library's extensive North Carolina Collection is among the finest in the state, bringing many out-of-towners to this public library for genealogical searches.

Media Information

Newspapers/Magazines

The *Sun Journal*, 638-8101, provides coverage of the tri-county area. The daily newspaper includes state, national and local news from Craven, Pamlico and Jones counties.

New Bern Magazine, 637-8188, is a monthly freebie that includes calendars of events and articles about coming events and matters of local interest. Art, music, performances, exhibits and festivals are all detailed in the magazine.

Vintage Times, P.O. Box 1149, New Bern, 28562, is a quarterly magazine for active, mature adults. Articles focus on health, retirement, investments and travel.

Television

New Bern is home to ABC affiliate **WCTI-TV 12**, 638-1212. The station covers New Bern and the surrounding area with news and weather reports. Other television stations close by include **WNCT-TV 9**, 355-8500, the local CBS affiliate; and **WITN-TV 7**, 636-2337, the local NBC affiliate.

Cable television service is available through **Cable TV** of New Bern, 638-3121.

Radio

Besides a good selection of rock 'n' roll, nostalgia and easy listening stations, New Bern is home to **WTEB, 89.3 FM**, 638-3434, a Public Broadcasting Service station at Craven Community College.

Other radio stations based in the area include **WNBR, Bear 94.1 FM**, 633-9401; and **WSFL, 106.5 FM**, 633-1065 or 633-2406.

Post Offices

There are numerous post offices throughout the area and in the surrounding towns and communities. The main New Bern Post Office, 638-6111, is at 1815 S. Glenburnie Road.

Zip Codes

New Bern is assigned five zip codes. Zip codes used within the city are 28560, 28561, 28562, 28563 and 28564. Other zip codes that might come in handy when requesting information include:

Bayboro	28515
Bridgeton	28519
Cherry Point	28533
Havelock	28532
Oriental	28571

Storm and Hurricane Information

Craven County Emergency Services Office, 636-6608, is charged with the responsibility of assessing storms and damage. Hurricanes are not frequent along the coast but should be taken seriously when predicted. For more information about hurricanes and ways to prepare, check this book's Crystal Coast Service Directory chapter.

Tax Rates

The Craven County 1994-1995 tax rate is 60¢ per $100 valuation and the New Bern tax rate is 47¢ per $100 valuation. These rates are subject to change July 1, 1995. North Carolina assesses a state income tax.

Utility Services Water and Sewer

The City of New Bern provides water service to customers living within the city limits. The city **Public Works Department**, 636-4025, is at 300 Pollock Street. **First Craven Sanitary District**, 633-6500, and **Neuse River Water & Sewer**, 636-6615, provide water and sewer services for those residents and business customers living outside the New Bern city limits.

Electricity

Carolina Power & Light, 1433 S. Glenburnie Road, 633-5688, serves residential and business customers in the areas surrounding New Bern. The **City of New Bern**, 249 Craven Street, 636-4000, provides electrical service to customers living within the city limits of New Bern and in Trent Woods.

Telephone

Carolina Telephone & Sprint-Carolina, 633-9011, serves the entire area.

IMAGINE...
LAND THAT FULFILLS
YOUR DREAMS.

Solitude was once the home to dreams, the place where spirits were renewed and senses restored by bountiful Southern waters and clean, gentle breezes. Today, rustic visionaries can find this same quiet beauty on the shores of eastern North Carolina, just 45 minutes from the historic towns of New Bern & Bath, with homesites beginning at $29,900.

Imagine . . . a new home, a new life.

Weyerhaeuser Real Estate Company, New Bern, NC
800-622-6297

New Bern
Real Estate
and Neighborhoods

It wasn't long ago that Craven County was listed as the fifth fastest-growing county in the state and North Carolina as the fifth fastest-growing state in the nation. Many factors are impacting recent growth, not the least being the growing personnel demands at nearby Cherry Point military base coupled with the tide of retirees finding New Bern to fit their requirements. It's not surprising then that New Bern's housing market has expanded substantially to meet the increasing demands of homeowners.

The city appears to be in the midst of a vibrant community renaissance. In downtown's historic neighborhoods, it is still not unusual to find a dilapidated structure in the midst of beautifully restored buildings, but this will be short lived. Any unrestored Georgian, Federal and Victorian edifices are quickly being purchased and restored, adding to the enhancement of the city's Colonial charm. Visitors are charmed by the restaurants, bed and breakfast inns and shops that now exist in restored structures in the downtown historic district.

Another big plus for the city is its location. Positioned at the joining waters of the Neuse and Trent rivers, New Bern is an hour's drive from the ocean and has a number of challenging and well-maintained golf courses. Its moderate climate and nearby recreational waterways offer added pluses in making it a popular va-cation, relocation and retirement spot for people from all walks of life.

With this in mind, New Bern's expanding homes market offers newcomers a wide range of neighborhoods and housing choices in styles and prices that are sure to appeal to any taste or income bracket. The range includes historic homes, contemporary structures, bungalows, ranch-style residences, riverfront condominiums, townhouses and building lots in ever-increasing new developments.

Because both waterfront and non-waterfront homes and lots are often within the same district, real estate values can vary widely within the same neighborhood. Prices for lots and houses quoted here are approximations and, of course, are subject to change. The following descriptions of neighborhoods will help orient you to the personality, price range and availability of New Bern housing.

Neighborhoods

Downtown Historic District

This is the mecca for those who desire to live in New Bern's oldest and most distinguished homes. The downtown historic district encompasses the point of land jutting into the confluence of the

Neuse and Trent Rivers and extends west to Queen Street.

The New Bern Preservation Foundation, in the years since its organization in 1972, has bought and restored approximately 40 structures of historic or architectural significance. This has stimulated private interests in the community that has resulted in the restoration of more than 150 private homes. A few of these date from the mid-1700s, shortly after New Bern was founded in 1710 by Swiss nobleman Christoph von Graffenreid.

The focal point of the downtown historic district is Tryon Palace on Pollock Street. The former home of the Carolinas' British governor, Tryon Palace, its gardens and associated buildings have been beautifully reconstructed or restored. The state historic site draws thousands of visitors each year. In the surrounding neighborhood, you can find tastefully renovated old homes, many of which are occupied by professional offices, businesses and bed and breakfast inns. The city has an astonishing total of 140 landmarks listed in the National Register of Historic Places, and most of these are found in the downtown district.

Facing the Neuse River north of the U.S. 17 bridge are approximately a dozen square blocks of pedigreed houses dating from the 18th, 19th and 20th centuries. Most are two- and three-story elegant restorations, and occasionally one is available for sale at a dear price. Smaller restored homes away from the river in this neighborhood are available in the

$100,000 range. The farther away you get from the river, blocks become more transitional and prices get lower.

The cost of homes throughout the entire downtown district varies enormously, depending upon location and the degree of restoration. Some homes along the fringes are offered in the $40,000- to $60,000-range, but you can bet they required a tremendous amount of work and TLC. Fully restored historic houses are offered for $160,000 to more than $300,000.

Riverside Historic District

This area includes National Avenue and the section east of it to the Neuse River. Noted as a historic district, this section unfortunately has fallen into disrepair over the years. Many of the larger homes were built between 1896 and World War II. They grew up around the lumber industry, which once flourished along the Neuse. Measures are being taken to rejuvenate this once-handsome neighborhood that is characterized by high-peaked, two-story Victorian structures, with wraparound porches and plenty of shade trees set well back from the road. Some of the homes have been beautifully renovated, while others are still a trifle run down. A few appear to have been abandoned and virtually cry out for restoration. On the cross streets running perpendicular to National Avenue and the Neuse are tidy rows of bungalows.

Homes along the River Drive waterfront are of an entirely different character. Here, you will find pretty brick ranch dwellings on small lots with plenty of trees and good landscaping. Real estate values vary widely, with some of the older bungalows offered in the $30,000- to $50,000-range. Renovated historic dwellings here start at about $125,000, with ranch-style houses along the shore selling for a bit more.

Ghent Historic District

This is the newest of New Bern's three historic districts, with homes dating from between 1913 and World War II. It includes the area encompassing Spencer, Rhem and parts of Park avenues. It was developed as a trolley car suburb in the days when working folks wanted homes away from the hustle and bustle of downtown New Bern. Today, Spencer Avenue is considered to be one of the prettiest streets in New Bern, with old-fashioned street lamps along a landscaped median separating two lanes of traffic.

Ghent has the appearance of an energetic, blue-collar neighborhood with a distinctly lived-in look. In recent years, it has become a highly desirable section for homeowners and has undergone a lot of sprucing up. Bungalows and cottage-style homes with neat lawns make up a large part of the neighborhood. Some residences feature antebellum column fronts, and many have open or screened porches for those warm summer evenings. One of the area's nicest amenities is a new, modern YMCA, which includes a Jr. Olympic-size swimming pool, a gymnasium, weight rooms and a racquetball court. It also offers day care and exercise classes. The Ghent neighborhood lies between Fort Totten Park, which has a baseball field and bleachers, and the larger Lawson Creek Park, a popular fishing spot. This park also has playing fields, nature trails, boat launches and picnic tables.

Homes here are larger than in many of the new housing developments surrounding New Bern, but many still require remodeling and renovation. Prices range from $65,000 to $120,000.

The Blades House — one of New Bern's fine old homes.

DeGraffenreid Park

This distinguished neighborhood lies between Trent and Neuse Boulevards, directly north of the Ghent Historical District. Homes here are generally large and well placed on spacious, beautifully landscaped lots. Sidewalks invite neighborhood walks, and streets carry names such as Queen Ann Lane and Lucerne Way.

Many of the more noteable residences are stately, two-story brick dwellings with dignified Federalist features. Brick walls and wrought-iron fences embellish many of the houses in the district. You can expect to pay between $100,000 to $200,000 for these homes.

Trent Woods

This large, mature development lies between New Bern and the Trent River. Over the years it has spread out from the central New Bern Golf and Country Club. Now its winding lanes contain some of the ritziest neighborhoods and poshest dwellings in the area. It also embraces many large, ranch-style homes. It has been incorporated into a town to give residents better control over their neighborhoods, and there is virtually no commercial development within its borders. It is a neighborhood well-suited to young families with children.

Most of the buildings here tend toward conservative rather than contemporary architectural styles and are constructed of wood, brick or stucco. Homes are large, with two and three stories, and usually have attached or separate two-car garages. Some homes have private docks along the Trent River waterfront. The lots are spacious, wooded and impeccably landscaped, often with Spanish moss draping towering trees. If you take a drive through Trent Woods in the spring, you'll be greeted by a stunning display of flowering trees and shrubs.

In addition to the country club, the area boasts other amenities such as the Eastern Carolina Yacht Club. The average price for a home in this area starts around $100,000; building lots are priced from the mid-$30,000s; and waterfront houses begin in the $300,000 range.

Olde Towne Harbour

This is one of the nicest subdivisions in New Bern, just east of Trent Woods and south of U.S. 70. Though just minutes from the downtown district and the shopping malls on U.S. 17, the area offers quiet seclusion in a lovely, natural setting. Here, one can find some of the most lavish, custom-built contemporary homes and condominiums in New Bern. The largest of these sprawl along the shores of the Trent River and Olde Towne Lake, (actually a river inlet). This is a strictly residential, built-in development, and it appears no expense has been spared by those who have recently purchased and built on these choice, waterfront lots. Lots here begin at about $45,000, condos at $175,000 and homes at $150,000. Waterfront homes, again, are another story, ranging upward into the $500,000 category.

River Bend

The 1,200-acre town of River Bend lies along a winding inlet on the north shore of the Trent River, about 5 miles south of New Bern. This location allows many of the homesites to have water frontage and private boat slips. The land

What New Bern Owes John Lawson

A great deal has been written about Baron deGraffenreid, the founder of New Bern, but only by delving into the annals of history do we learn of the important part John Lawson played in the establishment of the town.

John Lawson came to the Carolinas from England in 1700 when Native Americans ruled the land. Much of the territory was uncharted and thick vegetation and insects made traveling difficult.

It is believed that Lawson was educated at either Oxford or Cambridge. His extensive education is demonstrated in his approach to botanical collections and well-written texts. His book of 1709, *A New Voyage To Carolina*, is a fascinating chronicle of the terrain, wildlife, vegetation and Indians in eastern North Carolina from 1700 to 1711.

Lawson's wanderings through the eastern part of the state took him as far west as High Point, and his writings indicate that he explored more than 1,000 miles of territory in North and South Carolina. His travels brought him in contact with many of the Indian tribes of the day, and at one point he built a house in New Bern on "a pretty high piece of land by creekside" that today is known as Lawson's Creek. Lawson was eventually named Surveyor General of the province and played an important part in the founding of Bath and New Bern. In 1710, when deGraffenreid established a colony in New Bern, Lawson helped lay out the town.

Throughout his book, Lawson reported that "the Indians are really better to us than we have been to them," and added, as though forecasting his fate, "but the Indians are revengeful and never forget an injury done until they have reached satisfaction." Another entry states, "We have abandoned our own Native Soil to drive them out, and possess theirs."

By 1711, the Indians being crowded out were the fierce Tuscaroras. Lawson describes them as "well-shaped, clean-made" people, inclined to be tall and straight. "Their gate is sedate and majestic and they are dexterous and steady." Their eyes "are black or dark hazel" and "no people see better in the Night or Day." Their skin color, "is of a tawney, which would not be so dark did they not dawb themselves with Bear's Oil and a Colour like burnt Cork. This is begun in their Infancy and Continued for a long time, which fills the Pores and enables them better to endure the Extremity of the Weather. They are never bald on their Heads, which I believe proceeds from their Heads being always uncovered, and the greasing their Hair so often as they do with Bear's Fat which is a great Nourisher of the Hair, and causes it to grow very fast."

John Lawson met his fate at the hands of these people that he so admired on September 22, 1711, during a fact-finding trip up the Neuse River. Lawson, two slaves and Baron deGraffenreid headed out by boat to investigate the navigability of the upper Neuse and explore the surrounding land. Unknown to the exploration party was the Indians' plan to raid the white settlers. Lawson's excursion took place only a few days before the massacre occurred.

The first night, Lawson and his party arrived at the Indian village of Corutra and were immediately surrounded by armed Indians. They were forced to march all night to another village inland. The following morning the Assembly of the Great met, and after questioning Lawson and deGraffenreid, decided to free them. The next morning, however, Lawson got into an argument with village Chief Cor Tom and both Lawson and deGraffenried were sentenced to death. DeGraffenried pled for his life, and King Taylor, from whom the Baron had purchased the lands of New Bern, spoke in his favor. The Baron's life was spared but Lawson's was not. The Indians told the Baron of the planned massacre, but said New Bern would be spared.

It was six weeks before DeGraffenried, "quite lame, shivering with cold, nearly dead — my legs so stiff and swollen that I could not walk a step, but supported myself on two sticks," reached his New Bern home. He found the town partially destroyed and citizens frightened. While the Baron had been held captive, the Tuscarora Indians and their allies had carried out their plan of vengeance against the white settlers.

As for John Lawson, it is said that "his body was riddled with lightwood splinters to increase his agony. He knew these splinters contained enough pitch to guarantee them to burn profusely. His horror mounted as he watched the painted faces of his captors dance wildly about him."

was originally owned by the Odd Fellows, a fraternal group of black tenant farmers raising tobacco. During the recession of 1914, they were forced to sell their land to the "company store" for supplies and debts. During the first half of the century, the land was owned by a wealthy family that continued to have the land farmed for tobacco. In 1965, real estate speculator J. Frank Efird recognized the area's potential as a retirement development for people moving south from the northeast. He organized The Efird Company to acquire and develop the old Odd Fellows farm.

True to Efird's vision, large numbers of retirees now live in River Bend, although there are also a number of young families. The community has its own country club to service its 18-hole golf course. The club includes a well-stocked pro shop, a small sandwich shop, an outdoor swimming pool and four lighted tennis courts.

River Bend, which today has a population of approximately 3,000, incorporated into a town in 1980 in order to maintain roads and provide other services. The municipal building, finished in 1986, has a 99-seat meeting hall and is adjacent to a small park with a children's play area, baseball field and small dock. The development consists mainly of single-family dwellings, all with attached or detached one- and two-car garages. In recent years, clusters of townhouses and duplexes have been added to the community. Houses here begin at just more than $100,000 for a nonwaterfront location. Townhouse prices depend on the development, but the average range is between $60,000 and $150,000. The neighborhood is near New Bern Quinn Elementary and New Bern High School.

Fairfield Harbour

This expansive community is across the Neuse River off Highway 55 and 6 miles down Broad Creek Road. It is a 3,000-acre resort development featuring a large canal system, which gives many homes water access at their back doors.

The development is unique in that it is a combination of mostly single-family homes, with some condominiums, townhouses and timeshare condos added for good measure. In general, you can expect homes to start in the $80,000 range and continue on up into many thousands of dollars, depending upon proximity to the water.

Lots may be wooded, fronting one of two 18-hole golf courses, or on a canal where a private boat can be docked. Several hundred lots are available, with prices ranging from approximately $8,000 for an interior lot, $15,000 for a golf course lot, and from $44,000 to more than $100,000 for waterfront lots. Some waterfront sites have natural frontage, while others have bulkheads.

Condominiums and townhouses at Fairfield Harbour are arranged around small manmade lakes. Winding paths and roads connect all locations, and the combination of layout and landscaping gives a feeling of privacy, even with neighbors only a few feet away. The condos were built at different times, in different styles, and have varying levels of modern amenities. Jacuzzis and Jenn-Aire ranges are

common in most, as are balconies, decks and screened porches. Most have two or three bedrooms. One thing they all share is a respect for the trees that were there first. It is not unusual to see decks cut to accommodate a tree. Prices start in the $60,000 range for these maintenance-free homes.

The Harbour's combination of year-round residents and vacationers requires that a wide variety of activities be readily available. Established community activities are too numerous to list but include such interests as men's and women's golf associations, chorus, quilting, weaving, swimnastics, as well as garden, drama, book, bridge, RV, tennis and yacht clubs. The community features two 18-hole golf courses, one indoor and two outdoor pools, nine tennis courts, four of which are lighted, a country club with a restaurant, two pro shops, and two marinas on the premises. Boat rentals and cruises are available year round.

Brice's Creek

A number of subdivisions exist in this area southwest of New Bern, including the Lake Clermont subdivision, Snug Harbor, Oakview, Deer Run and River Trace. Some of these are fully built up, while others are in the beginning stages. The Brice's Creek region is just southwest of James City and south of the Trent River. Many homes are on interior lots, but the more elegant residences face the waterfront and are set well away from the road on large, wooded lots. They tend to be brick or stucco in contemporary styles. Homes on the waterfront generally sell in the $200,000- to $400,000-range depending on their water frontage. Houses away from the creek sell in the $90,000 to $175,000 range. The Craven County Airport, which only serves small aircraft, is just east of Brice's Creek.

Green Springs

Huge, contemporary dwellings on large, wooded lots grace the western banks of the Neuse River on Greensprings Road just off U.S. 70 E. between New Bern and Havelock. Waterfront homes start around $350,000, with lots in the price range of $125,000.

Farther east along Rivershore Drive, you can find older frame-houses and large cottages tucked into the river bluffs. Prices here vary greatly because of age, size and lot space. Just across the street and facing the water, though not on it, is a small development of brand-new, one-story contemporary homes on half-acre lots. Prices of these homes start at about $85,000, but the value is increasing rapidly.

River Bluffs

This is a new subdivision just off U.S. 70 E. outside of New Bern. It has half-acre interior lots as well as wooded waterfront lots on the Neuse River. It also has an inland lake. Lot prices range from $19,000 to $150,000. This developing neighborhood is well suited for retirees and young families with children.

Carolina Pines

About 11 miles south of New Bern off U.S. 70 on Carolina Pines Boulevard, Carolina Pines is a large, well-established residential resort golf community along the Neuse River. It offers a unique blend of quiet countryside living combined with country club flair and neighborly charm. Housing varies and includes modest patio homes, ranch styles and elegant two-story showplaces. Prices range from $125,000 to $160,000, with a variety of lot sizes available. A challenging golf course, a golf pro, a pro shop, tennis courts, pool, clubhouse with a restaurant and lounge and a patio overlooking freshwater lakes and the links are some of the extras residents enjoy. Homes and home sites are marketed by the Carolina Pines Real Estate Company, which is in the development. Call 447-8000 or (800) 654-5610 for more information.

West New Bern

This area is bounded by Neuse Boulevard on the northeast, Clarendon Boulevard on the southeast, U.S. 70 on the southwest and Glenburnie Road on the northwest. Homes in this attractive neighborhood are large, brick ranch and two-story dwellings on generous lots. This part of New Bern is well wooded, and there is plenty of undeveloped pine forest bordering many lots. Most of the homes have numerous large trees in the yards. Prices here begin at about $80,000 and go up to $100,000. These homes are very convenient to the West New Bern Recreation Center, which offers tennis courts, baseball fields, a basketball court and a supervised game room with pool tables. The center also offers reasonably priced craft classes and senior citizen discounts. The Trent Park Elementary School and Fields Middle School are also here.

Colony Estates

Homes in this completed development are approximately 10 to 20 years old. They are one-story brick and wood houses, with many attractive, contemporary features. The lots are about a quarter-acre. Yards are nicely landscaped, and the neighborhood is very neat and clean. There is some variety in architectural design of homes here, although they tend to be three-bedroom ranch dwellings with attached garages.

Derby Park

Farther west, the newer Derby Park subdivision has one-story homes with three or four different floor plans. The builders here varied the exterior designs with combinations of wood, brick and vinyl siding in light pastels. Houses have nice-size back yards but are squeezed closely together. Most have at least three bedrooms, and all have attached garages. Homes in both developments range in price between $65,000 and $85,000.

Greenbrier

Greenbrier is a distinguished 700-acre subdivision right in the middle of New Bern developed by the Weyerhaeuser Real Estate Company. It is off South Glenburnie Road and is a neighborhood well suited for families with young children, as well as an ideal location for retirees. Lots range from an eighth of an acre to more than a full acre, and excellent architectural planning has effectively blended a variety of home styles into a delightful community. Many homes are of contemporary brick designs, and all utilities are underground. Lot prices begin in the low $30,000s and go up to the high $80,000s. Homes on spacious lots begin at about $135,000. The entire development surrounds an 18-hole championship golf course managed by The Emerald Golf Club and designed by Rees Jones.

The clubhouse at The Emerald Golf Club at Greenbrier is often the chosen location for major local charity events. It contains an Olympic-size, Z-shaped pool and four lighted tennis courts. Golf club members can sharpen their skills on one of the finest new practice complexes in the state. A chipping green, fairway bunker and greenside bunker in association with the driving range are as popular as the nearby 11,000-square-foot practice putting green.

From Greenbrier's front gate, you are within 2 minutes of major shopping, 5 minutes from the local schools, hospital and adjacent to the campus of Craven Community College. The development phase at Greenbrier is nearly completed, and resales are handled by area real estate companies.

Real Estate Companies

There are many good real estate agencies in New Bern, and we have listed in alphabetical order some of those that come recommended. Likewise, there are a number of reliable building contractors in the area, and we have listed some of them for you. Also included is a list of building supply stores for the do-it-yourself homeowner. If you have questions about area real estate companies, consult the New Bern Board of Realtors, 636-5364. For questions about building contractors, contact Jean Overby of the New Bern-Craven County Home Builders Association at 633-1889.

CAROLINA PINES
REAL ESTATE COMPANY, INC.

390 Carolina Pines Blvd.   *447-2000*
(800) 654-5610

This 10-agent company specializes in new construction, resales, lots and acreage throughout Havelock and New Bern, particularly in the Carolina Pines subdivision south of New Bern off U.S. 70 E. It is a member of the Multiple Listing Service and is open seven days a week.

CENTURY 21 ACTION ASSOCIATES

1916 S. Glenburnie Rd.   *633-0075*
(800) 521-2780

This company is the oldest Century 21 franchise in New Bern and has more than 1,000 listings throughout the area. In addition to working with sellers, the company also offers a buyer's service, meaning it negotiates price and terms in the best interest of the buyer. Its agents pride themselves in providing good follow-up and personal care for their clients. The firm also offers property management and rental services.

CENTURY 21 ZAYTOUN-RAINES

1307 S. Glenburnie Rd.   *633-3069*
(800)548-3122
302 Tryon Palace Dr.   *636-1184*
(800)635-6454

George Zaytoun began building homes in 1964, and Marvin Raines began a real estate career in 1971. In 1986, they combined their expertise to create what has become one of the area's most successful real estate companies. The firm has been awarded Century 21's most distinguished award, the Centurion Award, presented to only eight of Century 21's 176 offices throughout North and South Carolina. It is impossible to drive through New Bern and not see Zaytoun-Raines "For Sale" or "For Rent" signs. The services of about 20 agents are available to handle residential, commercial and investment properties, as well as acreage and property management services.

COLDWELL BANKER
WILLIS-SMITH COMPANY

115 Middle St.   *638-3500*
(800) 334-0792

With more than 20 agents and a good reputation, this reliable firm recently combined its offices and relocated to its new Middle Street address along the New Bern waterfront. The company operates as a seller's and buyer's agency, offering a full range of services that includes residential brokerage and development and referrals to and from its national network. Its well-trained and experienced agents are knowledgeable about available housing in all of New Bern's long-established neighborhoods as well as about homes on the market in many of the area's new developments and subdivisions.

D. SEIPLE LAND MARKETING

48 Shoreline Dr.   *633-4520*

Farms, acreage, building lots and commercial properties are the specialties of this company. Clients in pursuit of business or industry locations often rely on Dick Seiple to provide currently marketed property appropriate to their purposes.

EASTERN SHORE REALTY, INC.

3317-D Hwy. 70 E.   *636-3050*

Eastern Shore Realty is the exclusive contact for the Eastern Shore townhouses in Bridgeton, which include both a garage and a boat slip for each condominium. It also can help you find acreage or homes in other areas of the county.

FAIRFIELD HARBOUR REALTY
750 Broad Creek Rd.   638-8011

Fairfield Harbour Realty operates in the Fairfield Harbour planned community. Its staff handles the sales of building lots, single-family homes, condominiums and timeshare condominiums.

HERITAGE REAL ESTATE
309 Metcalf St.   638-4663
(800) 728-4670

Heritage Real Estate is a growing and diversified agent-owned firm with offices in the historic district, just around the corner from Tyron Palace. Its agents specialize in relocation and work extensively with retirees.

Call ahead or stop by for an informative relocation packet, a brief orientation tour or an opportunity to have your questions answered. Heritage Real Estate's experienced agents are an excellent source of local knowledge about neighborhoods and home throughout the New Bern area. A warm welcome awaits you, and you'll be glad you called.

KELSO-WHEELER
BETTER HOMES AND GARDENS
1404 Neuse Blvd. 633-3043, (800) 638-1962
48 Shoreline Dr. 633-2434, (800) 846-0740

In business since 1962, the company's staff of more than 20 handles this nationally connected firm. It is a full-service real estate and insurance agency, and New Bern natives Chris Kelso and Gray Wheeler have an in-depth knowledge of homes and properties available throughout the area. The company handles both residential and commercial sales and has an in-house appraiser and builder.

LUPTON ASSOCIATES, INC.

2002 S. Glenburnie Rd.   637-6120
(800) 833-5671

Lupton Associates, Inc. is a full-service real estate agency and a well-known construction company that handles properties throughout New Bern and Craven County. It is a family-run business that has been doing well for more than 10 years. One of its specialties is the handling of lots in River Bend and in the River Bend subdivisions.

NANCY HOLLOWS REAL ESTATE

624 Hancock St.   636-3177

A one-woman dynamo, Nancy Hollows specializes in knowing everything there is to know about New Bern's historic homes. She has a good understanding of ordinances that govern historic district properties; however, she handles sales of all types of property throughout New Bern. Her forte is one-of-a-kind purchases, and she enjoys helping customers who are looking for unique waterfront locations. In addition, she has assisted buyers in acquiring bed and breakfasts and marinas. Her office is housed in a historic building next to her antique shop.

NEUSE REALTY

601 Broad Creek Rd.   633-4888
(800) 343-0186

Serving New Bern since 1977, this second-generation, family-owned firm focuses on relocation and total service, from the initial information-gathering process through site purchase, construction planning or resale services. Waterfront and upscale locations are a specialty as well as Fairfield Harbour properties. The firm is nationally affiliated with RELO, the largest inter-city relocation services and is a member of the New Bern and Havelock Board of Realtors, the Employee Relocation Council and the Craven County Committee of 100. Neuse handles a broad selection of rental properties.

NEW BEGINNINGS REALTY, INC.

220 E. Front St.   636-5858, (800) 331-8982

In business for 10 years, this company specializes in waterfront and golf areas for newcomers looking for retirement and relocation sites. It handles new residential homes, lots and resale of established homes. The firm has three agents who are happy to provide "no pressure," relaxed tours of available homesites in the area. A free cassette tape that describes New Bern and the surrounding vicinity as well as properties is available to those interested in relocating.

NEW BERN REAL ESTATE, INC.

1315 S. Glenburnie Rd., Ste. 9   636-2200
(800) 636-2992

This independently owned and operated full-service agency opened in 1985 and specializes in locating homes for retirees as well as local residents. Free brochures and newcomer packages are available to inquiring home seekers. Four knowledgeable and experienced agents conduct between two and five comprehensive home-finding tours per week, covering 48 miles in about 3.5 hours. Clients are provided with a free map, and the tour includes a complimentary low-calorie lunch.

RESORT HOMES OF THE CAROLINAS, INC.
530 Hwy. 55 E. 637-8080, (800) 892-8901

Resort Homes of the Carolinas is a full-service real estate company with a construction division as part of its operation. It handles sales of building lots, homes, condominiums, timeshare properties and rental property management. The company specializes in Fairfield Harbour resales and also offers new homes in River Bend and Lakemere. A home model is erected in Fairfield Harbour on Pelican Drive.

TRYON REALTY
233 Middle St. 637-3115

In business for more than 30 years, Tryon is a small company that specializes in building and development. It is the main developer of Olde Towne subdivision on the Trent River.

TYSON AND HOOKS REALTY
2402 Clarendon Blvd. 633-5766
(800) 284-6844

This firm has been in business since 1972. It offers general real estate services including commercial and residential lots and acreage. There are five agents associated with the firm.

WEYERHAEUSER REAL ESTATE COMPANY
101 Middle St. 633-6100, (800) 622-6297

Weyerhaeuser Real Estate Company is a subsidiary of Weyerhaeuser Company, the international wood and pulp giant. It offers an extensive inventory of home sites in New Bern and elsewhere in eastern North Carolina. In New Bern, the company handles real estate in its

Greenbrier community development, a 700-acre, upscale residential neighborhood surrounding the championship golf course, The Emerald. The development includes homes in Pinehurst Place. It also handles waterfront properties in nearby developments of Creek Pointe, Dawson Crossing, Sandy Grove and several other locations. Individual deep-water homesites vary greatly in size, ranging from a single acre to 50 acres and in clusters of eight to 54 homesites. The majority of Weyerhaeuser-developed properties offer homes directly on the water or on the golf course.

Builders/Contractors

BASS AND OUTLAW INC.
802 Broad Creek Rd. 633-4499

This is a family-operated contracting firm with a solid reputation for excellence in custom home building. Its services are organized into several categories, including design assistance and professional consultation before, during and after construction.

HOLLYBILLT, INC.
3303 Clarendon Blvd. 637-4173

Hollybillt is operated by Bill and Holly Willis and has been in business since 1982. The company specializes in construction of upscale homes — up to $250,000 — and also builds speculation houses and handles old-home restorations.

LUPTON ASSOCIATES, INC.
2002 S. Glenburnie Rd. 637-6120

Lupton Associates, Inc. began building in 1984 and specializes in low-maintenance, energy-efficient residential homes. It has a good reputation for well-built structures and constructs homes throughout Craven County.

NORTHWOOD BUILDERS
1315 Glenburnie Rd.   *637-3011*

Northwood Builders has been in business 16 years and specializes in the construction of new homes throughout the county. It can provide house plans or erect a customized home from plans chosen by the homeowner.

REGIONAL HOMES OF NEW BERN, INC.
2711 Nuese Blvd.   *633-6377*

Owner Dale Gupton has been n the building business 14 years. His company specializes in new construction and custom building but also does remodeling and old-home restoration.

RICHARD HOFF BUILDERS
210 Hancock St.   *633-4841*

Rich Hoff Builders specializes in custom homes with complex designs and unusual floor plans. Mr. Hoff avoids volume building and works with clients willing to spend $60 to $70 per square foot for a finished product. He also does remodeling and light commercial construction.

SCHEPER CONSTRUCTION, INC.
40 Shoreline Dr.   *637-9770*

Scheper Construction, Inc. is noted for its single-family homes at Canebrake in River Bend and townhouses at Pier Pointe. It specializes in custom-built homes, additions and renovations throughout the county.

TARHEEL ASSOCIATES
1911-A S. Glenburnie Rd.   *633-6452*

Tarheel Associates is a design-and-build company operated by Lucien Vaughn, Lewis Stowe and Bud Stilley. The firm works primarily on contract to construct custom-built homes and has a combination of 50 years of experience in the construction business.

ZAYTOUN & RAINES CONSTRUCTION
1307 S. Glenburnie Rd.   *633-0106*

Zaytoun & Raines Construction is one of three certified Master Builders for Greenbriar, which is Weyerhaeuser's prestigious development. It constructs homes ranging from $75,000 to $250,000, and each comes with a 10-year homeowner's warranty. The company also does remodeling.

Building Supplies

The following is a list of building supply businesses that carry the most complete line of building materials. They also make deliveries.

ASKEW'S, INC.
3600 Clarendon Blvd.   *633-5125*

LOWE'S OF NEW BERN
3310 Clarendon Blvd.   *633-2030*

NEW BERN BUILDING SUPPLY
(formerly General Wholesale Building Supply)
3321 Neuse Blvd.   *638-5861*

New Bern
Schools and Child Care

Educational opportunities in the New Bern area include public and private schools. In this chapter you'll find information about schools and several child-care facilities in New Bern.

Schools

Public Schools

The Craven County School System is a consolidated countywide system serving more than 14,000 city and county students. The county's public schools are fully accredited by the Southern Association of Colleges and Schools and the N.C. Department of Education.

The public school system employs about 900 teaching professionals, many of whom hold advanced degrees, and more than 600 support personnel. The average teacher-student ratio is 1-to-21 in kindergarten through 5th grade, 1-to-29 in 6th, 7th and 8th grade and 1-to-28 in high school.

Craven County's seven-member board of education is dedicated to helping schools increase student performance and positive student outcomes.

The school system offers a compre-hensive curriculum based on the North Carolina Standard Course of Study. Curriculum includes music, foreign languages, art, dance, theater, sports and computer classes, as well as all of the traditional academic offerings.

Among the high school offerings is the Comprehensive High School Concept, which focuses on individual students and early identification of problems that may lead students to be unsuccessful in school. Future Prep encourages students to specialize in one of three preparatory programs: occupational preparation, technical preparation or college preparation. Advanced placement courses are also offered.

Middle school students are involved in the middle school concept, which provides educational experiences that bridge learning between elementary school and high school for students in 6th, 7th and 8th grades. Among other programs, students are involved in team teaching and integration of subject matter, the teaching of language skills in a correlated fashion rather than as isolated subjects, and computer instructional labs. Elementary students are involved in hands-on science and math, and computer labs. A developmentally appropriate program in kin-

Contact the New Bern-Craven County Public Library, 638-7800, for a list of special children's programs being offered.

Insiders' Tips

dergarten through 3rd grade allows students to progress at their own pace academically.

The Craven County School System offers many support services including comprehensive testing, exceptional and academically gifted programs, student counseling services, dropout prevention and drug education programs and the services of school psychologists, social workers and nurses. Services are provided for students with visual, hearing, speech, orthopedic and other health impairments as well as for mentally handicapped, learning disabled and pregnant students.

Private Schools

New Bern offers a number of private schools, and another is located in Kinston, about 40 miles west. Additionally, the Yellow Pages section of the phone book lists a number of day camps and day schools for young children.

Ruth's Chapel Christian School, 2709 Oaks Road, 638-1297, is affiliated with Ruth's Chapel Free Will Baptist Church. The school serves about 215 students in kindergarten through 12th grade and an additional 35 students in day-care and before- and after-school programs. A structured program is also offered to 3 and 4 year olds.

St. Paul's School, 3007 Country Club Road, 633-0100, has about 300 students from preschool through 8th grade. The school provides before- and after-school care for its students and is affiliated with St. Paul's Catholic Church.

Arendell Parrott Academy, Kinston, 522-4222, offers nonsectarian instruction for students in pre-kindergarten through 12th grade and has a total enrollment of 515. The school offers transportation to out-of-town students.

Child Care

As is the case across the nation, the need for quality day care has grown in New Bern with the emergence of two-income and single-parent families. Here are just a few of the many day-care facilities in and around New Bern.

All About Children, 2610 Neuse Boulevard, 633-2505, accepts children from 6 weeks to 12 years old and offers before- and after-school care. Transportation to and from school is also provided.

Cobb's Child Care Center, 603 Gaston Boulevard, 638-8175, serves children from 6 weeks to 12 years old. The facility separates children into age groups and has its own kindergarten classes. Before- and after-school care and transportation to and from local schools are also available.

Colony Day Care and Kindergarten, 1108 Colony Drive, 633-2787, cares for children from ages 6 weeks to 12 years and has a van service to and from local schools. Before- and after-school care is also available.

Kid's Korner, 403 Ninth Street, 638-2957, and 3705 Old Cherry Point Road, 636-3791, accepts children from 6 weeks to 12 years. These two facilities offer before- and after-school care and transportation to and from schools.

New Bern
Retirement and Senior Services

New Bern is becoming a well-known retirement location for the senior set. Its combination of mild climate, relatively low-cost living, beautiful surroundings and friendly people seems too good to pass up. Fishing, golfing, sailing, hiking, boating — all are within a stone's throw of river city living. The colonial setting of the city itself is inviting, and a wide range of social, cultural and recreational activities enhances the attractiveness of living along the Carolina coast.

New residents find the city's excellent regional hospital, doctors' offices, shopping centers, quality restaurants and numerous religious denominations important factors in making a decision about changing their location. Those who decide to take the plunge and move to New Bern are seldom disappointed.

As more retirees settle in the area, a growing number of services and programs are being developed and tailored to meet their needs and interests. Agencies and public service organizations are expanding their offerings, and retirement communities are being designed to create stress-free environments. Housing options vary according to the needs of individuals, and agencies offer a variety of services aimed at assisting new and retired residents.

Housing Options and Facilities

Berne Village Retirement Community, 2701 Amhurst Boulevard, 633-1779, or (800) 634-7318, is a 15-acre retirement and assisted living complex near Highway 70 off Glenburnie Road. The village is a series of single-story apartment and service buildings set in a park-like environment.

The central building houses 60 rest home beds and is also the site of the community dining room, recreation facilities, library and barber and beauty shops. Facilities are available for the memory impaired, respite care and adult day-care services. In addition, the village has one- and two-bedroom, unfurnished apartments for independent living. Three financial arrangements are available: a rental plan, a year's lease, or a buy-in deposit. All three arrangements cover utilities, weekly cleaning, insurance, maintenance, transportation, 24-hour security, one meal a day in the dining room and personal emergency alert in each bedroom and bathroom. Apartment residents are required to pay for their own cable TV and telephone services.

The Christian Care Center Retirement Home on Efird Boulevard, 633-3455, is just off Highway 17 S. at the entrance to River Bend. Each of the facility's one- and two-bedroom apartments has a stove, refrigerator and hookups for washers and dryers. Independent living apartments are available, and a rest home is on site. A residents' council works with staff to plan activities, and the center staff maintains the apartments and grounds.

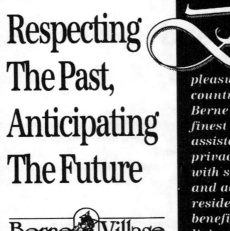
One month's rent plus a month's rent in advance is required for admission. Residents are responsible for their own electricity and phone charges, but water, sewer and garbage fees are included in the rent.

Nursing and Rest Homes

Twin Rivers Nursing Center, 1303 Health Drive, 633-8000, is owned and operated by Craven Regional Medical Center. It is a new facility and offers the advantage of being next door to the hospital should an emergency arise.

Britthaven of New Bern nursing home at 2600 Old Cherry Point Road, 637-4730, is equipped with rest home beds and nursing home beds. Additional nursing home beds have been added to a recently completed skilled Medicare unit.

A unique feature of the facility is its specially designed wing that accommodates Alzheimer's patients. The new wing has a well-equipped activities room and dining room, as well as two enclosed patios and a large hallway to allow patients to walk about without the dangers of becoming lost or injuring themselves. Requirements for persons entering the Alzheimer's program are that they be at least partially ambulatory, able to control their bladders and bowels and able to feed themselves.

Guardian Care of New Bern, 836 Hospital Drive, 638-6001, is a nursing bed facility adjacent to Craven Regional Medical Center. Permanent staff includes a full-time dietician, social worker and activities director. Activities for residents vary from holiday parties to plays presented at Easter and Christmas. Community groups often visit to provide entertainment and social interaction for residents.

Charles McDaniel Rest Home, 2915 Brunswick Avenue, 638-4680, has both private and semiprivate rooms. The facility provides basic rest home or custodial care, as well as transportation to the doctor and community events. A full-time activities director is on staff.

Agencies and Services

A number of agencies and organizations in New Bern are equipped to deal specifically with problems that may confront older people or their relatives. These agencies employ skilled staff members to handle delicate situations with empathy.

United Senior Services, Inc., 811 George Street, 638-3800, handles most of the city's services geared toward senior citizens. It offers a variety of programs and activities based at its Senior Citizens Center on George Street, where a daily meal is served. United Senior Services also operates in the communities of Havelock-Harlowe, Vanceboro, Dover and Trenton. Popular center pastimes include quilting, crafts, exercise programs, self-help and supportive services, health screenings and a wide variety of enrichment classes in cooperation with Craven Community College. The service operates a Senior Companion Program, a program in which seniors help seniors; Silver Crime Advocacy Program, for persons older than 60 who are victims of crime; Silver Friends, an inter-generational program involving youths and seniors; Elder Employment Program, which provides employment for eligible persons older than 60; Hastings Security Program, an in-home security service for seniors and the disabled; Elder Care Program, which meets special needs of seniors; N.C. Tar Heel Discount Program, which provides senior citizens shopping discounts with cooperating merchants; and the city's Meals-on-Wheels program.

The United Senior Services also operates the Craven County Information Line, 636-6614, an informational service that covers a wide variety of topics and requests of interest to seniors and the public at large, including phone numbers and referrals. The service conducts annual events such as Senior Awareness Day, Founder's Day, and Volunteer Recognition Day, as well as activities and celebrations on all major holidays. Tours, picnics, a grandparents' celebration, holiday dinners and birthday parties are also part of the regular activity schedule.

The **Department of Social Services**, 2818 Neuse Boulevard, 636-4900, offers information and assistance to seniors concerning health, Medicare and rest home and nursing home placement. The department operates an in-home aide program, a transportation program and an Adult Home Specialist Service. It also refers clients to other agencies and organizations for help with special situations.

The **Social Security Office**, 2822 Neuse Boulevard, 637-1703, administers the Social Security and Supplemental Security programs. It is open daily to provide information concerning Social Security guidelines and requirements and to answer other consumer questions. Clients are seen by appointment, and for those in Jacksonville or Morehead City, appointments can be made by calling (800) 772-1213.

Home Health Hospice Services, housed in the health department at 2818 Neuse Boulevard, 636-4930, serves homebound clients and those authorized for care by physicians. The organization provides in-home services, nursing, home health aid, nutritional care and physical, occupational and speech therapy. It also offers hospice care for the terminally ill and their families.

Area Agency on Aging, Neuse River Council of Governments, O'Marks Square, 233 Middle Street, 638-3185, works closely with the N.C. Department of Human Resources and is integrally tied to local governments in the area whose representatives make up the regional council policy board. The agency is responsible for direct contracting with local providers for priority services such as transportation, nutrition, in-home care, case management, housing and other services. It also provides technical assistance involving training, grant preparation, community coordination efforts, needs assessments and resource inventories. It additionally carries out regional ombudsman assistance to county-appointed nursing home and domiciliary home community advisory committees. The agency oversees development and implementation of aging programs, assists in the development of multipurpose senior centers and designates community focal point facilities for delivering services to the older population.

Home Care Services, a division of Craven Regional Medical Center, is housed at 1918 Clarendon Boulevard, 633-8182. The facility offers care for clients who have been authorized for services by their physicians. Home Care can provide skilled nurses, physical and speech therapy and home health aides. The organization is certified for Medicare.

Gold Care, 633-8902, is a program developed by Craven Regional Medical Center for adults 55 and older. Membership offers monthly health care seminars, a physician referral service, consultation to arrange home health care services, support groups, a Medicare hotline to assist with insurance and benefit matters, a quarterly newsletter and other activities. Annual membership is $15 for a couple or $10 for singles.

The **Professional Nursing Service,** 1425 S. Glenburnie Road, 636-2388, has licensed LPNs and RNs to assist with health care. The service can provide sitter companions, certified nursing assistance, private duty nurses and supplementary staffing.

New Bern
Volunteer Opportunities

Many of New Bern's public service agencies and nonprofit organizations rely heavily on volunteers' services and talents. Some simply could not operate without reliable volunteer assistance. New Bern has a number of spare-time opportunities, and new ones are popping up all the time. We've included several here, and you will find that volunteering with one organization often leads to developing interests in others. All organizations and agencies listed provide volunteer training.

The **New Bern Historical Society**, 510 Pollock Street, 638-8558, relies on volunteers for most of its vital functions. Volunteers make up the society's membership, education, marketing and program committees, serve as tour guides, staff the gift shop, organize and carry out fundraisers, put together the *Historical Society Journal* and a newsletter, help maintain historical buildings and grounds, and

Photo: Scott Taylor

Seems like everyone on the Crystal Coast likes to sunbathe.

coordinate special projects. Volunteers are in great demand during the city's Spring Homes and Gardens Tour and New Bern at Night Christmas Celebration. If you enjoy history and its preservation, you will find a niche here.

Like the Historical Society, the **New Bern Preservation Foundation**, also at 510 Pollock Street, 633-6448, counts on volunteers and uses their skills to operate its organization. Most volunteers are young retirees, and the foundation could not function without them. Docents serve as hosts or hostesses for home tours, help in the office, work to produce the Foundation's newsletter, help with the foundation's annual Antique Show and Sale in February, cater meals and assist with property cleanup and maintenance of historical buildings and grounds. They are also called upon to do archival work and help with special events.

The staff at **Tryon Palace**, 610 Pollock Street, 638-1560, manages most of the palace duties; however, during the Christmas season, when thousands of visitors and residents descend on the Colonial capital for day and candlelight tours, volunteer forces are called into action. Decking the palace halls with natural, handmade decorations requires the help of many, as does the making of confections and beverages in the palace kitchen. It is a very festive time, and volunteers seem to thoroughly enjoy their work.

Like any county-based arts organization, the **Craven County Arts Council**

and Gallery, 317 Middle Street, 638-2577, relies on volunteers to keep its wheels moving. Council volunteers serve as hosts in the main gallery, help in the office, assist with mass mailings, conduct programs such as the popular Jazz Sunday Showcase in February and Arts in the Schools, work on a variety of committees and assist with city-wide art projects, programs and fund-raising events throughout the year. If you have an affinity for art, this is your kind of place.

The **Craven County Convention & Visitors Bureau**, 219 Pollock Street, 637-9400, is a wonderful place to contribute some time acquainting visitors with the places they should see in New Bern. Volunteers are warm, enthusiastic and truly seem to love sharing the city of New Bern. It's also a great place to learn about New Bern if you are newly relocated and have volunteer time to offer.

The **American National Red Cross**, 1916 S. Glenburnie Road, 637-3405, is a well-known organization that uses volunteers to assist with bloodmobile clinics, serve as instructors for first aid and CPR, aid in disaster situations and help out in the office. When necessary, the Red Cross provides training for specific volunteer positions.

Officials at **Craven Regional Medical Center**, 2000 Neuse Boulevard, 633-8111, will tell you that the hospital would not run as well or as smoothly without its faithful volunteers. The center uses its 470-strong volunteer corps for everything from delivering mail to running the gift shop and snack bar. There is a junior volunteer group especially for 14- to 18-year-olds and a volunteer chaplaincy program for ordained ministers. Volunteers also help in the library, newborn nursery, emergency department and critical care waiting area. They operate the book cart and humor cart in the hospital, work in the office, assist in the nursing center and help with physical therapy and lifeline programs. The Gray Ladies and Gray Lads are perhaps the most active group, assisting with a wide variety of hospital-related duties. There's also an Auxiliary group that coordinates activities in 25 different areas. If you have time and energy to spare, the center can put them to good use.

The **Craven County School System**, 3600 Trent Road, 514-6300, welcomes volunteers to aid teachers and students in a variety of ways. Perhaps most in demand is assistance for children having problems in particular subjects, such as reading, English or math. Volunteers are also needed on field trips and in the library. Fund-raising is a constant cause, and the parent-teacher organization is always pleased to have volunteers help with special programs and projects to benefit the schools and students.

Craven County Emergency Services, 406 Craven Street, 636-6608, considers itself the right arm of the public and county government. It relies on an all-volunteer staff to oversee and operate 15 fire-fighting units and seven rescue squads. The service responds to emergency and nonemergency calls, hazardous materials cleanup standby, search and rescue, fire, and many other immediate-action situations.

The **New Bern-Craven County Public Library**, 400 Johnson Street, 638-7800, seeks volunteers to provide library services to hospitals by circulating books and magazines to patients. Its Friends of the Library group helps with fund-raising and programs, and area artists volunteer to exhibit work in the library's Artist of the Month display. If you enjoy books and literature, you may find this organization worth exploring.

The **Guardian Ad Litem** organization, 406 Craven Street, 633-0023, trains volunteers to advocate for children involved in a neglect or abuse court case. The volunteer is assigned to investigate the home situation, meet with the child and adults involved and report to the court. The information gathered is of particular assistance to the caseworker and can speed up the disposition of the case.

New Bern
Hospitals and Medical Care

The availability of quality medical care is a primary consideration for newcomers and residents of any area, and New Bern is particularly fortunate to be able to offer a wide range of top-notch professional services. The quality of life and the presence of an excellent medical center have attracted many physicians and specialized health professionals to the area.

With the influx of retirees in recent years, additional health care services, such as home care professionals, cardiac rehabilitation services and geriatric care, are now provided in New Bern — services not often available in a town of similar size. The Craven Regional Medical Center recently developed an open heart surgery unit that makes it the nearest hospital in North Carolina's mid-coastal region to offer the procedure. In addition, the medical center offers state-of-the-art diagnostic equipment and services at its New Bern Diagnostic Center and same-day surgery at New Bern Outpatient Surgery Center.

CRAVEN REGIONAL MEDICAL CENTER
2000 Neuse Blvd.   *633-8111*

Since it opened in 1962, the leaders at Craven Regional Medical Center have worked to keep up to date with equipment and services. Community leaders boast that the center is widely recognized as a leading medical facility serving eastern North Carolina and was the first in this part of the state to perform radiation therapy. The center is acutely attuned to quality medical care and implements a total quality management program.

The 314-bed facility offers a comprehensive range of services not often found outside larger urban areas. At least partly because of that, it has been named a primary health provider for a number of area counties and, most recently, for Defense Department beneficiaries in eastern North Carolina. An outstanding medical staff of more than 120 physicians, a dedicated professional and support staff of more than 1,100, and a progressive administration and board strive to combine the best of medical care with empathy for the patients.

All the major specialties are represented by the medical center's physicians and staff. Cardiac care is a focal point, with the area's most advanced services for diagnosing and treating heart disease including interventional cardiology and cardiac surgery. It was the first eastern North Carolina hospital to offer cardiac reha-

A would-be pharmacist from New Bern concocted a carbonate brew in the 1890s that he advertised as "exhilarating, invigorating and aids digestion" — thus birthed the Pepsi generation.

Insiders' Tips

bilitation on an outpatient basis. Its modern cardiac surgery suite includes surgical, recovery and intensive care rooms. Likewise, the medical center's oncology services lead the area in chemotherapy and radiation therapy on an inpatient or outpatient basis including support services.

The medical center's outpatient services include the New Bern Diagnostic Center, offering state-of-the-art diagnostic imaging equipment, mammography, ultrasound, nuclear medicine, X-ray and EKGs in a comfortable private setting. You can arrange same-day surgery at the New Bern Outpatient Surgery Center, which includes procedures for cataracts, hernias and an ever-expanding list of surgical treatments. It's Women's Center offers comprehensive gynecological care including outpatient procedures and laser surgical techniques, and it's Family Birth Place stresses family involvement in childbirth.

Specialty units include Crossroads, a 24-bed facility specializing in group-based care of adult mental health disorders, and the Coastal Rehabilitation Center, a 20-bed unit designed to help victims of stroke, orthopedic and neurological disorders.

Extended patient support services of Craven Regional Medical Center include home care and referral services, assuring that medical needs are met and services are provided.

EASTERN CAROLINA INTERNAL MEDICINE

New Bern Medical Arts Center 638-4023
1917 Trent Blvd. (800)676-8221

Eastern Carolina Internal Medicine is a large group practice with offices also in Havelock and Pollocksville. A team of 16 physicians specializing in general and subspecialty internal medicine provides care for infectious diseases, cardiology disorders, lung diseases, arthritis, digestive disorders, cancer diagnosis and treatment and hematology. The practice also specializes in aviation medicine. Its radiology department includes diagnosis and treatments involving ultrasound, CT and nuclear medicine.

NEW BERN INTERNAL MEDICINE AND CARDIOLOGY

702 Newman Rd. 633-5333

Eight physicians with internal medicine specialties provide a complete range of diagnostic and therapeutic medical care for nonsurgical adult health problems involving cardiac and pulmonary medicine, respiratory allergies, digestive disorders and cancer diagnosis and treatment. All physicians are certified by the American Board of Internal Medicine. Patients are seen by appointment, and office hours are 8:30 AM to 5 PM, Monday through Friday.

NEW BERN SURGICAL ASSOCIATES

701 Newman Rd. 633-2081
(800)682-0276 ext. 8419

The New Bern Surgical Associates practice involves five physicians specializing in laparoscopic procedures, general, vascular and pediatric surgery. All surgeons are board certified. Patients are seen by referral and by appointment during office hours, 9 AM to 5 PM, Monday through Friday. Emergency calls are received at 633-3557 at all other times.

COASTAL EYE CLINIC
802 McCarthy Blvd.   *633-4183*
(800)252-6763

Coastal Eye Clinic provides comprehensive medical, surgical and neuro-opthalmology services for patients with vision disorders. Five physicians and surgeons specialize in cataract surgery with lens implants, laser surgical techniques, glaucoma surgery and treatment, vitreous, retina and macular diseases, cosmetic surgery, pediatric ophthalmology and general eye examinations. Optical services allow for on-site selection of eyeglasses and contact lenses. Coastal Eye Clinic also has offices in Morehead City.

CRAVEN COUNTY HEALTH DEPARTMENT
2818 Neuse Blvd.   *636-4920*

Housed with other county services including the Department of Social Services in the Human Services Complex on Neuse Boulevard, the health department provides assistance and referrals in family planning, maternity care, child inoculation, adult and child health care, dental care, home health and health education.

New Bern
Higher Education and Research

Those interested in furthering their education have several options in the New Bern and Craven County area.

Whether you are pursing an associate's degree, credits to transfer to a four-year college or university, or continuing education courses, there are opportunities in New Bern.

CRAVEN COMMUNITY COLLEGE
S. Glenburnie Rd., New Bern   *638-4131*

Craven Community College offers two-year degrees and adult continuing education. Students are served in two-year associate's degree programs in the arts and sciences and more than 30 technical and vocational programs. The college offers basic adult education programs, two-year technical and transfer programs, one-year vocational programs and extension programs in occupational, practical and vocational courses of study. Craven Community College is part of North Carolina's 58-campus community college system.

EAST CAROLINA UNIVERSITY
Greenville   *328-6099*

East Carolina University in nearby Greenville is a state-supported university that offers a wide range of study areas for bachelor's, master's and doctoral degrees. The university has an enrollment of about 17,000 students. Two popular curriculum areas are education and health sciences. Many working adult students commute to the Greenville campus to pursue degrees. Craven Medical Center in New Bern is a clinical site for students enrolled in the ECU School of Nursing.

NORTH CAROLINA WESLEYAN COLLEGE ADULT DEGREE PROGRAM
New Bern Campus   *638-7209*

North Carolina Wesleyan College offers extension courses at its New Bern satellite campus, which is on the campus of Craven Community College. Students are offered three four-year degree programs — criminal justice, business administration and computer information. Wesleyan College's main campus is in nearby Rocky Mount. Call N.C. Wesleyan for a catalog to find out what courses are currently being offered.

New Bern
Commerce and Industry

Commerce and industry in New Bern are broad-based and receive strong support from the presence of Marine Corps military and civilian employees at Cherry Point Marine Corps Air Station and its affiliated Naval Aviation Depot (NADEP) in Havelock.

NADEP is one of the largest aeronautical maintenance, engineering and logistics support facilities in the Navy and is one of the largest civilian employers in eastern North Carolina. Managed by Marine officers, the facility has a work force of about 3,500 mostly civilian employees. That number is expected to grow to more than 4,000 this year as a result of the 1993 Base Closure and Realignment Study.

The depot refurbishes a variety of military aircraft and provides emergency repair and field modification teams to do repair work on aircraft unable to return to the depot. For more information about NADEP, see the Havelock chapter of this book.

Industries with large work forces in New Bern include Weyerhaeuser, Hatteras Yachts, Bosch Power Tool Company, Pepsi Cola and Moen.

Weyerhaeuser grows and harvests timber and processes it in a huge pulp mill just outside New Bern. The company employs about 700 people and owns more than 500,000 acres in eastern North Carolina.

Hatteras Yachts builds luxury watercraft in its New Bern plant and employs about 700 people. **Bosch Power Tool Company** has about 300 workers. A producer of plumbing fixtures, **Moen** has about 750 employees. **Maola Milk and Ice Cream** has about 160 workers, and **Chatsworth Products** produces computer stands and employs about 100 people.

Large non-industry employers include **New Bern-Craven County Schools, county government, Craven Regional Medical Center** and the **City of New Bern**.

The **New Bern Area Chamber of Commerce**, the **Committee of 100, Swiss Bear, Inc.**, the **Craven County Economic Development Commission** and the **Tourism Development Authority** all help to guide and encourage growth of area businesses and industries.

The Committee of 100 is a private group formed by area business leaders to stimulate business growth. The Committee owns the 519-acre Craven County Industrial Park that straddles U.S. 70 about 5 miles west of New Bern. The group owns two incubator facilities that offer free office and manufacturing space to new manufacturers. The Committee of 100 and the Economic Development Commission are constantly looking for new industries to move into the industrial park or into the county.

Photo: Scott Taylor

Cleared for takeoff!

Crystal Coast and New Bern
Airports

Passenger airline service is available at several airports convenient to the coastal area.

CRAVEN COUNTY REGIONAL AIRPORT
Hwy. 70, New Bern 638-8591

Craven County Regional Airport is the closest airport to Morehead City. Daily flights by USAir Express take passengers to the large hub airport of Charlotte. Charter services are available with Carolina Air, 633-1400. For information about car rental agencies based at the airport, see the New Bern Service Directory chapter of this book.

ALBERT ELLIS AIRPORT
Jacksonville (910) 324-1100

This airport is about 20 miles west of Jacksonville toward the town of Richlands. It is the closest airport to Camp Lejeune, the U.S. Marine Corps Base at Jacksonville. The airport offers commuter service on US Air, Henson and ASA Delta to the hubs of Charlotte and Atlanta.

MICHAEL J. SMITH FIELD
Hwy. 101, Beaufort 728-1777

Charter air service is available at Michael J. Smith Field in Beaufort. Beaufort Aviation is the fixed-base operator and handles all fueling, rental, flight instruction, charters and sightseeing flights. The airport was named for Capt. Michael J. Smith, a Beaufort native, who died aboard space shuttle *Challenger*.

RALEIGH-DURHAM INTERNATIONAL AIRPORT
Triangle Area 840-2123

This major international airport is in the middle part of the state and is about a 3-hour drive from the Crystal Coast. The airport is a major hub for domestic and international travelers and is served by all major and several feeder carriers.

Inside
Havelock

Welcome to the City of Havelock. Best known as the home to Marine Corps Air Station Cherry Point, the largest Marine Corps Air Station in the world, Havelock is a diverse city with much to offer visitors and residents.

Havelock and the base have a population of about 20,500, making it the largest city in Craven County and the 23rd largest in North Carolina. This is a far cry from the 100 residents recorded in 1950. Admittedly, Havelock gained a "few" residents when the base was annexed, but it is still one of the fastest-growing urban areas in the state. More and more people are choosing to locate in the city because of its good climate and proximity to the coast.

Havelock was named for Gen. Henry Havelock, a British general best remembered for his courageous rescues of hostage citizens during a bloody uprising in India in the mid-1800s. A marble bust of Havelock stands in the Havelock City Hall.

First called Havelock Station, the community saw action during the Civil War when troops from the Rhode Island Heavy Artillery came ashore in 1862 near what is now the base Officer's Club. From that point, Union troops captured New Bern and Fort Macon on Bogue Banks.

At one time, the production of tar and turpentine had more economic impact on Havelock than farming, but once steam engines began replacing wooden ships as transporters of goods, the market for tar and turpentine fell.

Because of its proximity to local waters and forests, Havelock gained notoriety in the late 1800s and early 1930s for its fishing and hunting opportunities. Area historians and artifact collectors value pictures of baseball great Babe Ruth, who often spent time in the area pursuing outdoor sports.

Today's residents and visitors to the Havelock area can enjoy being outdoors in the *Croatan National Forest*. This 157,000-acre forest spreads in a triangle between Morehead City, Cape Carteret and New Bern, and borders Havelock on three sides. The Croatan features many ecosystems, endangered animals, plant species and wildflowers. For more information about the Croatan National Forest, see the Crystal Coast Attractions chapter of this book.

Because of its continued growth, Havelock is experiencing more and more traffic, and the city has responded. Streets have been widened, turn lanes have been created and traffic lights have been synchronized. Additionally, a new back gate to the base was created a few years ago.

A bypass is also planned to guide traffic off the existing U.S. 70 just west of Havelock to take that traffic south of Havelock and reconnect it to U.S. 70 at the Craven County-Carteret County line on the east side of Havelock. This bypass will be connected to the city in several areas as it loops the city. Construction of portions of the Thoroughfare Plan are expected to begin in 1995 and continue over the next several years.

It will come as no surprise that the community shares in the pride and traditions of the **Marine Corps**. The most striking example of that pride is the Harrier monument in the center of town. Visitors and residents are reminded of their dependency on the military when a Harrier or an Intruder flies overhead. A sign in front of the base says it best: Pardon Our Noise — It's The Sound Of Freedom.

Havelock is often referred to as the "Gateway to Cherry Point." With more than 11,000 sailors and marines aboard the air station, Cherry Point is the largest Marine Corps Air Station in the world, and it ranks as the No. 1 industry for many of the surrounding counties.

The air station was first authorized by Congress in 1941. The arduous task of clearing the original 8,000 acres of swamp, farm and timberland began in August 1941, with actual construction beginning just 17 days before the attack on Pearl Harbor.

The air station was commissioned on May 20, 1942, as Cunningham Field, in honor of the Marine Corps' first aviator, Lt. Alfred A. Cunningham. In August 1942, the first troops arrived at the air station, and the Marine Aircraft Wing was officially formed in November 1942.

Although a number of rumors abound on how the base took the name Cherry Point, it is believed to have been adopted from an old post office established in the area years before. The post office, used by the Blades Lumber workers, was closed in 1935. The original "point" was just east of Hancock Creek, and "Cherry" came from the cherry trees that once grew there. The airfield itself, consisting of the runways and tower, is still technically named Cunningham Field.

In April 1946, the 2nd Marine Air Wing found a home at Cherry Point and was integral in training thousands of Marines for the Korean Conflict, Vietnam and the Persian Gulf War. Now, the 2nd Marine Air Wing has elements permanently stationed at MCAS Cherry Point, MCAS New River, North Carolina, and MCAS Beaufort, South Carolina. It is equipped with helicopters, fighters and attack and refueler/transport aircraft.

Over the years, Cherry Point has grown from a small airfield to one of the Marine Corps' most important air stations. The original 8,000-acre area has been expanded continuously and now encompasses more than 11,000 acres at Cherry Point and an additional 15,000 acres in assorted support locations. Built in 1941 at a cost of $14.9 million, the plant value of the base is now more than a staggering $1.6 billion.

The economic impact on the surrounding communities is enormous. An estimated $602 million is pumped into the local economy each year, including expenditures for materials, supplies and military payroll. The 10,000 military personnel draw in excess of $283 million in pay. Add to that the estimated 6,300 civilian jobs at Cherry Point, and the payroll approaches $500 million.

One stop at the **Havelock Chamber of Commerce**, 494 Westbrooke Shopping Center, 447-1101, will certainly help visitors or new residents. The friendly staff can provide maps and tons of information. With about 400 members, the Havelock Chamber serves as a visitors center and as a service-provider for its member-businesses. Chamber officials sponsor numerous events such as educational seminars, community services, social and business meetings, ribbon cuttings and workshops.

Havelock has a lot to offer. Don't just

view Havelock from Highway 70. Take a turn here or there. Stop at a few businesses — you might be surprised at what you find.

Here we offer a quick look at the city of Havelock. These sections are by no means comprehensive. One note about the addresses: Main Street is actually U.S. 70. So, if an address is on E. Main Street, it would be on the town's eastern end of Highway 70. West Main Street is on the New Bern side of the intersection of N.C. 101 and Highway 70.

Below, we have listed some general information about Havelock businesses, events and services. You'll find a listing of restaurants, accommodations, shopping, attractions, annual events, golf courses and real estate agencies. A service directory is offered with information about automotive services and tax rates. Information about area industry and military services follows.

Restaurants

From fast-food to family dining, Havelock is teaming with eateries able to satisfy whatever yen you may experience.

The restaurants listed alphabetically below represent only a small portion of the establishments in town. Ask locals for other recommendations, or stop by the Havelock Chamber of Commerce. The price code noted below the restaurant name will give you a general idea of the cost of dinner for two, including appetizers, entrees, desserts and coffee. Because entrees generally come in a wide range of prices, the code reflects an average meal — not the most or least expensive items.

Of course, lunch would cost less. The price code used in the reviews is as follows.

Less than $20	$
$21 to $35	$$
$36 to $50	$$$
More than $51	$$$$

CHOP STICKS

500 Miller Blvd.   447-1521
$

Chop Sticks serves wonderful Japanese cuisine and draws diners from all around. In a small building beside a Jim Dandy Food Store, Chop Sticks could easily be missed. But if you skip over this restaurant, you'll be sorry. Diners enjoy a variety of Japanese dishes featuring seafood, beef and pork. The restaurant's slogan is "Love At First Bite," and it is true.

CREATIVE CAFE & CATERING

424 W. Main St.   447-4669
$

Creative Cafe serves lunch each weekday and focuses on catering in the evenings and weekends. Lunch items include sandwiches on homemade whole wheat or in pocket bread and out-of-the-ordinary soups, salads and quiche. The cafe offers daily specials as well as Diet Center-approved salads and muffins. Desserts vary, but the mainstay is bread pudding. Dinner is served Wednesday, Thursday and Friday nights. Take-out orders can be arranged by calling the cafe. Catering services are available for just about any event — weddings, anniversaries, retirements or squadron parties.

EL CERRO GRANDE

314 W. Main St.   444-5701
$

El Cerro Grande offers Mexican food at its best and is a popular lunch and dinner spot. Appetizers include guacamole salad and dip, chile with cheese or nacho chicken. Entrees vary from combination plates with a choice of chicken, cheese, beef, potato or spinach fillings to special dinner platters that offer tostadas, burritos, steak ranchero and fajitas. El Cerro Grande also offers a vegetarian menu with a wonderful potato burrito and spinach enchilada. Desserts turn to such favorites as sopapillas and fried ice cream. The restaurant serves several Mexican beers, wine and mixed drinks — including fabulous Margaritas.

LA BAQUETTE CAFE

Westbrooke Plaza   447-3980
$

Stop by La Baquette for wonderful breads, rolls, croissants and pastries to take home or enjoy with coffee in the cafe. Everything is fresh-baked and delicious. Different specialty breads are prepared each day and vary from pumpernickel and Heidlerberg rye to raisin-walnut-whole wheat and sourdough. Croissants feature hazelnuts, cinnamon and chocolate. The international pastries are just plain tempting. You'll find Bavarian chocolate squares, poppyseed and apple strudel, custard raisin nut bars and so much more.

WINSTEAD'S FAMILY RESTAURANT

1222 E. Main St.   447-2036
$-$$

Winstead's is a family dining establishment with a casual atmosphere. This restaurant is very popular with locals as well as visitors. Opened in 1987 by the Winstead family, the restaurant offers a fabulous lunch and dinner buffet. The buffet features a multitude of seafood entrees and a chicken, beef and pork entree along with fresh hot vegetables, a salad bar, a number of "extras" and dessert. Guests can also enjoy the all-you-can-eat crab legs or the prime rib dinner. Winstead's recently expanded and is available for parties and banquets with seating for 175. The restaurant is open for lunch and dinner every day except Saturday, when only dinner is served.

Accommodations

Visitors to Havelock will be pleasantly surprised by the diverse accommodations offered. For years, only two motels served Havelock, with the majority of their clientele limited to traveling members of the armed services. With the increased popularity of nearby beaches and a local effort to attract industry to the area, new establishments have sprung up in recent years. We have only described a few in the section below.

For the purpose of comparing prices, we have placed each accommodation in a price category based on the summer rate for a double occupancy room. Please note that amenities and rates are subject to change, so it is best to verify the information when making inquires. The rate code is as follows.

$25 to $52	$
$53 to $75	$$
$76 to $99	$$$
More than $100	$$$$

BEST WESTERN HAVELOCK INN
310 E. Main St. 444-1414
$

Best Western currently has 38 rooms and is in the process of expanding. Guests will find a selection of sleeping arrangements. From a standard double to the Presidential and Honeymoon suites, there is a size and style to fit any traveler. The inn offers rooms with kitchenettes, balconies and Jacuzzies. A restaurant, lounge and outdoor pool are on site.

DAYS INN
Hwy. 70 E. 447-1122
$

Beside Winstead's Family Restaurant, Days Inn offers 73 rooms that open to an interior hallway. Part of a hotel chain, Days Inn offers comfortable and clean rooms. The inn also has an outdoor swimming pool, and special rooms are available for those traveling with pets.

HOLIDAY INN
400 Hwy. 70 W. 444-1111,(800) HOLIDAY
$$

This 102-room establishment offers guests room service during restaurant hours. Rooms vary in size and furnishings from a standard room to the executive suite, which features a small conference room and two adjacent bedrooms. Conference and banquet facilities for up to 350 people are also offered. A restaurant and lounge are accessible from the inn's main lobby, and an outside pool is open during the summer months.

HOSTESS HOUSE
449 McCotter Blvd. 447-3689
$

This unique "motel" might just revolutionize the way travelers think of hotels. Hostess House offers 59 rooms in several configurations, and most include kitchenettes for longer-staying guests. An expansion now under way will add 26 more rooms. Other features include an on-site laundry facility, a recreation room, barbecue grills and a miniature golf course and putting green. Hostess House is behind Food Lion grocery store at the east end of town. A Hostess House is also in Newport.

SHERWOOD MOTEL

Hwy. 70 W.   *447-3184*
$

The Sherwood Motel is well established, having been in business for many years. Guests will find a clean, quiet motel offering 89 rooms complete with cable TV, HBO and all the comforts expected. Kitchenettes are also available, and an outdoor swimming pool is open in the summer.

Shopping

Shopping opportunities continue to grow in Havelock. There are no shopping malls or major retail chain stores, but there is plenty of variety. Additionally, many Havelock residents shop in nearby Morehead City and New Bern, and military families have the opportunity to shop at the base exchange. Many of the shops in Havelock are service oriented video outlets, hair styling salons and laundry facilities. You'll also find a number of furniture stores, pawn shops and military surplus outlets. Below, we have chosen to highlight a few unique shops that are our favorites. Antique shops and flea markets are listed at the end of this section.

BOB CLARK'S PHARMACY

233 W. Main St.   *447-8102*

This pharmacy offers the usual items you would expect plus a wide selection of gift items. The store also has North Carolina souvenir items such as mugs, thimbles, etc., which are perfect for gifts for out-of-state or out-of-country friends.

BIKE DEPOT

Century Plaza, Hwy. 70 W.   *447-0834*

The Bike Depot offers Cannondale, Trek and Giant bicycles and makes repairs on all types. The store carries clothing, accessories, helmets and used bicycles. It's in the Century Plaza at the west end of town.

DOLLS GALORE

314 Hwy. 70 W.   *447-4147*

This shop offers shoppers all kinds of collector dolls. You'll also find wooden trains and stuffed animals.

MICHAEL'S FRAME & ART

488 Hwy. 70 W.   *447-3582*

Michael's offers a variety of arts and crafts materials, along with a large selection of needlepoint supplies. Custom framing is also available.

PALATE PLEASERS

U.S. 70 W.
Maxway Shopping Center   *447-2577*

This gourmet shop is a tempting place to browse. You'll find a good selection of gourmet foods, wines, cheeses, coffees and teas. Palate Pleasers also offers wonderful gift items or can prepare a gift basket for you.

Antiques/Flea Markets

HEIRLOOM SHOP

100 Jaycee St.
Commercial Shopping Center   *447-3154*

Lamps, lamps and more lamps. The Heirloom Shop can make a lamp from just about anything — a decoy, bottle, carving — then fit it with a lampshade made of silk, cotton, muslin, linen or other materials. This shop also sells antique furniture.

PLAZA TRADE CENTER FLEA MARKET

Hwy. 70 E.
Cherry Plaza   *447-3117*

This place offers a new concept in flea market retailing. With space for about 150 dealers, the Flea Market offers rental

booths to vendors. Each item is marked with the vendor's number. When a sale is made, whether the vendor is there or not, the market's cashier handles the transaction and credits the vendor's account.

Annual Events

Havelock hosts a number of events each year that are enjoyed by both residents of the city and visitors. We have listed a few of the larger and most popular events.

NORTH CAROLINA CHILI COOK-OFF CHAMPIONSHIP
U.S. 70 E.
Walter B. Jones Park   447-1101

Havelock hosts the state Chili Cook-Off Championships, and it really is a big deal. Folks come from all over to compete for prizes and to eat some of the best chili around. So, if you like chili, Havelock is where you need to be each October. Havelock plays host to 50 of the state's premier chili chefs, each vying for the title of state champion and the right to compete in the national cook-off contest. The festival also attracts cooking teams that travel the region. This is one event not to be missed, whether you like chili hot, mild or not at all. In addition to chili, music, crafts and other displays keep everyone busy. A number of local charities benefit from the profits.

CHERRY POINT AIR SHOW
MCAS Cherry Point   466-4241

This is one of the largest events in the area, with more than 60,000 people attending. It is a day the air station opens its gates to the public. The free air show features a wide variety of aerial displays from military and civilian aircraft. The numerous static displays allow visitors to get an up-close look at many of the military's high-tech aircraft. Cars are parked on the runways, so wear comfortable shoes — you may have to walk a ways. The show is conducted each April and alternates location from one year to the next between Cherry Point and Jacksonville.

FLOUNDER JUBILEE GOLF TOURNAMENT
Carolina Pines Blvd.
Carolina Pines Golf & Country Club 444-1000

The competition is sponsored by the

Men's Golf Association of Carolina Pines each June. There is no deadline for entering, but prior entrants are given first consideration. The event is a two-person superball competition.

EASTER EGG HUNT

U.S. 70 E., Walter B. Jones Park   444-6429

All children younger than 9 are invited to the park to hunt for eggs stuffed with gift certificates, money and toys. The day of the event changes each year, depending on when Easter falls, so call ahead. Children need to bring a basket.

SHERATON CRAVEN COUNTY 2-MAN GOLF TOURNAMENT

Area courses   447-1101

The 2-Man Golf Tournament is sponsored by the Havelock and New Bern chambers of commerce and draws a field of about 300 players. The tournament course varies from year to year.

OLD FASHIONED FOURTH OF JULY

U.S. 70 E., Havelock City Park   447-3212

As the name says, this is the city's Fourth of July celebration and is the prelude to the fireworks display later that evening. In prior years, crowds have enjoyed a wide variety of entertainment including musical groups, clowns and games. Food is available.

CHRISTMAS PARADE

Hwy. 70   447-1101

Like most area towns, Havelock hosts a Christmas parade each December. What makes this parade different is the fact that the featured performers are the members of the Marine Corps 2nd Marine Air Wing Band.

CHRISTMAS IN THE PARK

Hwy. 70 E., Havelock City Park   447-1101

This is one of the area's most unique Christmas celebrations. It is usually held each year on the Thursday before Christmas. The event consists of a Christmas carol sing-along and a live nativity scene.

Attractions

Although there are few bonafide attractions in and around Havelock other than Croatan National Forest, the ones that are here are must-sees for anyone traveling in the area.

CHERRY POINT BASE TOURS

It is possible to tour Marine Corps Air Station Cherry Point and see unclassified points of interest. The tours were first started in 1984 as a way to promote understanding between the air station and the surrounding community, and they continue today. Tours are offered every Thursday of the month from April through September. During the winter months, tours are offered on the first and third Thursday of each month. Those interested in taking a tour must go to the station's main gate early in order to obtain a visitor pass, (a driver's license and vehicle registration are required, and this takes a few minutes) and meet the tour guide no later than 8:45 AM. Reservations are needed for groups of 10 or more, and school groups are welcome. Tours vary depending on activities but could include a look at the weather and radar facilities, the military working dogs, the tower or a squadron. For exact times and details, call the Joint Public Affairs Office, 466-4241.

HARRIER MONUMENT

An AV-8A Harrier jump jet looms at the intersection of Highway 70 and Cunningham Boulevard. Mounted on a pedestal and encircled by flags, the AV-

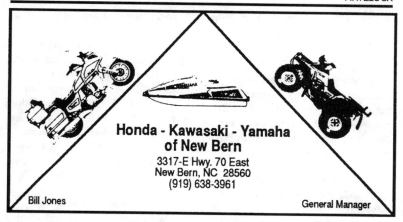
8A is a symbol of the past. Although Cherry Point is home to the largest number of Harriers in the world, the jet was taken out of service during the mid-1980s and replaced by the new AV-8B. The largest noticeable difference is that the landing gear on the "A" was located on the wing tips, while the "B" landing gear is closer to the center of the wings. This mounted jet was the second AV-8A military officials gave to civilians for display purposes. The first is on display at the Smithsonian in Washington, D.C.

Aircraft Viewing

The sound and sight of aircraft in flight is a regular occurrence for locals. However, it is often the very thing a visitor wants to experience. Although there is no designated or best spot for prime viewing, a good vantage point is along N.C. 101 near the main gate. Runway 5 ends here and, if the winds are right, is often used by Harriers, Intruders and C-130 cargo planes. The sound can be deafening, so a few words of caution: Brace yourself; warn your children; and protect infants from the noise.

Alfred A. Cunningham Air Museum

This isn't an attraction yet, but plans are in the works for a large air museum. Museum committee members hope to construct the first museum in the country dedicated to Marine Corps Aviation. Taking its name from the first Marine Corps aviator, Alfred A. Cunningham, the proposed museum would include such features as a military research library, a gift and book shop, a restaurant, a separate restoration facility and an observation tower where visitors could view flight operations on base. Museum officials currently have possession of more than 30 aircraft.

Croatan National Forest

This 157,000-acre national forest borders Havelock on three sides and offers visitors and residents a wide range of activities. Outdoor recreational activities include camping, picnicking, boating, hiking, hunting and salt- or freshwater fishing. For more information about the Croatan National Forest, see the Crystal Coast Attractions section, or contact the

Ranger's Office, 638-5628, 141 E. Fisher Avenue, New Bern, 28560.

Golf

Unless you have access to the golf course on the air station, you will end up traveling out of town to play. Numerous courses are on the Crystal Coast and in New Bern. The closest course to Havelock is described below.

CAROLINA PINES
GOLF & COUNTRY CLUB

Carolina Pines Blvd.   *444-1000*

Between Havelock and New Bern, this 18-hole, par 72 course is open year round. Carolina Pines is a residential resort development, and unlike most courses that get you in touch with nature, this course also gets you in touch with the neighbors. Residential homes dot the areas along the beautifully designed and challenging course.

Marinas

Those boaters with access to the air station also have access to a number of launching facilities. Two boat ramps will get you into either Slocum or Hancock creeks. Two other marinas, one on the Neuse River and the other on Slocum Creek, provide boat rentals and docking facilities. Without base access, your choices of marinas and ramps near Havelock are limited. Check the marina listings in the Crystal Coast and New Bern sections for nearby facilities. Below are a few of the closest choices.

MATTHEWS POINT MARINA

Temples Point Rd.   *444-1805*

At the mouth of Clubfoot Creek, this is a private membership marina, but often boaters are able to use an available wetslip overnight. A clearly marked entry channel is provided with facilities to accommodate both sail and power boats. The approach depth is between seven and eight feet. Open year round, the marina has ice, gas and diesel fuel available. Finding the marina by land is more difficult than by water. Seekers should follow Highway 101 toward Beaufort. Just a few miles out of Havelock, a church marks the corner of the highway and Temples Point Road. The marina is at the very, very end of Temples Point Road.

CAHOOGUE CREEK

The National Forest Service offers a boat ramp at Cahoogue Creek, which actually allows boats to access Hancock Creek and the Neuse River. In addition to the ramp, the facility provides grills, picnic tables and a small dock designed primarily to aid boarding. There are no bathroom facilities. Hancock Creek is great for water skiing because it is sheltered, and the surface of the creek can be as smooth as glass. This boat ramp is found at the end of Cahoogue Creek Road, a dirt road off Highway 101. There aren't really any landmarks to look for, so slow down and look for the road sign.

Real Estate

Residential housing is abundant, with prices ranging from around $35,000 to $250,000. The majority of homes in Havelock and surrounding areas are less than 10 years old. Many planned communities have popped up in the surrounding areas and are appealing to a wide range of individuals. Lured by the mild climate, low tax rate and relatively low cost of living, many retirees, both military and civilian, are finding a home in the Havelock area. Some of today's primary growth areas are the waterfront de-

velopments along the Neuse River and large creeks.

Because of the number of military entering and exiting the Havelock area, renting a place here for a period of time is a lot easier than in most areas. Rentals are abundant and come in many forms, including houses, apartments or mobile homes. Rental prices vary according to the type of accommodation and could range from $225 to $750 per month. Many storage units are also available and vary in size.

Century 21 Home Realty of Havelock, 447-2100 or (800) 858-4663, is in Westbrooke Shopping Center and is one of two Century 21 offices in Havelock. Home Realty offers sales in residential and commercial property and handles residential rentals. This is the place to find someone with extensive knowledge of the area and access to property in the surrounding four counties with multiple listing.

Century 21 Town & Country, 447-8188 or (800) 334-0320, 406 W. Main Street, is a good place to start looking for a home in or around Havelock. This is the oldest franchise real estate company in the city. Town & Country is an independently owned, full-service agency with a large market share of new and existing homes, residential and commercial rentals and investment properties for sale.

Carolina Pines Real Estate Company, 447-2000 or (800) 654-5610, markets new homes, resales, lots and acreage throughout Havelock and New Bern. Carolina Pines handles the Carolina Pines subdivision.

ERA Brickerd Realty, 444-2800, 450 Highway 70 W., has a very helpful staff. This is a good place to start looking for a home to buy or to rent. ERA Brickerd also has a full property management department.

First Carolina Realtors - Better Homes & Gardens, 447-7900 or (800) 336-5610, is easy to spot. The office is in an attractive two-story, home-type structure at the junction of highways 70 and 101. Stop by First Carolina Realtors for information about residential and commercial property for sale in the area.

The Property Shoppe, 447-1031, 957 E. Main Street, offers a wide range of services. Carol DeGennaro is the owner-broker and has been in the real estate business since 1977. The Property Shoppe is a well-established firm that handles sales of residential and commercial property in both Carteret and Craven counties, as well as rental property management.

Service Directory

Automobile Services

Serving the needs of the military is one of the prime objectives of all local businesses. As a result, and to no one's surprise, an abundance of new and used car dealerships and service centers dots the city.

Ballard Tire & Auto Service, 1202 E. Main Street, 444-1888, is a Goodyear dealer and carries other tires as well. Services include computerized wheel alignment and engine analysis, tune-ups, transmission and overall maintenance, exhaust, cooling and brake work, batteries and a number of other services.

AAA Tire Service, 174 Highway 70 W., 447-2121, carries Uniroyal and Michelin along with other tire lines and used tires. The business offers four-wheel alignment, brake work and computerized precision wheel and alignment balancing.

For quality tires and service, stop by **Super Tire Store of Havelock**, 447-1084. At 610 E. Main Street (Highway 70), the shop is owned by Allen Norris. Super Tire offers clients a full line of Michelin, Bridgestone and Kelly tires for any make or model automobile. Also offered are mag wheels at wholesale prices and complete exhaust work. Super Tire is celebrating its 27th year in business in 1995.

Tax Rates

The Craven County 1994-1995 tax rate and the municipal tax rates are based on $100 valuation and are subject to change at the end of the fiscal year. Craven County's rate is 60¢ and Havelock's rate is 39¢. New Bern's tax rate is 47¢. For information about Carteret County's tax rate or the rates of nearby cities, check the Service Directory in the Crystal Coast section of this guide.

Utilities

Utility service is provided by a number of companies. Here we have listed a few of the larger providers.

This pony lives on Carrott Island.

CABLE TELEVISION

CVI (for MCAS Cherry Point)   447-7101
Vision Cable (for service in Havelock) 447-7902

ELECTRIC COMPANIES

Carteret-Craven Electric
Membership Corporation   247-3107
Carolina Power & Light   447-9161

TELEPHONE SERVICES

Carolina Telephone   447-8958

WATER DEPARTMENT

Havelock City Water & Sewer   444-6404

TRASH COLLECTION

American Refuse Systems   633-6330

Commerce and Industry

The number of manufacturing companies in Havelock continues to grow. Through the years, a number of private firms have popped up and are helping to diversify the economic base of the city. This growth is in part thanks to the efforts of the Craven County Economic Development Commission (EDC) and Craven County's Committee of 100, 633-5300. The county has two incubator facilities and an industrial park. Here, we have highlighted a few of the largest industrial/manufacturing influences on Havelock's economy. Although it is not a private company, we have listed first the Naval Aviation Depot (NADEP) at Cherry Point because of its tremendous economic impact on the area.

NAVAL AVIATION DEPOT

MCAS Cherry Point   466-7999

NADEP is one of the largest civilian employers in eastern North Carolina. Managed by Marine officers, the facility currently has a work force of about 3,000. That number is expected to grow to 4,000 during this year as a result of the 1993 Federal Government Base Closure and Realignment Study. Other bases are being closed, and that work load and the associated employees are being moved to Havelock.

NADEP was originally established in 1943 as the Assembly and Repair Department at the air station. Since then, the facility has grown into one of the finest aeronautical maintenance, engineering and logistics support facilities in the Navy.

Its depot refurbishes a variety of military aircraft including the AV-8 Harrier, C-130 Hercules, H-46 Sea Knight helicopter, F-4 Phantom, A-4 Skyhawk, CH-53E Super Stallion and MH-53E Sea Dragon. NADEP also has extensive facilities designed to test and repair a number of different engines types, including the T58-400, which is used in the VH-3 presidential-executive helicopters. The depot also provides emergency repair and field modification teams to do repair work on aircraft unable to return to the depot. At a moment's notice, these field teams can be sent to any location around the world. Depot personnel were sent to various United States and overseas locations during the Persian Gulf War to perform such services.

JASPER TEXTILES INC.

103 Outer Banks Dr.   *444-3400*

Jasper Textiles was the charter member of the Havelock Industrial Park off Highway 101. The company manufactures men's knit sweaters under the "Outer Banks" label. Jasper Textiles opened the Havelock plant in 1991 and employs about 170 people.

UNITED PARCEL SERVICE

UPS offers express letter and parcel delivery, and the Havelock facility is a regional terminal. Opened in 1986, this facility currently employs about 50 people.

Military

The military plays a large part in the lives of all Havelock residents. More than 11,000 sailors and marines work aboard the air station.

Military Organizations

Cherry Point is home to two Marine Aircraft Groups, as well as a Marine Wing Support Group and a Marine Air Control Group.

MAG-14 consists of three All-Weather Attack Squadrons, currently flying the A-6E Intruder. These aircraft are expected to be phased out and replaced with the state-of-the-art F/A-18D. Cherry Point is expecting to have three full F/A-18 squadrons operational by 1995. In addition to the three A-6 squadrons, there is also one Tactical Electron Warfare Squadron of EA-6B, Prowlers, one Aerial Refueler and Transport Squadron with KC-130 aircraft and one Aerial Refueler and Transport Training Squadron.

MAG-32 came to Cherry Point in 1976, utilizing both the AV-8 Harrier and the A-4 Skyhawk. Since then, the Skyhawk has been totally phased out, and the original AV-8 aircraft has been replaced with the improved AV-8B. Cherry Point is home to five Harrier squadrons, including a squadron that trains all Harrier pilots for the Marine Corps. In addition to the AV-8B, the training squadron also utilizes the two-seat TAV-8B.

Two other groups also support operations for the 2nd Marine Air Wing. Some of their duties include air traffic control, weather, runway operations and air defense.

Services

A number of services are available to the military and their dependents ranging from housing to recreational facilities. All military personnel are entitled to live in base housing if they desire and if space is available. Often there is a wait to

get housing. More than 2,700 housing units are available for married personnel, ranging from apartments to houses. Three housing areas for noncommissioned officers are along the perimeter of the base and are accessible from Havelock. Thousands of barrack rooms are available for single personnel.

Military personnel are also able to utilize the new three-story Naval Hospital Cherry Point, which was dedicated last October in memory of Pharmacist Mate Second Class William D. Halyburton, a North Carolina native. The new $34 million, 201,806-square-foot hospital houses the most modern technology to support its 23 medical/surgery beds, two operating rooms, three birthing rooms and two labor and delivery rooms. Additionally, the hospital provides for the primary medical needs of our community.

Other facilities aboard the base are designed to afford military personnel a wide variety of conveniences and recreation. The Marine Corps Exchange offers a department store, grocery store, flower shop, liquor store and a number of small shops. There are also a child development center, a bank, dry cleaning and laundry facilities and a service center with a convenience store.

Recreational activities are also available and are geared to marines and their dependents. These include a large gymnasium, fitness center, three pools, an 18-hole golf course, a bowling center and a number of marinas.

Although the base offers many services for convenience and fun, the Marine Corps stresses the importance of improving one's education. The Joint Education Center provides a wide range of educational services. Offices are operated by Craven Community College, Southern Illinois University, Boston College and Park College. The center provides services such as admissions testing, independent study course catalogs, counseling and a basic skills education program. The base has one of the most comprehensive libraries in the area with everything from reference materials to children's books.

Many more services and facilities are on base. MCAS Cherry Point is a community in itself. For more information, call Base Information, 466-2811, or the Joint Public Affairs Office, 466-2536.

Inside
Oriental

Sitting beside the Intracoastal Waterway, Oriental is called the Sailing Capital of North Carolina. You won't find a big city with lots of fancy harbors and plush businesses, however you will find a town that has retained its small-village atmosphere, despite the record number of sailors who call Oriental home port or who visit there. And that small village feeling is just the way locals like it.

Oriental is in Pamlico County and is only a 20-minute ferry ride from the Crystal Coast or a short drive in the car via New Bern. The free Cherry Branch-Minnesott Beach Ferry leaves from outside Havelock (see our Ferry chapter), crosses the Neuse River and docks in Minnesott Beach. From there, it is only about 10 miles to Oriental.

The inspiration for the town's name came from the Federal Transport Ship *Oriental*, which sank off Bodie Island during a storm in May 1882. In 1896, when the community needed a post office, a name was put to a vote, and Oriental was selected.

Oriental is unlike many coastal communities. While most are dealing with new-found popularity and increased demands for housing and services, Oriental is enjoying a relaxed time. In 1910, the town's population was 2,500. Today, there are about 950 year-round residents. The tree-lined streets of downtown Oriental are perfect for strolling or biking. At the center of the older section of town is Raccoon Creek. Seafood plants with their rugged commercial trawlers line the docks alongside sleek yachts and sailboats. In recent years, new neighborhoods and marinas have sprung up around the town, offering waterfront lots, boat ramps and recreational areas.

Oriental's popularity soars on the Fourth of July weekend as thousands of visitors attend the annual **Croaker Festival** in celebration of that most vocal of fish. If you've never heard a croaker's croak, you need to spend more time on the water. Oriental's New Year's Eve community dragon run is very unique. Organized by community members, this **Chinese New Year** celebration attracts many visitors. There is an 8 PM dragon run for the children and an 11 PM run for the late-night revelers.

Oriental has a surprising number of businesses, and the fact that it is a haven for sailors is apparent by the number of sail makers and by the number of stores offering marine supplies, equipment and repairs. In the last few years many art studios and craft shops have opened. Oriental is the perfect getaway for relaxing, browsing, dining and enjoying the water. Oriental is in the 919 area code.

For those interested in getting outside, several businesses offer charters for half-day or full-day trips. There are sailing schools, creek cruises aboard a small trawler and boats and bicycles to rent. If you are interested in learning to sail, Oriental is home to a number of sailing schools. Try the **Oriental School of Sailing**, 249-0960, or **Carolina Sailing**, 249-0850.

Pelican Players is the community's performance company, and the group regularly has productions. For more information about coming plays, times and dates, call 249-1003.

Town maps are available outside beside the Oriental Motel and Restaurant and at most real estate offices. One you get the map, it is time to explore. Here are a few suggestions for places to go in Oriental.

Restaurants

The **Trawl Door Restaurant**, New Street, 249-1232, is the best-known restaurant and nightspot in town. The restaurant's dinner menu features seafood and beef with excellent prime rib, the featured entree on weekends. There is often live entertainment in the lounge, which has a special menu. The Trawl Door has all ABC permits and offers banquet rooms for private parties.

Village Restaurant, Broad Street, 249-1700, is very popular and offers lunch and dinner. The lunch salad bar and clam chowder are local favorites, along with the fresh-made hamburgers, trout and chicken sandwiches and shrimp burgers. Dinner favorites include the rib eyes and the fried or broiled seafood platters featuring shrimp, flounder, crabcakes and oysters. Also try the broiled salmon, tuna or grouper.

Accommodations

Accommodations can be found in motels or bed and breakfast inns. **Oriental Motel and Restaurant**, Hodges Street, 249-1818, is on the downtown harbor. The restaurant is very popular serving seafood, steaks and creative pasta dishes. **River Neuse Motel** at the corner of S. Neuse Drive and Mildred Street, 249-

1404, is a two-story motel is in a quiet residential area beside the Neuse River. This motel has a small cafe.

The Cartwright House, 301 Free Mason Street, 249-1337, is a Victorian bed and breakfast inn with private baths in each room. A favorite room is the cozy one on the third floor. Guests can make themselves at home on the wraparound porch, in the library or near the fireplace. Guests are served a hearty breakfast, and sailboat trips of any length can be arranged.

The **Tar Heel Inn Bed and Breakfast**, 205 Church Street, 249-1078, offers several bedrooms with private baths. Some of the rooms are in the original structure, and some are in an addition behind the country inn. Guests will find a brick patio, courtyard and gardens.

Shopping

Some people might call the **Ol' Store** on S. Water Street a curiosity shop, while others might call it a junk shop. Regardless of what it is, it is the best of its kind. The shop is jam-packed, filled to the brim with *stuff*. This place is really worth a look — you never know what you'll find, inside or out.

Inland Waterway Treasure Company, Hodges Street, carries marine hardware, charts, foul weather gear, books, gifts, T-shirts and nautical clothing. The company also rents bikes and boats.

Croakertown Shop, 807 Broad Street, offers a unique collection of gifts, books and antiques with a nautical flavor. The shop also is are best known as a fireplace shop.

Across the street is **Circle 10 Art Gallery**, a cooperative that features acrylics, oils, watercolors, basketry, fiber art, jewelry and much more.

Photo: Scott Taylor

To really get away from it all, take a quiet sail on the Neuse River.

The old hotel at the corner of Broad and Hodges streets was bought last year and is now filled with shops. The **Old Hotel Gallery**, offers unique ceramics and sculpture. Many pieces have a nautical theme. **White Heron Gallery**, is a wildlife and marine art shop that is filled with carvings, paintings and replicas.

Realty Companies

If youare interested in real estate in Oriental, either to buy or rent, there are several firms that can help.

Sail/Loft Realty Inc., Broad Street, 249-1787 or (800) 327-4189, handles sales of residential and commercial property, vacation and long-term rentals along with property management services, appraisals and storage units. **Coldwell Banker Harbor Realty**, Hodges Street, 249-1000, can help you locate a residential or commercial property to suit your needs and offers a limited number of rentals. **Village Realty**, Broad Street, 249-0509 or (800) 326-3317, offers patrons sales of residential and commercial property and vacation and long-term rentals. **Mariner Realty Inc.**, Broad Street, 249-1014, also offers residential and commercial property.

For more information about Oriental, contact the town hall, 249-0555.

Inside
Daytrips

Daytrips are the ideal way to see and enjoy more of this coastal area. Here's a quick guide to some of our favorite getaway spots. These places are close to the Crystal Coast and are Insiders' favorites for various reasons — the relaxed atmosphere, scenic beauty, unique restaurants, quiet evenings or lively nightlife. After learning more about these places, you might want to plan a longer visit.

The North Carolina Travel and Tourism Division of the Department of Commerce, Raleigh 27611, (800) VISIT NC or 733-4171, offers information about sights throughout the state. And the North Carolina Department of Transportation, P.O. Box 25201, Raleigh, 27611, can provide the latest state map, which features travel information and information about state bicycle paths. Also, you should check out the other available Insiders' Guides to various cities and regions near us. Descriptions of these publications and an order form are provided at the back of this book.

Outer Banks

Ocracoke

Visitors to Ocracoke love the slow, easy pace of this tiny island. From the time you arrive on the island until the time you leave, you will be on "Ocracoke Time." Slow down and enjoy the relaxed life.

The fact that you can get to Ocracoke only by water or air has something to do with the slow pace. Most visitors travel via state operated ferries, so there is no need to hurry up and go anywhere. You can only come and go when the ferry does. The island's airstrip is about 1 mile from the village.

From the Crystal Coast, daytrippers can take the Cedar Island-Ocracoke Ferry. This 2-hour and 10-minute ride ends in the heart of Ocracoke Village. Some choose to leave their cars on Cedar Island and walk or bike onto the ferry. Once in Ocracoke, visitors can walk just about anywhere. If you didn't bring your bike, rentals are available on the island, as are rentals of fishing equipment, sailboats and boards, beach umbrellas and chairs, and camping and hunting supplies.

Here is just a quick glimpse of Ocracoke. We suggest you read *The Insiders' Guide to North Carolina's Outer Banks* for more details.

Ocracoke was established as a port by

the colony of North Carolina in 1715. Early maps refer to the settlement as Pilot Town, because it was home to the men who were responsible for piloting ships safely into the harbor. About that same time, Edward "Blackbeard" Teach discovered the Outer Banks. The pirate and his crew robbed ships, murdered crews and terrorized island residents until 1718, when Lt. Robert Maynard of the Royal Navy and his crew ended Blackbeard's reign. Blackbeard was killed at a spot off Ocracoke now known as Teach's Hole. Legend has it that the pirate's head was mounted on Maynard's ship's bowsprit. Blackbeard's body was thrown overboard, where it swam around the ship seven times before it sank.

The island's solid white lighthouse was built in 1823 to replace the 1798 lighthouse that was just inside Ocracoke Inlet and remained in operation until 1818 when it was damaged in a storm. This is the oldest and shortest of the Outer Banks' lighthouses, measuring only 65 feet in height, or 75 feet with the lantern included. The light was manned by a keeper until 1929 when it was changed to electricity. It is now operated by the Coast Guard.

Ocracoke Village is nestled on the edge of Silver Lake on the southern end and the broadest part of the small island. There are docks for pleasure and commercial fishing boats, inns, gift shops, private homes, seafood wholesale and retail businesses, restaurants and marsh land surrounding the water. Some homes date back to the late 1800s, and many were built with timber from shipwrecks. As more visitors discover the island hideaway, more homes and lodgings are being built, and the face of the village is changing.

Highway 12, the main road in town,

begins at one ferry terminal and ends at the other. But much of the beauty of Ocracoke lies on the side streets. Howard Street is the most noted of the village's side streets. It was probably named for William Howard, who is said to have purchased Ocracoke Island in 1759 and is said to have served as Blackbeard's quartermaster.

Thirteen miles of undisturbed area stretch between Ocracoke Village and the Hatteras-Ocracoke Ferry terminal. On one side of the road is marsh leading to the sound and on the other is the Atlantic Ocean. This is the southern tip of Cape Hatteras National Seashore. This area is the perfect spot for shelling, fishing, sunbathing and ocean sports.

Because of the town's small size, many of Ocracoke's businesses do double duty. Restaurants are also nightspots; inns feature restaurants and restaurants offer gifts. Ocracoke has a surprising number of businesses. The more you explore the village, the more places you find tucked away.

Restaurant specialties vary from place to place, but you can rest assured that there is plenty of seafood. Restaurants that stay open during the winter often cut back on the number of menu items offered. Hyde County does not allow mixed drinks, but you can order beer and wine.

There are all types of accommodation choices on the island, including inns, motels, bed and breakfasts and rental cottages. While not all the places stay open year round, those that do offer some inviting winter rates. Here is a small sampling of the restaurants, shops and accommodations you will find on Ocracoke.

The village is dotted with arts, crafts, gift and apparel shops. **Island Ragpicker**, 928-7571, Highway 12, and **Village**

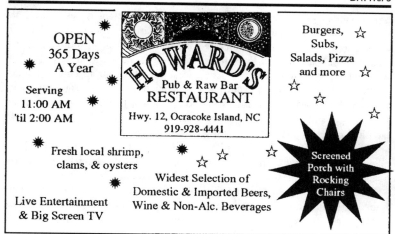

OPEN
365 Days
A Year

Serving
11:00 AM
'til 2:00 AM

HOWARD'S
Pub & Raw Bar
RESTAURANT
Hwy. 12, Ocracoke Island, NC
919-928-4441

Burgers,
Subs,
Salads, Pizza
and more

Fresh local shrimp,
clams, & oysters

Widest Selection of
Domestic & Imported Beers,
Wine & Non-Alc. Beverages

Live Entertainment
& Big Screen TV

Screened
Porch with
Rocking
Chairs

Craftsmen, 928-5541, on Howard Street are two favorites.

The Back Porch, 928-6401, serves diners in the relaxed atmosphere of its screened porch or in its dining room. The restaurant has become an island favorite with such offerings as smoked bluefish, crab beignets, pastas, salads, seafood prepared in creative ways, prime meats, secret sauces and freshly ground coffees. Unfortunately, it is closed in the winter.

Island Inn and Dining Room, Highway 12, 928-7821, is the oldest inn and restaurant on the Outer Banks. Guests are offered 16 traditional rooms in the 1901 country inn and 19 more modern rooms in another wing that fronts the island's only heated pool. The dining room is generally open for breakfast and dinner. Island Inn is open year round.

Howard's Pub & Raw Bar, Highway 12, 928-4441, is the home of the Ocracoke Oyster Shooter — a raw oyster covered with Texas Pete or Tabasco, a shot of beer and black pepper. Try it! This is the place to go for good food and a good time. Howard's doesn't close for hurricanes, holidays or winter, so chances are you'll find the place open from 11 AM to 2 AM.

Silver Lake Motel, Highway 12, 928-5721, overlooks Silver Lake and offers one wing with 20 rooms facing a shared porch. A new wing has 12 suites with private balconies and some extras, such as huge whirlpools. The rustic inn is open all year, and dock space is available for guests with boats.

Anchorage Inn, Highway 12, 928-1101, offers accommodations fronting Silver Lake Harbor. Chairs are scattered around the porches. The five-story inn

Insiders' Tips

stands high above the traditional island structures, and its brick exterior is not typical of other island structures. Guests are offered a pool, boat ramp and docks, along with rental sports equipment.

Pony Island Motel & Restaurant, Highway 12, 928-4411, offers rooms, efficiency units and cottages. This well-established motel has offered inexpensive accommodations for nearly 20 years. The adjoining restaurant is open for a hearty breakfast and for dinner.

The annual **Ocracoke Crab Festival** is held in the village on the first weekend in May. Festival-goers are given a mess of steamed crabs and then it is everyone for themselves as you finagle the tasty meat from the shells.

For more information about Ocracoke, stop by the **Ocracoke Museum and Visitors Center,** which is in the two-story yellow house near the ferry terminal.

Outer Banks Attractions

Venture a little farther than Ocracoke and discover all of North Carolina's Outer Banks. Of course, once you leave Ocracoke on the Ocracoke-Hatteras Inlet Ferry, you really aren't daytripping anymore — you're traveling.

The Hatteras Inlet Ferry actually puts passengers off at Hatteras Village. From there, the highway strings along the narrow islands to Corolla at the northern tip of North Carolina's Outer Banks.

An overview of the Outer Banks would take a whole book and, luckily, there is one. You can learn more about the Outer Banks by reading *The Insiders' Guide To North Carolina's Outer Banks.* As one of our sister books, it is laid out like this book, beginning at Corolla and taking you south through Ocracoke with

history, descriptions of restaurants, accommodations, shopping and much more. We are not going to attempt to duplicate that information here. Instead, we'll just whet your appetite with a description of a few of the larger attractions on the Outer Banks. So go on, pack the car and explore North Carolina's dynamic Outer Banks.

For additional information about North Carolina's Outer Banks, contact the Outer Banks Chamber of Commerce, Box 90CH, Kitty Hawk 27949, 261-3801, or the Dare County Tourist Bureau, Box 399, Manteo 27954, 473-2138.

ELIZABETH II STATE HISTORIC SITE
Elizabeth II State Historic Site
Manteo 473-1144

Elizabeth II is a 69-foot, square-rigged sailing ship representative of 16th-century English vessels. The ship is moored in the harbor in downtown Manteo and is open for touring. The visitors' center at Manteo offers educational programs and colorful exhibits describing the motives for exploration, shipboard life and the lives of the Native Americans encountered by the English colonists more than 400 years ago. Admission fees are $3 for adults, $2 for senior citizens and $1.50 for children 6 and older. Group discounts are available.

THE LOST COLONY
Fort Raleigh
Manteo 473-3414, (800)488-5012

Since 1937, more than 3 million people have experienced this rousing spectacle of song, dance, drama, fireworks and special effects. Written by Pulitzer Prize-winning playwright Paul Green, *The Lost Colony* is the nation's premiere symphonic outdoor drama, staged where most say the real-life events took place more than 400 years ago. The drama describes the circumstances of the 120 men, women and children who set sail from Plymouth, England, in the winter of 1586 to begin a new life in a strange land and vanished. Reservations are needed for this summer production. Performances are Sunday through Friday nights. Tickets cost $12 for adults, $11 for seniors and $6 for children younger than 12. On Mondays children 6 and younger get in for $3. On Fridays, senior citizens receive a $1 discount.

N.C. Aquarium
At Roanoke Island

Airport Rd., Roanoke Island   *473-3493*

This is a marine-oriented education and research facility. You'll find tanks of fish, lots of exhibits, films a touch tank and innovative displays. Guided tours and field trips can be arranged. The aquarium is one of three in the state. Others are in Pine Knoll Shores on the Crystal Coast and at Fort Fisher, near Wilmington. There is a small admission charge.

Outer Banks Lighthouses
Corolla, Bodie Island, Cape Hatteras

The 150-foot, red brick Currituck Beach lighthouse at Corolla was put into commission in 1875 and is still active. The lighthouses at Corolla and Hatteras are open to the public, and the long climb up is well worth it.

The 162-foot Bodie Island lighthouse was built in 1872 and is the third to stand at or near Oregon Inlet. It features black and white horizontal stripes. The visitor's center is in what used to be the keeper's quarters.

Cape Hatteras Lighthouse was built in 1872 and its black and white spiral design is probably the most recognizable of the Outer Banks structures. This landmark is 208 feet in height, making it the tallest brick lighthouse on an American coast. The former keeper's quarters serves as a visitor center. (For information about Cape Lookout Lighthouse, see the Crystal Coast Attractions section of this book, and for information about Ocracoke Lighthouse, see the Ocracoke section.)

Wright Brothers
National Memorial

Rt. 158, Bypass, MP 8
Kill Devil Hills   *441-7430*

Visitors can learn all about Orville and Wilbur Wright's first flight and other aviation pioneers at this site. The visitors center contains full-scale reproductions of the Wright's 1902 glider and of their 1903 flyer and documentation. On Kill Devil Hill, a 91-foot hill, visitors can go to the top of a 60-foot marker. The cost per entry at the guard gate is $2 per person or $4 per car.

Bath

The small, historic hamlet of Bath is North Carolina's oldest town. Located in Beaufort County, this coastal village is about 2 hours from the Crystal Coast. It can be reached by taking Highway 70 to New Bern to Highway 17, which will lead

Riding Ocracoke's trolley is a good way to relax and learn about the island's history.

Insiders' Tips

you to Washington, where you take Highway 92 to Bath. Another option is to take the more leisurely and scenic ferry route. Board the Cherry Branch-Minnesott Branch Ferry outside Havelock (see our Ferry chapter), which will take you to the other side of the Neuse River on Highway 306. Stay on Highway 306 to the Aurora-Bayview Ferry, which will deposit you on the other side of the Pamlico River. You will soon reach Highway 92, which you follow for a few short miles into Bath.

Incorporated in 1705, Bath has remained a small town, and seeing its historic sites can easily be done on foot. Today's residents take pride in their heritage, and the restoration of the town's significant 18th- and early 19th-century buildings began about 26 years ago. Before heading out on your own, stop by the visitors center on Carteret Street and view the orientation film *A Town Called Bath* as background for your walking tour. Although Bath is a small village, it has a number of historic sites well worth exploring.

Out the back door of the visitors center is a path leading to the c.1790 **Van Der Veer House**. The structure was relocated from the waterfront on the north edge of town. Continuing along the oyster shell walkway, you will come to the c. 1740 **Palmer-Marsh House**, with its large double chimney. The building is an excellent example of a large house from the Colonial period. Its architecture and history were the basis for its being designated a National Historic Landmark. The house opens for tours in April, and admission is by ticket obtained at the visitor center.

Crossing Water Street to Harding's Landing you will find a public boat dock that offers a picturesque view of the town shoreline. Heading south on Main Street

to the corner at Craven Street leads you to the **Glebe House**. This c.1835 structure was the residence of several notable 19th-century Bath citizens. It has been restored and is property of the Episcopal Diocese of East Carolina. It is not open to the public.

Behind the Glebe House is probably the town's greatest landmark, the **St. Thomas Church**. The church was built between 1734-'62 and remains the oldest church in the state. It has been restored, and services are conducted each Sunday. Visitors are welcome for self-guided tours. Continuing one block on Main Street will lead you to the **Bonner House**, c. 1830. The house was the home of the Bonner family, one of the distinguished families in Beaufort County history. It is an excellent example of North Carolina coastal architecture, which is characterized by large porches at the front and rear. Admission and a guided tour are by ticket, which can be obtained at the visitors center. Main Street in Bath is characterized by late 19th- and early 20th-century homes and commercial structures. Ballast stones taken from Bath Creek and used for walls and building foundations are reminders of Bath's maritime heritage. The town's historic district operates Monday through Saturday from 9 AM to 5 PM, and on Sundays from 1 to 5 PM.

For information before you go, call the visitor center at 923-3971.

Belhaven

If you've ventured as far as Bath, you'll be doing yourself a great disservice if you don't drive the few extra miles to scenic Belhaven. The riverside village is located on the shores of the Pungo River and has a population of about 2,500. The river provides many advantages — swimming, sailing, and skiing — and is a favorite fishing spot because of crabs and a wide variety of fish. The area is well-known among hunters of white tail deer, geese and ducks.

Located on the Intracoastal Waterway, the town is accessible by boat or car. From the Crystal Coast, you can get to Belhaven on four wheels by taking the Cherry Branch-Minnesott Beach Ferry and the Aurora-Bayview Ferry. By boat, simply follow the Intracoastal Waterway.

The main industries in Belhaven are fishing, farming, phosphates, forestry and garment manufacturing. The county is the state's largest crab meat processing center and soybean and pulpwood producer.

Belhaven has been celebrating the Fourth of July for the past 80 years with a parade, fish fry, ski show, art show, dances and concerts. The day of excitement ends with a fireworks display over the Pungo River.

Belhaven's **Memorial Museum** is one of the 14 sites on the Historic Albemarle Tour. The **City Hall**, which houses the museum, is included in the National Register of Historic Places. The museum, open seven days a week from 1 to 5 PM, has a unique collection of items depicting the area's past. The town also has an art gallery that displays a wide range of paintings, sculpture and artwork. There is a re-created Indian village and a Chamber of Commerce Welcome Center.

One of the most popular places in Belhaven is **River Forest Manor**, 600 East Main Street, 943-2151 or (800)346-2151, a rambling riverfront home that offers guest accommodations. Rooms are filled with antiques, and guest amenities include a hot tub, a swimming pool and a full service marina. The inn is famous for its wonderful Southern cuisine and lavish smorgasbord. The original owner, John Aaron Wilkinson, president of a lumber company and vice president of Norfolk and Southern Railroad Construction, began construction of the Victorian mansion in 1899. Italian craftsmen were called in to carve the ornate ceilings, and by 1904 the mansion was completed. There are carved oak mantels for each of the 11 fireplaces, cut glass leaded into windows, crystal chandeliers, mahogany features and two baths so large they include oversize tubs for two. In 1947, the house was purchased by Axson Smith of Belhaven, and the inn was opened. Mr. Smith's family continues to offer Southern hospitality.

For more information about Belhaven, contact the Belhaven Community Chamber of Commerce, P.O. Box 147, Belhaven 27810, 943-3770.

Lake Mattamuskeet Wildlife Refuge

OK, so a trip to Lake Mattamuskeet might require a bit more than a day. We have included it in the Daytrips chapter because it seems like an appropriate side journey if you make the jaunt to Oriental, Bath or Belhaven. The expansive wildlife refuge is located on Highway 264. Well-placed road signs make it easy to find.

Mattamuskeet National Wildlife Refuge stretches from Englehard on the east to Swan Quarter on the west. The refuge's 50,000 acres are made up of water, marsh, timber and croplands. The land is managed by the U.S. Fish and Wildlife Service. This beautiful area is most popular for the waterfowl it attracts. From October to March, the shallow 40,000-acre lake, which is said to be no deeper than a swan's neck, is a winter refuge for many birds. Waterfowl populations are at their peak from December through February, and so are bird watchers. The lake and adjacent canals are also popular for boating and sport fishing, with the taking of largemouth bass, striped bass, catfish, bream and other species from March 1 to November 1. Fishing for bass, catfish and bream is excellent in the canals and along the lake shore in spring and fall.

Herring dipping and blue crab fishing at the water control structures are very popular sports enjoyed by all ages. Herring dipping is permitted from March 1 to May 15, and crab fishing is permitted year round from the water control structures.

All fishing-oriented activities must be conducted in accordance with state regulations. Bow fishing for carp and other rough-fish is permitted during the fishing season.

The lake is 18 miles long and 5 to 6 miles wide, making it the state's largest natural lake. According to refuge information, more than 45,000 tundra swan winter at Mattamuskeet, and more than 150,000 birds gather at the lake between October and March. Thousands of snow

and Canada geese and 22 species of ducks are seasonal inhabitants. The refuge provides habitat for osprey, red-tailed hawks, coots, blue herons, green-winged teals, black and ruddy ducks, cormorants, widgeons, mergansers, loons and many other birds. The refuge is also home to otters, bobcats, deer and black bear. Several endangered bird species, such as the peregrine falcon and the bald eagle, seek refuge around the lake. The refuge provides public hunting of swans, ducks and coots in season. For current information on hunting dates and procedures, contact the refuge manager.

Prohibited activities in the refuge include camping, littering, swimming, molesting wildlife and collecting plants, flowers, nuts or berries. Fires and firearms are also prohibited without special authorization. The speed limit on refuge roads is 25 miles per hour, and no vehicles, such as overland vehicles or trail bikes, are allowed outside regularly used roads and trails. Boats may not be left on the refuge overnight without a special use permit.

Nearby accommodations can be found in Englehard, Fairfield, Swan Quarter and Belhaven. For additional information about area accommodations and restaurants, write or call Hyde County Chamber of Commerce, P.O. Box 178, Swan Quarter 27885, 925-5201.

For information about Mattamuskeet National Wildlife Refuge, contact the refuge headquarters, Route 1, Box N-2, Swan Quarter 27855, 926-4021.

Wilmington

A visit to Wilmington will probably require more than a day if you want to do more than drive into town, walk the waterfront and return to the Crystal Coast. This upscale but laid back river city is about 45 miles south of Jacksonville on Highway 17, about a 2-hour drive from the Crystal Coast area, and is a good jumping off point to explore several nearby beaches and attractions.

There is much to discover about this delightful city and its nearby attractions. For a complete guide to accommodations, restaurants, shopping, sightseeing and beaches, pick up a copy of *The Insiders' Guide to Wilmington and the Cape Fear Coast.*

There are two plantations that make interesting stops while in the Wilmington area. **Poplar Grove Historic Plantation**, (910) 686-9989, is an estate at Scotts Hill, 9 miles north of Wilmington on Highway 17. The 628-acre plantation is open to the public February through December and is listed on the National Register of Historic Places.

Orton Plantation and Gardens, just south of the city and a few miles off Highway 17, features a tour of the outbuildings; gardens of brilliant azaleas; Luola's Chapel, built in 1915; and an exterior view of Orton House, built in 1735. The house is now a residence. The plantation is open March through November. For information, call (910) 371-6851.

Several nearby beaches and attractions are a few minutes drive from downtown Wilmington. Fifteen minutes from the town hub lies '50s-style **Wrightsville Beach**, which is primarily a family beach and small island community that features a number of quality hotels, motels, apartments, cottages, condominium developments and many marvelous seafood restaurants.

Down U.S. Highway 421 is **Carolina Beach**, best known for its wide, uncrowded shore, swimming, surfing, pier fishing and deep-water charter boat fishing. Its shops, water slides, boardwalk and family amusement park offer something for everyone. **Carolina Beach State Park**, located on the Intracoastal Waterway at Carolina Beach, is known for its collection of diverse plants, including the endangered Venus's flytrap. The state park has 1,773 acres with a marina, picnicking, hiking and a camping area. Call (910) 458-8206 for general information or (910) 458-7770 for the marina.

Continuing down U.S. Highway 421 is **Kure Beach**, a site convenient to several attractions. It is adjacent to Historic Fort Fisher and is less than 2 miles from the N.C. Aquarium. The **Fort Fisher Historic Site** on U.S. Highway 421 is near the mouth of the Cape Fear River and includes the remains of the old fort, a visitors center, a museum with items salvaged from blockade runners and a reconstructed gun battery. Guided tours of the old earthenwork fortifications are available, and the site's 287 acres offer 4 miles of recreational beach, fishing and swimming areas, nature trails, boat ramps, picnic areas and refreshment facilities.

Nearby, the **N. C. Aquarium** houses display tanks, a shark tank, a hands-on touch tank and changing displays and exhibits. One of the state's three aquariums, it is open year round, and activities include films, talks, lectures, field trips, workshops and educational programs. For information, call (910) 458-8257.

Back to the river city of Wilmington. This historic town is home to one of the East Coast's fastest-growing deep-water ports. During the Revolutionary War, Wilmington gained importance as a point of entry, and its port was the last one on the Atlantic coast open to blockade runners during the Civil War. Continuous restoration and preservation make the town a history buff's delight. Its fast-growing population includes many students who attend the state university, UNC-Wilmington.

Almost everyone who visits Wilmington includes a tour of the **Battleship North Carolina** Memorial, (910) 762-1829, on the Wilmington waterfront.

Another "must see" in Wilmington is **St. John's Museum of Art**, (910) 763-0281, at 114 Orange Street in the historic district. Housed in three restored buildings dating from 1804, the museum exhibits one of the world's major collections of romantic color prints by renowned 19th-century American artist Mary Cassatt.

The **Bellamy Mansion Museum of Design Arts**, 503 Market Street, (910) 251-3700, is a classic Victorian example of Greek Revival and Italianate architecture. The mansion currently houses a museum of the design arts, embracing regional architecture completed in 1861, landscape architecture, preservation and decorative arts.

Another point of interest is **Brunswick Town**, the excavated ruins of a Colonial port town founded in 1726 and burned by the British in 1776. Displays include St. Philip's Church; Russellborough, the home of two royal governors; and the earthen mounds of the Confederate Fort Anderson.

Cape Fear Museum, 814 Market Street, (910) 341-7413, is a must for history buffs. The long-term exhibition, Waves and Currents: The Lower Cape Fear Story, follows the progress of the Lower Cape Fear from settlement to the 20th century and presents an expansive picture of southeastern North Carolina's heritage. Scenes come alive with life-size figures and miniature recreations of Wilmington's waterfront, c. 1863, and the Fort Fisher Battle paints a picture of Antebellum and Civil War times. Interac-

tive children's activities, videos, changing exhibitions and special events add vitality to this learning experience.

Thalian Hall, 310 Chestnut Street, (910) 343-3664 or (800) 523-2820, is a historic center for performing arts. The hall regularly hosts dramatic and musical performances, many featuring national stars.

For shopping, Wilmington's downtown streets are lined with unique stores and restaurants. Be sure to check out the **Cotton Exchange**. Housed in eight restored 19th-century buildings on the waterfront, it features distinctive shops and several good restaurants. **Independence Mall** at Oleander Drive and Independence Boulevard is home to more than 90 stores.

For an overnight stay, Wilmington has a number of fine chain hotels, and delightful bed and breakfasts have sprung up in the downtown historic district. The **Inn at St. Thomas Court**, the **Worth House** and the **Graystone Inn** are several noteworthy examples.

For gastronauts, the river city abounds with fine restaurants offering delectable food. Some that come highly recommended are **Frazier's, Elijah's, Pilot House, Caffe Phoenix, Cassidey's Eatery, Oceanic, Bridge Tender, Szechuan 132** and **Szechuan 130** and **d'Orso Importing Co.** But these are just a few of the many wonderful eateries available.

In spring, Wilmington's annual **Azalea Festival** draws visitors from miles around. Hundreds of lovely, old Southern homes on lots filled with huge trees draped with Spanish moss are surrounded by blooming azaleas. The entire community gets in on the act, with parades, contests and citywide celebrations. For information about the festival, call (910) 763-0905.

Index of Advertisers

Alan Shelor Real Estate	223	Coastal Carolina	229
American Chamber		Coastal Eye Clinic	374
Music Festival	121, 143	Coldwell Banker Spectrum	
Americare of Eastern Carolina, Inc	251	Properties	78, 227
Atlantis Lodge	63	Coldwell Banker Willis Smith	359
Beach Book Mart	94	Comfort Inn Morehead City	71
Benners Studio	339	Comfort Suites and	
Berne Village	366	Marina New Bern	279
Bogue's Pocket Cafe	45	Continental Shelf	158
Bourbon Street Cafe	35	Creative Lighting	107
Brandywine Bay	190	Crystal Coast Civic Center	17
Brynn Marr Behavorial		Crystal Queen	119
Health Care System	385	CVI	389
Cameo Boutique	107	Days Inn New Bern	277
Camp Sea Gull, Camp Seafarer	117, 185	Dee Gee's Gifts and Books	103
Captain Bill's Restaurant	47	Destinations de Travel	6
Captain Stacy	153, 151	Diamond Shoal Jewelers	104
Carolina Creations	300	DJ Shooters Restaurant	34
Carolina Princess	167	Eastern Carolina Internal Medicine	372
Carteret Community College	267	Eatmon, Ray	11
Carteret County Chamber		Emerald Isle Realty	74
of Commerce	xiv	Fabricate	97
Carteret County Economic		First Choice Mortgage	276
Development Council	268, 270	First Citizens Bank	Inside Front Cover
Carteret Craven		FSBO	225
Electric Cooperative	213	General Store	99
Carteret General Hospital	261	Golden Gull, The	107
Carteret Publishing Co.	xii	Golfin Dolphin	131
Cedars, The	69	Good Fortune	173
Century 21 Coastland Realty	9, 77	Gourmet Galley	111
Century 21 Home Realty	393	Granny's Diner	25
Century 21 Zaytoun Raines	272	Gull Isle Realty	7, 79
Cherry Point Federal Credit Union	382	Handscapes Gallery	97
Classy 103.3	8, 39, 237	Hearnes Jewelers	300
Clawson's Restaurant	43		

Holiday Trav-L-Park Resort for Campers	89
Honda-Kawasaki-Yamaha of New Bern	391
Howard's Furniture	219
Howard's Pub & Raw Bar	405
Inlet Inn	67
Ketterer Realty	82
Knowledge of Christ Book & Gift Shop	107
Larry Howard Insurance Agency	25
Lawrence Realty	18
Look Realty	83
Lynettes	107
Mail Boxes Etc	18
Mary's Flowers and Pastries	19
McGladrey and Pullen, CPA	15
Morehead General Medicine	263
Morehead Marine	163
Mystery Tours	122
New Bern Internal Medicine	375
New Bern Surgical Associates	376
No Name Grill & Lounge	37
North Carolina Maritime Museum	125
Northwest Creek Marina	329
Oceanana Family Resort	61
Ottis's Fish Market	31
Ottis Restaurant	31
Outer Banks Outfitters	165
Over The Rainbow	107
Painted Pelican	104
Pecan Tree Inn	68
Property Shoppe, The	398
Purple Pelican	
Ramada Inn, New Bern	293
Rapscallions	52
Realty World Clark Realty	80, 235
Rex Restaurant	33
Rocking Chair Bookstore	97
Royal Pavillion	62
Rucker John's Restaurant	41
Sailing Place	123, 169
Sheraton Grand New Bern	290
Skippers Cove	28
Sound 'n Sea Real Estate	79
Special Moments	94
Sports Center	183
Sprint Cellular	4
Stampers	99
Star Hill Golf Course	188
Sun Surf Realty	76, 233
Superior Carpet & Appliances	
Tetterton Management Group	81
Tom Togs	96
Truckers Toy Store	105
Tryon Palace	127
Turner Technical Service	25
Twin Rivers YMCA	334
Vacation Resorts International	295
Wachovia Bank and Trust	x
Walsh Marine	397
West Side Cafe	107
Weyerhaeuser	348
Whaler Inn	85
Windjammer Inn	62
Winstead's Family Restaurant	82
Wells Wayside Furniture	Inside Back Cover
Worthy Is The Lamb	129
WTKF	109, 155

Index

Symbols

115 Queen Street 41

A

AAA Tire Service 394
AB Jet Ski Rentals 167
ABC Day Care 247
ABC Stores 156, 324
Accommodations, Crystal Coast 59
Accommodations, Havelock 387
Accommodations, New Bern 291
Accommodations, Oriental 400
Aerie, The 291
Aerobics 182
AIDS Support Group for Patients and
    Families 262
Aircraft Viewing 391
Airports 381
Al Williams Properties 230
Alan Shelor Realty 230
Albert Ellis Airport 381
Alcoholics Anonymous 206
Aleopecia Areata Research
    Foundation 145
Alfred A. Cunningham Air Museum 391
Alger Willis Fishing Camps, Inc. 71, 195
Alive at Five Happenings 318
All About Children 364
All Saints Chapel 310
Alzheimer's Group 262
American Association of
    Retired Persons 253
American Legion, Post 46 254
American Music Festival 141, 200
American National Red Cross 206, 370
Americare of Eastern Carolina 250
Anchor Inn Restaurant
    and Lounge 44, 70, 155
Anchorage Inn 405

Anderson Audio 106
Animal Care Services 258, 345
Ann Street United Methodist
    Church 203, 246
Annabelle's Restaurant & Pub 281, 324
Anne Green Lane House 310
Anneliese's Surf & Turf 281
Annual Beaufort Old Homes Tour 146
Annual Events, Havelock 389
Annual Events, New Bern 317
Annual Turtle Release 142
Antique Depot 305
Antique Show and Sale 146, 318, 370
Antiques, New Bern 111, 304
Antiques/Flea Markets, Havelock 388
Apothecary Shop and Doctor's
    Office 117
Area Agency on Aging 368
Arendell Parrott Academy 364
Arrowhead Campsite 88
ART Gallery, Ltd. 341
Art Lessons 202
Arts and Drama Camps 140
Arts By the Sea 145
Arts, Crystal Coast 197
Arts From the Heart 141
Arts in the Schools 338, 370
Arts, New Bern 337
Atlantic 24
Atlantic Beach 6, 216
Atlantic Beach, Accommodations 60
Atlantic Beach, Restaurants 32
Atlantic Beach, Shopping 93
Atlantic Beach Surf Shop 93
Atlantic Coast Real Estate Service 235
Atlantic Dance Theater 337, 338
Atlantic Outlying Field And Piney
    Island (Marines) 271
Atlantic Photo 95
Atlantic Station Cinema 4 151
Atlantic Station Cinemas 94

Atlantic Station Shopping Center 94
Atlantic Veneer Corporation 269
Atlantis Lodge 63
Atlantis Lodge Sand Sculpture
    Contest 147
Attmore-Oliver House 309
Attractions, Crystal Coast 115
Attractions, Havelock 390
Attractions, New Bern 307
Autism Society 262
Auto Brite 106
Automotive Services, New Bern 345
Azalea Festival 412

B

B&R Lanes 323
Back Porch, The 405
Back Street Pub 154
Backyard Bears 304
Bagel Cottage 282
Bake Shoppe Bakery 95
Bald Headed Men of America 144
Bald Headed Men of America's Annual
    Convention 148
Ballard Realty 238
Ballard Tire & Auto Service 394
Bank of the Arts 312
Barber Shop Antiques and
    Collectibles 112
Barrier Island Adventures 167
Barrier Island Transportation
    Co., Inc. 195
Baseball and Little League, Crystal
    Coast 179
Basketball, Crystal Coast 180
Baskin-Robbins Ice Cream &
    Yogurt Shop 108
Bass and Outlaw Inc. 361
Bath 407
Battered Women Support Group 262
Batting cages 180
Beach Access Areas 159, 170
Beach Book Mart 94
Beach Tavern 152
Beachfront RV Park 88
Bear Island 90

Beaufort 11, 222
Beaufort, Accommodations 66
Beaufort By-the-Sea Music
    Festival 142, 200
Beaufort Christian Academy 246, 247
Beaufort Fisheries 48, 269
Beaufort Grocery Co. 40
Beaufort Harvest Time 148
Beaufort Historic Site 117
Beaufort Inn 66
Beaufort Land Conservancy
    Council, The 126
Beaufort Oars 167
Beaufort Old Homes Tour 118
Beaufort Parks 187
Beaufort Realty Company 235
Beaufort, Restaurants 40
Beaufort, Shopping 96
Beaufort Square Shopping Center 102
Belhaven 408
Belk 106
Bellair Plantation and Restoration 311
Bellamy Mansion Museum of
    Design Arts 412
Belle of New Bern 313
Bell's 102
Bereavement/Grief Support Groups 262
Bern Bear Gifts 303
Berne Restaurant 282
Berne Square 301
Berne Village Retirement
    Community 365
Bert's Surf Shop 93, 95
Best Western Buccaneer Motor Lodge 70
Best Western Havelock Inn 387
Better Breathers Support Group 262
Bettie 21
Bicycling, Crystal Coast 180
Big Oak Drive-In 64
Big Rock Blue Marlin Tournament 143
Big Sweep 147
Bike Depot 388
Billy's Ham and Eggs 282
Bird Shoal Peddler 98
Bistro By The Sea 32

Blackbeard Sailing Club's
    Winter Series 326
Blue Water Fishing Tournament 143
Bluewater Associates Better Homes and
    Gardens 232
Boardwalk By The Sea Arcade 137
Boat Ramps 162
Boating 166
Bob Clark's Pharmacy 388
Bob's Golf Range 191
Bogue Banks 5, 216
Bogue Banks Water Company 213
Bogue Banks Golf and Country Club 190
Bogue Inlet Fishing Pier 162
Bogue Sound Watermelon Festival 146
Bogue's Pocket Cafe 45
Bonner House 408
Bosch Power Tool Company 379
Bourbon Street Cafe 34
Bowling Alley 323
Bradham, Caleb 285
Branch's 103
Branch's of New Bern 303
Brandywine Bay Golf and
    Country Club 189
Breast Cancer Support Group 262
Brice's Creek 355
Bridgeview Family Campground 89
Britthaven of New Bern 366
Broad Creek 26
Broad Street Bar & Grille 292
Broman Rest Home 252
Brown and Swain Real Estate 236
Brunswick Town 412
Bryant-McLeod Ltd. 302
Brynn Marr Behavioral Healthcare
    System 260
Budget Inn 60
Builders/Contractors 239, 361
Building Supplies 241, 362
Bus and Taxi Service, Crystal Coast 206
Bus and Taxi Service, New Bern 345
Bushwackers Restaurant 40
Butcher Block Cafe 56
Byrd's 102
Byrd's Food Store 106

C

C.M. Hill Hardware 110
Cable Television, Havelock 395
Cahoogue Creek 392
Calico Jack's Inn & Marina 72
Calico Village Antiques and Carpentry
    Shop 112
Calypso Cafe 46
Cameo Boutique 108
Camp Albemarle 184
Camp Bryan Rod & Gun Club 181
Camp Morehead By The Sea 136, 184
Camp Sea Gull 136, 185
Camp Seafarer 136, 185
Camping 87, 180
Camping, New Bern 297
Cancer Support Group 262
Cannon & Gruber, Realtors 231
Cape Carteret 26
Cape Carteret, Shopping 110
Cape Fear Museum 412
Cape Lookout Lighthouse 129
Cape Lookout National
    Seashore 91, 128, 194
Cape Lookout Studies Program 118
Capps, John 144
Capt. Bill's Waterfront Restaurant 46
Capt. Charlie's Restaurant 55
Capt. Fannie's Billfish Tournament 146
Capt. Stacy 152
Capt. Stacy Fishing Center 164
Captain Ratty's Gear & Gifts 302
Captain's Quarters Bed & Biscuit 68
Car Rental, New Bern 346
Car Rentals 207
Carolina Air 381
Carolina Atlantic 104
Carolina Beach 411
Carolina Beach State Park 411
Carolina City Smoked Seafood 104
Carolina Creations 301
Carolina Cultured Shellfish 270
Carolina Kite Fest 138, 148
Carolina Linen 108
Carolina Marlin Club 222

Carolina Office Supply 103
Carolina Pines 319, 356
Carolina Pines Golf and Country
   Club 336, 392
Carolina Pines Real Estate
   Company 356, 394
Carolina Pines Real Estate
   Company, Inc. 358
Carolina Power & Light 212, 347
Carolina Princess 156, 164
Carolina Sailing 399
Carolina Telephone and
   Telegraph Co. 213, 347
Carolina Trailways 345
Carolina Water Service 213
Carteret Antique Mall 111
Carteret Arts Council 201
Carteret Arts Festival 145
Carteret Care Rest Home 252
Carteret Chorale 199
Carteret Community College 265
Carteret Community Theater 197
Carteret Contemporary Art 202
Carteret County Arts and Crafts
   Coalition Fall Show 147
Carteret County Arts and Crafts Coalition
   Spring Show 143
Carteret County Chamber of
   Commerce 269
Carteret County Chapter of N.C.
   Symphony 200
Carteret County Courthouse 117
Carteret County Economic Development
   Council, Inc. 269
Carteret County Emergency Management
   Office 210
Carteret County Home Builders
   Association 239
Carteret County Museum of History and
   Art 120
Carteret County News-Times 208
Carteret County Arts and Crafts
   Coalition 201
Carteret General Hospital 206, 259
Carteret Lanes 138
Carteret Writers 202

Carteret-Craven Electric Membership
   Corporation 212
Cartwright House, The 400
Catco 94
Catfish Lake 299
Causeway Marina 166
Causeway Pier 162
Cedar Creek Campground & Marina 90
Cedar Grove Cemetery 313
Cedar Island 24
Cedar Island National Wildlife
   Refuge 130
Cedar Point 26, 298
Cedar Point Open Air Flea Market 113
Cedar Point Tideland Trail 91
Cedar's Inn at Beaufort 68
Centenary United Methodist Church 342
Century 21 Action Associates 358
Century 21 Coastal Properties 231
Century 21 Down East Realty 236
Century 21 Home Realty of
   Havelock 393
Century 21 Newsom-Ball Realty 236
Century 21 Town & Country 393
Century 21 Waterway Realty 238
Century 21 Zaytoun-Raines 358
Century 21 Coastland Realty Inc. 232
Chachkas 98
Chadwick House 101
Chalk & Gibbs Realty 236
Channel Marker 152
Channel Marker Restaurant & Lounge 34
Charburger 282
Charles McDaniel Rest Home 367
Charles Slover House 311
Charter Boats 164
Charter Restaurant 46
Chatsworth Products 379
Cheek's Antiques 112
Chelsea — A Restaurant & Publick House,
   The 282
Chelsea, The 324
Cherry Branch - Minnesott Beach Free
   Ferry 194
Cherry Point Air Show 389
Cherry Point Base Tours 390

Child and Family Learning Center 246
Child Care 246
Child Care, Crystal Coast 243
Child Care, New Bern 363, 364
Children's Performing Arts 315, 337
Chinese New Year 399
Choice Seacoast Properties 236
Chop Sticks 386
Christ Episcopal Church 342
Christian Care Center Retirement
    Home 365
Christmas Candlelight Tours 322
Christmas Flotilla 148
Christmas Gallery Show 148
Christmas House 109
Christmas In The Park 390
Christmas Insider Tours 321
Christmas Open House 149
Christmas Parade 390
Chrysanthemum Festival 278, 321
Churches 203
Cinco de Mayo Fiesta 319
Cinema Triple 156, 323
Circle 10 Art Gallery 400
Circle, The 136
City Art Works, Inc. 341
City News Stand 104
City of New Bern 347, 379
City Side Cafe 296, 323
Civil War Museum 312
Clancy O'Hara's Restaurant
    and Lounge 284, 324
Clark-Taylor House 310
Clawson's 1905 Restaurant 42
Clayton Fulcher Seafood 270
Clayton White Remodeling and
    Repair 240
Coast Guard 205
Coast Guard Base Fort Macon 271
Coast Guard Station Swansboro 271
Coastal Carolina Christmas
    Celebration 149
Coastal Christmas Celebration 321
Coastal Christmas Flotilla 321
Coastal Coin Laundry 102
Coastal Crafts Plus 95

Coastal Eye Clinic 377
Coastal Invitational Showcase 146, 148
Coastal Jazz Society 200
Coastal Kiddie College 247
Coastal Rehabilitation Center 374
Coastal Riverside Campground 90
Cobb's Child Care Center 364
Codependents Anonymous 263
Coldwell Banker Harbor Realty 402
Coldwell Banker Willis-Smith
    Company 358
Coldwell Banker Spectrum
    Properties 231, 234
Colonial Carolina Pottery 106
Colony Day Care and Kindergarten 364
Colony Day Care Center 247
Colony Estates 356
Comfort Inn 70
Comfort Suites and Marina 292, 328
Commerce and Industry, Crystal
    Coast 269
Commerce and Industry, Havelock 395
Commerce and Industry, New Bern 379
Committee of 100 379
Consider the Lilies Florist 108
Containing Ideas 102
Continental Shelf 156, 166
Contractors 239
Cooks & Connoisseurs 304
Coor-Gaston House 311
Coors Light-Ramada Regatta 319
Coral Bay Shopping Center 95
Core Sound Decoy Carvers
    Guild 100, 113
Core Sound Decoy Festival 113, 149
Core Sound Waterfowl
    Museum 24, 101, 112, 120
Core Sound Waterfowl Museum
    Gift Shop 110
Country Aire Rental and U-Haul Inc. 210
Country Store 96
Courtney's Beach & Shag Club 152
Courts Plus 333
Cow Cafe 315
Crab Point 19
Crab Shack 38

Crafter's Emporium 302
Craven Arts Council
and Gallery 312, 318, 323, 337, 370
Craven Community Band 338
Craven Community Chorus 340
Craven Community College 378
Craven Concerts 317, 340
Craven County Board of
Commissioners 346
Craven County Convention and Visitors
Bureau 308, 370
Craven County Economic Development
Commission 379
Craven County Emergency
Services 347, 371
Craven County Information Line 367
Craven County Manager 346
Craven County Recreation & Parks 332
Craven County Regional Airport 381
Craven County School System 363, 371
Craven County Sheriff's Office 345
Craven County Water & Sewer
Department 346
Craven Historical Dancers 338
Craven Regional Medical
Center 259, 370, 373, 379
Craven Street Antiques &
Collectibles 112
Creative Cafe & Catering 386
Creative Carpentry 239
Creative Lighting 108
Creek Cafe 329
Crime Stoppers 206
Crisis Band 338
Crisis Helpline 206
Crisis Line 345
Croaker Festival 399
Croakertown Shop 400
Croatan National
Forest 91, 131, 308, 314, 391
Cross Creek Apparel 269
Crossroads 374
Crystal Coast 5
Crystal Coast Amphitheater 121
Crystal Coast Brass 106
Crystal Coast Choral Society 199

Crystal Coast Crafters 105
Crystal Coast Islands 132
Crystal Coast Rehabilitation Center 251
Crystal Palate 108
Crystal Queen 123, 154
Crystal Sports 106
Cunningham Field 384
Curtis Strange Golf Classic 335
Cutting-Allen House 310
Cutty Sark Lounge 153
Cypress Bay Plaza 108

D

D. Seiple Land Marketing 358
da Verrazzano, Giovanni 8
Dance 200
Dance Studios 200
David F. Jarvis House 311
Davis 22
Davis Beachwear Shop 94
Davis Island Hunting Club 181
Dawson-Clarke House 311
Days Inn 292, 387
Days Inn Suites 61
Daytrips 403
Decorating for the Holidays 321
Decorative Arts Symposium 318
Decoy Carvers Guild 120
Decoys 112
Dee Gee's Gifts and Books 102
Deer Run 355
DeGraffenreid Park 352
Delamar Inn Bed & Breakfast 69
Department of Social Services 367
Diabetes Support Group for Patients and
Families 263
Diamond City 9
Diamond Shoal Jewelers 105
Disabled American Veterans,
Chapter 41 254
Discovery Diving Company 169
Dixon-Stevenson House 308, 309
Dixon's Soda Shop 284
DJ Shooters Restaurant and Lounge 35
Dock House 154
Dolls Galore 388

Dolphins 171
Down East 21, 228
Down East, Accommodations 71
Down East Fish Fry 146
Down East Gallery 98, 201
Down East Public Schools 245
Down East, Restaurants 56
Down East, Shopping 110
Down East Togs 269
Down East Trading Post 102
Downtown Business & Professional
 Association 317
Downtown Historic District,
 New Bern 349
Dress Barn 108
Driftwood Campground 91
Driftwood Motel and
 Restaurant 56, 72, 183
Driving Ranges 191
Duck Creek Marina 329
Duke University Marine Biomedical
 Center 266
Duke University Marine Laboratory 266

E

East Carolina University 378
Easter Egg Hunt 142, 390
Easter Sunrise Services 142
Eastern Carolina Yacht
 Club 277, 326, 352
Eastern Carolina Internal Medicine 376
Eastern Carteret Medical Center 262
Eastern Gateway Realty 239
Eastern Shore Realty, Inc. 358
Eckerd Drugs 95, 102, 106
Econo Lodge Crystal Coast 71
Edward R. Stanly House and
 Dependency 311
Edwin Holt General Contractor, Inc. 240
EJW Bike & Tackle 160
EJW Outdoors 105
Ekklesia Apartments 250
El Cerro Grande 386
Elder Care Program 367
Elder Employment Program 367
Electricity, Crystal Coast 212

Electricity, New Bern 347
Eli Smallwood House 311
Elizabeth II State Historic Site 406
Elly's Personal Touch 96
El's Drive-In 47
Elusive Treasures 301
Emerald Golf Club 319, 357
Emerald Isle 10, 218
Emerald Isle Beach Music Festival 143
Emerald Isle Books & Toys 96
Emerald Isle Chapel By The Sea 203
Emerald Isle Fishing Pier 162
Emerald Isle Municipal Complex 180
Emerald Isle Parks and Recreation
 Department 187
Emerald Isle Realty 233
Emerald Isle, Shopping 95
Emerald Isle/Cape Carteret,
 Accommodations 64
Emerald Plantation 95
Emerald Plantation Cinema 4 96, 154
Emerald Properties 233
Emerald, The 335, 361
Emergency Phone Numbers 205
Emergency, Police, Sheriff 345
Environmental Services 258
ERA Brickerd Realty 394
ERA Carteret Properties 234
ETC 108
Eterna Riverview Stables 182

F

Fabricate Apparel 98
Fairfield Harbour 292, 335, 355
Fairfield Harbour Chorus 340
Fairfield Harbour Realty 359
Fairway Restaurant 57
Family Care Centers 252
Family Dollar Store 102
Fannie's Attic 104
Farmer's Market 304, 312
Favorite Gifts & Things 303
Ferries 192
Festival of Trees 148
Finz Grill & Eatery 42
Fire and Rescue 345

Fire Department 205
Fireman's Museum 312, 316
First Baptist Church 204, 342, 343
First Carolina Realtors - Better Homes & Gardens 394
First Craven Sanitary District 347
First Presbyterian Church 343
First United Methodist Church 204
Fisherman's Inn 72
Fishers Landing 298
Fishin' Fever 95
Fishing 159
Fishing and Water Sports, New Bern 326
Fishing, Crystal Coast 159
Fishing Reports 160
Fishing Schools 166
Fitness Centers, Crystal Coast 180
Fitness, New Bern 332
Flame, The 284
Flea Malls 113
Flea Market 111
Flounder Jubilee Golf Tournament 389
Flying Bridge, The 57, 156
Flying, Crystal Coast 182
Food Dock 95
Food Lion 95, 96, 102, 108
Fort Dobbs 124
Fort Fisher Historic Site 411
Fort Hampton 124
Fort Macon 124
Fort Macon State Park 124, 173
Fort Totten Park 334
Four C's, The 302
Fourth of July 146, 320
Frank and Clara's Restaurant & Lounge 39, 154
Fran's Beachwear 95
Fran's Gifts 95
Fred and Claire's 286
Freedom Park 187
Freeman's Bait & Tackle 160
Friday's 1890 Seafood 286
Front Street Grill 42
Frontier Home Builders 240
Frost Seafood House and Oyster Bar 39
Fudge Factory 102

Fun 'n' Wheels 136

G

Galleries 201
Garden Workshops 317
Gardeners' Weekend 319
Gazebo, The 96
General Rental 210
General Store, The 98
George Slover House 310
George Street Ballfield 334
Gerry Sadler Construction Company 240
Ghent Historic District 351
Ginny Agnew's Antiques & Collectibles
Ginny Gordon's Gifts and Gadgets 98, 105
Glebe House 408
Glenburnie Park 333
Gloria's Hallmark 108
Gloucester 22
Gold Care 368
Golden Gull, The 108
Goldman Metals 328
Golf 189
Golf & Shore Properties 237
Golf, Havelock 392
Golf, New Bern 335
Golphin' Dolphin 137, 191
Good Fortune 169
Goose Creek Resort 90
Gourmet Galley 105
Government Offices, Crystal Coast 207
Government Offices, New Bern 346
Governor's Walk 301
Grace Christian School 246
Graff's Fashions 108
Graham Academy 22
Gramercy Christian School 246
Granny's Diner 57
Grapevine, The 112
Gray Ladies and Gray Lads 371
Grayden Paul Jaycee Park 187
Great Lake 299
Great Mistakes 95, 101
Green Springs 356
Greenbrier 357

Guardian ad Litem 371
Guardian Care of New Bern 366
Gull Isle Realty 231

H

Hadnot Creek Farm 121
Halloween Parade 318
Hammock House 12
Hammocks Beach State Park 128
Hammocks Beach State Park Ferry 194
Hampton Inn 71, 292
Handscapes Gallery 102, 201
Harbor Island Club 181
Harbor Shop, The 98
Harborlight Guest House 66
Harborview Health Care
    Center 250, 252
Harborview Towers 249
Hardee's Annual Atlantic Beach King
    Mackerel Tour 147
Harkers Island 21, 100
Harkers Island Electric Membership 212
Harkers Island Fishing Center 72
Harlowe 17
Harmony House Inn 293
Harper's Oceanfront at the
    Jolly Knave 36
Harpoon Willie's Restaurant & Pub 42
Harrier Monument 390
Harris Family Care Center 253
Harry's Island Bar 61
Harvey Mansion, The 286, 292
Harvey W. Smith Watercraft Center 119
Harvey's Cellar Lounge 286, 324
Hastings Security Program 367
Hatteras Yachts 379
Havelock 383
Havelock Chamber of Commerce 384
Havelock Chili Festival 148
Hawks House 310
Head Boats 164
Healthy Choice Fitness Center 180
Hearne's Jewelers 301
Heirloom Shop 388
Henderson House Restaurant 286
Henry H. Harris House 310

Heritage Real Estate 359
Hi-Lites 94
Higher Education and Research 265
Higher Education and Research, New
    Bern 378
Hill's 302
Historic Beaufort Road Race 146, 184
Historic Preservation Commission 222
Hog Island 132
Holiday Inn 387
Holiday Inn Oceanfront 62
Holiday Trav-L-Park Resort 89
Holland's Shoes 102
Hollowell's Motel 60
Hollybillt, Inc. 361
Home Care Services 368
Home Finders Robinson and
    Associates 237
Home Health Hospice Services 368
Homeport Real Estate 236
Homes and Gardens Show 141
Horseback Riding, Crystal Coast 182
Hospice 148
Hospice of Carteret County 263
Hospitals and Medical Care,
    New Bern 373
Hospitals, Crystal Coast 259
Hostess House 387
Howard's Furniture Showrooms 105
Howard's Pub & Raw Bar 405
Hug A Bear Day Care 247
Huggins Island Fort 134
Human Care Services 258
Hunting, Crystal Coast 183
Hurricane Information 210

I

Indian Beach 6, 8, 218
Indian Beach Fishing Pier 162
Information Numbers 345
Inland Waterway Treasure Company 400
Inlet Inn 69
Iron Steamer Resort 63
Iron Steamer Resort and Pier 162
Island Beach and Racquet Club 185
Island Harbor Marina 167

Island Inn and Dining Room 405
Island Ragpicker 404
Island Restaurant 56
Island Rigs 95, 167

J

J.R. Dunn Jewelers 108
Jackson Press 98
Jacksonville Daily News 208
Jasper Textiles Inc. 396
Jazz Sunday Showcase 370
Jerkins-Duffy House 310
Jerry Lawrence General
  Contractor, Inc. 240
Jet Skis/Waverunners 167
Jewelers' Workbench 106
Jogging/Running, Crystal Coast 183
John H. Jones House 310
John Horner Hill House 310
John S. MacCormack Model Shop 120
John Wright Stanly House 308, 309
Jolly Knave Restaurant & Lounge 152
Jones Village Shopping Center 102
Josiah Bell House 117
Jungleland 136

K

Kafer Park 334
Karate 182, 184
Kelso-Wheeler Better Homes and
  Gardens 359
Kennels 206
Kerr Drug Store 110
Ketterer Realty 234
Kids Kampus 247
Kid's Korner 364
Kidstuff, Crystal Coast 135
Kidstuff, New Bern 315
Kidsville Playground 316
King George III's Birthday: Festival of
  Colonial 320
King's Arms Inn 294
Kinston Indians 179
Kite Flying 138
Kites Unlimited 95

Knowledge of Christ Books & Gifts 108
Kure Beach 411

L

La Baquette Cafe 386
La Musique Club of Carteret County 200
La Vaughn's Pottery 98
Ladies King Mackerel Tournament 146
Ladies' Shop, The 98
Lake Clermont 355
Lake Mattamuskeet Wildlife Refuge 409
Lands End 220
Langdon House 70
Latitude 35 287, 296
Laughing Gull Gallery 202
Lawrence, David 100
Lawrence Realty 238
Lawson Creek Park 334
Lazy Lyon's Auction Service 112
Lee's "Of Course" 103
Lennoxville 15
Lesbian Support Group 263
Libraries, Crystal Coast 207
Libraries, New Bern 346
Lifeline 254, 263
Light Within 106
Lighthouse Antiques 112
Lighthouses 407
Liquor Laws 156, 324
Loggerhead Turtles 115
LOOK Realty 234
Lookout Rotary Spring Road
  Race 142, 183
Lost Colony 133, 406
Lottie's Frocks & So Forth 102
Lucky Duck's 110
Lupton 132
Lupton Associates, Inc. 360
Luther Smith & Son Seafood 270
Lynette's 108

M

Mack Baker Construction 239
Magistrates 206
Magnolia House, The 294

Mailboat, The 208
Man Chun House Restaurant 36
Maola Milk and Ice Cream 379
Marina Market 329
Marinas 175
Marinas and the Intracoastal Waterway,
    New Bern 327
Marinas, Havelock 392
Marine Corps Air Station
    Cherry Point 384, 390
Marine Corps Auxiliary Landing Field 271
Mariner Realty Inc. 402
Mark Hannula Construction, Inc. 240
Marketplace, The 108
Marshallberg 22
Marsh's Surf Shop 93
Mary Catherine 166
Mary Elizabeth's 98
Mary Lou's Beach Club 152
Mary's Flowers and Pastries 103
Matthews Point Marina 330, 392
Mattie King Davis Art Gallery 98, 201
Maurice's 106
Max-Way 110
Mazzella's Italian Restaurant 57
McCauley Cleaners & Laundry 110
McLin-Hancock House 310
McMillan Builders Inc. 240
McQueen's Furniture and Interiors 108
Meals-On-Wheels 254, 367
Med Center One 262
Media 208
Media Information, New Bern 346
Medical Care, Crystal Coast 259
Menhaden Industry 48
Merchant's Park 187
Merrimon 16
Michael J. Smith Field 182, 381
Michael's Frame & Art 388
Michelob Cup Regatta 320
Middle Street Flea Market 305
Military 396
Military, Crystal Coast 271
Mill Creek 24
Mill Creek Oyster Festival 148
Minnesott Beach Yacht Basin 331

Miss Nancy's Early Learning Center 247
Mitchell Hardware —Since 1898 303
Moen 379
Molly's Beachside Bar 62
Moore's Barbecue 287
Morehead City 17, 224
Morehead City, Accommodations 70
Morehead City Country Club 190
Morehead City Floral Expressions 104
Morehead City Parks 187
Morehead City Public Schools 244
Morehead City Recreation
    Department 180, 187
Morehead City, Restaurants 44
Morehead City, Shopping 102
Morehead City-Carteret County Board of
    Realtors 230
Morehead Floral Market 104
Morehead Marine Inc. 167
Morehead Plaza 106
Morehead Plaza West 106
Morehead Twin 156
Morris Marina, Kabin Kamps and Ferry
    Service, Inc. 195
Morris Marina Kamps & Kabins 71
Movie Theaters 156, 323
Mrs. Willis' Restaurant 54
Mullet Festival 148
Multiple Sclerosis Support Group 263
Music 199
Mustard's Last Stand 287
My School 247
Mystery Tour 154
Mystery Tours 122

N

N. C. Aquarium 411
N. C. Coastal Federation 258
N. C. Kidsfest 140
N.C. Aquarium At Roanoke Island 407
N.C. Commercial Fishing Show 141
N.C. Maritime Museum 118, 202
N.C. Seafood Festival 184
N.C. Tar Heel Discount Program 367
Nancy Hollows Real Estate 360
Nancy's Nannies 246

National Oceanic and Atmospheric Administration 266, 327

NationalSound N' Sea Real Estate 231

Nature's Sake 101

Naval Aviation Depot 395

Naval Aviation Depot (NADEP) in Havelock 379

Naval Hospitals 260

Nearly Olde Shoppe 305

Neighborhoods, Crystal Coast 215

Neighborhoods, New Bern 349

Nelson Bay Challenge Sprint Triathlon 142, 186

Nervous Disorders Support Group 263

Net House Steam Restaurant & Oyster Bar 43

Neurology 264

Neuse Center for Mental Health 206

Neuse Realty 360

Neuse River Croatan National Forest 298

Neuse River Day 320

Neuse River Foundation 320

Neuse River Water & Sewer 347

Neusiok Trail 298

New Beginnings Realty, Inc. 360

New Bern 273

New Bern Academy Museum 308, 311, 319

New Bern Area Chamber of Commerce 319, 379

New Bern at Night Ghost Walk 321

New Bern Board of Realtors 357

New Bern City Water & Sewer Department 346

New Bern Civic Theater 337, 338

New Bern Diagnostic Center 374

New Bern Farmer's Market 317

New Bern Fire Department 345

New Bern Garden Club 367

New Bern Golf and Country Club 277, 336, 352

New Bern Historical Society 319, 321, 369

New Bern Internal Medicine and Cardiology 376

New Bern Magazine 346

New Bern Net & Craft Supplies 304

New Bern Police Department 345

New Bern Preservation Foundation 304, 307, 318, 350, 370

New Bern Real Estate, Inc. 360

New Bern Recreation Department 332

New Bern Rescue Squad 345

New Bern Spring Homes and Gardens Tour 319

New Bern Sunday Jazz Showcase 337

New Bern Surgical Associates 376

New Bern Tours 310

New Bern Trolley Tours 313

New Bern Yacht Club 326

New Bern-Craven County Home Builders Association 357

New Bern-Craven County Public Library 337, 346, 363, 371

New Bern-Craven County Schools 379

New Berne House Inn 294

New York Deli 36

Newport 24

Newport Development Center 246

Newport Family Practice Center 262

Newport Garden Center 110

Newport Pig Cooking Contest 142

Newport, Shopping 110

Newport-Morehead Flea Mall 113

Newspapers 208

Nightlife, Atlantic Beach 151

Nightlife, Beaufort 154

Nightlife, Crystal Coast 151

Nightlife, Emerald Isle 154

Nightlife, Indian Beach/Salter Path 154

Nightlife, Morehead City 155

Nightlife, New Bern 323

Nightlife, Pine Knoll Shores 153

Nightlife, Swansboro 156

Nikola's 47

No Name At The Beach 35

No Name Pizza & Subs 44

Noah's Ark 109

North Carolina Aquarium at Pine Knoll Shores 115

North Carolina Chili Cook-Off Championship 389

North Carolina Ducks Unlimited's Band the Billfish Tournament 146
North Carolina In-Water Boat Show 318
North Carolina Maritime Museum's Summer Science Series 135
North Carolina National Estuarine Research Reserve 266
North Carolina Port 269
North Carolina Seafood Festival 148
North Carolina Symphony 317
North Carolina Travel and Tourism Division of the Department of Commerce 403
North Carolina Wesleyan College Adult Degree Program 378
North Carolina Wildlife and Sportsman's Show 319
North River 16
Northwest Creek Marina 326, 328
Northwood Builders 362
Nuese Center for Mental Health 263
Nuese River Campground 297
Nursing and Rest Homes 366
Nursing Homes 251

O

Oak Grove Motel 64
Oakview 355
Oar House 328
Oar House Lounge 323
Obstetrics and Gynecology 264
Ocean 26
Oceanana Fishing Pier 162
Oceanana Resort Motel 60
Ocracoke 403
Ocracoke - Hatteras Inlet Free Ferry 194
Ocracoke - Swan Quarter Toll Ferry 193
Ocracoke Crab Festival 406
Oktoberfest 320
Ol' Store 400
Old Burying Ground 14
Old County Jail 117
Old Fashioned Fourth of July 390
Old Hotel Gallery 402
Old Island Store 95
Olde Variety Flea Market 305

Olympus Dive Center 169
Omni Real Estate 231
On The Wind Sailing School and Service 326
Onslow Memorial Hospital 260
Open Grounds Farm 269
Oriental Marina 331
Oriental Motel and Restaurant 400
Oriental School of Sailing 399
Orton Plantation and Gardens 411
Ottis' Fish Market 104
Ottis' Waterfront Restaurant 51
Outer Banks 406
Outer Banks Ferry Service 196
Outer Banks Outfitters 94
Outer Banks Wildlife Shelter 206
Over The Rainbow 108
Overeaters Anonymous 263

P

Painted Pelican, The 105, 202
Pak-a-Sak Food Store 94, 102
Palace Motel 295
Palate Pleasers 388
Palmer-Marsh House 408
Paper Plus 108
Parades 318
Paradise Restaurant 38, 61
Parker Marine Enterprises 270
Parkerton Inn 66
Parks, Crystal Coast 186
Parks, New Bern 332, 333
Parks, State and National 124
Parsons' General Store 105
Passport Lounge 38
Paul, Grayden 14, 15
Paul R. Taylor and Sons 240
Pecan Tree Inn 70
Pelican Players 400
Pelletier Harbor Shops 108
Pepsi Cola 379
Pete's Tackle Shop 160
Phillips Island 132
Phil's Barbecue Sauce 110
Piggly Wiggly 110
Pilentary Hunting Club 181

Pine Knoll Shores 6, 7, 216
Pine Knoll Shores, Accommodations 62
Pine Knoll Shores, Restaurants 37
Pine Knoll Shores, Shopping 95
Pine Ridge Arts & Crafts 106
Pirate Island Park 137
Pitt County Memorial Hospital 260
Piver's Island 133
Places of Worship, New Bern 342
Playland 137
Plaza Trade Center Flea Market 388
Police Departments 205
Pollock Gallery 304
Pollock Street Delicatessen and
   Restaurant 287
Pony Island Motel & Restaurant 406
Poor Charlie's Flea Market
   & Antiques 305
Poplar Grove Historic Plantation 411
Portsmouth Village 129
Post Offices 347
Post-traumatic Stress Disorder
   Support Group 263
PR Rentals and Sales 210
Presents 94
Private Schools, Crystal Coast 246
Private Schools, New Bern 364
Pro Sail Club 324
Pro Sail Lounge 296
Professional Nursing Service 368
Programs Just For Kids 138
Property Shoppe, The 394
Publick Days on Beaufort
   Historic Site 142
Purple Pelican 44
Purvis Chapel AME Zion Church 203
Putnam Real Estate Company 238

Q

Quarterdeck Gazebo & Bar 296

R

R. Rustell House 117
R.L. Kelly Construction 240

Rachel Carson Component of the North
   Carolina National Estuarine Research
   Reserve 126
Rack Room Shoes 108
Racquetball 180
Radio Island 133
Radio Shack 106
Radio Stations 209
Raleigh-Durham International
   Airport 381
Ramada Inn Oceanfront 64
Ramada Inn Waterfront and Marina 295
Ramada Marina 328
Ramada Steakhouse 288, 295
Rapscallions 52, 156
Re/Max Masters Realty 238
Real Estate Companies 230, 357
Real Estate, Crystal Coast 215
Real Estate, Havelock 392
Realty Companies, Oriental 402
Realty World-Clark Realty 234
Recycling 214
Red, White and Blueberry Festival 318
Redfearn's Nursery 111
Reef Restaurant and Lounge 152
Regional Homes of New Bern, Inc. 362
Rental Companies 78
Rental Services 210
Rescue Squad 205
Resort homes of the Carolinas, Inc. 361
Rest Homes 252
Restaurants, Crystal Coast 29
Restaurants, Havelock 385
Restaurants, New Bern 281
Retirement 249
Retirement and Senior
   Services, New Bern 365
Revco Drug Store 96, 102, 108
Rex Restaurant 52
Richard Hoff Builders 362
River Bend 352
River Bend Golf and Country Club 335
River Bend Yacht Club, The 328
River Bluffs 356
River Emporium General Store and Fudge
   Company 109

River Forest Manor 409
River Neuse Motel 400
River Trace 355
Riverside Deli & Cafe 55
Riverside Historic District,
    New Bern 350
Rivertowne Square 301
Riverwalk Deli & Cafe 53
Rocking Chair Book Store 102
Roses Stores 106
Rowing 167
Royal James Cafe 155
Royal Pavillion Resort 63
Rucker Johns A Restaurant & More 40
Rucker John's Restaurant and More 154
Russell's Island 134
Russell's Olde Tyme Shoppe 109
Ruth's Chapel Christian School 364

S

S.F. Ballou 239
S.M. Marshall Construction
    & Realty, Inc. 240
Saax Bradbury Playhouse 337
Safeway Taxi Co. 346
Sail/Loft Realty Inc. 402
Sailboarding 170
Sailing 167
Sailing Place, The 166, 167
Saints' Creations 302
Salter Path 6, 9, 218
Salter Path, Accommodations 64
Salter Path Clam and Scallop Festival 142
Salter Path Family Campground 88
Salter Path, Indian Beach, Shopping 95
Samuel Leffers Cottage 117
Sanddollar Transportation 196
Sandi's Beachwear 93, 98
Sandpiper Restaurant 288
Sanitary Fish Market & Restaurant 53
Sanitary Restaurant 175
Saunders Real Estate Company 238
Scalzo's 288
Scheper Construction, Inc. 362
School Daze 318
Schools 243

Schools and Child Care, New Bern 363
Scuba Diving 169
Scuttlebutt 98
Sea Harbour Marina 331
Sea Level 22
Sea Level Extended Care Facility 72, 252
Sea Level Inn and Restaurant 56, 72
Seaport Antique Market 112, 304
Sears Roebuck And Co. 108
Selling Team, Williams & Company 232
Senior Awareness Day 367
Senior Center 253
Senior Companion Program 367
Senior Games 254, 332
Senior Health Insurance Information
    Program 253
Senior Services 249
Service Directory, Crystal Coast 205
Service Directory, Havelock 394
Service Directory, New Bern 345
Sew It Seams 105
Shackleford Banks 130
Shackleford Banks and Carrot
    Island Ferry Service 196
Shackleford Realty 238
Sheraton Atlantic Beach Resort 61
Sheraton Craven County 2-Man Golf
    Tournament 390
Sheraton Grand New Bern Hotel and
    Marina 295
Sheraton Marina 328
Sheriff 205
Sherwood Motel 388
Shoe Splash 108
Shopping, Crystal Coast 93
Shopping, Havelock 388
Shopping, New Bern 301
Shopping, Oriental 400
Shorebird Boat Rentals 326
Show Boat Motel 60
Shrine Convention 318
Silver Creek Golf Club 190
Silver Crime Advocacy Program 367
Silver Friends 367
Silver Lake Motel 405
Simkhovitch, Simka 198

Sinbad's Bar and Grill 295, 324
Skiing 170
Skipper's Cove Restaurant and
    Lounge 37
Skipper's Cove Restaurant and
    Nightclub 153
Smith's Produce 111
Smyrna 22
Snorkeling 169
Snug Harbor 355
Soccer, Crystal Coast 184
Social Security Office 367
Softball, Crystal Coast 184
Somerset Square 101
Somethin' Special 110
Sonny's El Mex Restaurant 284
Sound Ace Hardware 96
South River 16
Southern Sampler 109
Southgate Cinema 6 323
Sparkle Fresh Cleaning & Linen 210
Special Moments 95
Special Olympics 332
Spooner's Creek Racquet Club 185
Sport Fishing Festival 146
Sports Center 180
Sports, New Bern 332
Sportsman's Pier 162
Sportsworld 138
Spouter Inn 44
St. Andrews Episcopal Church 204
St. Egbert's Catholic Church 204
St. Egbert's Catholic School 246
St. Egbert's School Track Club 184
St. John's Museum of Art 412
St. Patrick's Day Festival 141
St. Paul's Catholic Church 311, 343
St. Paul's Episcopal Church 204
St. Paul's School 364
St. Stephen's Congregational Church 204
St. Thomas Church 408
Stacy 22
Staebler Homes, Inc. 240
StageHands 338
Stamper's Gift Shop 98
Stamper's Jewelers 98

Star Hill Golfand Country Club 191
State Highway Patrol 206
Storm and Hurricane
    Information 210, 347
Straits 21
Straits Fishing Pier 162
Strange Seafood Exhibition 118, 147
Summer Camps 135, 184
Summer Palace Chinese Restaurant 53
Summer Science School for Children 138
Sun Photo 108
Sun-Surf Realty 234
Sunday Jazz Showcase 318
Sundowner Motel 60
Sunny Shores 232
Sunshine and Silks 109
Sunshine Garden Center 106
Sunsplash 95
Super Tire Store of Havelock 394
Superior Carpet & Appliance 106
Superior Structures 240
Surfing 170
Swansboro 19
Swansboro Antique Mall 112
Swansboro Oyster Roast 142
Swansboro Parks 187
Swansboro Public Schools 245
Swansboro, Restaurants 55
Swansboro United Methodist Child Care
    and Preschool 247
Swimming 170, 182
Swiss Bear Downtown Revitalization
    Corporation 321, 370
Swiss Bear, Inc. 274
Swissfest 318

T

T & W Oyster Bar and Restaurant 57
Tackle Shops 160
Tar Heel Inn Bed and Breakfast 400
Tarheel Associates 362
Taste Makers 103
Tax Rates, Crystal Coast 211
Tax Rates, New Bern 347
Taxi Service 206
Taylor, Brien 16

Taylor's Creek 12
Tea Room at The Aerie 291
Telephone, Crystal Coast 213
Telephone, New Bern 347
Televison Stations 208
Tennis, Crystal Coast 185
Texasgulf 269
Thalian Hall 412
Theater 197
Theodore Roosevelt Natural Area 126
Thomas Simpson Construction
    Company 240
Through the Looking Glass 104, 109
Tideland News 208
Tidewater Marina Co., Inc. 329
Tiller School, The 246
Timeshare 83
Tom Togs Factory Outlet 96
Tommy's Family Campground 90
Tom's Coins and Antiques 305
Tony's Beach Shop 94
Top Deck 98
Toughlove Parent Support Group 263
Tourism Development Authority 379
Tours, Crystal Coast 122
Tradewinds 38
Traditional Wooden Boat Show 119, 142
Trash 214
Trawl Door Restaurant 400
Trent River Coffee Company 302
Trent Woods 352
Triathlons, Crystal Coast 186
Triple S Fishing Pier 162
Truckers Toy Store 106
True Value Farm & Garden Center 102
Tryon Palace
    274, 317, 318, 321, 350, 370
Tryon Palace Christmas Celebration 321
Tryon Palace Gift and Garden Shops 302
Tryon Palace Historic Sites
    and Gardens 308
Tryon Palace Visitor Center 318
Tryon Palace's Drama Tours 320
Tryon Realty 361
Turner Technical Service 110
Turner Tolsen 304

Twin Book Stores 105
Twin Bridges Race 184
Twin Rivers Art Association 340
Twin Rivers Mall 301
Twin Rivers Nursing Center 366
Twin Rivers YMCA 332
Two-Man Classic Invitational
    Tournament 319
Tyson Building and Design 240

U

U.S. Marine Corps 269
Union Point Park 314, 329, 334
United Parcel Service 396
United Senior Services, Inc. 367
University of North Carolina Institute of
    Marine Science 266
Urgent Care 262
USAir Express 381
Utility Services, Crystal Coast 212
Utility Services Water and Sewer,
    New Bern 347

V

Vacation Rentals, Crystal Coast 75
Vacation Resorts International 296
Valente Construction Company 240
Van Der Veer House 408
Veterans' Groups 254
Veterans of Foreign Wars, Post 2401 255
Veterans of Foreign Wars, Post 8986 255
Veterans of Foreign Wars, Post 9960 255
Victims of Sexual Assault and Abuse 263
Video City 95
Video Plus 102
Village Craftsmen 404
Village Gift Shop & Beach Wear 95
Village Realty 402
Village Restaurant 400
Vintage Times 346
Volleyball, Crystal Coast 186
Volunteer Opportunities, Crystal Coast
    257
Volunteer Opportunities, New Bern 369
von Graffenried, Christoph 273

W

W.B. Blades House 310
W.B. Kelli's 36, 152
Wade House 311
Wadin' Creek Family Care Center 253
Wal-Mart 108
Walking, Crystal Coast 183
Walking Tour Attractions 310
Walking Tours 308
Walking/Running 180
Walsh Marine 330
Walston True Value Home Center 111
Walston's True Value Hardware 210
Water and Sewer 213
Water Sports And Rentals 166
Water Sports, Crystal Coast 159
Water Sports Rental 166, 167, 170
Waterfront Antiques & Collectibles 112
Waterfront Junction 103
Waterfront Seafood Deli & Cafe 54
Watersports Rentals & RV
    Campground 88
Watson-Matthews Real Estate 235
Waveriders Rentals 167
Week At Camp 254
West Carteret Medical Center 110
West Carteret Water Corporation 213
West New Bern Recreation Center 356
West Side Cafe 54
Western Auto 106
Western Carteret County 24
Western Carteret County Public
    Schools 245
Western Carteret County, Restaurants 56
Western Carteret Medical Center 262
Weyerhaeuser 269, 379
Weyerhaeuser Real Estate
    Company 357, 361
Whispering Pines Campground 90
White Heron Gallery 402
White House 310

White Oak Christian Academy 246
White Oak Gallery 202
White Oak River Cafe 55
White Sand Trail Rides 137, 182
Whittaker Creek Yacht Harbor 331
Widows' and Widowers'
    Support Group 263
Wild Birds Unlimited 111
Wildlife 206
Wildlife and Sportsman's Show 278
Will Gorges Antiques & Civil
    War Items 304
Williams and Company 232
Williams Hardware 106
Williston 22
Wilmington 410
Winberry Farm Produce 111
Wind Creations 105
Windjammer Inn 62
Windsurfing 170
Windward Gallery 103, 202
Wings 94
Winstead's Family Restaurant 386, 387
Winter Garden Tours 322
Woody's On The Beach 154
Worship 203
Worthy Is The Lamb 121, 145
Wreckreational Divers 60
Wright Brothers National Memorial 407
Writer's Organizations 202

Y

Yana's Ye Olde Drugstore Restaurant 55

Z

Zaytoun & Raines Construction 362
Zeigler Stables 182
Ziegler Motel 296
Zip Codes, Crystal Coast 214
Zip Codes, New Bern 347

ORDER FORM
Fast and Simple!

Mail to:
By The Sea Publications, Inc.
Hanover Center, PO Box 5386
Wilmington, NC 28403

Or:
for VISA or
Mastercard orders call
1-800-955-1860

Name ————————————————————————————

Address ————————————————————————————

City/State/Zip ————————————————————————

Qty.	Title/Price	Shipping	Amount
	Insiders' Guide to Richmond/$12.95	$3.00	
	Insiders' Guide to Williamsburg/$14.95	$3.00	
	Insiders' Guide to Virginia's Blue Ridge/$12.95	$3.00	
	Insiders' Guide to Virginia's Chesapeake Bay/$14.95	$3.00	
	Insiders' Guide to Washington, DC/$14.95	$3.00	
	Insiders' Guide to North Carolina's Outer Banks/$14.95	$3.00	
	Insiders' Guide to Wilmington, NC/$14.95	$3.00	
	Insiders' Guide to North Carolina's Crystal Coast/$12.95	$3.00	
	Insiders' Guide to Charleston, SC/$12.95	$3.00	
	Insiders' Guide to Myrtle Beach/$14.95	$3.00	
	Insiders' Guide to Mississippi/$12.95	$3.00	
	Insiders' Guide to Boca Raton & the Palm Beaches/$14.95 (8/95)	$3.00	
	Insiders' Guide to Sarasota/Bradenton/$12.95	$3.00	
	Insiders' Guide to Northwest Florida/$12.95	$3.00	
	Insiders' Guide to Lexington, KY/$12.95	$3.00	
	Insiders' Guide to Louisville/$14.95	$3.00	
	Insiders' Guide to the Twin Cities/$12.95	$3.00	
	Insiders' Guide to Boulder/$12.95	$3.00	
	Insiders' Guide to Denver/$12.95	$3.00	
	Insiders' Guide to The Civil War (Eastern Theater)/$14.95	$3.00	
	Insiders' Guide to North Carolina's Mountains/$14.95	$3.00	
	Insiders' Guide to Atlanta/$14.95 (4/95)	$3.00	
	Insiders' Guide to Branson/$14.95 (12/95)	$3.00	
	Insiders' Guide to Cincinnati/$14.95 (9/95)	$3.00	
	Insiders' Guide to Tampa/St. Petersburg/$14.95 (9/95)	$3.00	

Payment in full (check or money order) must
accompany this order form.
Please allow 2 weeks for delivery.

N.C. residents add 6% sales tax ————————

Total ————————

Who you are and what you think is important to us.

**Fill out the coupon and we'll give you
an Insiders' Guide® for half price ($6.48 off)**

Which book(s) did you buy? _____

Where do you live? _____

In what city did you buy your book? _____

Where did you buy your book? ❏ catalog ❏ bookstore ❏ newspaper ad
❏ retail shop ❏ other _____

How often do you travel? ❏ yearly ❏ bi-annually ❏ quarterly
❏ more than quarterly

Did you buy your book because you were ❏ moving ❏ vacationing
❏ wanted to know more about your home town ❏ other _____

_____

Will the book be used by ❏ family ❏ couple ❏ individual ❏ group

What is you annual household income? ❏ under $25,000 ❏ $25,000 to $35,000
❏ $35,000 to $50,000 ❏ $50,000 to $75,000 ❏ over $75,000

How old are you? ❏ under 25 ❏ 25-35 ❏ 36-50 ❏ 51-65 ❏ over 65

Did you use the book before you left for your destination? ❏ yes ❏ no

Did you use the book while at your destination? ❏ yes ❏ no

On average per month, how many times do you refer to your book? ❏ 1-3 ❏ 4-7
❏ 8-11 ❏ 12-15 ❏ 16 and up

On average, how many other people use your book? ❏ no others ❏ 1 ❏ 2
❏ 3 ❏ 4 or more

Is there anything you would like to tell us about Insiders' Guides? _____

_____

_____

Name _____ Address _____

City _____ State _____ Zip _____

**We'll send you a voucher for $6.48 off any Insiders' Guide© and a list of available
titles as soon as we get this card from you. Thanks for being an Insider!**

BUSINESS REPLY MAIL

FIRST CLASS   PERMIT NO. 20   MANTEO, NC

POSTAGE WILL BE PAID BY ADDRESSEE

The Insiders' Guides®, Inc.
PO Box 2057
Manteo, NC 27954